REVIEW OF RESEARCH IN
EDUCATION, 30

Special Issue on

*Rethinking Learning: What Counts as
Learning and What Learning Counts*

REVIEW

OF

RESEARCH

IN EDUCATION
30
2006

JUDITH GREEN
Editor
University of California, Santa Barbara

ALLAN LUKE
Editor
Queensland University of Technology

PUBLISHED BY THE
AMERICAN EDUCATIONAL RESEARCH ASSOCIATION
1230 Seventeenth Street, NW
Washington, DC 20036-3078

Copyright © 2006
American Educational Research Association
Library of Congress
Printed in the United States of America
ISBN 0-935302-33-6
ISSN 0091-732-X

CONTRIBUTORS

Alfredo J. Artiles
Carol Christensen
Sherman Dorn
Michael J. Ford
Ellice A. Forman
Brian J. Girard
Laura C. Haniford
Elizabeth B. Kozleski
Wan Shun Eva Lam
Pamela A. Moss
Jean-Yves Rochex
Julian Sefton-Green
Jennifer A. Vadeboncoeur
Olga A. Vásquez

Contents

Introduction
Rethinking Learning: What Counts
as Learning and What Learning Counts

JUDITH GREEN
University of California, Santa Barbara
ALLAN LUKE
Queensland University of Technology

The rapid transformations of social, economic, and cultural worlds of learners in school and nonschool settings that we are facing today are reminiscent of the transformations that accompanied the industrial revolution at the turn of the 20th century. In 1900, John Dewey characterized the impact on education in the following way:

One can hardly believe there has been a revolution in all history so rapid, so extensive, so complete. Through it the face of the earth is making over, even as to its physical forms; political boundaries are wiped out and moved about, as if they were indeed only lines on a paper map; population is hurriedly gathered into cities from the ends of the earth; habits of living are altered with startling abruptness and thoroughness; the search for the truths of nature is infinitely stimulated and facilitated, and their application to life made not on practicable, but commercially necessary. Even our moral and religious ideas and interests, the most conservative because the deepest-lying things in our nature, are profoundly affected. That this revolution should not affect education in some other than a formal and superficial fashion is inconceivable. (p. 9)

Much of what Dewey argued over 100 years ago can be viewed as characteristic of the current shift to an information society of the 21st century. Like those at the turn of the 20th century, education researchers and their constituencies (e.g., students, teachers, community members, and policy makers) are faced with a series of questions: How are we to respond to the educational challenges of this new millennium? How do we engage with new forms of learning, the influence of new media on children's lives, changing community dynamics, and many long-standing and tenacious educational and social problems? And how can research and theory constructively and critically engage with the demands and imperatives of government educational and social policies?

In this issue of *Review of Research in Education,* we bring together, with the support of our international Advisory Board, an intergenerational group of researchers who represent both new and long-standing perspectives and debates on the shapes, definitions, and processes of learning in the context of global cultural and economic change. These authors revisit the concept of learning from different methodological, theoretical, and national perspectives. They focus variously on the social, cultural, and psychological dynamics of classroom life, changing student identities and lives, powerful new policy and assessment imperatives, and blends of new media and emergent forms of learning in schools and nonschool programs. They review empirically rich and theoretically complex research on diverse groups of students and youth in North America and other nations or continents (e.g., France, Australia, United Kingdom, China, Africa, among others). Taken together, these chapters frame a new version of the fundamental question raised by Dewey at the turn of the last century and provide insights into how this question can be addressed across the broader research community: *How and in what ways can we, as an intellectual and scholarly community, revisit, rethink, and reformulate research in response to the significant and unprecedented educational challenges of new cultural, economic, and social contexts?*

Across these chapters, readers have a unique opportunity to examine how researchers are seeking theoretically and empirically sound ways of responding to policy directions of governments and local communities seeking to address perceived educational problems. Further, the authors of these chapters bring new insights into issues of the relationship among research, theory, practice, and policy. Several of the chapters caution researchers about the risk of narrowing the directions by focusing solely on one group of stakeholders, rather than expanding the range of paradigmatic views of what might count as teaching and learning and their consequences to different constituencies at this historical point of dynamic change. Several authors present new theoretical and empirical approaches to addressing complex problems involved in research on learning in school and out-of-school contexts. Others explore how policy makers and researchers in different countries have sought new ways to forward schools and education research in an era where the very institutions and practices of modernity have become less stable and more fluid. Yet others have turned to work in adjacent fields of research — from applied linguistics to cultural studies — seeking new understandings of learning. Together they raise questions about what counts as learning, where and when learning counts, and how research and policy relationships support and constrain our understandings of learning.

By deliberately expanding the purview of research on learning, our aim in this volume was to provide a rich and diverse body of scholarship that would enable readers to explore once again what counts as learning; how definitions and understandings of learning are being shaped and reshaped by teachers, learners, and policy makers as well as researchers and educational theorists; and to explore the research on how situated views of learning are made to count in new institutional and policy contexts. Thus the chapters in this volume constitute a broad multidisciplinary and transnational collection that focuses on four major themes:

1. New and diverse cultural contexts for learning;
2. The impacts of new communications media on learning;
3. The study of learning in school and nonschool settings; and
4. The national and cross-national assessment of learning.

The chapters represent reviews grounded in a broad range of empirical and interpretivist traditions. In their reviews, we asked authors to work with a set of developmental reviewers to provide an overview of current research directions, contextual issues, and policy debates — an educational "problematic" in Dewey's sense — and to weave a theoretical and conceptual argument that could lay a foundation for future directions. Each chapter brings to the fore particular sites for exploring the issues of learning in context, and each identifies both residual and emergent methodological, theoretical, and policy issues.

These chapters, therefore, can be viewed as "making the familiar strange," a process that ethnographers argue is central to examining and re-examining cultural assumptions underlying everyday work of researchers as well as those in our research studies. Without this process, much of what counts as learning across various groups, constituencies, and research traditions would remain invisible; could be assumed to be neutral, natural, or understood; and, therefore, would remain unexamined. As the authors illustrate in different ways, the challenge as we move into the 21st century, just as it was at the turn of the 20th century as Dewey argued, is to re-examine the most basic questions of who is learning what, for what purposes, under what conditions, and with what educational, social, and cultural outcomes and consequences for learners, communities, and nations. While in the past, the field of education research and policy makers have engaged in vigorous debates over method, policy, and educational practice, these studies show that such debates often mask more basic issues, including what counts as learning. Dewey (1902, pp. 3–4) captures the challenges and issues facing education research and its stakeholders and constituencies succinctly:

[a]ny significant problem involves conditions that for the moment contradict each other. Solution comes only by getting away from the meaning of terms that is already fixed upon and coming to see the conditions from another point of view, and hence in a fresh light. But this reconstruction means travail of thought.

The diversity of perspectives, research traditions, topics of study, and ways of conceptualizing learning in this volume will challenge all. We encourage readers, therefore, to read across these chapters, rather than to select those within your own area of expertise, and to rethink, re-examine, and reconsider what counts as learning not only in the chapters but also in your own programs of research. As the authors of the various chapters in this volume demonstrate in multiple ways, no one research tradition, theoretical perspective, or methodological approach can address the full range of complexity entailed in seeking to understand both what counts as learning and its counterpart, what learning counts. The collection, therefore, provides a rich and varied body of work, which those new to educational research as well as those with long histories of research on learning will find informative, insightful, and challenging. The authors also lay a foundation for revisiting and rethinking the complex issues and debates on what counts as research on learning in this transformative moment at the onset of the 21st century.

ACKNOWLEDGMENTS

The editors would like to thank Cesar Coll, University of Barcelona, Spain; Adrienne Dixson, The Ohio State University; David Gillborn, Institute of Education, London, UK; and Chris Thorn, University of Wisconsin for editorial comments at the initial stages of the development of Volume 30.

REFERENCES

Dewey, J. (1900). *The school and society.* Chicago: University of Chicago Press.
Dewey, J. (1902). *The child and the curriculum.* Chicago: University of Chicago Press.

Chapter 1

Redefining Disciplinary Learning in Classroom Contexts

MICHAEL J. FORD AND ELLICE A. FORMAN
University of Pittsburgh

Repeatedly, for more than a century, educational reformers have reminded us that students enter and leave school with a very limited notion of what the disciplines they study are actually about (Shulman & Quinlan, 1996; Stevens, Wineburg, Herrenkohl, & Bell, 2005; Wineburg, 1991). This concern led us to focus on the relatively recent "practice turn" in sociocultural learning theory, which we believe offers an innovative opportunity for conceptualizing disciplinary learning in classrooms. We found, however, that making something of this opportunity requires a perspective that is broader than educational psychology (even that provided by the sociocultural approach), a perspective that provides a firmer understanding of the academic disciplines themselves. We therefore appeal to another "practice turn," in the philosophy and sociology of science literature,[1] to provide a disciplinary anchor for effectively conceptualizing learning in the area of science education. Although we focus on science education as an example, we more generally assert that scholarship on disciplinary practices can inform research on learning in other content areas as well (see Putnam, Lampert, & Peterson, 1990, and Wineburg, 1991, for similar efforts that made use of different disciplinary examples).

Another concern that motivates our examination of disciplinary practices is the frequent assertion by educational reformers that students should be engaged in the activities of historians, mathematicians, scientists, or literary analysts rather than just learning about the results of those practices. This trend can be seen in standards documents in many fields, including mathematics (National Council of Teachers of Mathematics, 2000) and science (National Research Council, 1996) education. Although this mandate to incorporate authentic disciplinary practices into classroom instruction has become a standard rhetorical move in journal articles and policy documents, it is rarely elaborated or adequately supported by evidence about those practices. In addition, there has been little explicit attention given to the fundamental aspects of a discipline that students should experience. To adequately design instruction or assessment to include aspects of authentic scientific practice, we need to justify the disciplinary practices that should be represented in classrooms and clarify how to implement those practices in our long-term and short-term learning objectives.

This concern with disciplinary learning is not new. Dewey had a vision in which school curricula would reflect the intellectual activities of mature subject-matter experts as well as the developmental needs of students. Shulman and Quinlan (1996) pointed out that Dewey's vision was a means of "psychologizing" the subject matter, because it blended authentic aspects of disciplines with ideas about how learning occurred. Shulman and Quinlan attributed the relative lack of attention to this approach since Dewey to a series of events early in the 20th century that redirected the field of educational psychology toward Thorndike's program of systematizing a science of educational psychology. Largely because of Thorndike, behaviorist learning theory eclipsed serious consideration of disciplines by defining learning as generic processes (stimulus-response connections, motivation) and outcomes (skill attainment). Behaviorist learning theory was then augmented by a similar research approach that appealed to cognitive learning theories in the middle of the 20th century.

Whatever their shortcomings, behavioral and cognitive learning theories have been quite influential in education, among other reasons because they provide clear ways for teachers, curriculum designers, and testers to organize their work around well-defined learning objectives. For behaviorists, the learning objectives were defined in terms of behavioral skills; for cognitive psychologists, they were defined in terms of mental structures (e.g., concepts or procedures). These new behavioral or mental learning objectives were thought to be "acquired" by students if they had been effectively taught in their classrooms. As a result, the educational enterprise was and still is framed in terms of teaching strategies designed to encourage the acquisition of such learning objectives and assessment strategies to verify that they have been acquired.

The recent "practice turn" in sociocultural[2] learning theory has challenged this conceptualization of learning objectives that can be evaluated in terms of behavioral skills or mental structures by reorienting a focus from the individual to people's activities within their social context (Packer, 2001; Sfard, 1998). A substitute for the acquisition of behavioral skills or mental structures has been offered as "participation in a practice," a notion elaborated in broadly influential and extremely helpful ways by Lave and Wenger (Lave, 1988; Lave & Wenger, 1991; Wenger, 1998). If we are to apply the notion of participation to research on learning in classrooms, however, we need some notion that can substitute for the acquisition of behavioral skills or mental concepts as learning objectives. Although participation can be considered one of several learning objectives, participation itself is not "acquired." That is, we need to address ways in which the individual is affected by such participation and what resources he or she "takes away" from these instructional experiences.

Despite the theoretical advances of sociocultural learning theory, by and large these advances have not broadly transformed classroom instruction. Cognitive learning theory has been more influential in education (as was behaviorism before it). Cognitive theory offers a way of thinking about subject-matter learning objectives in terms of acquired disciplinary concepts and procedures. In science classrooms, for example, the discipline has been largely framed for instruction as a focus on understanding vocabulary and use of the scientific method. These concepts and procedures can be readily assessed through a combination of standardized tests and performance assessments. In contrast, how does one evaluate students' ability to participate in scientific practices after having engaged in episodes of authentic scientific work? Sociocultural learning theory cannot, in itself, help us articulate what participation in authentic disciplinary practices can provide students as resources for further learning. In this chapter, we provide a framework for examining the discipline of science that can also be useful for assessing its impact on students.

What aspects of an academic discipline's practices should be considered fundamental and therefore central to sociocultural learning objectives? Participating in any practice means acting appropriately, and "appropriateness" is judged as whether or not one's actions "mesh" with those of other individuals in the practice for forwarding the community's aims. In any academic discipline, the aim of the practice is to build knowledge or, in other words, to decide what claims "count" as knowledge, distinguishing them from those that do not. Deciding what counts as knowledge implies authority, and thus the raison d'etre of academic practices is how these practices ground disciplinary authority. In regard to educational concerns, therefore, these practices that ground authority for deciding what counts as knowledge in disciplines are the ones that students should engage in classrooms if their participation is to be authentic and they are to learn fundamentally what the practice is about.

Following this general analysis, subsequently we articulate classroom learning objectives in science as a familiarity with how the discipline decides upon knowledge claims, a familiarity we refer to as a "grasp of practice"[3] (Ford, in press; see Lehrer & Schauble, 2006, for an interesting parallel among three images of science and metaphors for scientific literacy: science as logical reasoning, science as [conceptual] theory change, and science as practice).

The scientific disciplines (physics, chemistry, biology, and so forth) are social endeavors in which participants both collaborate and compete by debating what should be accepted as knowledge. These disciplines have ways of deciding upon knowledge claims that are neither arbitrary nor dogmatic. Authority emerges as an outcome of debates, and so it is the way that debates are decided that provides access to disciplinary authority. From this perspective, students need to learn from their experiences in classrooms that neither do they have authority to decide "what counts" as knowledge nor is this authority inaccessible to them. Rather, students need to learn the difference between a personal (or political) perspective on a scientific issue and a scientific perspective. Scientific understanding implies a familiarity with the roles of agents and how they interact in the ways science grounds authority for knowledge claims.

From a sociocultural perspective, teaching students about any disciplinary practice requires that they be engaged authentically in the activities of individual agents and group members that are necessary for a practice to achieve its aims. Although sociocultural theory can point to this general need, the details about the necessary activities of a particular community require scholarship on the disciplinary practices of this community as well. In the sciences, individuals typically work on research teams in which different actors collaborate to define research questions, collect data, quantify and display data, write research papers, produce posters for professional meetings, and design inventions (Latour & Woolgar, 1986). However, of themselves, these actions do not, in most cases (successful frauds aside), provide access to a disciplinary authority by which "what counts" as a knowledge claim is decided. Merely holding a test tube or making a poster, for example, is not fundamental in a disciplinary sense. If students are to attain a "grasp" of how a practice works, they need to engage in those aspects of the practice that are responsible for the grounding of authority and deciding what counts as knowledge. In the next section, we articulate candidates for these aspects of practice in one discipline, that of science.

A FRAMEWORK FOR REDEFINING DISCIPLINARY LEARNING IN SCIENCE CLASSROOMS

In developing this account of classroom learning objectives, we draw from science as an example, not least because the basis of scientific claims has been a long-standing focus of attention in philosophical literature. A recent "practice turn" in this literature has highlighted how scientific practices can account for science's historical production of reliable knowledge claims. Rather than focusing exclusively on the reasoning of individuals, philosophers of science have appealed to a larger level of description, that of the community, to explain how the institution of science "works." This appeal to communities of practice in philosophy of science, of course, parallels a similar appeal in sociocultural psychology of learning, offering a convenient overlap for reconceptualizing disciplinary learning. Against this backdrop, our aim in this chapter is to review recent, sociocultural studies of classroom-based research in science education in light of a sample of practice-based research within the field of science studies. Our framework for conceptualizing disciplinary learning in science is organized around three points from the science studies literature.[4]

1. *Social aspect of scientific practice:* In scientific practice, communities of investigators engage in public debates about explanatory accounts of nature using socially negotiable but largely stabilized norms and means.
2. *Material aspect of scientific practice:* The ultimate arbiter (and therefore basis of authority) in community debates is the "behavior" of nature. In science, nature does not address investigators' explanatory accounts directly but rather is framed, measured, and represented in particular ways to do so. A large part of scientific work involves this framing, measuring, and representing of nature's behavior to support arguments in the public realm about the explanatory accounts under debate.
3. *Practice as an interplay of Roles:* Both the social and the material aspects of scientific practice are necessary to explain the overall functioning of the scientific enterprise, particularly the grounding of disciplinary authority. These aspects of practice can be represented (simplistically but fruitfully) as two Roles[5]: Constructor of claims

and Critiquer of claims. These Roles interact in ways that support the function of the institution overall, are played by all individual scientists in the public realm at different times, and are part of the private realm when experienced scientists consider the likely impact of their work on their colleagues.

Whereas the social and material aspects of practice address how scientific authority is grounded by the part nature plays in debates, "practice as an interplay of Roles" formulates these aspects as patterns of interactions among agents. It is an understanding of these patterns of interaction and their rationale in light of the enterprise's function, or a "grasp of practice" that we offer as a classroom learning goal.

Given this summary of our argument, next we provide a historical overview and conceptual review of the "practice turns" in two fields: in the psychology of learning and in science studies. Then we summarize some recent work in science studies along the lines of the three points and apply our understanding of these issues to a small sample of the literature on learning in science classrooms to illustrate the value of this approach. In our conclusion, we speculate about the ways a "grasp of practice" might serve as a disciplinary resource for students, in contrast to the more familiar notion of "transfer."

HISTORICAL OVERVIEW AND CONCEPTUAL REVIEW
Trends in the Psychology of Learning

One important historical development in psychology has been the "practice turn" in the study of learning, exemplified by concepts such as "situated learning," "cognitive apprenticeship," and "legitimate peripheral participation in communities of practice" (Brown, Collins, & Duguid, 1989; Greeno, 1998; Holland, Lachicotte, Skinner, & Cain, 1998; Lave & Wenger, 1991; Rogoff, 1990, 2003; Sfard, 1998; Wenger, 1998). This movement has shifted focus on learning from something that occurs exclusively inside people's heads to something that is played out in our everyday activities in communities. This perspective has been influencing schools in various ways, from policy documents describing disciplinary standards in the United States, Great Britain, and elsewhere in the postindustrial world (e.g., American Association for the Advancement of Science, 1993; Millar & Osborne, 1999; National Council of Teachers of Mathematics, 2000; National Research Council, 1996) to research methods for studying classroom processes and outcomes (Eisenhart, 1988; Erickson & Gutierrez, 2002; Green, Dixon, & Zaharlick, 2003).

At the beginnings of the field of psychology, Wundt and others proposed a need for two psychologies: one version to study elementary mental functions (e.g., sensation, perception) experimentally and one to study higher mental functions (e.g., memory, reasoning, and language) descriptively (Cole, 1996). In the United States and Western Europe, these two psychologies were merged into one, with the experimental and reductionist version predominating. Explanations of both elementary and higher mental functions were reduced to accounts previously applied to only the former.

And, of course, this explanatory assertion was accompanied by a methodological one based in behaviorist theory (Bazerman, 1988; Cahan & White, 1992) that looked to the natural sciences for models of experimental design and inferential statistics, rejecting descriptive methods (such as ethnography) as being insufficiently scientific for the new field. While behaviorist theory grew, the second psychology survived in a few places: in Germany with Gestalt psychology, in France with Durkeim (a sociologist), in Switzerland with Piaget, and in the United States with the pragmatism of Mead and Dewey (Cole, 1996).

The Soviet Union was one of the few places where a version of the second psychology flourished early in the 20th century in the work of Lev Vygotsky and his colleagues, Alexander Luria and Alexei Leontiev (Cole, 1996). Dewey briefly played a homologous role in the United States (Popkewitz, 1998). Both Dewey and Vygotsky opposed the dominant view of universalistic psychology. Unfortunately, neither theorist had much influence on education in their lifetimes (Popkewitz, 1998).

Leaders of the constructivist movement in education at the end of the 20th century reinterpreted the theories of both Dewey and Vygotsky to serve a new set of historical and cultural needs. As Popkewitz (1998) proposed, Vygotsky's and Dewey's theories were used to articulate a position that "knowledge is socially constructed" (p. 547), which paralleled similar movements in many other disciplines (e.g., anthropology, linguistics, philosophy, sociology, psychology). He argued that current versions of constructivism were attracted to Vygotsky's position on the role of speech in thinking and to Dewey's pragmatic philosophy and emphasis on the important role of community in learning.

Like Wundt, Vygotsky (1978) divided thinking into two basic types: elementary mental functions (e.g., sensation, perception, basic memory and attention, conditioned learning) and higher mental functions (e.g., selective attention, voluntary memory, logical reasoning, and complex problem solving). According to Vygotsky, higher mental functions were voluntary, conscious, and self-regulated, whereas the elementary functions were not. Unlike many other psychologists, however, Vygotsky stressed that higher mental functions required semiotic mediation and had social origins. That is, he argued that higher mental functions are learned first through social interaction (usually in the company of experts) and that this learning requires communication (semiotic mediation) and involves tools (physical, symbolic, or both). Another key concept in Vygotsky's theory is genetic analysis. He proposed that to understand any psychological phenomenon, one needs to investigate it historically (cf. Wertsch, 1985).

One more Soviet-era theorist from the early and mid-20th century, Mikhail Bakhtin, has emerged as an influence on psychology and education since the 1980s. A number of contemporary theorists see a close conceptual tie between the work of Vygotsky and that of Bakhtin, even though there is no evidence that they met or were directly influenced by each other (Holland et al., 1998; Wertsch, 1991).[6]

Bakhtin's[7] theory is perhaps even less well understood than Vygotsky's theory by educational researchers (Matusov, in press). Wertsch (1991) integrated some Bakhtinian ideas into sociocultural theory, especially in places where Vygotsky's own work was incomplete or inadequate. For example, Vygotsky's writings about inner speech (what occurs when social speech is internalized) were quite vague and misleading to investigators interested in understanding how speech is transformed when it is used for self-regulation. Unfortunately, Vygotsky's early death prevented him from constructing, elaborating, or borrowing notions from others that would have been necessary to fully develop what he meant by inner speech or internalization of social speech. In contrast, Bakhtin's notion of dialogicality (as well as heteroglossia, authoring, and addressivity) helps us better understand how people *appropriate* (rather than merely *internalize*) the speech of others.

Dialogicality is the idea that a single individual may conduct an inner conversation with multiple voices or perspectives (as do the characters in Dostoyevsky's later novels). "Language, when it *means,* is somebody talking to somebody else, even when that someone else is one's own inner addressee" (Bakhtin, 1981, p. xxi). Thus, when dialogicality occurs, a speaker or writer or thinker is addressing a seen or imagined audience (the addressee). It may also be the case that more than one individual is carrying on a monologue, if the more powerful person silences or fails to address the less powerful. This occurs when the authoritative speech of a single speaker dominates in a one-sided conversation.

Utterance is the basic unit of analysis in Bakhtin's theory: Language in use is more important to his theory than any formal, abstracted linguistic code. Nevertheless, utterances are multifaceted (i.e., heteroglossia). Heteroglossia means that all utterances embody two fundamental aspects of communication: a static system of formal rules and dictionary meanings and a context-dependent system. The context changes, elaborates, contradicts, or restricts the situational meaning we derive from our understanding of the fixed system (Bakhtin, 1981). Another aspect of heteroglossia involves the tension between authoritative and internally persuasive discourse in Bakhtin's theory.

The authoritative word demands that we acknowledge it, that we make it our own; it binds us, quite independent of any power it might have to persuade us internally; we encounter it with its authority already fused with it. (Bakhtin, 1981, p. 342)

Holland and her colleagues (1998) relied on both Vygotsky's and Bakhtin's theories to articulate a framework on identity development within cultural contexts that is neither socially determined nor individually determined. In their view, cultural contexts (e.g., a caste society) are collective imaginary constructions ("figured worlds") that position individuals as actors in their larger social systems (e.g., as low or high caste). They relied on Bakhtin's notion of authoring to show how individual agency must be included to counterbalance these ascribed positions.

The world must be answered—authorship is not a choice—but the form of the answer is not predetermined . . . authorship is a matter of orchestration: of arranging the identifiable social discourses/practices that are one's resources . . . to craft a response in a time and space defined by others' standpoint in activity, that is, in a social field conceived as the ground of responsiveness. Human agency comes through this art of improvisation. (Holland et al., 1998, p. 272)

Although Holland et al. identified "discourses/practices" as resources, the distinction we offer here is that through participation in a disciplinary or classroom community, people come to learn the various roles that exist in that practice. Subsequently, these roles serve as disciplinary resources. Recent work of other researchers in education has also drawn on the advances of Holland and her colleagues to highlight the importance of considering student agency so as to acknowledge the dynamic and multifaceted notion of identity (e.g., Boaler & Greeno, 2000; Brown, Reveles, & Kelly, 2005; Nasir, 2002).

Students' willingness to learn from their teachers and peers in classrooms requires, in part, an act of imagination and emotional commitment to a view of themselves as becoming highly educated: a potential mathematician, scientist, writer, architect, and so forth. To achieve these personal outcomes, they must become motivated to appropriate disciplinary resources. This act of appropriation is likely to require integrating the authoritative speech of science with their internally persuasive speech (Cazden, 1993). Teachers can play an important part in this process by acknowledging students' agency through dialogical interchanges in the classroom that may create a third (intermediate) space between the authoritative speech of science and students' own speech (Gutierrez, Baquedano-Lopez, & Tejeda, 1999).

Another related idea from sociocultural theory that is useful for conceptualizing how meanings are made and shared in communities is intertextuality. "We can make meanings through the relations between two texts; meanings that cannot be made within any single text" (Lemke, 1992, p. 257). This idea is based on the assumption that a "text" is not just language that is written or spoken; it can also include a wide variety of social practices (e.g., gestures, intonation patterns, drawings, physical models, maps and other forms of inscription). Texts can be linked in a variety of ways: in terms of content, attitudes, activity structures, and speech genres. Lemke (1990, 1992) discussed intertextuality in light of Bakhtin's theory of semantics.

Bakhtin (1981) showed his awareness of intertextuality when he wrote about the multiple voices of dialogic speech (within a single speaker or between several speakers). Intertextuality may be used by teachers to connect students' own internally persuasive speech with the authoritative speech of science in the intermediate or third space identified by Gutierrez and her colleagues (1999).

In summary, a revised and expanded version of sociocultural theory provides us with a number of theoretical tools for understanding learning as practice in disciplinary and classroom communities. For example:

- Thinking and learning occur in the social activities of our everyday lives: Knowledge is socially constructed.
- Descriptive analysis can provide a detailed picture of how people play their roles in collaborative activities that involve acts of communication.
- Communication requires a speaker and an audience; these roles are interchangeable and must take account of each other.

- Social roles (or positions) are not fixed or determined, because people are capable of authoring their own identities (or positioning themselves) in practices.
- Practices have a history: They build on the memories and products of the past and provide resources for the future.
- Participants in a practice engage in intertextuality that explicitly or implicitly links authors and texts across time and space.
- Dialogic speech requires that the agency of less powerful participants in a community be acknowledged and addressed by the more powerful; dialogic speech makes the creation of a third space possible (between authoritative speech and internally persuasive speech).

What can this version of sociocultural theory tell us about learning science in classrooms that we may not have been able to learn using other theoretical approaches? Can it help us understand how science is learned or what science is learned in classrooms? To address these questions, we now turn to a survey of historical trends in the study of learning in classrooms.

Trends in the Study of Learning in Classrooms

Research on classroom learning in general has at least two distinct historical roots (Shulman, 1986) from within educational psychology as the study of teaching effectiveness (Shulman & Quinlan, 1996) and from within sociolinguistics as the study of language and social interaction (Green, 1983; Hicks, 1995; Mehan, 1998). Both branches developed during the second half of the 20th century, although they involved different theoretical frameworks and distinct methodologies. The version that developed within educational psychology was influenced by the dominant behavioral theory and experimental methods and sought to relate teacher behaviors to student outcomes on standardized tests. Because this approach correlated teaching behaviors (process variables) and student outcomes (product variables), it was called "process-product" research (Shulman & Quinlan, 1996). Attention to context was limited to quantifiable features such as class size or students' socioeconomic status. Subject matter was viewed as merely another contextual variable that could be easily categorized by level and content (e.g., middle school algebra).

In contrast, the sociolinguistic research on classrooms focused on context and process using descriptive and interpretive methods (Erickson, 1986). This work by microethnographers depended upon videotape or audiotape records (or both) to capture the dynamics of face-to-face interaction (Mehan, 1998) that are lost when predetermined observational checklists and rating scales are used (as in the process-product tradition). As Mehan argued, the sociolinguistic approach raised different research questions.

Instead of asking questions that seem to imply a correlational answer . . . microethnographers asked questions that call for a constitutive answer. "What is the interactional work of . . . [disability, identity, school success]?" (1998, pp. 247–248)

When the early sociolinguistic research was being conducted in the 1970s and 1980s, activities such as reading groups and sharing time in elementary classrooms were frequently studied (Mehan, 1979; Michaels, 1981). During this period, mathematics and science were typically taught in a way that severely constrained students' interaction and discourse (Stodolsky, 1988). Thus, the face-to-face dynamics in these subject areas were so scripted (monologic) or infrequent that microethnography seemed unnecessary. This situation changed in at least a few classrooms after publication of the mathematics and science standards in North America during the late 1980s and 1990s, when teachers were encouraged to engage their students in doing and talking math (Kieran, Forman, & Sfard, 2001; Lampert & Blunk, 1998) or doing and talking science (Cornelius & Herrenkohl, 2004; Lemke, 1990). Similar changes occurred in Western Europe, Japan, Israel, and parts of Latin America. Much of the microethnographic research in math and science education has involved an instructional design methodology that requires frequent and careful formative assessment to fine-tune the tasks, talk, and tools employed (Brown, 1992; Burkhardt & Schoenfeld, 2003; Cobb, Confrey, diSessa, Lehrer, & Schauble, 2003; Ford & Forman, 2006).

During the past 15 years, numerous microethnographic studies have been conducted in science classrooms (e.g., Bianchini, 1997; Kelly & Brown, 2003; Ritchie, 2002; Warren & Rosebery, 1996). Given its emphasis on the dynamics of face-to-face interaction in classrooms, microethnography seems ideal for explicating *how* science is learned but perhaps not capable of explicating what students "take away" from their engagement in scientific practices. As Sfard (1998) and others have argued, the dominant educational psychology approach is to view learning as acquisition of skills or concepts. This version of learning was clear about what is learned in terms of cognitive structures (e.g., concepts and their connections). In contrast, the dominant metaphor for learning within the sociocultural paradigm is learning as participation. Research conducted in a sociocultural framework tends to articulate *how* learning occurs in classroom communities (e.g., via participant structures, narratives, or argumentation) but rarely examines *what* students take away or how they are changed by those experiences.

A recent article by Engle and Conant (2002) moves us closer to answering these questions about what is learned as well as how. Engle and Conant characterized effective learning environments for science by differentiating among engagement, disciplinary engagement, and productive disciplinary engagement. After reviewing previous research on successful mathematics and science classrooms, they derived their design principles for effective learning environments in math and science classrooms: provide appropriately challenging activities, allow students to take authority over their learning while ensuring that their work can be scrutinized by others (teachers and students), and use criteria acceptable to scientific disciplines (e.g., logical consistency, explanatory power). In addition, students must have access to the resources they need (texts, laboratory equipment, recording devices) to evaluate their claims and communicate them to others.

Engagement requires evidence that students are sufficiently active (e.g., Are they involved in classroom activities? Are they responding to each other? Do they seem interested?) in the curriculum. Evidence of productive engagement requires that students' activities lead somewhere (e.g., that their arguments become more sophisticated over time, that they make more connections between ideas with time, that they generate new questions for investigation or design new studies). In this fashion, Engle and Conant attempted to connect productive work with learning, that is, learning through participation.

Many aspects of Engle and Conant's (2002) article are quite useful and informative. However, similar to many of the studies conducted from a sociocultural perspective, Engle and Conant succeeded more in describing the nature of participation than in articulating what students "took away" from it or what disciplinary resources they had acquired.[8] Although their attention to features of student work in classrooms helps us scrutinize whether participation is *productive,* Engle and Conant's effort was less successful in identifying activity that is *disciplinary.* Their framework provides criteria from psychological task analysis and curriculum design to guide judgments of productive disciplinary engagement (e.g., increasingly complex conceptual networks or increasingly elaborated, articulated, and integrated arguments). Engle and Conant repeatedly referred to "disciplinary norms," "disciplinary issues and practices," and "disciplinary questions and connections" without adequately defining these terms or referring to the literature of science studies.

The attention that the "practice" turn in sociocultural learning theory has brought to classrooms has been extremely valuable. Ethnographies and linguistic analyses have provided detailed accounts of the way classroom activities unfold, and reviews such as that of Engle and Conant have offered principles that can guide the design and management of activities for engaging students in productive "science-like" work. In this way, the field has an increasingly varied toolkit for thinking about student activity in classrooms.

Two questions must be addressed if this body of work is to connect classroom activities with scientific activities. First, we need to know how to determine whether the activities students engage in should be considered authentically scientific. If the work of students is merely "science-like," then what aspects of similarity exist, and how central are they to what distinguishes science as a knowledge-producing discipline? If students are merely engaged in trivial aspects of science (e.g., holding a test tube), then it is unlikely that they are "taking away" what is deemed important in that discipline. Second, we need to know how to consider what students learn from authentic disciplinary engagement when it does occur. That is, when students do authentically engage in the aspects of scientific work that are crucial to the functioning of the discipline, how should we think about *what* they learn?

Answering these two questions requires appeal to the science studies literature. Whereas the "practice turn" in learning theory has reformulated learning in terms of participation, another "practice turn" in science studies has appealed to the practices of scientists, as individuals and groups, to account for the relative reliability of

scientific claims. This literature helps us define authentic scientific practice as constituted by the Roles in that practice and how they interact to make the institution
"work." Thus, "authentic disciplinary engagement" could be defined as accurate
engagement in these Roles, and what students learn from this can be considered as
a "grasp of practice."

Trends in Science Studies

History, philosophy, and sociology of science have recently turned their attention to "practice" in recontextualizing science[9] as a discipline. These literatures aim
to account for the performance of science, that is, its apparent generation of reliable
explanatory accounts of nature. Long-standing arguments appealed to universal logic
and methods and idealized science in terms of objectivity in a largely influential
movement broadly referred to as the positivist endeavor (e.g., Comte & Martineau,
1853; Popper, 1968). More recently, a sociological and historical orientation began
questioning the idealized objectivity of science, drawing attention away from a basis
in logical rules of inference and toward how research programs are based on theoretical frameworks and accompanying methods (e.g., Kuhn, 1970; Lakatos, 1970).

Subsequent efforts aimed to debunk the privileged position of science by challenging its anchor in rationality. This challenge pointed out that individual scientists do
not abide by logical rules of inference but also are susceptible to subjective social and
political considerations. This "social turn," largely a reactive movement to positivist
assertions, produced explanations varying in the degree to which social factors were
asserted to govern science (an extreme version aptly named the "Strong Program"
[Barnes & Bloor, 1982]).

Social Aspect of Scientific Practice

In the wake of this "social turn" in the science studies literature, there has also
been a "practice turn," an effort to account for the relative reliability (and thus intersubjectivity, if not objectivity) of scientific claims through the practices of scientists
as individuals and groups. It is now becoming increasingly accepted that scientific
communities play an important role in negotiating what research questions count as
worth pursuing, which programs of research are viewed as most productive, how
debates are framed, and what drives scientific discovery (Latour, 1987, 1999; Latour
& Woolgar, 1986; Pickering, 1995; Rouse, 1996). More important, the social "practices" of scientific communities have become a way to explain science's *rationality,*
thus replacing the positivist formula whereby logical reasoning played this role. For
example, Longino (2002) argued that the influence exerted by public critique and
peer review on ideas results in publicly accepted "scientific claims" being more effective in explaining nature than those that any individual could produce alone.

Scientists debate ideas that involve matters of fact, method, and values (Laudan,
1984). Scientists share these ideas with each other and, in the process, encounter
alternative assertions of fact, method, and values and are stimulated to resolve dis-

putes regarding which alternatives will best continue the community's work. Scientific ideas are those that have passed community muster and are elevated to the status of "public." Ideas are not considered "scientific" until this occurs. Note that this notion of scientific claim is considerably narrow. The individual scientist who wakes up with an innovation does not have a scientific claim, at least not until it is presented in a public forum and seriously considered by the scientist's peers.

At first glance, this seems a recapitulation of Popper's (1968) critical rationalism. Popper, however, if not strictly a positivist, thought in terms of the positivist account, which focused on logical rules of inference. These rules, of course, did not appeal to social forces because such forces were seen merely as a source of bias that would taint the ideal workings of pure logic. Indeed, apparently for Popper (1972), isolating social aspects of practice from the process of criticism was important enough to have them inhabit a different "World." Popper's World Three was constituted by statements that can be related to each other by logic, whereas social forces were relegated in his theory to World Two. Hence, Popper's mechanism of criticism does not draw on the subjective experience of scientists, neither as individuals nor as a community, but is a matter of logical evaluations between objective statements. Note that, under Popper's account, the explanation is the same at both the individual and communal levels of description—at both levels, the model of criticism is the same. Longino (2002), in contrast, identified social forces as integral to the critical process that supports the rationality of science. Although individual scientists can be biased by social forces, the ways that scientists interact at the communal level are responsible for science's rationality.

The social aspect of scientific practice includes both communal and individual components. Authority resides with the community, which is composed of individuals. The community can be considered as involving two distinct Roles: Constructor of claims regarding matters of fact, method, and values and Critiquer of such claims. The Constructor floats arguments and the Critiquers publicly identify errors in those arguments, at which point the presenter returns to production work and attempts to remove errors. In this way, peer review is an iterative process of both collaboration (as a community) and competition (as individuals). Individuals play both Roles at different times, so their individual contributions to the practice can vary. On a larger level of description, however, the basic function of the enterprise overall is constant. That is, through these Roles, science produces considerably reliable explanatory accounts of nature.

Material Aspect of Scientific Practice

Any account of science is incomplete without its material aspect. It is this aspect of the discipline that distinguishes the basis of authority from that in other disciplines such as mathematics[10] (cf. Stevens et al., 2005). The material aspect is intertwined with the social aspect, because it characterizes *what* the public discussions are about and *why*. Crucially, the material aspect is what ultimately arbitrates subjective disagreements about scientific claims (Bazerman, 1988). "Data decide" because nature is indifferent to our beliefs or claims about it. Because it provides a constraint on and guide to ideas, nature's behavior serves as a referent against which arguments about beliefs and claims are decided. Although the indifference of nature to our beliefs is a fact, the use of this indifference to systematically arbitrate disagreements in science is a foundational value and key aspect of how the endeavor "works." Without the grounding of claims with reference to the behavior of nature, science would not produce explanatory accounts of nature that are as reliable as they are.

At the same time, of course, nature's "voice" in such arguments is not purely independent but is brought to the table by scientists *through material aspects of practice*. This does mean that "data are theory laden" (e.g., Duhem, 1969; Hanson, 1958), because the ways scientists frame, measure, and represent nature to support arguments are directly related to the theoretical notions they are asserting. However, this does not mean that we can make whatever we want of nature's behavior (e.g., Pera, 1994). To express the extent to which nature acts as a constraint on ideas, some philosophers have argued that it is best to think of nature as exerting "material agency" in scientific debates (e.g., Pickering, 1995), as another party at the table, so to speak (Pera, 1994).

There are two interrelated senses of the material practice. In one sense, scientists probe nature by manipulating material to make aspects of it visible and isolated from others. For example, ramp experiments can focus on the patterns by which constant acceleration due to gravity changes the speed of a ball. Although we are familiar with gravity and may even witness freefall in everyday observations, ramp experiments allow a more focused and scientific look at patterns of speed change in isolation. Of course, identifying these patterns requires more than mere observation—the phenomenon must be isolated, framed, and related to some sort of systematic scale. Measurement and the requisite isolation and framing of the phenomenon constitute a substantial amount of scientists' work (Hacking, 1983; Pickering, 1995; Rouse, 1987, 1996).

The reason scientists invest so much time in these efforts is that, through them, they come to learn new things about how nature behaves and are then able to share what they have learned with their peers. Making nature's behavior apparent for peers to support arguments about theory is the second aspect of material practice (Goodwin, 1994; Latour, 1990). Whereas the first aspect of material practice is more about what scientists do to get nature to "speak," the second aspect is more about the way nature's "voice" is portrayed, to convince oneself and others of the existence of a pattern in nature. As noted, scientists argue about nature's behavior in communities. These arguments are *about what is made apparent* through portrayals of what the presenting scientist did and how nature responded; in other words, the crux of the arguments is "explicit connections" to nature's behavior (Rouse, 1996). Of course, it is the arguments that demonstrate something new about nature's behavior that are considered compelling.

The material and social aspects of science are, of course, intertwined. Although it is true that there are particular ways of talking in science (e.g., Lemke, 1990), these ways of talking are intertwined with and dependent upon the material aspect of practice. It is the "capture" or "marshalling of material agency" and the subsequent representation of nature in scientific arguments that convince peers and therefore are the source of authority in science.

Scientific Practice as Interplay of Roles

Thus, we have an account of scientific practice that, although complex in the details of each case, is considerably simple in its basic structure. Scientists construct explanatory accounts of nature and debate with other scientists about these accounts, drawing on information they have gathered on nature's behavior as an arbiter for specific points in their arguments. The community as a whole comes to a consensus regarding the account that explains most and conforms best to nature's behavior, which is how individual scientists' claims become the community's scientific claims. With this basic model of practice, we can pull out the specific Roles played by individuals—Constructors and Critiquers of claims. These Roles play out in both public and private spheres.

Consider how these two Roles relate to the basic model of scientific practice described here and how they are, in practice, two sides of the same overall activity. Table 1 provides a model of how this occurs. In this model, the Roles of Constructor and Critiquer involve both the social and material aspects of science. The social aspect is represented by the movement patterns through the numbered cells and the material aspects by the activities of framing, measuring, and representing nature's behavior occurring within these cells. Consider a claim Constructor conducting an experiment (Stage 1). He or she subsequently presents this claim to his or her community of peers, the Critiquers, where it is evaluated in terms of the ways nature's behavior, as seen through data collection, analysis, and representation, sufficiently or insufficiently demonstrates an "explicit connection" to the claim (Stage 2). The Constructor returns to his or her private realm and revises the claim itself or the data collection, analysis, or representation process. In either case, the aim is achieving a better "explicit connection" between the claim and nature's behavior (Stage 3). In this stage of private revision, the community of peers is not physically present but is still present in a way, because the Critique has become a part of the way the scientist reasons about and conducts Construction (signified by a split of Stage 3 between

TABLE 1 A Sequence Through Roles and Realms in Social and Material Practices of Science

	Constructor Role	Critiquer Role
Private and individual (e.g., laboratory)	1, 3	3
Public community (e.g., conferences, journals, reviews)	4	2

Constructor and Critiquer Roles). Finally, the Constructor returns to the community of peers where, if the claim is informative and the community can find no other objections about its Construction, the claim is accepted. Acceptance of the claim elevates it from a product of an individual to a product of the community (Stage 4).

Although they are *analytically separable,* the two Roles depend integrally on each other and how they interact in practice for their sense and rationale. Therefore, we consider them *psychologically inextricable.* As an example of this essential integration, consider how individual efforts to Construct claims (i.e., collecting, analyzing, and representing data) in practice become governed by features of Critique appropriated from the social level. Indeed, the Roles themselves are to a significant extent constituted by each other. One would not be able to act as an appropriate Critiquer without also being able to be a Constructor, and vice versa. Learning a practice involves becoming able to play both Roles appropriately, with *appropriateness* appealing to the rationale of how these Roles interact toward the overall function of the practice. Knowing a Role includes not only the local action but an awareness of how one's action interacts with the actions of other Roles to support the function of the practice overall. We refer to this holistic knowing about Roles and how they interact at a community level as a "grasp of practice" (Ford, in press).

Our aim in summarizing the social studies of science literature is to explicate key aspects of authentic disciplinary practice in science. Although educational researchers such as Engle and Conant (2002) have developed design principles for fostering productive disciplinary engagement in classrooms, these principles have ignored two important questions: How do we distinguish between science-like and authentic disciplinary activities? and What do students "take away" from their productive disciplinary engagements? To provide authentic access to disciplinary practices, classroom activities need to simulate both the social and the material aspects of science. Through such engagement, students attain a "grasp" of how the enterprise works through their activity in the Roles of Constructor and Critiquer of claims. Because disciplinary authority in science is based in the community and these ways of interacting, a "grasp of practice" represents access to the discipline at its most fundamental level and serves as a basic yet powerful disciplinary resource. Before turning to elaborate on the value of this resource, in the next section we use this vision of authentic disciplinary engagement to critique several programs of classroom research in science education.

PROGRAMS OF RESEARCH IN SCIENCE EDUCATION

We have selected four programs of educational research to discuss in light of our analysis of the literature on science studies. Our aim is to use our framework to evaluate the degree to which these programs are likely to foster authentic engagement with the social and material practices of science and to familiarize students with the integration of those practices with the Roles of Constructor and Critiquer of claims. The first two programs of research highlight the discourse of science classrooms; the second two programs show how discourse is linked to material practices in classrooms. The first of the research groups, Osborne, Erduran, and Simon, use Toulmin's (1958/1964) model of argumentation to help teachers and students analyze the important components of a valued scientific discursive practice. The second group, Mortimer and Scott and their colleagues, use Bakhtin's notion of dialogicality to investigate classrooms where students are able to author their own scientific explanations. Varelas and Pappas and their colleagues (the third group) employ the notion of intertextuality to understand how students and teachers connect oral and written language with their instructional histories and classroom activities. Finally, Lehrer and Schauble and their colleagues argue that learning science involves at least three interrelated activities: "rhetoric, representation, and modeling" (Lehrer, Schauble, & Petrosino, 2001, p. 251).

Research Based on Toulmin's Model of Argumentation

Osborne, Erduran, and Simon and their colleagues (Driver, Newton, & Osborne, 2000; Erduran, Simon, & Osborne, 2004; Osborne, Erduran, & Simon, 2004; Simon, Erduran, & Osborne, 2006; Simon, Osborne, & Erduran, 2003) have chosen to focus on an important rhetorical genre in science education: argumentation. They propose that "the teaching of argumentation through the use of appropriate activities and pedagogical strategies is . . . a means of promoting epistemic, cognitive and social goals as well as enhancing students' conceptual understanding of science" (Simon et al., 2006, p. 236). Their aim is to change the view of science that classrooms often implicitly endorse (as a set of canonical truths) to a perspective on the discipline that emphasizes its contested and emergent nature. Whereas a focus on explanations and concepts has been a popular learning goal for science education, Simon and her colleagues include argumentation as a learning goal. In their view, argumentation is a central practice in science: the social, logical, and empirically grounded way that competing claims are ultimately judged within a disciplinary community. Thus, they feel that teachers and students need to use argumentation in classrooms so that students can learn, first hand, appropriate scientific norms for the practice (e.g., supporting claims with evidence); can become comfortable with the rhetoric of science; and can experience its power and utility (Driver et al., 2000).

Toulmin's (1958/1964) theory of argumentation has served as a tool in their work with teachers and students, following up on its use in previous research in science and math education (e.g., Forman, Larreamendy-Joerns, Stein, & Brown, 1998; Jimenez-Aleixandre, Rodriguez, & Duschl, 2000; Kelly, Drucker, & Chen, 1998; Krummheuer, 1995). Toulmin's model specifies the main components of any contested knowledge claim and their connections: data, claim, warrants, and backing. Qualifiers and rebuttals are also specified in his model. While admitting the limitations of this abstract scheme for educators, they recognize that argumentation needs to be explicitly taught if one hopes to instill it in classrooms (Driver et al., 2000; Simon et al., 2006).

In one study of a professional development program with 12 middle school teachers in the United Kingdom, Simon and her colleagues (2006) used a socioscientific task (whether a new zoo should receive funding). They asked their teachers to design detailed lesson plans and encourage their students to brainstorm for or against this proposal. Teachers were then provided with additional activities for fostering argumentation and asked to teach nine argument-based lessons over a year (approximately once per month). The zoo lesson was observed and taped twice for each teacher (at the beginning of the first year and at the beginning of the second year with a new group of students).

Simon et al. (2006) found that their teachers varied quite a bit in their comfort with and goals for argumentation. They also found that the teachers used argumentation in their classrooms in a multitude of ways: in whole-class debate, in small groups of students, and in whole-class reflections. Over a 1-year period, some teachers' classrooms showed increasingly complex arguments (exhibiting claims, data, warrants, and backing), while others did not (exhibiting claims and data only).

How can we evaluate this program of research in light of our review of the science studies literature (i.e., according to our original three points)? The emphasis on the social nature of arguments in this body of work clearly supports our first point: the social aspect of scientific practice. Simon, Erduran, Osborne, and their colleagues have been working diligently with teachers to help increase their familiarity with orchestrating public debates in classrooms that are based, in part, on science content. They emphasize the need for the teacher to play "devil's advocate" or, in their terms, be a "hole-seeker" providing critique and pressing students to revise their arguments in light of this criticism. Thus, the social aspect of science is clearly represented in their work.

However, the material aspects of scientific practice are harder to find in this body of research—beyond their recognition that arguments must be grounded in empirical data. That is, the work of framing, measuring, and representing through which empirical data are constructed is not given substantial attention, and the point of such work, to achieve authority for one's claims, also seems missing. Finally, the integration of social and material practices as an interplay of Roles is merely hinted at in this approach to argumentation, and it is not clear whether students are actually invited into these Roles authentically through the support provided by a general argument structure.

Toulmin's framework was derived from abstracting the final, well-formed arguments of experts and not from novices' beginning attempts to articulate and defend their claims. Simon and her colleagues used this abstract framework to help teachers support and motivate their students' argumentation. Thus, the rationale for developing a mature scientific argument may be obscure for both teachers and students who are using the Toulmin system. The scope of what students could argue about is also considerably constrained. It is unclear whether matters of method and values are as open for debate in these classrooms as are matters of fact. For example, despite the centrality of debates in science about ways to measure and inscribe data, it is not clear whether such debates would be part of this approach to teaching argumentation. In contrast, our framework of scientific practice emphasizes the importance of anchoring arguments (and the reason for arguing) in the material behavior of nature.

Similar points were made by Lehrer et al. (2001) about the training of students in experimentation. If students and teachers are not fully aware of why argumentation (or experimentation) is useful, then they have failed to understand their role as designers and interpreters of experiments and observations and have failed to participate in a disciplinary practice. If students and teachers are not aware of or interested in authoring truth claims, then training them to use argumentation would not be sufficient for inculcating a disciplinary approach in science education. By implication, the Roles they would learn would not be Constructor and Critiquer of claims as they exist in practice.

Research Based on Bakhtin's Dialogicality

Mortimer and Scott and their colleagues have chosen to focus on the discursive dynamics of authoring in classrooms, using Bakhtin's theory. One aspect of their framework involves the tension between authoritative and internally persuasive discourse in Bakhtin's theory: the authoritative word of the teacher, textbook, and discipline versus the internally persuasive word of each student's intuitions, feelings, experiences, and interests (cf. Forman, McCormick, & Donato, 1998). For Bakhtin, every utterance can potentially embody this tension between the authoritative and internally persuasive voices—this is the essence of his notion of dialogicality. Nevertheless, some utterances are monological: They are only authoritative. Mortimer and Scott are interested in investigating the degree to which classroom discourse is monological (or authoritative) versus dialogic.

Building from Bakhtin's theory, Mortimer, Scott, and their colleagues (Mortimer & Scott, 2003; Scott, Mortimer, & Aguiar, 2006) differentiate between four different classes of communicative acts and their functions over time in science classrooms: interactive/dialogic, noninteractive/dialogic, interactive/authoritative, and noninteractive/authoritative. They argue that during the course of a teaching episode (within or across lessons), teachers' purposes for using different types of discourse may change, resulting in a different pattern of authoritative and dialogic communication among individuals and groups.

For example, an early lesson on thermal physics in a Brazilian high school class involved students brainstorming about their senses of temperature (after a demonstration) and justification of their reasoning (Scott et al., 2006). In this lesson, dialogic and interactive communication predominated to support a teaching goal of generating hypotheses and backing up claims. In later lessons, when the historical origins of ideas about heat were linked to students' intuitions, speech became more authoritative and interactive. Scott and his colleagues propose that this contrast was intentional on the part of the teacher and consistent with a disciplinary norm that holds students accountable for their claims (Engle & Conant, 2002). Scott et al. continue by arguing that this disciplinary norm "encourages students to take ownership of the scientific point of view" (p. 13). Although Scott and his colleagues emphasize (like Bakhtin) the inherent tension between authoritative and dialogic (or internally persuasive) utterances, they see this tension as quite productive. "The tension which we refer to in this article develops as dialogic exploration of both everyday and scientific views requires resolution through authoritative guidance by the teacher" (p. 19). They view the dynamic between speech forms and functions as dialectic: A predominance of one pattern in a given lesson can provoke the predominance of the other in a future lesson. Thus, the teacher intentionally created a third space (Gutierrez et al., 1999) where students' intuitions about temperature, scientific explanations, and the norms of scientific argumentation create a hybrid dialogue within and across lessons.

How does this second body of research address the three points of our framework? Mortimer and Scott's research clearly aligns with the first of our three points from the science studies literature: the social aspect of scientific practice. The second point, the material aspect of scientific practice, is deemphasized in this work, except as it functions as empirical support for claims. Finally, does it address the third point (practice as an interplay of Roles)? We believe that it has the potential to come closer to this theme if they expand their theory to deal with Bakhtin's notion of addressivity.

Hayes and Matusov (2005) have used addressivity in their work to critique the notion of ownership in educational research. They argue that ownership of ideas or intellectual products (as used by Scott et al., 2006) is theoretically incoherent (e.g., more monologic than dialogic) and less educationally useful than a construct such as addressivity that refers to mutual respect and integrated activity in the service of collective goals. Addressivity was defined by Volosinov (another important member of the Bakhtinian school) in the following manner:

Each person's inner world and thought has its stabilized *social audience* that comprises the environment in which reasons, motives, values, and so on are fashioned . . . the *word is a two-sided act*. It is determined equally by *whose* word it is and *for whom* it is meant. . . . I give myself verbal shape from another's point of view, ultimately, from the point of view of the community to which I belong. (Volosinov, 1929/1986, pp. 85–86)

By focusing on addressivity in science classroom discussions, we believe that research on learning could come closer to the third theme in our framework. The Roles of Constructor and Critiquer of claims are characterized by addressivity. As scientists compile their activities (experiments, observations, material practices, written and oral communications, inscriptions), they must keep in mind the likely counterarguments of their critics (e.g., competitors, journal reviewers, funding panels, institutional review boards, tenure and promotion committees). The process of presenting and answering competing claims in science involves complex decisions about authorship. For example, reviewers and editors play a substantial part in making sure that authors appropriately address their journal's audience. Nevertheless, reviewers and editors do not share ownership with the authors of articles. Thus, we believe that our third point could be adequately addressed in science education if investigators examined the potential of classrooms for fostering addressivity as well as dialogicality. Another aspect of Bakhtin's theory, intertextuality, provides educational practice the option of integrating, in a workable and coherent way, our second theme (material practices) with social aspects of practice and the Roles of Constructor and Critiquer.

Research Based on Intertextuality

Pappas and Varelas and their colleagues (e.g., Pappas, Varelas, Barry, & Rife, 2003; Varelas, 1996; Varelas & Pappas, 2006) have employed the notion of intertextuality to explore the connections within and across classroom resources for learning science (especially in the primary grades). They define "texts" quite broadly to encompass written documents (fiction and nonfiction books, writing on the board and on classroom posters, books from home and elsewhere, drawings), shared oral texts (songs, poems, rhymes, media events), current and prior classroom discourse, recounted events, and hands-on data explorations (inside or outside the classroom) (Varelas & Pappas, 2006). As in the previous two programs of research, Pappas and Varelas are interested in maximizing authentic and meaningful engagement with science in classrooms (especially among teachers and young children in urban classrooms in the United States). Like Lemke (1990, 1992), they endorse the notion that creating connections among texts is both a general meaning-making process and a valued practice in the discipline of science.

In one illustrative study, Varelas and Pappas (2006) employed information books and read-aloud activities along with hands-on explorations to foster scientific activities in two urban primary school classrooms. After they coded seven read-aloud sessions in both classrooms for instances of intertextuality of various types, they found that event links (recounts from personal and impersonal experiences or from generalized experiences) were the most frequent category, followed by connections to hands-on activities and links to prior classroom discourse. They also saw a shift over time from "narrative to scientific language, which was accompanied by a decrease in event intertextuality and an increase of intertextual links to hands-on explorations" (p. 252). They argued that connecting theory and data, which intertextuality involves, could be seen in its early form when children relate their hands-on experiences with information texts (as well as with personal experiences). In addition, when they compared the two classrooms, they found that the second graders were more likely than the first graders to ask "why" questions (e.g., the causes and meaning of an event or hypotheses about an alternative event), which they viewed as a version of theorizing essential to science. Therefore, it appears that the teachers in these classrooms were able to create a third space (Gutiérrez et al., 1999) where students' experiences and intuitions could be heard by teachers and connected via intertextuality with authoritative scientific information texts.

Lemke (1992) helped us connect intertextuality to the discipline of science when he argued that the aim of science is not to repeat texts but to understand how texts are structured or patterned in the scientific community.

In science, unlike some other subjects (e.g., literature), it is only the *pattern* that counts as the content of the subject, not any particular text which instances it. Mastery of the pattern, the ability to "say it in your own words," means reproducing the pattern, not the text. Learning the pattern, like learning a genre, requires exposure to many differently worded instances of it (necessary, but not sufficient). The pattern is an intertextual formation, characteristic of a community; it is not predictable from knowledge of the syntax or lexicon of the language used to say it, or even from the semantic potential of the language. (p. 262)

A related idea is "intercontextuality": the linkages among events in the past, present, and future (Bloome, Power, Morton, Otto, & Shuart-Faris, 2005; Engle, in press; Floriani, 1994; Heras, 1994). Science advances when authors cite previous investigations as justification for current investigations. Educators are also proposing that students be made aware of how their present activities relate to their instructional histories (Engle, in press; Strom, Kemeny, Lehrer, & Forman, 2001) and to their likely futures (Forman & Ansell, 2001). Engle (in press) argues that when students are active agents in their own investigations, teachers need to support the long-term generativity of those practices by linking them explicitly to their use in other situations via intercontextuality. The aim is not merely to promote the "transfer" of isolated skills, but of an entire activity system.

By employing the notion of intertextuality, Varelas and Pappas (2006) help us understand the beginnings of links between concrete experiences and explanations that can engage even young children in an activity that is a key characteristic of scientific communities. In this way, children can be familiarized with the *pattern* of connections in science (e.g., between experiments and claims, between one's own argument and other arguments). This body of research appears to show that even primary school classrooms can engage students in science as a social and material practice. Their transcripts indicate that students were listening to each other, to some degree, and responding to the teachers' thoughtful questions and comments about their theorizing.

However, it is not clear in several respects whether these students were engaged in disciplinary authenticity or merely "science-like" activities. First, it is not obvious that the students saw their Roles as Constructors and Critiquers of scientific investigations (as in our third point). Second, it is not obvious whether the teachers who worked with Pappas and Varelas emphasized intercontextuality as well as intertextuality. Because intercontextuality may be necessary for helping students understand how today's lesson is linked to last week's or next year's, it is important that such extratextual connections be made explicitly as well as implicitly in order for those activities to serve as learning resources. Finally, Pappas and Varelas have not conducted as careful an analysis of the "hands-on" activities as they have of the different types of literary and discursive activities that constitute their typology of intertextual links. Thus, it is possible that those "hands-on" activities are not connected to key scientific models (e.g., of energy and matter) or the central aspects of practice in science that are developmentally appropriate. This is where our fourth and final program of research (that of Lehrer, Schauble, and their colleagues) provides a useful contrast to the previous three research programs.

Research Based on Rhetoric, Representation, and Modeling

Lehrer, Schauble and their colleagues have been investigating children's mathematical and scientific problem solving in U.S. elementary schools for many years (a recent review of this work appears in Lehrer & Schauble, 2006). Unlike the previous three research programs, Lehrer and Schauble do not often conduct detailed analyses of classroom discourse (Strom et al., 2001, is an exception). However, they view argumentation, data representation, and modeling as three integrated aspects of scientific practice and classroom practice (Lehrer et al., 2001). In addition, Lehrer, Schauble, and their colleagues explicitly reference and employ many of the sources we have cited from the science studies literature when they write about their project and when they design their instructional activities. Thus, these investigators have anticipated our framework for evaluating studies in science education.

Lehrer and Schauble are critical of research that focuses on experimentation by itself as being foundational in science education. "Experimentation is always embedded in a context of argument or rhetoric about the model-appropriateness of the materials, procedures, instruments, objects, and manipulations that are employed" (Lehrer et al., 2001, pp. 257–258). Likewise, they see argument as being merely one aspect of an integrated disciplinary practice. For Lehrer and Schauble (2006), science is about creating and evaluating causal models of the world, whereas arguments and inscriptions (representations) are the resources used by scientific communities to support or refute those models. Their educational research program is based on this concept of scientific practice and their belief that even young children can engage in important aspects of it.

One example of how they integrate modeling, representation, and argumentation in their classroom work appears in Lehrer, Schauble, Carpenter, and Penner (2000). In this chapter, they described a sequence of classroom lessons in U.S. elementary school classrooms (second and third grades) in which one group of students first investigated inclined planes and freefall and then investigated plant growth. During the first investigation, students found that they needed to invent the notion of steepness to compare ramps and discovered, after extensive discussions (i.e., instructionally orchestrated and supported arguments), that the ramps could be viewed as right triangles (representations) that varied in angle of inclination. In this way, arguments and representations were employed in the service of modeling freefall, that is, constructing a conceptual framework for linking ideas to framed, measured, and represented aspects of that phenomenon.

This same group of students, in a second investigation, plotted growth curves of Wisconsin fast plants. On the surface, these disparate activities would seem unlikely to demonstrate learning gains using standard educational psychology criteria, because they may not appear to be connected to the same content. Nevertheless, as students attempted to explain changes in growth over the life span of a plant, which on a graph appears to have an S shape, one of them realized that using the right triangle from their earlier work with ramps would help them quantify the slope of a graph at some key intervals and explained it to her classmates. Thus, the triangle became not just a tool that framed a key feature of a ramp for measurement; it was used to generalize rates of change across different intervals of time on a growth curve. In this way, the triangle became a key symbolic means in this classroom community: a representation that proved its value in two arguments conceptually involving foundational ideas in science. Although the authors did not explicitly link these lessons to the literature on intertextuality and intercontextuality, it appears that those notions could help explain the long-term advantages of instruction that builds like this from one investigation to the next (Engle, in press).

Applying our framework to the Lehrer and Schauble research indicates that their work incorporates at least the first two points from the field of science studies: science as a social practice and science as a material practice. Students were encouraged and supported to debate the relative usefulness of alternative ideas that they brought to the table, and these discussions were purposefully orchestrated by framing, measuring, and representing particular physical phenomena for scrutiny. We would also argue that it embodies the third point as well, science as an interplay of Roles. This is because the students were genuinely engaged in investigating questions that interested them (why objects roll or plants grow in particular ways) and in constructing ways of representing answers to those questions (e.g., graphs of growth curves) that could be used to support their claims about causal mechanisms. To address the counterclaims of their classmates or teachers, they needed to anticipate those claims by rejecting solutions to their investigations that were inadequate. These arguments and investigations were classroom-community wide and occurred throughout the academic year as one investigation led to another. Just as in the history of science (e.g., Pickering, 1995; Rouse, 1987, 1996), students in the Lehrer and Schauble program pursue new questions after they emerge and invent new tools or employ old tools for new purposes to record and debate the results of their investigations of the material world. It is not surprising that this fourth program of research is more closely aligned with our framework for examining disciplinary learning in classrooms given that the investigators have intentionally modeled their classroom practices on aspects of the science studies literature.

CONCLUSIONS AND IMPLICATIONS FOR EDUCATIONAL RESEARCH

Has our framework, adapted from the science studies literature, helped us come closer to answering our initial question: What counts as disciplinary learning in a classroom context? We believe that we have begun to answer this question for the discipline of science. An initial answer to this question was the notion of productive disciplinary engagement first articulated by Engle and Conant (2002). We feel that we have gone beyond their notion in at least two ways. First, we have been able return to Dewey's notion of psychologizing the subject matter in terms of sociocultural learning theory by examining a sample of current work in science education in terms of our three points: social aspects and material aspects of scientific practice and practice as the interplay of Roles. We believe that a focus on these three points allows us to distinguish between science-like activities and activities that are genuinely scientific.

Second, we feel that our framework moves us closer to understanding what students are "taking away" in terms of disciplinary resources from authentic scientific activities. This issue is very important when one begins to redefine "what counts" as learning science in classrooms (i.e., learning objectives). The aspects of a discipline that arbitrate between competing knowledge claims are the source of a discipline's authority. If students are to grasp how disciplines and their products can serve as resources in their lives, this basis of disciplinary authority is fundamentally necessary.

Kelly's (2005) reading of a slightly different sample of the science studies literature made him cautious about using that work to go beyond *describing* scientific practices to *prescribing normative* educational practices. As he argued, some of this research tends to view science as relativistic: Knowledge claims are determined more by social power dynamics in a community than by rationality. Kelly cautioned that naively importing these notions to science education could encourage teachers to allow the free flow of competing ideas without a way of arbitrating between them. We agree with Kelly's concerns, but our reading of a different sample of science studies publications suggests that a corrective to extreme relativism is available within that field in the added focus on material practices and on the integration of social and material aspects of science with the interactional Roles of Constructor and Critiquer of knowledge claims. Nevertheless, we also agree that classroom norms are necessarily responsive to nondisciplinary (i.e., psychological and institutional) constraints. For example, teachers face many challenges when they attempt to modify their instructional approaches, including limited time, energy, and resources.

Nevertheless, if we believe that providing access to disciplines is an important objective of classroom learning, and if the basis of disciplinary authority is through its practices, then what students "take away" needs to include a "grasp" of how the discipline works. A turn to meta-disciplinary scholarship, especially scholarship that explains the discipline in terms of its practices, is thus an essential resource in considering what students should be learning. The conceptual innovation presented here is that this grasp of the scientific enterprise necessarily involves the ways that the Roles of Critiquer and Constructor are integrated and reflects both material and social aspects of science. This is a small but important step, because if we are serious about supporting learning though participation in disciplinary practices, we need a way of thinking about which ones are of most consequence, both for the discipline and for students. We believe that the aspects of a practice of most consequence are those that ground the discipline's authority, arbitrating between competing knowledge claims.

This innovation, of course, will require more work to explicate psychologically how a grasp of these disciplinary practices can serve as a personal resource. Here we follow Packer (2001), who offered a proposal to expand sociocultural approaches to learning in school by providing a new ontology of the person and a revised view of the goals of schooling. Packer drew on Lave (1988) and Dewey (1916) to critique the traditional, "functionalist" account of schooling, which is based on two anachronistic assumptions: (a) It conceives of what is learned in terms of conceptual structures, and (b) it views society in terms of a closed, deterministic system of people interacting in their use of these conceptual structures. Although schools continue to operate on these two assumptions, there is considerable scholarship that shows that these two underpinnings of this functionalist account of schooling are badly misguided. First, the notion of learning conceptual structures followed by their transfer for valued competencies does not align with what we know about human abilities (Brown, 1992). Second, society, as many have noted (e.g., Dewey, 1916; Luke, 2004; Packer, 2001), is hardly static but is rather a dynamic and complex emergent result of many dimensions of social negotiation. Thus, training students to "fit into" a static social position is counterproductive and, it could be said, irresponsible. Packer (2001) argued that schools need to recognize their responsibility for preparing students to transform themselves instead of focusing exclusively on the transfer of isolated skills, concepts, or strategies across static contexts. "Schooling itself must be reconceptualized as a praxis wherein children are transformed, in the face of multiple, often contradictory, political and economic demands" (p. 510).

Our notion of the "grasp of practice" represents learning objectives as fundamentally different from conceptual structures or behavioral skills. We believe that classroom contexts that familiarize students with the essential Roles of the discipline can equip them to flexibly respond to a large range of complex problems instead of training them to use a narrow set of skills or strategies in limited circumstances (Engle, in press; Ford, 2005; Greeno, 2006). We agree with Holland and her colleagues, who argued that human agency involves acts of improvisation and of orchestration of social roles or positions from within a practice (Holland et al., 1998). What one can do in a situation builds upon prior experiences with one's Roles in a community but is not restricted by them. Instead, prior experience can be a resource for generating alternative Roles, as new life is breathed into that resource for a novel purpose and effect. A Role is necessary for "positioning" oneself and others in various ways. In addition, as noted earlier, Roles are mutually constitutive because in a practice actors must be responsive to each other, as in Bakhtin's and Volosinov's notion of addressivity (Volosinov, 1929/1986).

Society is not static but is an emergent result of social negotiation. Roles are resources for negotiation that stem from disciplines. When one appeals to a Role in a situation, it casts that situation (or frames it) as part of a practice, positioning other actors as potential players in the practice (Holland et al., 1998). How a situation is framed is fundamentally what is at stake in social negotiations. If schools could provide Roles that link to traditional disciplines (e.g., math, science, history, literature), then they could provide students with disciplinary resources that have their basis in perhaps the most fundamental and shared cultural stores available to our society, those that are perhaps most "broad in scope" (Dewey, 1916).

We have explicated this notion of disciplinary resource using a framework derived from a selective reading of one discipline. Other readings of the science studies literature may provide additional frameworks for critiquing classroom research in science education. Other disciplines have models for authority and influence that also involve social negotiation but different criteria of "what counts" as knowledge and "what counts" as the basis of authority. The notion of Roles as learning objectives could be explicated for other disciplines as well, bringing together what we know about these disciplines with sociocultural learning theory to design curricula that appeal appropriately to both psychology and disciplinary domains (Shulman & Quinlan, 1996).

For a sociocultural vision of schooling to take hold, a conception of disciplinary resources is necessary but not sufficient. Other work needs to help us understand the forms of instruction that provide students opportunities to learn the grasp of practice. Students need to be positioned (Holland et al., 1998) as players in a practice and be afforded opportunities to position or author themselves in that practice. Considerable work remains for us to clearly articulate visions of those practices that matter most and then to design forms of instruction that would position students as disciplinary players. It is this grounded work that may succeed in changing the way schools function, and a grasp of practice can organize a way of thinking about the kinds of people we aim for our students to become.

ACKNOWLEDGMENTS

The order of authorship is alphabetical; the contribution of both authors was equal. We acknowledge the valuable feedback we received on earlier versions of this chapter from Judith Green; our two reviewers, Neil Mercer and Martin Packer; and from members of the Pittsburgh Interaction Analysis Group: Jim Greeno, Gaea Leinhardt, Stephen Pelethy, Sarah Starr, Gabriel Stylianides, and Carla van de Sande.

NOTES

[1] We refer to this literature as "science studies" because it includes work by philosophers, anthropologists, linguists, psychologists, and sociologists that attempts to depict the essential practices of scientists in the natural sciences.

[2] We use the term "sociocultural theory" to refer to this family of theories within psychology and education. One of the founders of this theory, Lev Vygotsky, referred to his work as cultural historical theory (Cole, 1996).

[3] We use the term "grasp of practice" deliberately to denote an understanding that does not need to reside "in the head" but includes "know-how." In the remainder of this chapter, we plan to present a broad picture of what we mean by scientific "know-how" or a "grasp of practice."

[4] We have chosen these three points from the science studies literature to focus our review of that literature and our review of the literature in science education. We have also chosen them because, in our view, they are more consistent with our overall argument about the grasp of scientific practice. Other scholars may prefer to summarize this literature using different themes.

[5] We have decided to capitalize Roles when we refer to the specific subject positions of Constructor and Critiquer of claims in a scientific community or a classroom science community modeled after the discipline. Keep in mind that this notion of Roles in science is not fixed but negotiable, as with the norms of science or aims of any investigation.

[6] A closer connection between Dewey and Vygotsky is likely. Prawat (2000) proposed that Dewey met Vygotsky during his trip to the Soviet Union in 1928 at the invitation of leading Russian educators. Cole (1996) noted that Vygotsky and his colleagues read Dewey as well as Piaget and other important theorists of their era.

[7] Bakhtin was a literary theorist, so his "data" were texts, such as the dialogic novels of Dostoyevsky (e.g., Bakhtin, 1984).

[8] In a more recent article, Engle (in press) addresses the issue of what students "take away" directly by providing her own reconceptualization of "transfer."

⁹ We recognize that the natural and life sciences comprise a variety of explanatory models and methods; some are experimental, others are historical. For the purposes of this chapter, we survey philosophical, historical, linguistic, and sociological work that draws from physics, engineering, biology, chemistry, and other pure and applied sciences. Thus, we see a value in using "science" rather than any one particular science in our argument.

¹⁰ Social and material practices unite the subfields within the physical and living sciences. Biologists as well as physicists must base their truth claims on evidence from the natural world. Of course, social scientists also base their claims on evidence from the human world. Thus, some aspects of our argument could apply to disciplines other than the natural sciences.

REFERENCES

American Association for the Advancement of Science. (1993). *Benchmarks for science literacy.* New York: Oxford University Press.

Bakhtin, M. M. (1981). *The dialogic imagination: Four essays* (C. Emerson & M. Holquist, Trans.). Austin: University of Texas Press.

Bakhtin, M. (1984). *Problems of Dostoyevsky's poetics* (C. Emerson, Trans.). Minneapolis: University of Minnesota Press.

Barnes, B., & Bloor, D. (1982). Relativism, rationalism, and the sociology of knowledge. In M. Hollis & S. Lukes (Eds.), *Rationality and relativism* (pp. 21–47). Oxford, England: Blackwell.

Bazerman, C. (1988). *Shaping written knowledge: The genre and activity of the experimental article in science.* Madison: University of Wisconsin Press.

Bianchini, J. (1997). Where knowledge construction, equity, and context intersect: Student learning of science in small groups. *Journal of Research in Science Teaching, 34,* 1039–1065.

Bloome, D., Power, C. S., Morton, C. B., Otto, S., & Shuart-Faris, N. (2005). *Discourse analysis and the study of classroom language and literacy events: A microethnographic perspective.* Mahwah, NJ: Erlbaum.

Boaler, J., & Greeno, J. G. (2000). Identity, agency, and knowing in mathematics worlds. In J. Boaler (Ed.), *Multiple perspectives on mathematics teaching and learning* (pp. 171–200). Westport, CT: Ablex.

Brown, A. L. (1992). Design experiments: Theoretical and methodological challenges in creating complex interventions in classroom settings. *Journal of the Learning Sciences, 2,* 141–178.

Brown, B. B., Reveles, J. M., & Kelly, G. J. (2005). Scientific literacy and discursive identity: A theoretical framework for understanding science learning. *Science Education, 89,* 779–802.

Brown, J. S., Collins, A., & Duguid, P. (1989). Situated cognition and the culture of learning. *Educational Researcher, 18*(1), 32–42.

Burkhardt, H., & Schoenfeld, A. H. (2003). Improving educational research: Toward a more useful, more influential, and better-funded enterprise. *Educational Researcher, 32*(9), 3–14.

Cahan, E. D., & White, S. H. (1992). Proposals for a second psychology. *American Psychologist, 47,* 224–235.

Cazden, C. B. (1993). Vygotsky, Hymes, and Bakhtin: From word to utterance and voice. In E. A. Forman, N. Minick, & C. A. Stone (Eds.), *Contexts for learning: Sociocultural dynamics in children's development* (pp. 197–212). New York: Oxford University Press.

Cobb, P., Confrey, J., diSessa, A., Lehrer, R., & Schauble, L. (2003). Design experiments in educational research. *Educational Researcher, 32*(1), 9–13.

Cole, M. (1996). *Cultural psychology: A once and future discipline.* Cambridge, MA: Belknap Press of Harvard University Press.

Comte, A., & Martineau, H. (1853). *The positive philosophy of Auguste Comte.* London: Chapman.

Cornelius, L. L., & Herrenkohl, L. R. (2004). Power in the classroom: How the classroom environment shapes students' relationships with each other and with concepts. *Cognition and Instruction, 22,* 389–392.

Dewey, J. (1916). *Education and democracy.* New York: Macmillan.

Driver, R., Newton, P., & Osborne, J. (2000). Establishing the norms of scientific argumentation in classrooms. *Science Education, 84,* 287–312.

Duhem, P. (1969). *To save the phenomena: An essay on the idea of physical theory from Plato to Galileo.* Chicago: University of Chicago Press.

Eisenhart, M. A. (1988). The ethnographic research tradition and mathematics education research. *Journal for Research in Mathematics Education, 19,* 99–114.

Engle, R. A. (in press). Framing interactions to foster generative learning: A situative explanation of transfer in a community of learners classroom. *Journal of the Learning Sciences.*

Engle, R. A., & Conant, F. R. (2002). Guiding principles for fostering productive disciplinary engagement: Explaining an emergent argument in a community of learners classroom. *Cognition and Instruction, 20,* 399–483.

Erduran, S., Simon, S., & Osborne, J. (2004). Tapping in argumentation: Developments in the application of Toulmin's argument pattern for studying science discourse. *Science Education, 88,* 915–933.

Erickson, F. (1986). Qualitative methods on research on teaching. In M. Wittrock (Ed.), *Handbook of research on teaching* (3rd ed., pp. 119–161). New York: Macmillan.

Erickson, F., & Gutierrez, K. (2002). Culture, rigor, and science in educational research. *Educational Researcher, 31*(8), 21–24.

Floriani, A. (1994). Negotiating what counts: Role and relationships, texts and contexts, content and meaning. *Linguistics and Education, 5,* 241–274.

Ford, M. J. (2005). The game, the pieces, and the players: Generative resources from alternative instructional portrayals of experimentation. *Journal of the Learning Sciences, 14,* 449–487.

Ford, M. J. (in press). 'Grasp of practice' as a reasoning resource for inquiry and nature of science understanding. *Science and Education.*

Ford, M. J., & Forman, E. A. (2006). Research on learning and instruction in science: Elaborating the design approach. In C. Conrad & R. C. Serlin (Eds.), *Sage handbook for research in education: Engaging ideas and enriching inquiry* (pp. 139–155). Thousand Oaks, CA: Sage.

Forman, E. A., & Ansell, E. (2001). The multiple voices of a mathematics classroom community. *Educational Studies in Mathematics, 46,* 115–142.

Forman, E. A., Larreamendy-Joerns, J., Stein, M. K., & Brown, C. A. (1998). "You're going to want to find out which and prove it": Collective argumentation in a mathematics classroom. *Learning and Instruction, 8,* 527–548.

Forman, E. A., McCormick, D., & Donato, R. (1998). Learning what counts as a mathematical explanation. *Linguistics and Education, 9,* 313–339.

Goodwin, C. (1994). Professional vision. *American Anthropologist, 96,* 606–663.

Green, J. L. (1983). Research on teaching as a linguistic process: A state of the art. In E. W. Gordon (Ed.), *Review of research in education* (Vol. 10, pp. 151–252). Washington, DC: American Educational Research Association.

Green, J. L., Dixon, C. N., & Zaharlick, A. (2003). Ethnography as a logic of inquiry. In J. Flood, D. Lapp, J. R. Squire, & J. M. Jensen (Eds.), *Handbook of research on teaching the English language arts* (2nd ed., pp. 201–224). Mahwah, NJ: Erlbaum.

Greeno, J. G. (1998). The situativity of knowing, learning, and research. *American Psychologist, 53,* 5–26.

Greeno, J. G. (2006). Theoretical and practical advances through research on learning. In P. B. Elmore, G. Camilli & J. Green (Eds.), *Complementary methods for research in education* (pp. 795–822). Washington, DC: American Educational Research Association.

Gutiérrez, K., Baquedano-Lopez, P., & Tejeda, C. (1999). Rethinking diversity: Hybridity and hybrid language practices in the third space. *Mind, Culture, and Activity, 6,* 286–303.

Hacking, I. (1983). *Representing and intervening.* Cambridge, England: Cambridge University Press.

Hanson, N. R. (1958). *Patterns of discovery.* Cambridge, England: Cambridge University Press.

Hayes, R., & Matusov, E. (2005). From 'ownership' to dialogic addressivity: Defining successful digital storytelling projects [online]. *Technology, Humanities, Education, Narrative (THEN) Journal.* Retrieved October 24, 2006, from http://thenjournal.org/feature/75

Heras, A. I. (1994). The construction of understanding in a sixth-grade bilingual classroom. *Linguistics and Education, 5,* 275–299.

Hicks, D. (1995). Discourse, learning, and teaching. In M. W. Apple (Ed.), *Review of research in education* (Vol. 21, pp. 49–95). Washington, DC: American Educational Research Association.

Holland, D., Lachicotte, W., Skinner, D., & Cain, C. (1998). *Identity and agency in cultural worlds.* Cambridge, MA: Harvard University Press.

Jimenez-Aleixandre, M. P., Rodriguez, A. B., & Duschl, R. (2000). "Doing the lesson" or "doing science": Argument in high school genetics. *Science Education, 84,* 757–792.

Kelly, G. J. (2005). Discourse, description, and science education. In R. K. Yerrick & W.-M. Roth (Eds.), *Establishing scientific classroom discourse communities: Multiple voices of teaching and learning research* (pp. 79–104). Mahwah, NJ: Erlbaum.

Kelly, G. J., & Brown, C. (2003). Communicative demands of learning science through technological design: Third grade students' construction of solar energy devices. *Linguistics and Education, 13,* 483–532.

Kelly, G. J., Drucker, S., & Chen, C. (1998). Students' reasoning about electricity: Combining performance assessments with argumentation analysis. *International Journal of Science Education, 20,* 849–871.

Kieran, C., Forman, E., & Sfard, A. (Eds.). (2001). Bridging the individual and the social: Discursive approaches to research in mathematics education. *Educational Studies in Mathematics, 46*(1–3).

Krummheuer, G. (1995). The ethnography of argumentation. In P. Cobb & H. Bauersfeld (Eds.), *The emergence of mathematical meaning: Interaction in classroom cultures* (pp. 229–269). Hillsdale, NJ: Erlbaum.

Kuhn, T. (1970). *The structure of scientific revolutions* (2nd ed.). Chicago: University of Chicago Press.

Lakatos, I. (1970). Falsification and the methodology of scientific research programmes. In I. Lakatos & A. Musgrave (Eds.), *Criticism and the growth of knowledge* (pp. 91–196). Cambridge, England: Cambridge University Press.

Lampert, M., & Blunk, M. L. (Eds.). (1998). *Talking mathematics in school: Studies of teaching and learning.* New York: Cambridge University Press.

Latour, B. (1987). *Science in action.* Milton Keynes, England: Open University Press.

Latour, B. (1990). Drawing things together. In M. Lynch & S. Woolgar (Eds.), *Representation in scientific practice* (pp. 19–68). Cambridge, MA: MIT Press.

Latour, B. (1999). *Pandora's hope: Essays on the reality of science studies.* Cambridge, MA: Harvard University Press.

Latour, B., & Woolgar, S. (1986). *Laboratory life: The construction of scientific facts* (2nd ed.). Princeton, NJ: Princeton University Press.

Laudan, L. (1984). *Science and values: The aims of science and their role in scientific debate.* Berkeley: University of California Press.

Lave, J. (1988). *Cognition in practice: Mind, mathematics and culture in everyday life.* New York: Cambridge University Press.

Lave, J., & Wenger, E. (1991). *Situated learning: Legitimate peripheral participation.* New York: Cambridge University Press.

Lehrer, R., & Schauble, L. (2006). Scientific thinking and scientific literacy. In W. Damon, R. Lerner, K. A. Renninger, & E. Sigel (Eds.), *Handbook of child psychology* (6th ed., Vol. 4, pp. 153–196). Hoboken, NJ: Wiley.

Lehrer, R., Schauble, L., Carpenter, S., & Penner, D. (2000). The inter-related development of inscriptions and conceptual understanding. In P. Cobb, E. Yackel, & K. McClain (Eds.), *Symbolizing and communicating in mathematics classrooms* (pp. 325–360). Mahwah, NJ: Erlbaum.

Lehrer, R., Schauble, L., & Petrosino, A. J. (2001). Reconsidering the role of experiment in science education. In K. Crowley, C. D. Schunn, & T. Okada (Eds.), *Designing for science: Implications from everyday, classroom, and professional settings* (pp. 251–278). Mahwah, NJ: Erlbaum.

Lemke, J. L. (1990). *Talking science: Language, learning, and values.* Norwood, NJ: Ablex.

Lemke, J. L. (1992). Intertextuality and educational research. *Linguistics and Education, 4,* 257–267.

Longino, H. (2002). *The fate of knowledge.* Princeton, NJ: Princeton University Press.

Luke, A. (2004). Teaching after the market: From commodity to cosmopolitan. *Teachers College Record, 106,* 1422–1443.

Matusov, E. (in press). Application of Bakhtin scholarship on discourse and education: A critical review essay. *Educational Theory.*

Mehan, H. (1979). *Learning lessons: Social organization in the classroom.* Cambridge, MA: Harvard University Press.

Mehan, H. (1998). The study of social interaction in educational settings: Accomplishments and unresolved issues. *Human Development, 41,* 245–269.

Michaels, S. (1981). Sharing time: Children's narrative styles and differential access to literacy. *Language in Society, 10,* 423–442.

Millar, R., & Osborne, J. (1999). *Beyond 2000.* London: King's College.

Mortimer, E., & Scott, P. (2003). *Meaning making in secondary science classrooms.* Philadelphia: Open University Press.

Nasir, N. A. (2002). Identity, goals, and learning: Mathematics in cultural practice. *Mathematical Thinking and Learning, 4,* 211–245.

National Council of Teachers of Mathematics. (2000). *Principles and standards for school mathematics.* Reston, VA: Author.

National Research Council. (1996). *National science education standards.* Washington, DC: National Academy Press.

Osborne, J., Erduran, S., & Simon, S. (2004). Enhancing the quality of argument in school science. *Journal of Research in Science Teaching, 41,* 994–1020.

Packer, M. (2001). The problem of transfer, and the sociocultural critique of schooling. *Journal of the Learning Sciences, 10,* 493–514.

Pappas, C. C., Varelas, M., Barry, A., & Rife, A. (2003). Dialogic inquiry around information texts: The role of intertextuality in constructing scientific understandings in urban primary classrooms. *Linguistics and Education, 13,* 435–482.

Pera, M. (1994). *The discourses of science.* Chicago: University of Chicago Press.

Pickering, A. (1995). *The mangle of practice: Time, agency, and science.* Chicago: University of Chicago Press.

Popkewitz, T. S. (1998). Dewey, Vygotsky, and the social administration of the individual: Constructivist pedagogy as systems of ideas in historical spaces. *American Educational Research Journal, 35,* 535–570.

Popper, K. R. (1968). *The logic of scientific discovery* (rev. 2nd ed.). New York: Harper & Row.

Popper, K. R. (1972). *Objective knowledge.* Oxford, England: Oxford University Press.

Prawat, R. S. (2000). Dewey meets the "Mozart of psychology" in Moscow: The untold story. *American Educational Research Journal, 37,* 663–696.

Putnam, R., Lampert, M., & Peterson, P. L. (1990). Alternative perspectives on knowing mathematics in elementary schools. In C. B. Cazden (Ed.), *Review of research in education* (Vol. 16, pp. 57–150). Washington, DC: American Educational Research Association.

Ritchie, S. M. (2002). Student positioning within groups during science activities. *Research in Science Education, 32,* 35–54.

Rogoff, B. (1990). *Apprenticeship in thinking: Cognitive development in social context.* New York: Oxford University Press.

Rogoff, B. (2003). *The cultural nature of human development.* New York: Oxford University Press.

Rouse, J. (1987). *Knowledge and power: Toward a political philosophy of science.* Ithaca, NY: Cornell University Press.

Rouse, J. (1996). *Engaging science: How to understand its practices philosophically.* Ithaca, NY: Cornell University Press.

Scott, P. H., Mortimer, E. F., & Aguiar, O. G. (2006). The tension between authoritative and dialogic discourse: A fundamental characteristic of meaning making interactions in high school science lessons. *Science Education, 90,* 605–631.

Sfard, A. (1998). On two metaphors for learning and the dangers of choosing just one. *Educational Researcher, 27*(2), 4–13.

Shulman, L. S. (1986). Those who understand: Knowledge growth in teaching. *Educational Researcher, 15*(2), 4–14.

Shulman, L. S., & Quinlan, K. M. (1996). The comparative psychology of school subjects. In D. C. Berliner & R. C. Calfee (Eds.), *Handbook of educational psychology* (pp. 399–422). New York: Simon & Schuster.

Simon, S., Erduran, S., & Osborne, J. (2006). Learning to teach argumentation: Research and development in the science classroom. *International Journal of Science Education, 28,* 235–260.

Simon, S., Osborne, J., & Erduran, S. (2003). Systemic teacher development to enhance the use of argumentation in school science activities. In J. Wallace & J. Loughran (Eds.), *Leadership and professional development in science education: New possibilities for enhancing teacher learning* (pp. 198–217). London: RoutledgeFalmer.

Stevens, R., Wineburg, S., Herrenkohl, L. R., & Bell, P. (2005). Comparative understanding of school subjects: Past, present, and future. *Review of Educational Research, 75,* 125–157.

Stodolsky, S. S. (1988). *The subject matters: Classroom activity in math and social studies.* Chicago: University of Chicago Press.

Strom, D., Kemeny, V., Lehrer, R., & Forman, E. A. (2001). Visualizing the emergent structure of children's mathematical argument. *Cognitive Science, 25,* 733–773.

Toulmin, S. E. (1964). *The uses of argument.* Cambridge, England: Cambridge University Press. (Original work published 1958)

Varelas, M. (1996). Between theory and data in a seventh-grade science classroom. *Journal of Research in Science Teaching, 33,* 229–263.

Varelas, M., & Pappas, C. C. (2006). Intertextuality in read-alouds of integrated science-literacy units in urban primary classrooms: Opportunities for the development of thought and language. *Cognition and Instruction, 24,* 211–260.

Volosinov, V. N. (1986). *Marxism and the philosophy of language* (L. Matejka & I. R. Titunik, Trans.). Cambridge, MA: Harvard University Press. (Original work published 1929)

Vygotsky, L. S. (1978). *Mind in society: The development of higher psychological processes.* Cambridge, MA: Harvard University Press.

Warren, B., & Rosebery, A. S. (1996). "This question is just too, too easy!": Students' perspectives on accountability in science. In L. Schauble & R. Glaser (Eds.), *Innovations in learning new environments for education* (pp. 97–125). Mahwah, NJ: Erlbaum.

Wenger, E. (1998). *Communities of practice: Learning, meaning, and identity.* New York: Cambridge University Press.

Wertsch, J. V. (1985). *Vygotsky and the social formation of mind.* Cambridge, MA: Harvard University Press.

Wertsch, J. V. (1991). *Voices of the mind.* Cambridge, MA: Harvard University Press.

Wineburg, S. S. (1991). On the reading of historical texts: Notes on the breach between school and academy. *American Educational Research Journal, 28,* 495–519.

Chapter 2

Cross-National Explorations of Sociocultural Research on Learning

OLGA A. VÁSQUEZ

University of California, San Diego

... human learning presupposes a specific social nature and a process by which children grow into the intellectual life of those around them. (Vygotsky, 1978, p. 88)

Scholars, practitioners, and laypeople at one time or another have questioned what learning is and how it can be measured once it is defined. Many use the term interchangeably with growth, change, development, knowledge, education, cognition, or acquisition as it is commonly considered in educational practice (Kozulin, 2003). However, most generally assume a vague and unstated understanding of learning. Despite this apparent consensus, few will disagree that the notion of learning is complex and indistinct. This chapter focuses on research that seeks to account for this complexity by characterizing learning as a product of social and cultural processes. This perspective regards learning as achieved through a social process that is intimately related to cultural and cognitive development—a viewpoint that dates back to the work of Lev Vygotsky, the father of Soviet psychology, in the 1920s and 1930s. Scholars who follow this tradition see learning as analogous to a theory of culture in mind.

Much has been written on the theoretical formulations of Vygotsky's perspective on learning and development. In this chapter, however, I focus on learning in the actual classroom, the theorized classroom, and out-of-school settings, with special emphasis on research in after-school activities that grows out of the work of the Laboratory of Comparative Human Cognition directed by Michael Cole at the University of California, San Diego. I map out the landscape of the Vygotskian sociohistorical or cultural historical approach (see Cole, 1995, 1996), appropriated in the West as sociocultural research (Ageyev, 2003; Wertsch, Del Rio, & Alvarez, 1995), and then follow it back to the international arena as cross-national explorations of learning that have implications for understanding classroom learning but may or may not be specifically situated in the classroom. Given space constraints, minimal attention is given to activity theory research, although its history is intimately intertwined with sociocultural research and its antecedents, sociohistorical and cultural historical research, to the present (Wertsch et al., 1995).

33

I begin with a brief historical sketch of the search for the relationship between culture and cognition that dates back to Darwin, "when the idea of evolution dominated the imagination of those concerned with the study of man" (Jahoda & Lewis, 1988). I examine the objectives and methodologies used to track the effects of culture on behavior and everyday life and follow these ideas as they move into the international arena as variability studies. Next, I turn to studies on learning that hold education as the comparative structure, beginning with those that explore learning in the social world and the world of theory and follow with those studies that focus directly on classroom learning. In the latter section, I give special emphasis to a select group of studies that examine cultural variation within and across human experience—e.g., studies that apply Vygotskian notions of learning and development to multiculturalism, biliteracies, abilities, poverty, social change, and identity—what Joseph Glick calls "the intra-Psychology" (personal communication, 2006). I follow these studies with a case study of after-school activity systems (technology intervention programs) that builds on Vygotskian ideas of creating optimal learning environments. Finally, I conclude by summarizing how the key ideas of learning have evolved in time and forecast new areas of study that will logically emerge as sociocultural theory gains momentum and the world changes radically to accommodate the influences of globalization.

WHAT MAKES RESEARCH CROSS-NATIONAL

Given the multiple uses of learning and its multifarious explorations, it is noteworthy to discuss what I mean by "learning" and the idea of "cross-national." Vygotsky (1978) equated development with higher intellectual functions and not physical development as such, although the two are intricately related. He saw learning and development as separate but also as parts of the same process. In this vein, I link learning to thinking, cognition, and problem solving and use them interchangeably. In doing this, I am following Rogoff, who argues that:

. . . cognition and thinking are defined broadly as problem solving. I assume that thinking is functional, active, and grounded in goal-directed action. Problem solving involves interpersonal and practical goals, addressed deliberately (not necessarily consciously or rationally). (1990, p. 8)

Using these terms interchangeably does not imply that learning is equated with thinking, cognition, or problem solving. Rather, it indicates that the appropriation of culture, achieving a new developmental stage, solving a problem, and thinking through a goal-directed action all assume a learning process, and to separate them tells only half the story. Learning is integrally related to thinking, problem solving, and cognition in the same way that individual fibers are woven into an object called a braid; when the fibers are separated into individual strands, its identity as a braid is undetectable but latent with the possibility. The same is true for learning and cognition, problem solving, and thinking. Vygotsky made the same analogy between the relationship of thought and speech and the constituent components of water, oxygen, and hydrogen. Analyzing either of the two separately no longer reveals much of characteristics of water other than to compare to all kinds of water (Vygotsky, 1987).

Explorations on the social embeddedness of learning make visible the comparative nature of sociocultural research, occasionally blurring the lines among culture, nation, language, and other arbitrary distinctions. The arising comparison, too, invites a clarification of the idea of cross-national. In much of the research I cover in this chapter, the notion of cross-national is vague and indistinct as Western researchers cross into foreign lands to conduct cross-cultural studies, as foreign scholars appropriate ideas, and/or as studies on distinctions and relations among and across groups are conducted within the same national context. The most notable Western researchers who blur national boundaries as they seek to understand "how cultural differences are reflected in cognitive differences" (Childs & Greenfield, 1980, p. 71) include Mead (1978); Scribner and Cole (1981); Greenfield and Childs (1997); Greenfield, Maynard, and Childs (2000); Beach (1995); Saxe (1982); and Stigler and Perry (1990)—many of whom are discussed in the methodologies section.

These differing conditions suggest the need to reconsider the concept of cross-national. In this chapter, I make a case that it is not sufficient, for example, to limit cross-national research to a simultaneous comparison across two or more countries where geography and arbitrary physical borders separate presumably distinct cultural groups. Although this is the common distinction that characterizes some of the early cross-cultural studies that I already noted, this definition fails to capture the variations that later studies found within and across cultures situated both within and across national borders. Thus, I highlight the variability of difference that sociocultural theory touches on throughout its brief history, some of which has been conducted cross-nationally and some that has been cross-national only because the ideas and/or the researcher cross the border to establish a tacit, if not explicit, comparison. Recent sociocultural research addresses the differences in the schooling process as much for those who are part of the cultural fabric of the American classroom as for those who are not. I focus on studies of difference in the section on classroom research on learning.

Another perspective on cross-national explorations is the appropriation of Vygotsky's ideas across national contexts. Elhammounmi's (1997) published bibliography illustrates the cross-national transportability of Vygotsky's ideas into 33 countries. A cursory examination of the articles shows that for the most part, these articles primarily elaborate Vygotsky's ideas, signaling the highly theoretical tradition of cultural historical research. A comprehensive review of the full range of ways in which Vygotsky's work has influenced the field is beyond the scope of this article. However, to illustrate the potential of a Vygotsky perspective, in the remaining sections, I focus on small portion of this work, mostly research coming out of the United States, with a few references to work conducted in Europe to provide an in-depth exploration of this research area.

LEARNING FROM A VYGOTSKIAN PERSPECTIVE

Two central concepts distinguish Vygotsky's perspective on learning: (1) the notion of the zone of proximal development that conceptually draws a line around the dynamic relationship between learning and development and (2) the genetic law of cultural development that conceives the natural course of the development of culture in the individual as leading from the social to the psychological level, that is, "first between people as an intermental category then within the child as an intramental category" (Vygotsky, 1978). Both of these constructs deem learning as central to the relationship between the learner and others in the social world. Learning is a dynamic process of relationship as Hedegaard (2001) specifies: "learning can be seen as a change in the relations between the person and the world, through the subject's appropriation of tool use and artefactual knowledge" (p. 15).

Vygotsky saw learning as a means of promoting subsequent, higher levels of development. He proposed that learning promotes development where it is possible to create a zone of proximal development that he describes as:

. . . distance between the actual level of development as determined by independent problem solving and the level of potential development as determined through problem solving under adult guidance or in collaboration with more capable peers. (1978, p. 86)

In laying the foundation for the next level of development, learning is not independent of or equal to development, but rather is in "advance of development" (Vygotsky, 1978, p. 89), creating it as a by-product of a dynamically charged interconnected process. For Vygotsky, understanding this relationship is vital to designing educational practices that enhance all children's learning potential (Newman & Holzman, 1993). This is a point of divergence, with much conventional practice that aims instruction to past rather than future development, a strategy Vygotsky considers as a "refrain from understanding child development" (Vygotsky, quoted in van der Veer & Valsiner, 1993, p. 239).

Conceptually, the zone of proximal development also exemplifies another key principle of sociocultural theory—the notion that the path of learning and development proceeds from the sociocultural (intermental) to the individual (intramental) levels of organization. That is, what an individual comes to know and believe is largely based on the social and cultural processes in which he or she is raised. As learners interact with others in their social environment, they not only acquire new forms of knowledge and skills but also acquire the ideas, language, values, and dispositions of the social group, making their experience a "culture learning experience." It is through the process of acquiring these cultural resources that learners achieve membership in the social group, as the introductory quote makes clear.

Another crucial point in considering the social aspect of learning is the notion of mediation. Mediating agents (i.e., symbolic tools, human beings, and organized learning activities [Kozulin, 2003]) are instrumental to the social processes that give rise to cultural and cognitive development. In contrast to previous explanatory models that represent human action as linear, discrete, and easily measured, the theory of mediation attempts to shed light on the active construction of mental processes that underlie behavior and by extension explains the nature of human beings. It argues that human beings are not simply organisms predisposed to the whims of external forces, as the stimulus-response model posits. Rather, the notion of mediation casts a tenuous net across a complex, interactive relationship between the individual and the social environment that extends far beyond the patterned responses captured by the Cartesian and Stimulus-Response model. From this perspective, human beings are neither determined by their social conditions nor completely independent of them. Instead, their thoughts and actions are actively constructed in a give-and-take that is imbued with personal and cultural history grounded in the beliefs and expectations of a particular context (Cole, 1996; Hedegaard, 2001). In 1993, activity theorists led by Yrjö Engeström concluded that:

The transformation of individuals and their community, which result from the fact that human beings do not merely react to their life conditions but that they have the power to act and therefore the power to change the very conditions that mediate their activities. (Holzkamp, cited in Roth, 2004, p. 1)

The key contribution of the idea of mediation is not that human beings simply stand apart from their objective world, but that they construct it and are constructed by it through their use of technical and symbolic tools.

Accordingly, the goal of Vygotsky's approach is to understand the relationship of learning to the sociocultural context, or as Wertsch and colleagues (1995, p. 11) explain, the goals are "to explicate the relationships between human action, on the one hand, and the cultural, institutional, and historical situations in which this action occurs, on the other." Human action, in this case, refers to behavior that is intentional, dynamic, and active (Bronckart, 1995)—in other words, thoughtful action on the part of the individual. Hence, to study learning involves the study of the social context, social practices, and intervening mediating agents as they intertwine in an interactional relationship whether it is situated in the community, family, class-room, or after-school activity.

CULTURE AND LEARNING

The analysis of culture's role in child development and learning has a comparative foundation that can be traced back to Darwin when the theory of variability became the driving force behind scientific explorations (Jahoda & Lewis, 1988). The evolutionary perspective—the idea of the increasing complexity and divergence in nature—gave rise to categories comparing the developmental trajectories of human groups. Early anthropologists interpreted this as cultural progression from primitive to civilized society, and the psychologists applied it to the recapitulation of this continuum in human development (Johado & Lewis, 1988). Widespread attention was given to the origins of the species and the differences in social, cultural, and intellectual development among societies. In particular, the emergent fields of psychology and anthropology in the early 20th century laid the ground-work for understanding the relationship between the history of the species and individual development, or more specifically, as Cole and colleagues (1971) argued, for understanding the ways in which humans adapt to different cultural and natural environments.

According to Cole (1996, p. 14), these cross-cultural studies were grounded on three basic assumptions: (1) "social evolution as a process of increasing differentiation and complexity of social life," (2) all human beings have a basic mental structure (i.e., "the psychic unity"), and (3) there is "an intimate relationship between culture and mind." Initially, based on others' accounts and influenced by a mentality of colonialism, these studies sought to prove a distinction between the social and/or mental development of "civilized" societies and "savage" groups (Pennycook, 1998).

Many paths led to the idea of the relationship between culture and thought. However, available evidence indicates that it was the work of Vygotsky and the progenitors of sociohistorical and cultural historical theory that brought it to prominence in the 1920s and 1930s. Cole (1996), for example, traces the origins of the ideas of culture in psychology back to Giovanni Vico's proposition that truth is substantiated through the products of "being social" rather than simply through individual action. Linguistics goes even further back to ancient India to the Sanskrit scholar Bharatrihari, who posed that language is fundamentally related to human existence and awareness. In anthropology, Boas is generally credited with posing the relation between the human mind and the environment. However, these ideas can be traced back to the Enlightenment thinkers who maintained that reason depended on sensory experience to know anything about the world, "excluding the mind's own concoctions" (Tarnas, 1991, p. 334).

Although linguistics, anthropology, and psychology follow different paths to the study of culture in thought, they converge to form the backbone of sociocultural theory after World War II, when a current of internationalism swept over a prevailing pessimism. Anthropology's focus on the study of human diversity is realigned to E. B. Taylor's notion that the study of culture is the study of human thought. The work of Mead, Malinowski, and Read, for example, lays the foundation for linking culture to thinking through their examination of kinship, socialization practices, and informal learning (Jahoda & Lewis, 1988). It was Mead (1978), for example, who prompted Piaget to change his views regarding the difference in thinking of civilized and uncivilized groups, starting what Jahoda and Lewis (1988, p. 12) call a "veritable industry of world-wide comparative studies." At the time, linguistics extended its focus from the evolution of human languages to consider a different kind of relativity, one based on language. Generally known as the Sapir-Whorf's hypothesis of language relativity, this idea argues that differences in human thinking are influenced by the group's language rather than its culture (Agar, 1994). Psychology, on the other hand, extends its focus on the problem of the adaptation of human beings to their environment to the study of the higher psychological functions, or what Wundt called "Völkerpsychologie" (Cole, 1996). This new psychology took on a cultural perspective that required history, language, and expressive culture to explain mental functioning. The resulting cross-fertilization across these three fields gave birth to new fields and approaches, such as psycholinguistics, cognitive anthropology, and cross-cultural psychology, which serve as the perspectives from which sociocultural research is approached today.

Methodologies

The problem of method has a long history, but it was not until the emergence of modern science in 16th and 17th centuries that it received considerable attention (Newman & Holzman, 1993). It is the first challenge researchers face when blazing new paths of study. This is especially true of the pioneers in the fields of linguistics, psychology, and anthropology who stepped away from conventional paradigms to relate culture to mind. In calling for a different view of human diversity—a cultural relativism rather than a ranking of social structures—Boas and Malinowski, for example, proposed participant observation as the method for the study of culture, a method that has become the keystone of cultural anthropology. The same can be said of Marx's proposal of a dialectical materialism methodology, which he developed "to challenge the fundamental epistemic (how we know) and ontic (what there is) categories of Western cognition" (Newman & Holzman, 1993, p. 32), a revolutionary and controversial method that has received considerable attention throughout the years. Marx's objective was to uncover the effects of the class structure on social consciousness through the study of a dialectal form of historical materialism, i.e., the opposing forces of society, economics, and history. In believing that "to study something historically means to study it in the process of change; the dialectical method's basic demand" (Vygotsky, 1978, p. 65), Vygotsky advances Marxism as a methodology and as a revolutionary practice (Newman & Holzman, 1993). To change the world, both Marx and Vygotsky suggest a radical shift in the approach to perceive it. Both believe that a "revolutionary methodology" that "challenges how we challenge and introduces a qualitatively different (practice of) method" (p. 33) is necessary to understand the relationship between human beings and society.

The problem of method is of critical importance to Vygotsky. He opposes the belief that "only nature affects human beings and only nature determines historical development" and rather sees human behavior as "a transformative reaction on nature" (Vygotsky, 1978, p. 60). He argues that this new conception of the human condition requires a new method and a new analytic framework:

The search for method becomes one of the most important problems of the entire enterprise of understanding the unique human forms of psychological activity. In this case, the method is simultaneously pre-requisite and product, the tool and the results of the study. (1978, p. 65)

Vygotsky defines method beyond the notion of instrumentation (i.e., tool). Instead, he sees it as a practice that is inseparable from "the experimental content and results, i.e., from that for which it is a method" (Newman & Holzman, 1993, p. 33). "It is neither a means to an end nor a tool for achieving results. Rather it is, in Vygotsky's formulation, a "tool and result" (pp. 33–34). His method of practice is "purposeful" and has "no completed or generalized identity," and its "defining feature is the activity of their development rather than their function" (Newman & Holzman, 1993, p. 38). This is particularly evident in Vygotsky's signature construct—the zone of proximal development. The zone of proximal development is at once a practice of cognitive development and a method in that it refracts back the developmental trajectory of a learner that the adult or more capable peer has scaffold through strategic intervention, providing progressively more clues and information to spur the learner's understanding and performance of the task (Brown & French, 1979).

Essentially, Vygotsky's views on learning are methodological as well as theoretical. According to Daniels (2001), Vygotsky insisted on the "elucidation of the 'explanatory principle' the object of study (or analytic unit) and the dynamics of the relations between the two" (p. 31). His was a developmental approach that focuses on process, not products, explanation rather than description, and future level of development instead of the level in which functions are automatic and routinized (i.e., fossilized) (Vygotsky, 1978). His focus is on the social context of human interaction—"the person-environment interface or the scene" (Cole, Hood, & McDermott, 1978)— and not the individual isolated from others. His aim is to determine the "genesis of causal-dynamic relations"; in words relevant to the objective of this article, he is interested in tracking the developmental trajectory of learning. "It is here," he says, "that the past and the present is seen in the light of history" (Vygotsky, 1978, p. 64). To study this dynamic in action, Vygotsky proposes an "experimental-developmental" method that:

> . . . artificially provokes or creates a process of psychological development. This approach is equally appropriate to the basic aim of dynamic analysis. If we replace object analysis by process analysis, then the basic task of research obviously becomes a *reconstruction of each state* in the development process: the process must be turned back to its initial stages. (1978, p. 62, emphasis added)

From this perspective, this new approach rejects the stimulus-response framework that views humans as passive objects susceptible to the random forces of nature. Instead, Vygotsky argues that the stimulus response approach fails to describe anything greater than elementary cognitive functioning and cannot account for the "revolutionary shifts" in development (Wertsch, 1985, p. 19). "At best, it can only help us record the existence of lower, subordinated forms, which do not capture the essence of the higher forms" (Vygotsky, 1978, p. 60). In the West, similar concerns were raised against the conclusions derived from data used by the proverbial "armchair anthropologist" and the methods born of laboratory inquiry after World War II. Accounts of travelers and explorers were deemed inadequate to account for how and what things are known and acted on in a given society. The same held true for laboratory explorations, a "methodology" that was just beginning at the time of Vygotsky. The critique here centers on the inability of the laboratory method to account for the social aspects of thinking, problem solving, and remembering. Adhering to this critique, many scholars began conducting field experiments on a multitude of cognitive tasks out in the social world as I describe below (Childs & Greenfield, 1980; Mead, 1978; Scribner & Cole, 1981).

In the 1970s, the adaptations of the laboratory method were also questioned as researchers asked, "How can we with any degree of validity generalize to everyday life when the strict laboratory conditions 'isolate' variables and constrain people's activities so that the object under study can be examined 'purely'?" (Newman & Holzman, 1993, p. 21). "How does performance on one occasion relate to performance on another occasion" was another question that many sought to answer with a multitude of approaches, including coding schemes and observation techniques (Griffin, Cole, & Newman, 1982). However, it was the issue of validity that produced considerable debate.

In particular, it was "ecological validity," that is, the area of study concerned with the intersection of an individual's "life space" and his social physical environment (Lewin quoted in O'Neil, 1976, p. 99) and representative sampling (Bronfenbrenner, 1979; Cole, Hood, & McDermott, 1978) that produced the greatest methodological challenges facing researchers interested in studying the social embeddedness of cognitive tasks (Cole et al., 1978). On the one hand, they questioned the ability of the laboratory method to fully capture the intervening social and cultural factors in the performance of tasks. On the other, they critiqued the study of behavior in the social world because it, too, was influenced by "laboratory's methodological assumptions as is research conducted in the laboratory itself." (Newman & Holzman, 1993, p. 23). Recreating the experimental design out in the social world compromised the natural order of life and therefore the ability to uncover the effect that the environment has on cognition.

The notion of method as practice in real-life contexts prompted Newman, Cole, and Griffin (1989) to see the sociohistorical perspective as a methodology in and of itself. Today, systematic collection of data on the person-environment interface by various means—particularly ethnographic methods, such as participant observation, interviews, evocative measures (cognitive tests), and video and audio recordings of discourse—constitute the storehouse of sociocultural methodology. Scholars continue to elaborate on past methodological accomplishments from multiple angles. Cole (1995), citing Lamb and Wozniak's criteria for good research as a starting point, offers a cultural-genetic methodology for studying cultural mediation. He builds on the following criteria to study change at multiple levels within a single setting in what he calls a "mesogenetic approach" (1995, p. 94)—the approach of studying the intellectual and social development of youth participating in especially designed activity systems:

1. dynamic analysis of the flow of events over time;
2. interactional analysis of dyads, triads, and larger units;
3. pattern analysis of the interrelatedness of variables;
4. transactional analysis of person-environment interactions;
5. multicultural and historical analyses; and
6. willingness to deal with the messy interactions outside of laboratories.

Cole (1995), for example, uses the notion of culture-as-medium (i.e., as garden) to frame the mediational nature of cultural activities arranged in an after-school activity system known as the Fifth Dimension. He is able to show the role of culture "in helping things grow" by contrasting newcomers and old timers and several different contexts in which the Fifth Dimension operates. These contrasts highlight the process of enculturation in the participants and the differential effect the amount of culture of the Fifth Dimension has on the development of shared knowledge—one of the key features of the Fifth Dimension.

Rogoff's (1995a) study of the transformative nature of participation in sociocultural activities also offers new methodological perspectives on the social and cultural foundations of human action. She illustrates how process *is* the product by focusing on development from three perspectives—the community, interpersonal, and personal.

These 'planes' are mutually constituting elements of sociocultural activity. None exists separately. Still, the parts making up a whole activity or event can be considered separately as foreground without losing track of their inherent interdependence in the whole. (p. 159)

Rogoff uses the example of Girl Scouts selling and distributing Girl Scout cookies to point out the need and the accomplishments of such a broad analytic framework, as well as to propose a different view of apprenticeship, guided participation, and appropriation and internalization. In later work, Rogoff (1998) elaborates these ideas further as they relate to cognition as a collaborative process.

The study of historical change provides another methodological perspective on the effects that culture has on thinking. Initiated by Luria (1976) in central Asia in the 1930s, this method attempts to show the fundamental shifts in mental processes brought about by rapid cultural-historical changes, in this case, a change from the subsistence farming of cotton to collective agricultural production and industrialization. The shift brings forth a new economic system and an extensive formal schooling system. Using various cognitive tests dealing with logical reasoning, perception, and classification, Luria attempts to demonstrate that becoming "acquainted not only with new fields of knowledge but also with new motives for action" has an affect on the way people think (1976, p. 13). Methodologically, Luria's findings raised two important issues that ecological psychologist questioned later (1) the generalizability of his field derived conclusions to activities in everyday life outside of the experimental setting and (2) the adequate representation of the process of change from concrete-graphic to theoretical thinking in his experimental activities (Cole, 1998). Although Luria's clinical interview methods have been highly regarded, they, too, were questioned because the strategy of interviewing subjects was an unfamiliar discourse for the people of that region at the time of the study (Cole, 1998).

Researchers such as Beach (1995); Greenfield, Maynard, and Childs (2000, 2003); and Saxe (1982, 2005) have extended Luria's efforts to study the effects of the exposure to new cultural practices on mental functioning. These researchers conduct a form of cross-national research in developing countries experiencing rapid cultural and socioeconomic changes. They highlight the effect that larger scale changes have on the community's everyday practices. In particular, they are interested in how the introduction of schooling affects everyday teaching and learning.

Beach, for example, examines the coexistences of both indigenous and introduced forms of measurement—the traditional measurement using body parts and the modern metric measurement using a ruler. He was interested in tracking the changes in the use of school and nonschool mathematics as they are practiced in everyday shop keeping by schooled subjects who are apprenticed to shopkeepers and the shopkeepers themselves who are enrolled in adult education. Beach finds that both groups demonstrated some amount of flexibility in using both forms of measurement but that the socialization of school and shop keeping strongly affected the respective participants' full appropriation of the alternative form of calculations, that is, the status of being schooled prompted the schooled apprentices to display the use of written forms of mathematics, and the notion of "doing shopkeeping" reinforced the shopkeepers' need for using traditional measurement.

Saxe (1982) and Saxe and Esmonde (2005) conducted similar research among the Oksapmin of Central New Guinea. Seeking a framework for a practice-based approach to studying the effects of cultural change on learning and development, Saxe entered the Oksapmin community, first looking at counting and number conservation and later at the effect that economic change had on the indigenous number system. The Oksapmin use a traditional mode of counting with a 27-digit number system based on body parts, beginning with the little finger of the right hand and moving up the arm, around the head and down to the left arm, ending at the little finger of the left hand. In the span of 20 years, Saxe found that the uses of the traditional number system were influenced by the amount of exposure individuals had to the uses of money, life outside the community, and money itself. Those with more exposure, especially those with more schooling, were more easily disposed to using the base-10 system learned in school.

Greenfield and colleagues (2000, 2003) also demonstrate the effects of ecological change on learning and development. Using longitudinal methodology, they showed how each "ecology emphasizes a different set of skills, different developmental pathways and different process of socialization or informal education" (Greenfield et al., 2000, p. 353). Greenfield and Childs (1977) first studied the cultural influences and cognitive development of the Zinacantec Maya in the state of Chiapas, Mexico, in 1969 and 1970 and returned in 1991 and 1993 to study changes in learning and cognition of the second generation. They found that the shift from subsistence farming to a market economy had a direct effect on cultural apprenticeship, creativity, and cognitive representation. In a space of a generation, they documented greater independent cultural learning, abstract representation, and innovation than had been evident in past research. In other words,

... weaving apprenticeship moved from a more interdependent to a more independent style of learning, woven textiles changed from a small stock of defined patterns to widely varied and innovative patterns, and cognitive representation of woven patterns became less detailed and more abstract. (1977, p. 351)

The influx of new cultural forms and socialization practices was reflected in the shift from a strict adherence to traditional modes of weaving and pattern representation to modes of weaving that were more tolerant of innovation.

Together these studies set up a within-cultural comparison using ethnographic and longitudinal data to examine culture change and the effects it has on cognitive tasks played out in everyday life. They also set up a tacit cross-cultural comparison between practices found in these communities and those back in the home country, which some of these researchers pursue in their later work (Greenfield, 1984; Saxe, 1994).

EXTENSIONS AND FORMULATIONS OF VYGOTSKIAN THEORY TO CLASSROOM LEARNING

During the last three decades, neo-Vygotskians have increasingly elaborated, reformulated, and extended Vygotsky's ideas regarding the influence that cultural and social processes have on the human condition. Much of this work examines, from multiple perspectives, the factors that influence the acquisition of knowledge in situ, but a substantial amount addresses education, if not in practice, in theory. This is particularly true after the 1990s, when sociocultural theorists realigned their focus to center on education, specifically on what Moll (1990) calls "research in practice." The impetus for this newfound attention is twofold. First, Vygotsky's theorizing and methodologies, although provocative and concerned with education, were not fully completed or empirically tested before his untimely death in 1934 (Wells, 2000). Today, theorists who reformulate and extend his ideas to new contexts and to new sociohistorical periods also endeavor to understand exactly what he meant by these ideas in the first place— e.g., some of the contemporary debates focus on what Vygotsky meant by speech and language, the notion of method, internalization (Hedegaard, 2001; Rogoff, 1995b) and the concept of the zone of proximal development.

Second, Vygotsky was an educator long before he became a psychologist, and he "regarded education not only as central to cognitive development but as the quintessential sociocultural theory" (Moll, 1990, p.1). Vygotsky returned to the problem of teaching in school in his later life (van de Veer & Valsiner, 1993), but his early writings—six of the first eight articles—focused on educational issues (Blanck, 1990). One of his main concerns was that psychology go beyond theory to practice in the study of education and directly "intervene in human life and actively help in shaping it" (Leontiev & Luria, 1968, p. 367). He considered schools and other informal educational settings to be the best "cultural laboratories" to study thinking (Blanck, 1990; Riviere, quoted in Moll, 1990) because these contexts provide the opportunity to reorganize mental functioning in a systematic organized way. Säljö (1991), concurs that Vygotsky found it necessary to understand "the new attitudes of the world that are invoked and the set of learning priorities that are imposed by the schooling process" to develop successful methods for instruction and, by extension, to serve nonnormative learners. Thus, Vygotsky acknowledges the transformative power of schooling but importantly, he also advocates an interventionist approach to research and practice, as is evident in much of the research covered in this chapter. Essentially, this research endeavors to not only study but also to promote change in the classroom and, increasingly, in the education of diverse learners.

Sheldon White, for example, makes this point in the Preface to Cole's (1996) *Cultural Psychology:* "If we want to change the pattern of a human being's activities, we need to address the *surrounding situations* in which those activities live (xiv, emphasis added)." Moll's (1990) groundbreaking edited volume also highlights clearly the value of Vygotsky's theory for bringing about educational change:

> Given Vygotsky's emphasis on the social context of thinking, the study of educational change has important theoretical and methodological significance with this approach: It represents the reorganization of a key social system, and associated modes of discourse, with potential consequences for developing new forms of thinking. (Moll, 1990, p. 2)

Understanding the "surrounding situations" of learning through Vygotsky's theoretical formulations and improving our human condition is what makes neo-Vygotskian research unique (Wells, 2000). It provides the conceptual means for us to understand the social nature of behavior and to identify the points of intervention.

An extensive review of the literature on sociocultural research on learning, particularly research reported in English and in the West, reveals three types of studies that relate to classroom learning: (1) studies on learning in the social world that have strong implications for schooling, (2) studies that extend Vygotsky's theoretical formulations to education, and (3) studies that test, extend, and reformulate Vygotsky's ideas on learning in the classroom. With few exceptions, cross-national studies that focus on learning in the social world and are not particularly situated in settings commonly considered as educational fall into the first category. In the following section, I begin with those studies on learning in the social world and the classroom.

Learning in the Social World

Given the emphasis sociocultural theorists attribute to culture and the social context, it should be no surprise that their concern with education would begin with explorations on learning in the outside world and only slowly turn to classroom studies more directly. Classed under the rubric of "everyday cognition" (Rogoff & Lave, 1984), these studies were primarily concerned with the effects of everyday practice on cognition, but they were also interested in the flow of knowledge and skills from the social world to education and back again. Whether they tracked cognition beyond the classroom and laboratory to the workplace, the streets, and the courtyards or created their own laboratories in the natural environment to test theory in practice (Lave, 1988; Scribner & Cole, 1981), school was the implicit comparative structure from which behavior and culture were judged. Lave believed, for example, that it was, "impossible to analyze education—in schooling, craft apprenticeship, or any other form—without considering the relations with the world for which it ostensibly prepares people (1988, p. xiii). Thus, most, if not all, of the inquiries into the role of the social context on learning implicitly—and at times explicitly—referenced education as the standard of quality, form, or frequency (Gallimore & Tharp, 1990; Tudge, 1990, 2004).

In essence, these studies sought to understand learning in places where it was commonly not believed to inhabit. However, examining skills typically considered the purview of schooling—that is, math, literacy, and problem solving—as functions of everyday practice in the world raised several challenges, one of which was the lack of a sufficiently adequate analytic framework to examine learning outside a laboratory setting. Much like explorers paving new paths, sociocultural theorists such as Lave, Murtaugh, and de la Rocha (1984); Rogoff (1981); Scribner (1984); and Stigler and Perry (1990) all faced well-established norms that qualify scientific inquiry in their exploration of "outdoor psychology" (Geertz, quoted in Lave, 1988, p. 1). At issue were such things as the time-honored distinctions between scientific and everyday thought that privileges the former over the other (Lave, 1988). They argued the importance of social context on learning and development and drew conceptual boundaries around it. They endeavored to make sociality visible as White and Siegel point out, "Children in experimental rooms and classrooms are not engaged in solitary achievement. They are working with other humans" (1984, p. 239). Rogoff (1990) makes the same point in *Apprenticeship in Thinking*. She argues that the social context is inseparable from the child and the social partners: "The roles of the individual and the social world are mutual and not separable, as humans by nature engage in social activity with their contemporaries and learn from their predecessors" (p. viii).

The move to the social context, however, does not solve the issue of finding the source or the primacy of cognitive skills. Rather, researchers find that cognitive skills vary according to the social situation in which they are practiced—e.g., the same tasks performed poorly in laboratory settings are executed with great success in the social world. For example, White and Siegel conclude that: "to understand cognitive development across time and space requires seeing it deeply embedded in a social world of occasions, formalities, etiquettes and dramaturgy" (1984, p. 239). The specificity of context, thus, is implicated in the performance of cognitive skills, and their generalizability is seriously limited (Cole et al., 1978; Griffin et al., 1982; Newman, Griffin, & Cole, 1984; Rogoff, 1984; Scribner & Cole, 1981). Scribner and Cole (1981) illustrate this point effectively in their study of literacy practices among the Vai people of Liberia. The local practice of three distinct literacies—English, Koranic, and Vai—each emphasizing different cognitive skills, such as memorization, decoding, and abstraction, demonstrated limited generalizability across contexts. Cognitive skills embedded in each of the literacies transferred only to narrow contexts that resembled the function and social practice of the cognitive sills related to the particular type of literacy.

Elaborations in the Classroom

Vygotsky's interest in development, particularly the development of higher intellectual functions, carried onto the classroom. He believed that instruction, like learning, precedes development, and concluded that, development creates the potentialities and instruction realizes them (Vygotsky, 1987, p.175). He argued that development of everyday cognition and scientific thinking—i.e., learning in the course of everyday living and learning through systematic teaching—differ developmentally, methodologically, and in the motives that drive them and that these differences have direct implications for teaching. As I pointed out, Vygotsky believed that schools and other formal educational institutions were the ideal sites for the exploration of thinking, especially the relationship between everyday and scientific thought.

Vygotsky considered understanding the relation between instruction and the mental development of the child of practical importance for studying numerous questions relating to teaching and learning. He conducted a series of studies that examined various aspect of development: (1) the level of cognitive development necessary for learning subject matter—that is, reading and writing, grammar, arithmetic, natural science, and social science; (2) the relationship between the learning curves of teaching and development; and (3) the issue of transfer of knowledge across school subjects (Vygotsky, 1987). Using the zone of proximal development as the analytic frame, he advocated teaching to the mental age of the learner rather than to the chronological age. The following studies that I review follow in the same tradition, asking basically the same type of questions that captivated Vygotsky almost eight decades ago.

As Kozulin (2003) highlights, the work of Vygotsky:

. . . prompts us to inquire into the nature of knowledge used in the classroom, for example, knowledge as information versus knowledge as concept formation. His theory makes us aware of our vision of students, for example, children defined by their age and IQ versus culturally and socially situated learners. It forces us to formulate our ideal of a teacher, for example, role model versus mediator, and so on. (p. 2)

The central concern of classroom researchers today continues to focus on explicating the relationship between learning and development, exploring the role of the social context and prior knowledge, and testing various aspects of Vygotskian theories, such as mediation, scaffolding, internalization, and the ubiquitous zone of proximal development. Implicit in this more theoretical endeavor is the concern with improving education to make a difference in the individual, as well as improving the society-at-large (Moll, 1990; Wells, 2000; Wertsch, 1985).

In the following sections, I provide a brief sketch of a select group of studies dealing with language and literacy, subject matter, teaching, and Vygotsky's most widely deliberated concept, the zone of proximal development. I select these studies to reflect on the series of studies I mentioned above and that Vygotsky (1987) conducted back in the 1930s in which he relates these areas of study to speech development. Although many of the studies cited touch on all of these topics, I arbitrarily separate them into those dealing with language, literacy, and writing and those dealing with teaching, subject matter, and the zone of proximal development. I also arbitrarily separate those studies that focus on aspects of difference to give them special emphasis. All of these studies have an empirical base and focus specifically on what Moll (1990) calls, "research in practice."

Language, Literacy, and Writing

Vygotsky found the understanding of the relation between scientific and everyday concepts of practical importance to education and instruction. In particular, he equates the learning of a native language to learning spontaneous concepts and learning a foreign language and the acquisition of written language to learning scientific concepts. The difference, he maintains is based:

... on spontaneous development and systematic instruction. In a certain sense, one may call the development of one's native language a spontaneous process, and the acquisition of the foreign a nonspontaneous process. (Vygotsky, 1987, p. 161)

Spontaneous development and systematic instruction have different origins, developmental trajectories, and functions that have important implications for instruction outcomes. Each process of knowledge acquisition: "reveal(s) different attitudes toward the object of study and different ways of its representation in the consciousness" (p.161). Vygotsky exemplifies this difference in the example of the acquisition of the words "brother" and "exploitation." The former is learned in the course of everyday life, and the child is able to absorb it without much difficulty because he or she has lived its meaning. The word exploitation, on the other hand, is introduced in the school for the first time. The child begins to form the concept of "exploitation" at the moment that he or she learns the meaning of the word. The concept cannot be absorbed ready-made into the child's everyday understanding without systematic instruction and without making connections to and modifications of previous knowledge and understanding. As Smolka, De Goes, and Pino (1995) point out, the word is "a historical product and production" evolving in its meaning in the encounters with others and in the case of scientific concepts, in close relation with the teacher.

Today, language, reading and writing studies produce variants of these ideas. Wells (1999, 2000), for example, relates the importance of language in human development, particularly to an emergent curriculum "in which teacher and students dialogically make sense of topics of individual and social significance" (2000, p. 98). His central goal is to call attention to the use of psychological tools—i.e., language—to build communities of inquiry in the classroom that will help improve the well-being of not only the learners but also society as well. Lantolf (2002) narrows the focus to the process of foreign-language learning in which private speech makes evident that the first language and the discourse of educational contexts mediate the process language learning. He differentiates between adults and children, noting that adults do not use as much private speech as children as a function of having learned what is expected in the classroom. Alanen (2003) also shows the influence of significant others in learner beliefs that children have about second foreign-language learning.

Clay and Cazden (1990), Dyson (2000), and McLane (1990) examine writing in a similar vein—as an emergent, complex, cultural activity. Working with low-performing children, Clay and Cazden highlight how the teacher strategically guides the reading process, doling out assistance in accordance with the growing competence of the child, a collaborative strategy particular to the framework of the zone of proximal development. Dyson and McLane continue the exploration of writing as a social process, extending their inquiry into the influence that community has on learning to write. Dyson's goals to "link learning to write" to "learning to participate in a complex community marked by sociocultural differences" focuses more specifically on the meaning-making of small children (2000, p. 128). She argues that:

Written words, like oral ones, are a means for participating in an always changing social community, a never-ending process of societal history-making and thus their meaning, their appropriate use, is always changing too. (p.144)

McLane examines the social aspect of writing outside of school, with collaboration from teachers and adults in charge of after-school activities out in the community. She demonstrates that with adult support, children learn not only to write but also to write for a purpose—i.e., to explore relationships, experiment, and play.

Collectively, these studies make visible the need to examine literacy learning as a situated process across times and places. These studies extend Vygotsky's assertion of the relationship between speech development and language, literacy, and writing by adding the broader community as an integral component in the respective developmental processes. The situated and generative nature of literacy learning in contexts of writing is integrally related to social others in the cultural community.

Teaching, Subject Matter, and the Zone of Proximal Development

Most studies of classroom teaching and learning from the sociocultural tradition can well be studies about how Vygotsky's ideas of everyday and scientific concepts are taught and learned in the classroom, as well as how the concept of the zone of proximal development plays a role in instruction and learning. These studies typically answer the questions that Säljö, 1991 asked about the relationship between Vygotsky's ideas and education:

What sense can we make of instruction when we approach it with the conceptual tools provided by the socio-historical school? What do we see when we begin to think in terms of zone of proximal development, when we utilize a genetic perspective or try to follow the transitions from mental to intra-mental processes? (p. 72)

What we see is the child's level of development and the developmental possibilities that exist for creating optimal learning conditions. Thus, this perspective allows us to see the change in the learners, the teachers, and the social context that is brought about by interweaving teaching, subject matter, and the zone of proximal development.

Haenen, Schrijnemakers, and Stufkens (2003); Hedegaard (1990); and Martin (1990), for example, seek to understand how to teach school knowledge in ways that mobilizes teachers' knowledge as well as the child's prior knowledge. Hedegaard (1990) uses the zone of proximal development as an analytic tool for promoting and evaluating children's development in school. Following Vygotsky's ideas of everyday and scientific concepts, Hedegaard makes a distinction in empirical knowledge and theoretical knowledge, claiming a difference in acquisition, epistemology and uses in the classroom for promoting subject matter learning. She proposes that teachers make a double move in instruction in which they use general laws to guide instruction while the children participate in exploratory activities that elicit and facilitate practice and acquisition of theoretical knowledge. Martin (1990) adds video technology to the connection between science problem solving and children's everyday knowledge. She finds that there is much more to learn about the role that mediating material (i.e., video technology) can play in facilitating conceptual connections between everyday experience and knowledge of an experience system; however, she concludes, "children in each class learned, at least for the day, what it means to identify a problem and solve it" (p. 398).

Au (1990), Haenen and colleagues (2003), and Tharp and Gallimore (1988) follow in the same vein, with the exception that they focus more directly in facilitating the socialization of novice teachers and the development of optimal learning environments. Haenen and colleagues examine the systematic teaching of historical concepts by helping teacher trainees explore their own as well as the children's zone of proximal development. They help teachers concur that "telling isn't teaching" and to see teaching as a heightened awareness of when, what, and how to facilitate a child's developmental process. At the same time, teacher trainees fine-tune their disciplinary knowledge and accept that historical concepts are socially constructed in the field and the classroom. Au (1990) and Tharp and Gallimore (1988) also attempt to create environments for both teacher and student development. They design and study an integrated instructional program that draws heavily on community resources called the Kamehameha Elementary Education Program (KEEP). The aims of the program are to both socialize teachers to an integrative perspective on teaching and learning and to teach general literacy and language development. In her study, Au reports on the acquisition of this integrative model of instruction by a novice teacher in dialogue with the researcher. As the teacher systematically explores her implicit theories of learning and her personally held belief system, the researcher supports the development of an enhanced perspective on teaching and learning. Using a Vygotskian perspective to examine the dynamic character of teacher's consciousness, the researcher strategically scaffolds "the teacher's discovery of solutions" (p. 285), in the process helping her to recognize the source and the application of expertise.

The study of the zone of proximal development often focuses on its relevance as a practical tool for enhancing learning and development. Thus, studies often focus on interactional routines that support learning and development in the learning setting. The study of adult-child interaction by Petitto (1988) demonstrates how the zone of proximal development is applied to support the acquisition of procedural knowledge, in this case, the hierarchy of goals and subgoals that characterize remainder division. Petitto's findings strongly suggest a type of teaching and teacher expertise that pays close attention to changes "in the specifics of a plan while retaining the plan's overall goal structure" (p. 235). Interestingly, Petitto finds that teachers differentially assist children according to their achievement levels. She concludes that:

A careful analysis of lesson content and goals to enable educators to find ways that children with different levels of prerequisite skills can receive maximum instruction on the relevant aspect of the current lesson, even though certain elements of presentation and external support might be different. (p. 267)

Tudge (1990), on the other hand, makes a case to reexamine the conditions of peer-peer interaction within the framework of the zone of proximal development. Although much research highlights the value of adult-child interaction, Tudge argues that peer-peer collaboration can also be beneficial given certain conditions—i.e., when the partner is more competent and confident and the materials provide feedback. Without these conditions, the possibility that the children regress in their development is high. He argues that the effect of feedback "overshadows any effects of discussion with a partner" (p.167) and demonstrates again that it is not sufficient to think that the zone of proximal development can be achieved on its own—the teacher must remain vigilant of the developmental process and intervene in whenever necessary.

In summary, the life of the classroom in itself is full of complexity, intrinsically dialogic (Gutiérrez & Stone, 2000), socially constructed and negotiated (Putney, Green, Dixon, Durán, & Yeager, 2000) even without aspects of difference that are discussed in the following section. In both situations, complexity has critical implications for language and literacy development (John-Steiner & Mann, 1996; Gutiérrez & Stone, 2000; Mercer, 1995; Wells, 1999), cultural mediation in teaching (Moll, 2002), and context development (Vasquez, 2003, 2006). The studies cited point to the adeptness of the analytic framework of sociocultural theory to manage the complexity in the classroom from the most minute aspects of task analysis to the nuances of interactional encounters and imperceptible shifts in understanding. Although some implicitly deal with cultural diversity (these are listed in the following sections), I focus on studies that make variations within and across languages, cultures, and abilities the focus of the analysis.

The Study of Difference and Change

Perhaps one of the most perplexing challenges facing sociocultural theorists at the dawn of the 21st century is the issue of diversity in culture, literacy, ability, income, schooling, and identity. The challenge goes beyond the obstacles facing researchers whose goals are to optimize teaching and learning as discussed in the classroom studies discussed earlier, although these new perspectives may have the potential to disrupt the core of education that Elmore (1996) characterizes as intractable. However, the challenge of diversity is more wide ranging than how we do education. Sociocultural theorists face the challenge of how to do society, particularly how to treat diversity not as a deficit or a pariah, but rather as part and parcel of the social unit. As an interventionist approach, sociocultural theory has much to offer for understanding, integrating, and enhancing the intellectual and material resources of an increasingly diverse student population. It allows us to understand, manage, and marshal the complexity that diversity generates to facilitate the development of the individual and society.

According to Kozulin (2003), the conceptual resources of sociocultural theory potentially offer, "one of the best theoretical frameworks for educating culturally and socially diverse learners" (p. 10). Conceptually, this theory creates the lens to distinguish old and new knowledge and to imagine how in theory these resources play a critical role in the teaching and learning processes. For example, this theory allows us to examine the role that culture and discourse play in classroom learning (Gutiérrez, Rymes, & Larson, 1995), to conceptualize the value of community resources as important tools for learning and development in the classroom (González, Moll, & Amanti, 2005; Moll & Diaz, 1987; Moll & Greenberg, 1990) and to establish the effects of program effect on the long-term social and economic integration of communities of difference (Martínez & Vásquez, 2006; Vásquez, 2003, 2006). Importantly, it also affords us the possibility to create environments in which old and new knowledge can be marshaled to achieve optimal achievement (Vásquez, 2003). Following, I highlight only a select group of studies that allows us to see difference from a different perspective from what has been done.

To study diversity is to study complexity within and/or across cultures, national boundaries, socioeconomic variables, abilities, and identities. To study it from a Vygotskian perspective is to study the constitutive relation of this complexity to cognitive and cultural development; that is, to deem difference as a viable resource in the learning process. Some of the angles from which researchers on diversity approach this perspective include (1) how individual actors relate to conflicting cultural norms in the classroom; (2) how cultural resources can be identified, interpreted, and drawn on in the instructional program; and (3) how learning contexts in the community can be linked to classroom learning. Researchers such as Gutiérrez and Stone (2000), Ishiguro (1996), Putney et al. (2000), Smagorinsky & O'Donnel-Allen (2000), and Smardon (2004) are a few who clearly illustrate the complexity in the classroom and the individual successes and tensions that arise out of this complexity for learners of diverse backgrounds. Occasionally, differences are central to the analysis; at other times, they await expectantly in the background ready to influence the tweaking of the theoretical framework, the practice, or the individual's process of integration into the culture of the classroom. In the following section, I give a brief sketch of work done in these three areas.

Putney and colleagues (2000) layout in great detail the complexity of life in the classroom as revealed by the conjoining of three analytic frames—interactional ethnography, sociocultural theory, and critical discourse analysis. They track a child's development as a point of view across time and events to make evident the consequential effect that cultural resources of a community of practices have on the individual's opportunities for learning. They argue that lived experiences seen from such an expanded analytic frame show much promise for answering the questions that continue to plague researchers and practitioners about learning, specifically the recurrent question, What is learning? Ishiguro's (1996) study demonstrates the tensions and successes of assimilation to a new community of practice. He tracks the process of appropriation of a new voice by a Ukrainian child in a Japanese nursery school and points to the complexity children must negotiate in the classroom, often, at a high cost to the child's language and sense of self. The costs include the disparagement of being spoken in "baby talk" and the rejection of the native language to fit in, experiences foreign-language speakers encounter worldwide. Yet, despite these tensions, Ishiguro points to the appropriation of classroom discourse styles as a positive aspect of becoming part of the community of practice. He suggests that the concept of appropriation extends the analytic possibilities of the zone of proximal development.

Rueda (1990), on the other hand, addresses another kind of difference that has critical implications for the teaching of literacy and learning disabilities. He concurs with others already cited in this chapter that teachers or other adults are of great importance to literacy development. His findings support Ishiguro's conclusions that nonschool talk by teachers has implications for learning; this time it is positively related to learning as opposed to the negative affect of "baby talk" in Ishiguro's article. He finds that the teacher's personalized response has a greater effect on the children's grasp of written language as a communication tool than school talk. Teachers, he argues, play a crucial role in "assisting students in internalizing the concept of written language as a medium for expressive and communicative purposes" (p. 407). McDermott and Varenne (1995) extend this perspective even further and show how the label of disability (i.e., the inadequate performance on tasks) is arbitrary and socially constructed. The label of disability is free flowing, and anyone in the classroom is subject to being labeled as such.

Cultural resources that children bring to the classroom can play a powerful role in influencing classroom teaching and learning once they are identified, interpreted, and drawn on in the instructional program. Gutiérrez and Stone (2000), for example, argue that learning "is not always a benign activity; thus conflict, tension, and contradiction contribute to the idiosyncratic nature of learning activity" (p. 151). Cultural variability in the classroom can lead to positive and fruitful dialogue or to conflict that provokes disillusion or alienation. Gutiérrez and colleagues (1995, 2000) borrow the notion of "third space" to describe "a discursive space in which alternative and competing discourses and positionings transform conflict and difference into rich zones of collaboration and learning" (p. 157). Smardon (2004) also shows how conflicting cultural resources, discourses used in different context—one "decent" (presumably the language of school), one "street" (the language of the community)—are mobilized in the classroom to achieve either effective or conflicting outcomes. From the teacher's and researcher's perspectives, street code provokes a series of misinterpretations, lost opportunities, and intractable discontinuities. It is not until a careful analysis of video data is conducted that the strategic use of street code is recognized as a mechanism for maintaining a personal identity in the midst of conflicting cultural norms. The finding is that street code has little predictive value for the acquisition of knowledge of science but has important implications for teachers who often misjudge students' use of cultural codes in the classroom.

According to Kozulin (2003), "cultural funds of knowledge, culturally appropriate, or culturally compatible pedagogies, and so many other important concepts related to modern multicultural education" (p. 15) are not found in Vygotsky's theorizing. However, these concepts are exactly the ones that researchers interested in making a change in education and society use. The groundbreaking work of Moll and Diaz (1987), Moll and Greenberg (1990), and González et al. (2005) link learning contexts as a means of "transforming classrooms into more advanced contexts for teaching and learning" (p. 344) and consequently, mediate the social and academic integration of non-mainstream groups (Vásquez, 2003, 2006). Cultural resources, namely Vygotsky's notion of prior history, from this perspective are important intellectual tools for training teachers in creating optimal learning environments (González et al., 2005), facilitating comprehension (Moll & Diaz, 1987), enhancing the development of biliteracy and thinking (Moll, October 1992), and maintaining the first language and acquiring the second language (Vásquez, 1993, 2003).

These studies on difference are but a few that are challenging how we do education and society at a time of great social change. Much more must be done to address the complexity that diversity brings into the learning setting both in after school contexts and classrooms. Although after-school contexts based on cultural historical and sociocultural approaches have much to offer the classroom in terms of radical-local teaching and learning (Hedegaard & Chaiklin, 2005) and developmental approach to cultural relevance (Vásquez, 2003, 2006), it is the classroom that will make the difference in the child and the society. As Dyson (2000) points out, we must incorporate the study of the "ideological fluidity of cultural symbols or human identities" (p.144) to help children learn how to talk about the differences in which they live and to familiarize teachers the realities of society at the dawn of the 21st century.

LEARNING IN CONSTRUCTED ACTIVITY SYSTEMS

The most influential force in the spread of sociocultural theory and practice has been the Laboratory of Comparative Human Cognition (LCHC) under the leadership of Michael Cole. Although Vygotsky recognized that he needed a new analytic framework and a new methodology to study the social nature of thought, Cole created the environment in which to test, extend, compare, amalgamate, and disseminate ideas emerging from this new science. Newman and Holzman (1993) reckon that:

Recognizing that one could not develop a new science without building an environment where such a new methodology, would be nourished, Cole designed the lab as a challenge to traditional institutional organization and structure of academia. (p. 20)

The laboratory became a forum for innovation in thought and action where "almost no work . . . was out of bounds; obscure, radical and alternative writings and research were studied" (p. 20). For almost 30 years, collaborators at the laboratory have spearheaded some of the most critical discussions of social science in the 20th century— e.g., the issues of ecological validity, generalizability, context, and diversity. The laboratory's newsletter—*The Quarterly Newsletter of the Laboratory of Comparative Human Cognition*—and its successor—*Mind, Culture and Activity*—have been a major voice in the discussion of these issues. Articles in the LCHC newsletter are recognized as:

"... important benchmarks in the history of a discussion of context, culture and development. The central theme of this discussion can be posed as a question: How shall we develop a psychology that takes as its starting point the actions of people participating in routine cultural contexts? This question engenders a second: What kind of methodology does the study of human behavior in context entail? (Cole et al., 1997, p. 1)

Long before it became fashionable, the classroom became one of those cultural contexts of interest to collaborators at the laboratory (Moll, 1990; Newman et al., 1989). The laboratory itself became a methodology onto itself "to understand the relations between learning and development in order to come up with educational practices which maximize the learning and development of all children" (Newman & Holzman, 1993, p. 24).

LCHC has also distinguished itself in three other critical ways: its national and international collaboration has been singular, it has been a leader in experimenting with information and communication technologies to create new forms of distributed academic research and teaching, and it has promulgated a method for studying and enhancing human development in powerful activity systems. In many regards, LCHC characterizes all three definitions of the notion of cross-national research I proposed earlier. Not only have collaborators come from diverse backgrounds, but also diversity has been the focus of the laboratory's research both locally and internationally. The laboratory's extensive, technology supported, collaborative networks have been critical to the flow of ideas into every corner of the world. Collaborators from all parts of the world—many of whom are cited in this review—have spent time at the laboratory or have participated in one of its many electronic supported seminars or online discussions.

The laboratory has also been one of the pioneers in the use of information and communication technologies to engage in collaborative dialogue with colleagues worldwide, offer distance-learning both locally and internationally, and design experiments (Brown, 1992) that create powerful activity systems to study culture and development. These telecommunication technologies have made it possible for a distributed group of scholars to greatly enrich the experiences of the local participants by actively participating in course discussions and sometimes coauthoring articles online through an extended discussion list called XLCHC or through video-conference technology. These technologies provide local participants the opportunity to test their ideas in a greater context and to form collegial relationships with scholars worldwide. Here, however, I want to give special attention to two of LCHC's quasi-experimental activity settings that focus primarily on the study and support of learning and development; the Fifth Dimension and one of its many innovations, *La Clase Mágica.*

The Basic Design of the Fifth Dimension

In its earliest incarnation, the Fifth Dimension was a computer-based curriculum for academically challenged children attending an after-school academy housed in the library of an elementary school near University of California, San Diego, where LCHC is located. Efforts to develop a model system for the in-school study of learning disabilities eventually led LCHC researchers to after-school hours—where they were free to manipulate the curriculum and relations of power to achieve maximum interaction between children and adult participants. With support of students enrolled in a practicum course, researchers created a fictional world in which the power of adults was diminished in direct proportion to the increases in the power of the participating children (LCHC, 1982). Thus, the Fifth Dimension developed into a model system involving university and community institutions to both create and study the viability of activity systems to promote learning and development and to sustain themselves independent of the university sponsorship (Cole, 1997).

Today, the Fifth Dimension is a design experiment (Brown, 1992) in which researchers are able to study some of the fundamental ideas of sociohistorical theory discussed earlier—mediation, zone of proximal development, an interventionist methodology, diversity, and culture. Theories deployed to study and develop a model system to enhance learning and development in after-school contexts have led researchers to:

. . . think simultaneously about the social organization of activity, the various tools used to carry out the various tasks (computers, pencils, paper, task cards, wizard, modems), social roles, modes of participation, and the relation of the activity to its context. (Cole et al., 2006)

Researchers worldwide have appropriated this methodology and constructed activity systems to study local issues relating to language and literacy practices (Gutierrez, Baquedano-López, & Tejeda, 1999; Moll, 1992), the relationship of school to social integration of minority groups (Lalueza & Crespo, 2006; Vásquez, 2003) and linking of important contexts to human development (González et al., 2005).

La Clase Mágica

One of the Fifth Dimension's offspring that has focused specifically on diversity and education from a Vygotskian perspective is a bilingual bicultural, five-tier research initiative known as *La Clase Mágica* (see Vásquez, 2003, for details). *La Clase Mágica* adds bilingualism and biculturalism to the original curriculum, a life-span approach to its pedagogy, and a revamped practicum undergraduate course specifically designed to theorize the practice of minority education from outside the system in an after-school computer program where conditions can be tweaked to achieve optimal outcomes (Vásquez, 2006b). Building on Vygotsky's interventionist methodology, *La Clase Mágica* made the study of the academic achievement of minority youth and their representation in higher education key components of its research agenda. It has also sought to link important contexts for human development in a cross-system collaborative effort that circulates knowledge and resources throughout the system spawning continuous reflective change.

During the last 17 years, the research agenda of *La Clase Mágica* has concerned itself with understanding and enhancing the learning potential of its participants and the social and academic integration of minority youth and their families (Martínez & Vásquez, 2006). Its guiding questions have included: What makes for an optimal learning environment for diverse learners? (Vásquez, 1994, 2003); How best to create a culture of learning that supports the acquisition of both mainstream and minority cultural knowledge? (Vásquez, 2005); What role do bilingualism and biculturalism play in learning and development? (Vásquez, 1993); How best to link important contexts related to human development through equitable and sustainable relations of exchange between researchers and community members (Vásquez, 1996, 2003); and How best to integrally involve parents as equal partners in their children's schooling? (Vásquez, 2003).

As the social conditions change as a result of the economic and cultural globalization processes, *La Clase Mágica* has increasingly shifted its theoretical and research lens to the concern of how best to tweak the learning context to prepare diverse learners for the new realities of the 21st century (Vásquez, 2006a). In particular, it has emphasized how technology-supported environments can influence learning and development of individuals but also spur relevant change in the contexts linked to human development (Vásquez, 2006a, 2006b).

A BEGINNING, NOT A CONCLUSION

The idea of the social nature of human thought, or "culture in mind," as the cultural historical and sociocultural theorists call it, dates back a long time as I discussed, but it was the work of Vygotsky that gave this area of study, its theoretical framework, its methodology, its unit of analysis, and basically its raison d'etre. Sociocultural research on education is in its infancy, less than 20 years old according to Moll (1990). The potentialities of its development can be only be realized through research—to borrow Vygotsky's notion of the relationship between development and instruction—as is evident in the work described in this chapter. The elaboration of Vygotsky's theoretical concepts, the incorporation of other analytic frames (Newman & Holzman, 1993; Putney et al., 2000), and the focus on quasi-formal learning contexts, such as the laboratories reported by Moll and colleagues (2000, 2005), Cole, (1996), Hedegaard and Chaiklin (2005), and Vásquez (2003), will continue to expand the potential of sociocultural theory to understand and marshal the complexity of learning contexts that not only serve to enhance teaching, but also serve to enhance individual development and the betterment of the society-at-large.

Given the changes that must be made in education at a time in which the world is in constant flux, when educational institutions are confronted with the insurmountable complexity of diversity of all types, sociocultural research on learning, specifically research dealing with difference in the learning context will be ever more important in the coming years. The cultural changes occurring worldwide will necessitate cross-cultural work of the ilk that engages cross-national collaboration to solve global issues in the local stemming from the flows of people, ideas, technology, and capital. Out of the need to address the increase in immigration and its attendant issues, such as poverty, unemployment, academic failure, and violence, education and other cultural institutions will, out of necessity, turn to the notion of connecting learning contexts important to child development (González et al., 2005; Moll, 2000; Vásquez, 2006) that include those in the home country or other locales to solve societal, as well as individual problems. Thus, not only will researchers or ideas cross national boundaries but collaboration will also cross national borders to achieve greater resolution of issues related to the academic and social integration of minority groups of foreign or indigenous backgrounds. I envision an integrative collaboration that operates within a community of practice in which each collaborating entity is a fully engaged partner with equal role in helping to change how we do education and society (John-Steiner, 2000). Comparative studies of language, the most important symbolic and material tool instantiating the relation of culture in mind, will no doubt receive greater emphasis along the lines begun by Alanen (2003) and Lantolf (2003), as well as continue to tease out the processes, both functional and ideological, of second-language acquisition. I anticipate that the pluralities of cultural resources, aims, and purposes driving literacy, language, and writing development will continue to captivate the analytic curiosity of researchers and practitioners for some time to come. Finally, I anticipate that activity theory will turn its focus more prominently on classroom learning and that future research on learning will make stronger connections between the spontaneous learning in after-school contexts and the systematic instruction in the classroom for the benefit of both settings. The study of how new information and communication technologies will be central to finding ways to establish these connections and to promote the type of cultural and cognitive change that the new realities of the 21st-century mandate.

REFERENCES

Agar, M. (1994). *Language shock: Understanding the culture of conversation.* New York: William Morrow.

Ageyev, V. (2003). Vygotsky's educational theory in cultural context. In A. Kozulin, B. Gindis, V. Ageyev, & S. Miller (Eds.), *Vygotsky in the mirror of cultural interpretations* (pp. 432–449). Cambridge, UK: Cambridge University Press.

Alanen, R. (2003). A sociocultural approach to young language learners' beliefs about language learning. In P. Kalaja & A. M. Ferreira Barcelos (Eds.), *Beliefs about SLA: New research approaches* (pp. 55–58). Boston: Kluwer Academic Publishers.

Au, K. H. (1990). Changes in a teacher's views of interactive comprehension instruction. In L. C. Moll (Ed.), *Vygotsky and education. Instructional implications and applications of socio-historical psychology* (pp. 155–172). Cambridge, MA: Cambridge University Press.

Beach, K. (1995). Activity as a mediator of sociocultural change and individual development: the case of school-work transition in Nepal. *Culture and Activity: An International Journal, 2*(4), 285–302.

Blanck, G. (1990). Vygotsky: The man and his cause. In L. Moll (Ed.), *Vygotsky and education: Instructional implications and applications of socio-historical psychology* (pp. 31–58). Cambridge, MA: Cambridge University Press.

Bronfenbrenner, U. (1979). *The ecology of human development.* Cambridge, MA: Harvard University Press.

Bronckart, J. (1995). Theories of action, speech, natural language, and discourse. In J. Wertsch, P. Del Rio, & A. Alvarez (Eds.), *Sociocultural studies of mind* (pp. 37–55). Cambridge, MA: Cambridge University Press.

Brown, A. L. (1992). Design experiments: Theoretical and methodological challenges in creating complex interventions in classroom settings. *The Journal of the Learning Sciences, 2*(2), 141–178.

Brown, A. L., & French, L. A. (1979). The zone of potential development: Implications for intelligence testing in the year 2000. *Intelligence, 3,* 255–279.

Childs, C. P., & Greenfield, P. M. (1980). Informal modes of learning and teaching: The case of Zinacanteco weaving. In Warren, N. (Ed.), *Studies in cross-cultural psychology, Vol. 2* (pp. 269–316). London: Academic Press.

Clay, M. M., & Cazden, C. B. (1990). A Vygotskyian interpretation of reading recovery. In L. C. Moll (Ed.), *Vygotsky and education: Instructional implications and applications of socio-historical psychology* (pp. 206–222). Cambridge, MA: Cambridge University Press.

Cole, M. (1995). Socio-cultural-historical psychology: Some general remarks and a proposal for a new kind of cultural-genetic methodology. In J. V. Wertsch, P. Del Rio, & A. Alvarez (Eds.), *Sociocultural studies of mind* (pp. 187–214). Cambridge, MA: Cambridge University Press.

Cole, M. (1996). *Cultural psychology: A once and future discipline.* Cambridge, MA: The Belknap Press of Harvard University Press.

Cole, M. (1998). Culture and cognitive development in phylogenetic, historical, and ontogenetic perspective. In D. Kuhn & R. Siegler (Eds.), *Handbook of child psychology: Fifth edition. Vol. 2: Cognition, perception, and language.* New York: John Wiley & Sons.

Cole, M., Engeström, Y., & Vásquez, O. A. (1997). *Mind, culture, and activity: Seminal papers from the Laboratory of Comparative Human Cognition.* Cambridge, MA: Cambridge University Press.

Cole, M., Gay, J., Glick, J. A., & Sharp, D. W. (1971). Culture and thinking. *The cultural context of learning and thinking: An exploration in experimental anthropology* (pp. 3–24). New York: Basic Books.

Cole, M., Hood, L., & McDermott, R. P. (1978, April). Concepts of ecological validity: Their differing implications from comparative cognitive research. *The Quarterly Newsletter of the Laboratory of Comparative Human Cognition, 2*(2), 34–37.

Daniels, H. (2001). *Vygotsky and pedagogy.* New York: Routledge.

Dyson, A. (2000). Linking writing and community development through the children's forum. In C. Lee & P. Smagorinsky (Eds.), *Vygotskian perspectives on literacy research: Constructing meaning through collaborative inquiry,* (pp. 127–149). Cambridge, MA: Cambridge University Press.

Elhammounmi, M. (1997). *Socio-historicocultural psychology.* Lanham, MA: University Press of America, Inc.

Elmore, R. (1996). Getting to scale with good educational practice. *Harvard Educational Review, 66*(1), 1–2.

Gallimore, R., & Tharp, R. (1990). Teaching mind in society: Teaching, schooling, and literate discourse. In L. Moll (Ed.), *Vygotsky and education* (pp. 175–205). Cambridge, MA: Cambridge University Press.

González, N., Moll, L., & Amanti, C. (2005). *Funds of knowledge: Theorizing practices in households, communities, and classrooms.* Mahwah, NJ: Lawrence Erlbaum Associates.

Greenfield, P. M. (1984). A theory of the teacher in the learning activities of everyday life. In B. Rogoff & J. Lave (Eds.), *Everyday cognition: Its development in social context* (pp. 117–138). Cambridge, MA: Harvard University Press.

Greenfield, P. M., & Childs, C. P. (1977). Weaving, color terms, and pattern representations: Cultural influence and cognitive development among the Zinacantecos of Southern Mexico. *International Journal of Psychology, 11,* 23–48.

Greenfield, P. M., Maynard, A. E., & Childs, C. P. (2000). History, culture, learning, and development. *Cross-Cultural Research: The Journal of Comparative Social Science, 34*(4) 351–374.

Greenfield, P. M., Maynard, A. E., & Childs, C. P. (October-December, 2003). Historical change, cultural learning, and cognitive representation in Zinacantec Mayan children. *Cognitive Development, 18*(4), 455–487.

Griffin, P., Cole, M., & Newman, D. (1982). Locating tasks in psychology and education. *Discourse Processes, 5,* 111–125.

Gutiérrez, K., Baquedano-López, P., & Tejeda, C. (1999). Rethinking diversity: Hybridity and hybrid language practices in the third space. *Mind, Culture, and Activity, 6*(4), 286–303.

Gutiérrez, K. D., Rymes, B., & Larson, J. (1995). Script, counterscript, and underlife in classrooms: James Brown vs. Brown vs. Board of Education. *Harvard Educational Review, 65,* 445–471.

Gutiérrez, K., & Stone, L. (2000). Synchronic and diachronic dimensions of social practice: An emerging methodology for cultural-historical perspectives on literacy learning. In C. Lee & P. Smagorinsky (Eds.), *Vygotskian perspectives on literacy research: Constructing meaning through collaborative inquiry* (pp. 150–164). Cambridge, MA: Cambridge University Press.

Haenen, J., Schrijnemakers, H., & Stufkens, J. (2003). Sociocultural theory and the practice of teaching historical concepts. In A. Kozulin, B. Gindis, V. Ageyev, & S. Miller (Eds.), *Vygotsky's educational theory in cultural context* (pp. 246–266). Cambridge University Press.

Hedegaard, M. (1990). The zone of proximal development as basis for instruction. In L. C. Moll (Ed.), *Vygotsky and education: Instructional implications and applications of sociohistorical psychology* (pp. 349–371). Cambridge, MA: Cambridge University Press.

Hedegaard, M. (Ed.). (2001). *Learning in classrooms: A cultural-historical approach.* Denmark: Aarhus University Press.

Hedegaard, M., & Chaiklin, S. (2005). *Radical-local teaching and learning.* Denmark: Aarhus University Press.

Ishiguro, H. (1996). On the relation between new voices and old voices: What does a newcomer appropriate? Paper presented at the Second Annual Conference for Socio-cultural Research, Geneva, September 12.

Jahoda, G., & Lewis, I. M. (1988). *Acquiring culture: Cross cultural studies in child development* (pp. 1–34). New York: Croom Helm.

John-Steiner, V. (2000). *Creative collaboration.* New York: Oxford University Press.

John-Steiner, V., & Mann, H. (1996). Sociocultural approaches to learning and development: A Vygotskian framework. *Educational Psychologist, 31*(3/4), 191–206.

Kozulin, A. (2003). Psychological tools and mediated learning. In A. Kozulin, B. Gindis, V. S. Ageyev, & S. M. Miller (Eds.), *Vygotsky's educational theory in cultural context* (pp.15–38). Cambridge, MA: Cambridge University Press.

Laboratory of Comparative Human Cognition. (1982, July). A model system for the study of learning difficulties. *The Quarterly Newsletter of the Laboratory of Comparative Human Cognition, 4*(3), 39–65.

Lantolf, J. P. (2002). Sociocultural theory and second language acquisition. In R. B. Kaplan (Ed.), *The Oxford Handbook of Applied Linguistics* (pp. 104–114).

Lave, J. (1988). *Cognition in practice.* Cambridge, MA: Cambridge University Press.

Lave, J., Murtaugh, M., & de la Rocha, O. (1984). The dialectics of Arithmetician grocery shopping. In B. Rogoff & J. Lave, (Eds.), *Everyday cognition: Its development in social context.* Cambridge, MA: Harvard University Press.

Leontiev, A. N., & Luria, A. R. (1968). The psychological ideas of L. S. Vygotskii. In B. B. Wolman (Ed.), *Historical roots of contemporary psychology* (pp. 338–367). New York: Harper & Row Publishers.

Luria, A. R. (1976). *Conclusion. Cognitive development* (pp. 161–164). Cambridge, MA: Harvard University Press.

Martin, L. (1990). Detecting and defining science problems: A study of video-mediated lessons. In L. Moll (Ed.), *Vygotsky and education: Instructional implications and applications of sociohistorical psychology* (pp. 372–402). Cambridge, MA: Cambridge University Press.

Martinez, M., & Vásquez, O. A. (2006). *Sustainability: La clase mágica beyond its boundaries.* Unpublished manuscript.

McDermott, R., & Varenne, H. (1995). Culture as disability. *Anthropology & Education Quarterly, 26*(3), 324–348.

McLane, J. (1990). Writing as a social process. In L. Moll (Ed.), *Vygotsky and education: Instructional implications and applications of sociohistorical psychology* (pp. 304–318). Cambridge, MA: Cambridge University Press.

Mead, M. (1978). The evocation of psychologically relevant responses in ethnological fieldwork. In G. D. Spindler (Ed.), *The making of psychological anthropology* (pp. 87–139). Berkeley: University of California Press.

Mercer, N. (1995). *The guided construction of knowledge.* Clevedon, UK: Multilingual Matters.

Moll, L. C. (1990). Introduction. In L. Moll (Ed.), *Vygotsky and education: Instructional implications and applications of sociohistorical psychology.* Cambridge, MA: Cambridge University Press.

Moll, L. C. (October, 1992). Biliteracy and thinking. *The Quarterly Newsletter of the Laboratory of Comparative Human Cognition, 13*(3), 51–65.

Moll, L. C. (2000). Inspired by Vygotsky: Ethnographic experiments in education. In C. Lee & P. Smagorinsky (Eds.), *Vygotskian perspectives on literacy research: Constructing meaning through collaborative inquiry* (pp. 256–267). Cambridge, MA: Cambridge University Press.

Moll, L. C. (2002). Through the mediation of others: Vygotskian research on teaching. In V. Richardson (Ed.). *Handbook of research on teaching* (4th ed.). Washington, DC: American Education Research Association.

Moll, L. C., & Diaz, S. (1987). Change as the goal of educational research. *Anthropology and Education Quarterly, 18*(4), 300–311.

Moll, L., & Greenberg, J. (1990). Creating zones of possibilities: Combining social contexts for instruction. In L. Moll (Ed.), *Vygotsky and education: Instructional implications and applications of sociohistorical psychology* (pp. 319–348). Cambridge, MA: Cambridge University Press.

Newman, D., Griffin, P., & Cole, M. (1984). Social constraints in laboratory and classroom tasks. In J. Lave & B. Rogoff (Eds.), *Everyday cognition: Its development in social context* (pp. 172–193). Cambridge, MA: Harvard University Press.

Newman, D., Griffin P., & Cole, M. (1989). *The construction zone: Working for cognitive change in school.* Cambridge, MA: Cambridge University Press.

Newman, F., & Holzman, L. (1993). *Lev Vygotsky revolutionary scientist.* London: Routledge.

O'Neil, P. (1976). Educating divergent thinkers: An ecological investigation. *American Journal of Community Psychology, 4*(1), 99–107.

Pennycook, A. (1998). *English and the discourses of colonialism.* New York: Routledge.

Petitto, A. L. (1988). Division of labor: Procedural learning in teacher-led small groups. *Cognition and Instruction, 2*(3/4), 233–270.

Putney, L. G., Green, J., Dixon, C., Durán, R., & Yeager, B. (2000). Consequential progressions: Exploring collective-individual development in a bilingual classroom. In C. Lee & P. Smagorinsky (Eds.), *Vygotskian perspectives on literacy research: Constructing meaning through collaborative inquiry* (pp. 86–126). Cambridge, MA: Cambridge University Press.

Rogoff, B. (1981). Schooling and the development of cognitive skills. In H. C. Triandis & A. Heron (Eds.), *Handbook of cross-cultural psychology* (Vol. 4) (pp. 233–294). Boston: Allyn & Bacon.

Rogoff, B. (1984). Introduction: Thinking and learning in social context. In B. Rogoff & J. Lave (Eds.), *Everyday cognition: Its development in social context* (pp. 1–9). Cambridge, MA: Harvard University Press.

Rogoff, B. (1990). *Apprenticeship in thinking: Cognitive development in social context.* New York: Oxford University Press.

Rogoff, B. (1995a). Developing understanding of the idea of communities of learners. *Mind, Culture, and Activity: An International Journal, 1*(4), 209–229.

Rogoff, B. (1995b). Observing sociocultural activity on three planes: Participatory appropriation, guided participation, and apprenticeship. In J. V. Wertsch, P. Del Rio, & A. Alvarez (Eds.), *Sociocultural studies of mind* (pp. 139–164). Cambridge, MA: Cambridge University Press.

Rogoff, B. (1998). Cognition as a collaborative process. In D. Kuhn & R. Siegler (Eds.), *Handbook of child psychology: Fifth edition. Vol. 2: Cognition, perception and language* (pp. 679–744). New York: John Wiley & Sons.

Rogoff, B., & Lave, J. (Eds.). (1984). *Everyday cognition: Its development in social context.* Cambridge, MA: Harvard University Press.

Rueda, R. (1990). Assisted performance in writing instruction with learning-disabled students. In L. Moll (Ed.), *Vygotsky and education: Instructional implications and applications of sociohistorical psychology* (pp. 401–426). Cambridge, MA: Cambridge University Press.

Säljö, R. (1991, July). Vygotskian lessons. *The Quarterly Newsletter of the Laboratory of Comparative Human Cognition, 13*(3), 71–74.

Saxe, G. B. (1982). Developing forms of arithmetic operations among the Oksapmin of Papua, New Guinea. *Developmental Psychology, 18*(4), 583–584.

Saxe, G. B., & Esmonde, I. (2005). Study cognition in flux: A historical treatment of Fu in shifting structure of Oksapmin mathematics. *Mind, Culture, and Activity, 12*(384), 171–225.

Scribner, S. (1984). Studying Working Intelligence. In B. Rogoff & J. Lave (Eds.), *Everyday cognition: Its development in social context* (pp. 9–41). Cambridge, MA: Harvard University Press.

Scribner, S., & Cole, M. (1981). *The psychology of literacy.* Cambridge, MA: Harvard University Press.

Smagorinsky, P., & O'Donnell-Allen, C. (2000). Idiocultural diversity in small groups: The roll of relational frameworks in collaborative learning. In C. Lee, P. Smagorinsky (Eds.), *Vygotskian perspectives on literacy research: Constructing meaning through collaborative inquiry* (pp. 165–190). Cambridge, MA: Cambridge University Press.

Smardon, R. (2004). Streetwise science: Toward a theory of the code of the classroom. *Mind, Culture and Activity: An International Journal, 11*(3), 201–223.

Smolka, A. L. B., De Goes, M. C. R., & Pino, A. (1995). The constitution of the subject: a persistent question. In J. V. Wertsch, P. Del Rio, & A. Alvarez (Eds.), *Sociocultural studies of mind* (pp.165–184). Cambridge, MA: Cambridge University Press.

Stigler, J. W., & Perry, M. (1990). Mathematics learning in Japanese, Chinese, and American Classrooms. Indexicality and socialization. In Stigler, J. W., Shweder, R. A., Herdt, G.

Cultural psychology: Essays on comparative human development (pp. 328–353). Cambridge, MA: Cambridge University Press.

Tarnas, R. (1991). *The passion of the western mind: Understanding ideas that have shaped our world view.* New York: Ballantine Books.

Tharp, R., & Gallimore, R. (1988). *Rousing minds to Life: Teaching, learning and school in social context.* Cambridge, MA: Cambridge University Press.

Tudge, J. (1990). Vygotsky, the zone of proximal development, and peer collaboration: Implications for classroom practice. In L. Moll (Ed.), *Vygotsky and education: Instructional implications and applications of sociohistorical psychology* (pp. 155–172). Cambridge, MA: Cambridge University Press.

Tudge, J. (2004). Practice and discourse as the intersection of individual and social human development. In A. Perret-Clermont, C. Pontecorvo, L. B. Resnick, T. Zittoun, & B. Burge (Eds.), *Joining society: Social interaction and learning in adolescence and youth* (pp. 192–203). Cambridge, MA: Cambridge University Press.

Van der Veer, R., & Valsiner, J. (1993). *Understanding Vygotsky: A quest for synthesis.* Cambridge, MA: Blackwell.

Vásquez, O. A. (1993). A look at language as resource: Lessons from *La Clase Mágica.* In B. Arias & U. Casanova (Eds.), *Bilingual education: Politics, research, and practice* (pp. 199–224). Chicago: National Society for the Study of Education.

Vásquez, O. A. (1994). The magic of *La Clase Mágica:* Enhancing the learning potential of bilingual children. In A. Luke, C. Luke, & J. Carr (Eds.), *Cultural studies in the classroom: critical practices. The Australian Journal of Language and Literacy, 17*(2), 120–128.

Vásquez, O. A. (1996). Model systems of institutional linkages: Transforming the educational pipeline. In A. Hurtado, R. Figueroa, & E. Garcia (Eds.), *Strategic interventions in education: Expanding the Latina/Latino pipeline* (pp. 137–166). University of Santa Cruz: Santa Cruz, CA.

Vásquez, O. A. (2003). A participatory perspective on parent involvement. In J. Mora & D. Diaz (Eds.), *Research in action: A participatory model for advancing Latino social policy.* Binghamton, NY: Haworth Press.

Vásquez, O. A. (2005). Social action and the politics of collaboration. In P. Pedraza & M. Rivera (Eds.), *Educating Latino youth: An agenda for transcending myths and unveiling possibilities.* Mahwah, NJ: Laurence Erlbaum.

Vásquez, O. A. (October, 2006). Technology and culture: Taming the complexity of diversity. Paper presented at the Russian Regional Meeting of ISCAR, Moscow State University of Psychology and Education, Moscow, Russia.

Vásquez, O. A. (April, 2006a). A pedagogy of the future. Inaugural issue of *Pedagogies: An International Journal.* Nanyang, Singapore, 2006.

Vásquez, O. A. (2006b). Technology and culture: Taming the complexity of diversity. Paper presented at the International Conference, Cultural-Historical Psychology: Current Situation and Perspectives, October 3–4, 2006, Moscow State University of Psychology and Education. Moscow, Russia.

Vygotsky, L. S. (1978). Interaction between learning and development. In M. Cole, V. John-Steiner, S. Scribner, & E. Souberman (Eds.), *Mind in society: The development of higher psychological functions* (pp. 79–91). Cambridge, MA: Harvard University Press.

Vygotsky, L. (1987). *Thought and language.* Cambridge, MA: The MIT Press.

Wells, G. (1999). *Dialogic inquiry: Toward a socialcultural practice and theory of education.* Cambridge, UK: Cambridge University Press.

Wells, G. (2000). Dialogic inquiry in education: Building on the legacy of Vygotsky. In C. Lee, & P. Smagorinsky (Eds.), *Vygotskian perspectives on literacy research: Constructing meaning through collaborative inquiry* (pp. 51–85). Cambridge, MA: Cambridge University Press.

Wertsch, J. V. (1985). *Vygotsky and the social formation of mind.* Cambridge, MA: Harvard University Press.

Wertsch, J. V., Del Rio, P., & Alvarez, A. (1995). Sociocultural studies of mind: history, action, and mediation. In J. V. Wertsch, P. Del Rio, & A. Alvarez (Eds.), *Sociocultural studies of mind* (pp. 1–34). Cambridge, MA: Cambridge University Press.

White, S. H., & Siegel, A. W. (1984). Cognitive development in time and space. In B. Rogoff & J. Lave (Eds.), *Everyday cognition: Its development in social context* (pp. 238–279). Cambridge, MA: Harvard University Press.

Chapter 3

Learning in Inclusive Education Research: Re-mediating Theory and Methods With a Transformative Agenda

ALFREDO J. ARTILES AND ELIZABETH B. KOZLESKI
Arizona State University
SHERMAN DORN
University of South Florida
CAROL CHRISTENSEN
University of Queensland

Inclusive education is a highly visible yet contentious notion in contemporary education reform because of conceptual, historical, and pragmatic reasons. From a conceptual perspective, the definition of inclusion is still debated, ranging from physical placement in general education classrooms to the transformation of entire educational systems. However, inclusive education is defined in many professional and popular contexts as the mere placement of students with specialized needs in mainstream programs alongside individuals who are not disabled. Yet even when inclusion is defined in such simplistic terms, the evidence suggests *where* a student with disabilities is educated has important correlates. For instance, a study of 11,000 students in the United States shows that students with disabilities who spend more time in general education classrooms are absent less, perform closer to grade level than their peers in pull-out settings, and have higher achievement test scores (Blackorby et al., 2005). On the other hand, in the same study, students with disabilities generally perform more poorly than their same-grade peers without disabilities. In particular, unlike students with learning and sensory disabilities, students with mental retardation and autism cluster around the low end of standardized achievement tests. Although some outcome differences were found between students with various kinds of disabilities, overall the study confirmed that students with disabilities in general education settings academically outperformed their peers in separate settings when standards-based assessments were used.

This finding is corroborated by the second National Longitudinal Transition Study (NLTS-2), which found that secondary students with disabilities who take more general education classes have lower grade point averages than their peers in pull-out academic settings, but they score closer to grade level on standards-based assessments of learning than their peers in math and science, even when disability classification is considered (Wagner, Newman, Cameto, & Levine, 2003).

From a historical perspective, special education was created as a parallel system for serving students with specific identifiable needs and disabilities. This created ongoing dilemmas related to allocation of resources, divisions of professional labor, professional identity issues in personnel preparation, and barriers for the education of disabled populations to access mainstream practices and contexts. The educational project of inclusion aims to change this historical separation. In this historical context, it is not surprising that inclusive education is more visible in the special education literature, even though it purportedly addresses the needs of *all* students.

Moreover, the student populations historically served in special education have been predominately poor ethnic minority students. However, the effects of cultural and economic globalization are changing the characteristics and experiences of the student population and the climate in which educators serve these students. For example, teachers are working in educational systems where accountability and standards are increasingly more stringent with the goal of preparing a workforce that can compete globally. These pressures are creating significant tensions for teachers and administrators as they are also being asked to respond to equity questions related to inclusive education. Meanwhile, U.S. ethnic minority students are increasingly being educated alongside immigrant students whose languages and cultures differ markedly from the nation's mainstream society. A greater proportion of students are crossing cultural and geographic borders. This entails actual transnational, regional, and local mobility of populations; ubiquitous intercultural contact; and expanded exposure to a globalized popular and media culture (see Lam, Sefton-Green, this volume). A major consequence is that student, teacher, school, and community cultures are blending and hybridizing in unprecedented ways precisely at a time when accountability reforms are pushing educational systems to homogenize its "clients."

Pragmatically, these conditions raise many complex questions about how practitioners construct and sustain inclusive practices. For instance, given the trends outlined, what are the governance structures, professional development models, curriculum approaches, and collaborative processes that support positive learning outcomes for all students? Are researchers asking programmatic questions, and do study designs rely on multiple methods? More importantly, how do we know these efforts are having a positive affect on learning? Is learning in this research defined from single or multiple theoretical perspectives? Although we do not expect to obtain simple and straight answers to these multifaceted questions, we must take stock of the findings from the emergent empirical knowledge base on inclusive education.

The purpose of this chapter is to examine and expand the evidence on inclusive education, with particular attention to the views of learning that inform this work. The first challenge was to work with a clear understanding of what counts as a learning theory. We found the work of Lave (1996) and Bransford, Brown, and Cocking (2000) useful to address this question. Lave (1996) explained a theory of learning embodies three types of stipulations: a *telos*—"that is, a direction of movement or change of learning (not the same as goal directed activity)"; a *subject-world relation*—"a general specification of relations between subjects and the social world (not necessarily to be construed as learners and things to-be-learned)"; and *learning mechanisms* ("ways by which learning comes about)" (Lave, 1996, p. 156).

Lave (1996) explained that the focus on telos compels researchers to examine how learners change over time. From a practice-based view of learning, this means to document the trajectories of becoming kinds of persons. Subject-world relation is traditionally addressed by asking where reality lies (in the subject or in the world) and how a person comes to know it (which is contingent on where it lies). She proposed, in contrast, that a practice-based model sees subject-world relations concerned with the following question: "How is the objective world socially constituted, as human beings are socially produced, in practice?" (p. 156). Lave described learning mechanisms in most learning theories as concerned with techniques, strategies, and tools. A practice-based learning model focuses instead on participation—i.e., "ways of becoming a participant, ways of participating, and ways in which participants and practices change" (p. 157). In turn, Bransford et al. (2000) distinguished among learning approaches that are community, assessment, learner, and subject centered.

We use some of these constructs, when relevant, as we review the research on inclusive education and in the final discussion of the chapter. Rather than an exhaustive scrutiny of studies on the topic, we analyze two broad strands of inclusion research grounded in distinct units of analysis, namely whole-school and classroom-based research. We cite studies selectively within each research strand to highlight broad trends and patterns in this body of work. First, however, we define inclusive education and outline various discourse strands in this work. Next, we summarize the historical trajectory of inclusive education and analyze the two inclusion research programs. We conclude with reflections about theory and research methods for future inclusive education work.

INCLUSIVE EDUCATION DEFINED: DISCOURSES, ASSUMPTIONS, AND INTERSECTIONS

Inclusive education is an ambitious and far-reaching notion that is, theoretically, concerned with *all* students. The concept focuses on the transformation of school cultures to (1) increase *access* (or presence) of all students (not only marginalized or vulnerable groups), (2) enhance the school personnel's and students' *acceptance* of all students, (3) maximize student *participation* in various domains of activity, and (4) increase the *achievement* of all students (Booth, Ainscow, Black-Hawkins, Vaughan, & Shaw, 2000; Kalambouka, Farrell, Dyson, & Kaplan, 2005). Yet, inclusive education is rooted in conceptions of inclusion, the movement of students in special education (particularly those with severe disabilities) from separate and isolated facilities and classrooms into neighborhood schools and general education classrooms. Indeed, systematic searches of the literature consistently suggest research on inclusive education focuses on the *inclusion* of certain vulnerable groups, particularly students with special education needs and disabilities.

Links between special and inclusive education are particularly strong in wealthy, industrialized countries that began to create policies and programs in the 1970s to serve the educational needs of students with disabilities. Because the concept of specialized education was instantiated in policy and bureaucratized in practice, evolving concepts of practices were constructed in response to existing programs. The 1994 Salamaca Statement endorsing inclusion as an important value in special education—"those with special educational needs must have access to regular schools which should accommodate them within a child-centered pedagogy capable of meeting these needs" (United Nations Educational, Scientific, and Cultural Organization [UNESCO], 1994, p. viii)—came while many developing countries had (and many continue to have) weak education systems in general, particularly for their students with disabilities. This historic coupling of inclusive and special education, particularly in countries that adopted special education policies and systems before 1980, may produce the types of disconnects between the theory and its practice made visible in current research synthesis, such as that by Dyson, Howes, and Roberts (2002).

Dyson et al. (2002) intended to conduct a comprehensive and systematic review of research on school-level actions for promoting participation by all students. Although they designed the review to examine research in schools that had taken a holistic approach to inclusion (i.e., a focus on *all* students, emphasis on multiple forms of participation), they found that most "studies reported population composition in outline, but presented detailed data only on one or a limited number of distinct student groups and on how schools were responding to these groups . . . the majority of studies included a focus on students with special educational needs and disabilities" (p. 27). Similar trends have been reported elsewhere (Kalambouka et al., 2005).

Dyson (1999) identified multiple professional discourses about inclusive education that are grouped under two broad categories, namely discourses to *justify* the need for inclusive education and discourses on the *implementation* of inclusion. One set of arguments to *justify* inclusion rests on a *rights and ethics* perspective, that is, individuals with disabilities ought to be educated in inclusive programs because it is their inalienable right. In addition, the justification of inclusive education can be based on an *efficacy* critique. Accordingly, inclusive education is needed because segregated/ separate special education programs have not shown a positive effect on students with disabilities. Many of these studies documented informants' (e.g., teachers and students) views on the need, support for, and feasibility of inclusive education programs (Artiles, 2003). Many of these studies relied on survey instruments and rendered mixed results.

In contrast, the *implementation* of inclusive education discourse is supported by arguments that stress *political* struggles. The thesis is that the change from a traditional separate special education system to an inclusive system cannot occur without political labor and disputes. A second implementation discourse addresses *pragmatic* considerations that explore the question: "How does it work?" The pragmatic discourse on inclusive education focuses on the nature and characteristics of programs and schools (Dyson, 1999). This scholarship is perhaps the most voluminous and includes descriptions of the philosophical foundations of these programs, various (governance, curricular, and pedagogical) practices, school climate, and professional learning opportunities. Additional research addresses the perspectives (e.g., beliefs and perceptions) of students, parents, teachers, and administrators about inclusive education programs. Another set of research on inclusive education focuses on its achievement outcomes for students with and without disabilities.

Although the term *inclusive education* might suggest a straightforward definition, in practice the construct has multiple meanings that range from physical integration in general education classrooms (e.g., Magiera & Zigmond, 2005) to the transformation of school buildings (e.g., Bulgren & Schumaker, 2006), and even the reconfiguration of entire educational systems (e.g., Ferguson, Kozleski, & Smith, 2003). Despite these multiple meanings, it is fair to argue that the telos (i.e., "a direction of movement or change of learning" [Lave, 1996, p. 156]) of the inclusive education movement has been to give access to and enhance the participation of individuals with disabilities in normative contexts and practices (i.e., nondisabled cultures) despite efforts to broaden the construct and definition. Therefore, tensions between the theory of inclusive education and its practice remain. Inclusive education is theorized as a broad, boundary-blurring agenda across multiple perspectives that enrich learning, such as culture, language, migration, experience, ability, and religion for *all* students. This perspective is juxtaposed with a pragmatic concern about where and how students with disabilities will be educated. A historical perspective helps to explain how these tensions remain.

A HISTORICAL MAP OF INCLUSIVE EDUCATION

Detailing the history of inclusive education rhetoric, policies, and practices is more difficult than identifying patterns of special education history. Putnam (1979) suggested that the development of special education was largely determined by a country's wealth. An empirically tested, international, historical map of inclusion does not exist. However, for heuristic purposes, one can divide countries' special education services by two questions: Had their systems developed into mature infrastructures by the early 1980s, and by then, had political, legal, or administrative pressures challenged school systems to move toward more inclusion?

In the 1960s and 1970s, pressures for inclusion affected school systems in several industrialized countries (e.g., France, the United States, and the United Kingdom) that had long-established special education systems (much of it separate from general education) (Braswell, 1999; Woll, 1999). For some countries, such as Italy, there is some disagreement about the extent of policy support for inclusion since the 1970s (e.g., Cocchi, Larocca, & Crivelli, 1999). For other countries with mature systems, the earlier wave of inclusion left them unaffected: The Netherlands, Hungary, the former Soviet Union, Brazil, Hong Kong, Taiwan, and Japan are notable in this group (Abe, 1998; Csányi, 2001; Eglér Mantoan & Valente, 1998; Shipitsina & Wallenberg, 1999). Among some countries, totalitarian or otherwise politically restricted regimes either interfered with the development of special education or encouraged the development of largely separate systems in China, Mexico, Spain, South Africa, and the Palestinian territories (Arrendondo & Ryan-Arrendondo, 1999; Deng, Poon-McBrayer, &

Farnsworth, 2001). Certainly, one could also place Brazil and the Soviet Union in this category as well, historically. Yet even apart from the effects of dictatorship, poverty remained a significant barrier to the development of systems in these countries, as well as in others, such as India and Pakistan (Khan, 1998; Misra, 1999).

A second wave of inclusion instituted by some countries, followed by the signing of the Salamanca Statement by 92 nations, should be understood as evidence of the multiple pressures producing inclusive education responses. For instance, some countries that signed the Salamanca Statement are engaging in debates over inclusion similar to the one contested in the United States. One example is South Africa, whose new constitution and a new education law in 1996 enshrined broad rights, but where the result was a debate over the continuum of services (Gwalla-Ogisi, Nkabinde, & Rodriguez, 1998). Second, in undeveloped systems, students with disabilities may be in general education classrooms but without the types of services and supports needed to access the curricula and hence, learning. To characterize this as inclusion may be a misnomer. Third, in many of the second-wave inclusion countries, the society or educators have resisted inclusion efforts to some degree. In particular, Nutbrough and Clough's (2004) identification of a "yes-but" response—yes in principle, but not always in individual cases—is similar to reactions identified in the Western-focused literature review of Scruggs and Mastropieri (1996).

Of Boundaries and Margins

There are many reasons why those outside special education should pay attention to special education's practices and history. All teachers are responsible at some point for the education of students with disabilities. In addition, in many countries, students with disabilities have specific rights. Third, school system behavior is tied to what happens at the margins of the system. Not only is the education of students with disabilities more expensive on average than that of other students, but also the debate over inclusion has set the boundaries of who *belongs* in school communities (Cobb-Roberts, Dorn, & Shircliffe, 2005). The structure of U.S. special education law is an established fact of educational politics with robust constituencies. The tacit agreement is as important because the continuing conflict for delineating who belongs to schools for most Americans and who is still excluded from that understanding of a school community.

The result of the U.S. legislative and legal battles in the 1970s was a political and legal compromise. The general rights of children with disabilities were established legally. However, the 1982 U.S. Supreme Court decision limited the substantive educational obligations of school districts to providing programs that were likely to provide some benefits to children (*Board of Education v. Rowley*, 1982; Weatherley & Lipsky, 1977), and educators discovered that the majority of students with disabilities had tolerable cognitive and behavioral problems at worst (e.g., Scruggs & Mastropieri, 1996). Yet some children, especially those with severe intellectual disabilities and behavioral problems, have remained the focus of battles over inclusion, *not* commonly recognized as valuable (or even legitimate) members of schools. After the

Supreme Court limited suspensions for students with disabilities—defining suspension of more than 10 days as a change in placement that triggered due-process protections and thus setting a practical limit to suspensions without parent approval—educators both resisted and then openly fought those rules.

In the 1990s, school officials convinced U.S. Congress to modify the limits on disciplining students with disabilities. One myth that spread in the late 1980s and early 1990s was that schools *could not* legally discipline students with disabilities, because of both the Supreme Court's interpretation of federal law and the threats that parents would sue the local schools. This myth was incorrect—federal law left schools with several options apart from suspension, and schools had several ways to separate students with disabilities from school—but it provided fodder for educators, parents, and eventually lawmakers who believed that federal special education law established double standards for behavior (e.g., Alpert, 1996). In the early 1990s, the U.S. Congress explicitly included students with disabilities when it gave local schools the authority (and mandate) to suspend and move children who brought guns and other weapons to school. In 1997, the reauthorization of federal special education law created a new compromise. One part of the compromise was authority given to school officials to provide an alternative 45-day placement for children whose behavior was dangerous to other students, teachers, or staff. The other part of the *de facto* compromise was the requirement that students' annual programs have support for positive behavior where appropriate. Even with a compromise, the battle over discipline in the 1990s clearly marked the boundaries of "easily-accommodated" students—those who had behavior problems were not necessarily welcome in the general classrooms of local public schools. Although U.S. educators and communities now acknowledge that the "borders" of the school community include the majority of children with disabilities, they still patrol the borders for students who transgress the rules (Yell, Rozalski, & Drasgow, 2001).

Institutions and Normative Expectations

The institutional focus on the margins—students with behavior problems and debates over full inclusion—have come with both practical and symbolic arguments. Debates over behavior and placement revolve around pragmatic questions. The simultaneous existence of practical and values questions illustrate the link between institutional settings and normative expectations. The practices of institutions can both establish and violate norms, and well-established practices frame future debate, creating a legacy for how one discusses the issue. Inclusion in particular split the special education community. When signed in 1975, Public Law 94-142 provided an ambiguous mandate: Students must be in the "least restrictive environment," with as much contact with nondisabled peers as was consistent with an appropriate education. There has been some controversy about the appropriate extent of *mainstreaming* students (the term used before the advent of inclusive education) but little among advocates for special education rights. In the early 1970s, the primary concerns were basic: access to school for those who had been excluded before, fair assessment, the inclusion of parents in individualized educational planning, and due-process protections. This focus on access has occurred in dozens of other countries as well. Although the statistics from the 1960s and early 1970s are sketchy, parents and advocates observed that several hundred thousand of students with sensory impairments and mild cognitive disabilities were unnecessarily separated from nondisabled peers in self-contained classes and that tens of thousands of students with more involved cognitive disabilities were in separate schools with no possibility of contact with nondisabled peers. Although there was resistance from some educators, most advocates were firmly convinced that the majority of students with disabilities needed and had a right to more contact with nondisabled peers (20 U.S. Code §1412(5)(B)) (Sarason & Doris, 1979; Sigmon, 1983).

By the early 1990s, in contrast, the majority of students receiving special education services *did* have meaningful, frequent contact with nondisabled peers in school (U.S. Office of Special Education and Rehabilitative Services [OSERS], 2002). Public Law 94-142 had significantly changed *where* students spent their time in school, in part through its continuum of placement options, from full-time placement in a general-education classroom without any help to residential institutionalization, and within 15 years the majority of students were concentrated much closer to the nonrestrictive end of the continuum than in 1975. By the 1990s, students with disabilities were far more likely to spend the school day in ordinary school buildings than in separate settings; for all students aged 6–17 receiving special education services in 1990–1991, 69% spent at least 40% of their time in the general education setting, with nondisabled peers (U.S. OSERS, 2002). That did not mean that most students with disabilities spent all of their time with nondisabled peers or that they were succeeding academically in a general classroom setting. A plurality received services in resource rooms and other part-time settings where special education teachers have juggled responsibilities for groups of students who shuttle in and out for pull-out academic instruction during the day. Other students had limited social contact with nondisabled peers, outside academic instruction—a more common routine for interaction between nondisabled peers and students with more severe intellectual disabilities. Among all 6- to 21-year-olds labeled mentally retarded in 1990–1991, 58% spent 60% or more of their time in a separate classroom and another 12% were outside regular schools entirely. Yet other students with disabilities spent academic instructional time in general education classrooms with little support (U.S. OSERS, 2002).

This dramatic change in the placement patterns of special education helped ignite additional debate about moving students more systematically into general education settings—what educators and parents began to call inclusion in the 1980s. Having some success in changing where schools placed students, some advocates pushed for more inclusion (Osgood, 2005). Beginning in the late 1980s, some parents, researchers, students, educators, and advocates for children with the most severe intellectual disabilities argued that *any* separation from a general education classroom was inappropriate, and they began to argue for the full inclusion of all students with disabilities in classrooms with nondisabled peers (e.g., Lipsky & Gartner, 1996; Stainback & Stainback, 1996).

Quickly, other parents, researchers, students, educators, and advocates *within special education* argued against full inclusion and against some other inclusion proposals. Some called themselves preservationists (seeking to maintain the continuum of placement options). Much of the split came between different areas of special education. The most visible advocates of full inclusion were tied to the education of individuals with severe intellectual disabilities, an area that was still on the margins of many schools more than a decade after Public Law 94-142. Curriculum for students with severe intellectual disabilities stressed learning the social and survival skills necessary for adulthood. On the other hand, many of the most visible opponents of full inclusion were tied to the education of individuals with relatively mild cognitive disabilities, whose most urgent concerns were effective academic instruction, not social contact with nondisabled peers. Parents, students, researchers, educators, and advocates closely tied to other areas of special education had their own particular concerns that they used to judge inclusion proposals. Some concerns focused on whether most general classroom teachers had skills or time to reward good behavior. Other concerns focused on how full inclusion (or something close to it) might endanger the ties between students with hearing impairments and the deaf community that many adults with hearing impairments identified with (e.g., Fuchs & Fuchs, 1994; Gallagher, 2001; MacMillan, Gresham, & Forness, 1996; Zigmond, Jenkins, Fuchs, Deno, & Fuchs, 1995).

Legally and politically in the 1990s, full inclusion advocates faced an uphill struggle. Legally, the ambiguous wording of the least restrictive environment mandate did not clearly require full inclusion. Despite claims to the contrary, full-inclusion advocates were unable to convince judges that the law required full inclusion. Where a school system followed due process guidelines and provided documentation of decision making, courts have generally accepted the professional judgment of educators about various discretionary matters in special education, including the appropriate placement for students with disabilities. Politically, full-inclusion advocates have faced the opposition of many educators and some parents of students with disabilities. Part of the administrators' opposition has been concern with the practical problems of full inclusion, especially the potential for students whose proper curriculum was not academic in focus to distract from the academic education of other students.

However, the vigorous nature of the debates over full inclusion in the 1980s and 1990s—for example, AFT President AL Shanker's (1994–1995) vociferous argument against full inclusion—is not well explained by the practical discourse. It is better explained in some ways by several issues that are tied to symbolism and values. Part of the sometimes-bitter nature of the debate may well be related to a residual exclusion of students with severe intellectual disabilities from educators' notion of a school community. Part may be tied to the evolution of special education as a community with common interests, and, since 1975, somewhat diverging sets of interests.

Part may be related to cooling support for integration as a value of public schooling. In all of these ways, the organization of schools became a lens through which advocates with different perspectives viewed appropriate norms.

The Pull and Limits of Standardization

The existence of institutionalized norms has a complex relationship with efforts to individualize or standardize educational programs and practices. On the one hand, efforts to individualize education have run into bureaucratic practices. Several countries have experimented with individualization as both a best-practice standard for special education and an affirmation of values or rights for students with disabilities. In the United States, the legal right to individualization is instituted as the individualized education plan. In many countries, the values are expressed in language norms, such as the effort to push for *person-first* language (e.g., students with disabilities instead of disabled students). Yet in each case, there are limits to the efforts to individualize education either programmatically or in language. As Smith (1991) pointed out, drafting individualized plans in the United States all too often became a routine, bureaucratic process that endorsed existing practices. Tomlinson (1982) illustrated how British schools adopted Warnock's "special needs" phrase but without the "*student with* special needs" emphasis on the student rather than a deficit. The limits to individualization in the past few decades may be a function of school bureaucracies of a long history of routines that are budged, modified, and appended but rarely torn apart (e.g., Tyack & Cuban, 1995). While coeducation developed informally and without significant debate in the loose, unsystematic set of early 19th century North American primary schools (Tyack & Hansot, 1990), the expansion of schooling for students with disabilities in the past half century occurred in a bureaucratic environment. Special education itself could be considered a dramatic success of a system that accepts additions but not revolutions (Cuban, 1996).

Yet that historical development of standardization is incomplete. Schools are highly standardized in formal rules, textbook purchases, and some matters of record keeping, but they are highly nonstandardized in everything humans have day-to-day authority over—instructional methods, classroom management, and handling human crises that inevitably occur in a building with several hundred or thousand students. Organizational theorists call this a *loosely coupled system* (Weick, 1976) or *street-level bureaucracy* (Weatherley & Lipsky, 1977), but it is the inevitable result of attempting to systematize an activity that is personal in nature and where the majority of costs are in personnel. Thus, the great problem of innovative techniques is "scaling up" (Healey & De Stefano, 1997), school systems drop easy-to-use programs with demonstrated success, and Florida primary teachers under a mandate to take data for formative assessment frequently misunderstand its purpose and use (K. Powell, personal communication).

An alternative interpretation of these limits to individualization focuses on the neo-liberal push for efficiency. Individualized education was a key element of initial legislative reforms through the Individualized Education Programming mandate and fit well both with egalitarian and social-mobility goals for education. In other words, advocates for greater access and inclusion argued that to benefit from education and to have equality of opportunity, students with disabilities needed to have their specific needs addressed. However, individual provision undermines some aspect of neo-liberal agendas that threaten to dominate a globalized economy, an efficiency view increasingly used to justify education reforms as rationalization. Individualization is more expensive, and it is unstandardized by definition. However, such tensions have been largely submerged in the existing literature on inclusion. A focus on implementation and techniques, or the practical discourse, can appeal, and in the past has appealed to those interested in both egalitarianism and social mobility and efficiency.

The Globalization Context

Although this is not the first era in history with a global interchange of ideas, goods and services, people, and even diseases, the most recent wave of globalization has pushed economic, political, and social relations in a new direction. We use the term globalization to refer to the transformations in social, economic, political, and governance structures that have occurred throughout the world in the last two decades. These changes have had a dramatic and pervasive effect on the societies in which they have occurred.

Rizvi, Engel, Nandyala, Ruthowski, and Sparks (2005) argue that globalized societies are characterized by mobility of capital, information, and communication technologies, as well as mobility of people, culture, and management systems. This rapid movement throughout nations and societies is underpinned by belief in free and open markets and competition policies. Thus, there has been an 'inexorable integration of markets, nation-states, and technologies to a degree never witnessed before in a way that is enabling individuals, corporations, and nation-states to reach around the world faster, deeper, and cheaper than ever before' (Friedman, 2000, p. 7). In brief, neo-liberalism promotes (1) minimal regulation and withdrawal of state from intervention in the economy; (2) withdrawal of the state from social intervention and the privatization of social support to citizens; (3) deregulation of labor markets and rejection of labor policies, such as minimum wage and collective bargaining; (4) emphasis on economic efficiency, productivity, and profitability; (5) emphasis on public accountability; (6) openness of competition; and (7) free flow of global capital, labor, and resources among many other features (Castells, 1996; Rizvi et al., 2005; Strange, 1996).

These two concepts, globalization and neo-liberalism, have immediate relevancy for constructing and sustaining inclusive education agendas within nations. First, globalized populations mean that schools must prepare for new students who may detach their identities from particular times, places, and traditions. Many transnational students today are staying in ever closer contact with their home nations, thus preserving cultural practices, creating hybrid national identities, and cultivating a steady flow of economic and cultural exchanges among nations (Garcia Canclini, 1995).

Accessible mass communication means that events at home countries and in the host society continuously affect the daily routines of students and the communities in which they participate (Artiles & Dyson, 2005; Suárez-Orozco, 2001).

Second, neo-liberalism means that governments have new interests in schooling both in how investments are made in schooling infrastructures and the results that are achieved. Although Labaree (1997) argued that social mobility (and consumerism) once dominated much of the U.S. education system, the ideology of neo-liberalism emphasizes social efficiency. The social efficiency view suggests that education plays a fundamental role in the production of capable workers to contribute to the economic health of the nation and the corporations that employ them. The social efficiency view also requires that educational systems work efficiently. They must produce workers who have the knowledge and skills to contribute to the knowledge economy. Additionally, they must have efficient organizational structures, so that there is an economic return on society's investment. The social efficiency view sees education as a both public good and private benefit because it enhances the individual's ability to compete effectively within the labor market. In both cases, education is linked to organizational efficiency and economic productivity (Rizvi et al., 2005). Thus, globalized economies have pursued an agenda that redefines the purposes of education to focus on developing the capacity of productive workers who have a strong grounding in basic literacy and numeric skills and who are flexible and creative, multiskilled, and competent in information and communication technologies.

In globalized societies, social efficiency has been endorsed by intergovernmental organizations, large corporations, and individual citizens, as well as increasing numbers of national governments. The emerging market-driven educational paradigm has important implications for students who are considered outliers in a homogenizing system, such as students with disabilities. Unfortunately, this emerging educational paradigm does not consider the historically rooted systems of disadvantage that structure access and opportunity for various groups in globalized societies. In the United States, for example, the rapid racial (re)segregation of schools and the concomitant unequal distribution of resources between minority and nonminority schools (Orfield & Eaton, 1996) shape access to curricula and technologies that apprentice learners into the literacy and numeric skills required for successful participation in the emerging globalized societies.

To conclude, the processes of globalization in conjunction with neo-liberal economic theory have changed the landscape of educational thought so that social efficiency has become an overriding goal of education policy makers in many countries at a time when student populations are becoming increasingly culturally and linguistically diverse. These policy directions, with an emphasis on production of knowledge-rich citizens who can become flexible, efficient workers in a competitive global environment, have profound implications for students with disabilities and inclusive education. There is emerging evidence, for instance, that English-language learners (ELLs) (immigrant and nonimmigrant) are disproportionately placed in special education in some regions of the United States (Artiles, Rueda, Salazar, & Higareda,

2005). This state of affairs raises still another set of questions that focuses on inclusive programs on a broader level: How are inclusive education programs serving students who inhabit transnational contexts? How are inclusive programs considering the lives of students who navigate multiple cultural worlds? Do we have evidence about the effect of globalization and neo-liberal policies on the consolidation of inclusive education?

LEARNING IN INCLUSIVE EDUCATION RESEARCH

Inclusive education research has a broad focus and addresses many interrelated questions. The bulk of this literature addresses the *implementation* of programs, and thus we summarize and analyze such research. We should note that most of the research on inclusive education has been conducted in the United States and United Kingdom. The research can be grouped in two categories, namely research on inclusive education from a whole-school perspective and research on aspects or components of inclusive education, which is generally classroom based.

Whole-School Models of Inclusive Education

We have two goals in this section. First, we outline the main findings from major reviews of the literature to set the context for our second goal, namely to present a more detailed analysis of a research program on whole-school models of inclusive education implemented in the United Kingdom. The literature reviews were concerned with school efforts to enhance the participation of all students (Dyson, Howes, et al., 2002) and the effect of inclusion on students without disabilities (Kalambouka et al., 2005). Although other reviews have been reported in the literature (Harrower, 1999; Manset & Semmel, 1997; Salend & Duhaney, 1999), the two selected syntheses are among the most comprehensive and systematic efforts to date. Some of the main findings from the Dyson, Howes, et al. (2002) review include:

1. Studies included in the review (*n* = 27) were based on case study designs about the structures and processes of inclusion models.
2. Most of this research was cross-sectional and conducted in primary schools that were self-identified as inclusive or selected by researchers or other informants as pursuing an inclusive agenda.
3. Many studies had considerable methodological weaknesses and offered poor reports.
4. The evidence was based mostly on interviews and unstructured observations.
5. Interviews were often conducted with teachers and other stakeholders (e.g., administrators, parents, and students) and generally focused on participants' descriptions of school inclusive cultures (e.g., features of such cultures and factors that supported an inclusive school culture). Teacher perspectives dominated research reports. Hence, the evidence on school cultures is mostly grounded in teachers' beliefs and views about their schools.

6. The studies did not coalesce around a set of overarching questions, frameworks, or settings. Thus, the reviewers did not find evidence of a programmatic agenda in inclusive education research.

7. Most studies "simply reported on some aspect of diversity, action, or participation while a smaller number presented what we judged to be *detailed* data" (p. 3, emphasis in original).

8. Inclusive school cultures embraced the value of respect for differences and a commitment to support the presence and participation of all students. Strong leadership committed to inclusive cultures had a visible presence in these schools. Despite the presence of tensions and disruptions in inclusive schools, participatory approaches that included all stakeholders (e.g., pull-in instructional models and constructivist pedagogies), collaborative practice, and collective problem solving were distinctive features of these school cultures.

9. Most of these studies privileged schools' cultural cohesion, that is, researchers assumed the schools they studied had cogent and seamless cultures that supported inclusion. Contradictions and anomalies within school cultures were neither documented nor examined.

10. Systematic analysis of the links among participants' beliefs and values, school structures and practices, and student outcomes were not examined. In most cases, such links were merely stated or self-reported. According to Dyson et al. (2002), "the assumption seems to be that the strong assertion of inclusive values by teachers leads inevitably and unproblematically to greater inclusion for students" (p. 50).

11. Student outcome data were not always reported, and it was not uncommon to find outcome data reported by school personnel or "inferred from an account of teacher practices. . . . Direct reports of outcome data are rare" (Dyson et al., 2002, p. 50).

The literature review reported by Kalambouka et al. (2005) offers the following conclusions:

1. The analysis of 26 studies on the effect of inclusion on nondisabled students suggests that many studies included pupils with intellectual and learning difficulties. Unfortunately, research reports were not always clear on the types of special needs represented in the study samples; thus, "it is difficult to provide direct conclusions regarding the impact of including pupils with a specific type of [special needs] on the academic and/or social or other outcomes of all school pupils" (p. 4).

2. More than 50% of the selected studies were published in the 1990s ($n = 15/26$), and the majority were conducted in the United States ($n = 22/26$).

3. Studies documented academic outcomes (e.g., standardized tests, class tests, and teacher ratings) and social outcomes; almost half of these studies (12) documented only academic outcomes.

4. The nature of inclusion in this research was defined as either the proportion of students with special educational needs in a general education classroom or the num-

ber of hours spent in a general education classroom every day (or week). However, the authors expressed a serious concern about the slightly loose or uncertain way in which the term "inclusion" was defined. . . . It was not always clear whether the inclusion arrangements involved fulltime placement in mainstream class, whether and to what extent such placements were supported, and whether pupils were withdrawn to other special classes for certain lessons and for how long. All this means that it is not possible to judge from the review whether certain types of inclusion arrangements were associated with particular academic or social outcomes (p. 64).

5. Previous literature reviews offered mixed results on the effect of inclusion on nondisabled students. In contrast, these reviewers concluded the inclusion of students with special needs and disabilities in regular schools does not have a negative effect on the academic and social performance of students without special needs and disabilities, particularly if a support system was an intricate component of the inclusion model—there was a slightly greater positive effect for academic outcomes. The only exception was (compared to the other groups of special needs/disabilities) when students with emotional/behavioral disorders were included, there were more negative outcomes. It should be noted that the data on the effect of inclusion was not examined across various curriculum subjects.

6. Successful inclusive education programs are the result of intensive, coordinated, and systematic work that is grounded in a strong and explicit commitment to an inclusive vision of education on the part of parents, students, and professionals. Moreover, "programmes of work have to be carefully planned and reviewed regularly; and support staff need to work flexibly as a team and receive appropriate support and training" (p. 5).

In summary, although there are promising findings in the reviews of the empirical knowledge base on inclusion (e.g., features of inclusive school cultures), significant gaps and limitations were identified in the conceptual and methodological bases of this research. The reviewed work purportedly has the characteristics of an *emergent* knowledge base in which an emphasis on descriptive accounts pervade, conceptual refinement and strengthening of methodological rigor are needed, and a lack of understanding about the complexities of the phenomenon are apparent (e.g., causal links between practices and outcomes, interactions between types of interventions, subpopulations, and setting types).

Because the focus of our analysis is views of learning in inclusive education research, we were surprised to find a lack of attention to this construct. When research was framed from a community-centered perspective of learning (Bransford et al., 2000) (i.e., inclusive school cultures), measures of outcomes were indirect (e.g., teacher reports). It was equally unexpected to find an explicit attention to learning outcomes *with a particular emphasis on students without disabilities* (as opposed to *all* students). Although a focus on academic outcomes has been stressed, we asked whether a closer look at a research program would help us understand better the views of learning used in inclusion research.

A Closer Look at Learning in Whole-School Inclusive Education Research

To address this question, we concentrated on a research program conducted in recent years in the United Kingdom by Ainscow, Booth, and Dyson (2006) because it represents a sustained effort to document the processes that unfold in schools to develop inclusive education models. These researchers use the whole school as the unit of analysis, and their work is based on a broad definition of inclusive education, that is, "reduce barriers to learning and participation that might impact on a wide range of students" (Ainscow, Booth, & Dyson, 2004a, p. 2). Note the view of inclusion is framed with an explicit equity focus (i.e., reduce barriers) and is aligned with the definition outlined in a preceding section that encompasses presence, participation, acceptance, and achievement. Consistent with the inclusion literature discussed thus far, although the target population in this program of research is identified in rather ample terms (e.g., all students and a wide range of students), the main group of interest is students with special needs and disabilities—at least as reflected in most examples provided in the work published by this team of investigators.

One aspect of interest for this team is how schools address the tension found in the current education reform climate in the United Kingdom between the social justice agenda of the inclusive education movement and the neo-liberal economic competitiveness rhetoric that permeates the standards reforms. Ainscow and his colleagues identify two stances toward this situation that they label pessimistic and optimistic views. The former argues that the standards movement grounded in market driven policies hinder the creation of school cultures supportive of inclusive education. In contrast, the optimistic view contends inclusive practices are "likely to emerge under appropriate organizational conditions" (Ainscow et al., 2004a, p. 15). From this perspective, it is argued that schools can engineer processes and structures that buffer the anti-inclusion pressure of the standards reforms.

Project Focus and Design. The project was framed as a school-change effort, and the guiding premise of the work was that "outsiders" (university researchers) can work collaboratively with "insiders" (teachers, parents, and students) to gain a better understanding of and develop ways to address barriers to participation and learning (Ainscow, Booth, & Dyson, 2004b). The team created a network based on an action research approach to work in 25 schools throughout three local education agencies (LEAs) in a 4-year period (1999–2004). The questions addressed in this work include (Ainscow et al., 2004b) (1) an exploration of students' barriers to participation and learning, (2) identification of the practices to address those barriers, (3) how identified practices contribute to improved learning outcomes, and (4) ways to sustain and encourage successful practices. Participants included three university teams (Manchester, Canterbury, and Newcastle) and approximately 100 teachers and school personnel. Teams of school personnel and university researchers collaborated in the analysis, design, and implementation of inclusive practices. The project allowed participants to be responsive to local needs and priorities. Although there was variability throughout sites, schools generally relied on a common model: a small leadership team was appointed, which typically included the principal, among others, that led efforts to identify a work agenda. The process included an analysis of current practices and the creation of a plan and its implementation to transform the school into an inclusive organization. Support from the university and LEA teams was available through regular meetings in which evidence collected by each party was shared and examined critically. Meetings with other schools within and throughout LEAs, and national conferences were used as means of support. The academic teams created a support system within the network that included regular meetings, communications, and sharing of analytic papers and memorandums about developing themes and patterns. The evidence included parent, professional, and student interviews; observation data (field notes and videos); notes from meetings; school evaluation data; materials produced by university and school participants; and conference products. An online database was created with private and public levels of access to support the work of the teams (Ainscow et al., 2004b).

In contrast to prior inclusive education work, the research team opted to recruit so-called "typical schools" that were grappling with the changing demands of an increasingly diverse student population in a standards-based policy environment. LEAs initially invited schools to join the university teams in the examination of "participation in teaching and learning, and taking action to improve it" (Ainscow, Howes, Farrell, & Frankham, 2003, p. 229). Most of the schools that joined the Manchester research team had recently appointed principals, and half of the schools had been classified as "being in serious difficulties" (p. 229).

Ainscow and his colleagues (2004a) characterized their project as "critical collaborative action research" in which inclusive education tenets were used inductively to examine local practices and develop action plans to become more inclusive. The work of school-university teams was also concerned with a critical analysis of the standards movement and how it might affect their inclusion-oriented work. More importantly, the analytic and planning labor was deliberately concerned with using school personnel's agency in the creation of opportunities to navigate the anti-inclusion pressure of the standards movement while they worked to build inclusive programs.

Learning in Whole-School Models: Overview and Issues With Core Constructs. Ainscow and his colleagues (2004a) explain that their work is concerned with the creation of collaborative school cultures that "support particular kinds of professional and organizational learning, which in turn promote the development of inclusive practices" (p. 6, emphasis added). This is an ambitious vision, indeed. A community-centered perspective (Bransford et al., 2000) is emphasized in this research program as reflected in its concern for engineering school cultures that are grounded in inclusive practices. In fact, Ainscow and his colleagues acknowledge the influence of sociocultural theories, particularly Wenger's (1998) work on communities of practice. From this perspective, the consolidation of inclusive practice communities is the goal of their efforts in which learning is regarded as "a characteristic of practice" (Ainscow et al., 2004a, p. 7). It is explained that, "practices are . . . ways of negotiating meaning through social action" (Ainscow et al., 2004a, p. 7). Aligned with Wenger's work, meaning is created through participation and reification. As members of school communities participate in daily routines and build collective histories, they construct shared meanings of notions, such as "inclusion," "competence," or "unacceptable behavior." At the same time, school communities create reifications of their practice— i.e., tangible means and strategies to represent what they do (e.g., planning artifacts, behavioral rules, and flow charts to outline prereferral interventions). Ainscow et al. (2003) cite Wenger to explain that the interconnections between reification and participation constitute learning in communities of practice.

A closer look at this work raises questions about the nature and boundaries of "practice" (Little, 2002). More specifically, teams of researchers and practitioners gather outside of classrooms and other settings in which their routine professional work occurs to analyze such work. The practice of analysis in these distal settings is expected to change the routine professional practices enacted in classrooms, assessment rooms, etc. What constitutes the core practices of these communities? Is the central practice what teachers do in classrooms or what they do in the meetings where evidence is analyzed? If it is both, what are the intertextual processes that mediate professional learning (Floriani, 1993)? Do these communities prescribe rules or criteria for acceptable forms and means of representation of practitioners' practices? What is, to borrow from Little (2002), the "situational relevance," of the evidence that teachers bring to these analytic sessions (e.g., anecdotes, stories, work samples, questions)? Is learning expected to unfold in both settings? How is learning accounted for in each setting? Unfortunately, these issues about the idea of practice are not clearly addressed in this work.

The focus on interpretive processes that mediate how communities of practice make meaning is an important assumption of this team's work because it foregrounds the agency of communities and the dialectics of microprocesses and macroprocesses. More specifically, these authors argue that, "external agendas cannot simply be imposed on communities of practice . . . external policy agendas, however powerfully enforced, have to be endowed with meaning within a local context before they can inform practice" (Ainscow et al., 2004a, p. 9). This assumption helps us understand why there is considerable variation in schools' responses to national reform agendas, such as standards. An apparent gap in this work, however, is the lack of documentation and analysis of specific local episodes that would enable researchers to link people's agency and labor with larger historical and institutional processes and forces (Engestrom, Miettinen, & Punamaki, 1999).

The authors stress a normative dimension of communities of practice in which schools achieve cohesion as a way of building inclusive practices. They favor a situated perspective in which local understandings of ideas (e.g., inclusion) are emphasized and the shared histories of participants contribute to crafting distinctive communities of practice in particular schools. Although we find in this work an acknowledgment of the tensions and issues that arise in the process of building inclusive school cultures, the end point of such labor is embodied in a monolithic view of inclusive school culture. We see, therefore, that the notion of tensions or contradictions can be examined in at least two different ways. First, contradictions, disagreements, and tensions can arise among participants as a result of the work that is done in schools to investigate local practices. Ainscow and his colleagues report such disturbances as school personnel struggle to become more inclusive. However, a point that is not recognized in this work is that such contradictions could contribute to the formation of various groups or coalitions that form their own communities as school strive to become inclusive. This means that the development of inclusive schools might encompass the configuration and reconfiguration of a multiplicity of practice communities that result from the negotiations and deliberations of the school personnel. From this perspective, inclusive schools do not have monolithic cultures; unfortunately, a sizable proportion of the inclusive education literature endorses the assumption of thoroughly cohesive school cultures.

A second way in which contradictions can be examined is as the impetus for change. Reminiscent of cultural historical activity theory (Engestrom et al., 1999), Ainscow and his colleagues (2003) explain that anomalies or contradictions in school local practices can be the engines of change, though not all instances of emerging contradictions resulted in transformed school practices. School traits help explain the differences in responses to these anomalies (e.g., principal's leadership style, engagement with evidence, and the cohesion of a community of practice). They describe disruptions as *external* (e.g., planned interventions from university staff and observations of other schools) and *internal* (e.g., school teams' identification of disturbances in data analysis sessions of their own practice) (Ainscow et al., 2004a). These activities or incidents compel school personnel to question what is taken for granted (e.g., beliefs, premises, and assumptions), and sometimes such interpretive processes result in the reformulation of standard or routine practices. It should be noted, however, that school change was not smooth. Indeed, resistance and multiple contradictions often coexisted in the participating schools.

Gallannaugh and Dyson (2003), for instance, documented how school personnel initially interpreted low student attainment and the school's failure to achieve the prescribed standards as the result of students' social class disadvantages. Through the collaborative analysis of evidence, however, school personnel gained increasingly sophisticated understandings of their labor, and the deficit views they first espoused about their students were gradually transformed as they witnessed what students were able to do. Examples of tools or contexts used to mediate professionals' action research efforts included advisory teachers that led teacher study groups, visits to other schools, and examination of evidence, such as student and parent interviews, case studies, teacher interviews, observations of other teachers' classroom practices, video recordings of teaching episodes, test results, attendance registers, exclusion records, and observations in other schools in the LEA. The critical point about these exercises is that the analyses or discussions of evidence create conditions to question assumptions taken for granted and making the familiar unfamiliar to explore alternatives for the renewal of practice (Ainscow et al., 2003). Thus, this work stresses the role of mediation in learning that is distinctive of a social constructivist metaphor. Unfortunately, although research techniques have been developed to document school change processes (Ainscow, Hargreaves, & Hopkins, 1995), we could not find thick descriptions of change processes. Aside from researcher statements or participants' self-reports about these mediating experiences (e.g., "Some school staff reported learning a lot from an environment where sharing difficulties was encouraged, rather than presenting accomplishments.") (Ainscow et al., 2004b, p. 132), a detailed documentation of how mediating processes were constructed in interpersonal contexts is needed. This lack of analytic attention to actual interpersonal processes is consistent with research on practice communities with teachers for the purpose of professional development (Little, 2002; Wilson & Berne, 1999). It seems *learning* (changing participation) in this research includes both, *changes in practice* and in *organizations' problem solving approaches.* Similar to the research on teacher change (Richardson & Placier, 2001), this work is grounded in the assumption that changes in practice index improvement. However, it is not clear whether the available research evidence supports this assumption.

An important theoretical extension of the community of practice idea is that learning is constituted in identity projects because people are always becoming someone else in the process of participation (Lave, 1996). The whole-school model of inclusion research has not used this core notion thus far.[1] Attention to the idea of identity projects as part of the notion of changing participation has the potential to enrich this program of research. For instance, we raise questions above about the implicit assumption of monolithic inclusive school cultures and about the lack of attention to the formation of subcommunities as inclusive school cultures are forged. It is feasible, for example, that people resist or engage in "nonparticipation" in these whole school projects. Hodges (1998) explains that individuals in practice communities might not identify with the identities that signal membership in a practice community, yet they accommodate through some way of participating in the community's normative practice. As she describes it, nonparticipation defines a clash between participation and identification; "It is a split between a person's activities and their relations with participation, a rupture between what a person is actually doing, and how a person finds [herself] located in the 'community.' Nonparticipation describes how a person might be participating in the contexts of grappling with possible, albeit mutable, identities" (pp. 272–273).

A documentation of identity projects as a form of changing participation in inclusive schools will help understand the micropolitics of school change and how members of communities might (mis)align with visions of inclusive education. Ainscow et al. (2004b) alluded to schools in which the notion of inclusive education is defined in alternative ways that were not always consistent with the researchers' vision. They found, for instance, that "many schools are interpreting 'inclusion' to mean enabling low-attaining students to meet national targets in key areas. In this sense, the target setting agenda has colonized the liberal/rational notion of 'inclusion' " (p. 135). What happens when school staff "dis-identifies²" with inclusive communities of practice and subscribes to a standards agenda, yet they manage to participate in the emerging inclusive school culture? Are exclusion processes triggered for these individuals? To borrow from Hodges, how do such "agonized compromises" (p. 279) affect the culture of the school and the identities of these individuals? What forms of *difference* are created in these inclusive contexts? How is such identity work interactionally achieved?

Theoretical and methodological benefits will be gained from addressing these ideas and challenges. For instance, researchers will be compelled to disentangle the constructs of *participation* and *identification* in practice communities. This, is turn, will enable future research to address the role of power and privilege in the construction of communities of inclusive practice by examining the construction of identities and marginalized positions within communities. Methodologically, researchers will need to document and analyze interactional and discursive processes from microperspectives and situated perspectives.

Tensions Between an Individual vs. a Community Focus. Ainscow and his colleagues (2004a) argue that a condition for organizational learning is that "someone in particular has to recognize a problem as an anomaly and to convince others . . . individuals can be powerful inhibitors or facilitators" (p. 12). This is an interesting emphasis because it addresses one of the criticisms of community-based models of learning—i.e., that the role of the individual tends to be underexamined, thus losing important information about what a learner actually learns in a community. In this work, learning (i.e., changes in a community's practices or problem-solving approaches) is contingent on professionals' agency. In fact, some of this research has focused on teacher learning (defined as changes in thinking and practices), but the report relies on researchers' descriptions and participants' (Howes, Booth, Dyson, & Frankham, 2005).

The individual is also acknowledged from the students' perspective. One way in which this is done is through the analysis of outcome evidence by subgroups of students. It could be argued that an implicit assumption of such exercise is a requirement for monitoring potential exclusionary practices for different types or groups of students with distinctive traits (e.g., "at-risk" pupils). At the same time, the inclusion view used in this program of work is critical of "the assumption that some students' characteristics are such that they require a different form of teaching from that offered to the majority of students" (Ainscow et al., 2003, p. 239). It is interesting that student traits are dismissed as an analytical category in the context of instructional prescriptions, but they become a legitimate focus of examination for equity purposes. This means that, in addition to a community-centered perspective, a learner-centered model of learning (Bransford et al., 2000) is used, though rather distinctively.

Another way the individual student perspective is acknowledged in this work is in the discussion of student responses to the current standards movement in the United

Kingdom (Dyson, Gallannaugh, & Millward, 2002). The accountability movement in this nation compels practitioners and students to achieve certain outcomes. However, teachers face a uniquely difficult situation as they strive to routinize their professional practice in the midst of rapidly changing complex conditions that incorporate non-inclusive accountability policy demands, pressures to build inclusive schools, uncertainty about how accountability mandates are to be implemented, and a changing student population. Thus, students witness and respond to teachers' struggles to enact inclusive education practices in policy and organizational climates that discourage inclusion and are dissonant with the student population's experiences and realities (Ainscow et al., 2004a; Dyson, Gallannaugh, et al., 2002). It follows that school ecologies are fraught with tensions and contradictions and students do not always respond in the ways anticipated by inclusion advocates. As Ainscow et al. (2004a) explain:

. . . some evident mismatch between the established practices of the school and the actual outcomes of that practice has become apparent. This might relate to a group of students whose exclusion from classrooms ceases to be taken for granted, or a number of students who "disrupt" establish practices, or large numbers of students who "fail" to reach national targets. (p. 14)

Again, the attention to student perspectives and "realities" strengthen the emphasis on learner-centered models of learning. Ainscow and his colleagues explain that the focus of their work is to develop inclusive schools, which can be characterized as "a process of learning about how to learn from differences" (Ainscow et al., 2003, p. 233). Now, by alluding to the need to understand pupils' realities and lives (in the context of contemporary standards reforms), these researchers open a space for a more critical analysis of inclusive education. It would be possible, for example, to examine how race, gender, social class, language, and immigration status mediate students' experiences of inclusive education and standards. How does such a "cultural-historical baggage" (Hodges, 1998, p. 283) in a class-stratified and racist society (Diniz, 1999) mediate student experiences in schools that are grappling with inclusive and standards agenda in this globalization era? Ainscow and his colleagues recognize the need to focus on such contentious forms of difference (e.g., Ainscow et al., 2003, p. 239), but evidence in which such analysis is conducted in missing in this body of work. The idea of difference is addressed through a (dis)ability perspective.

The Elusive Quest for Outcomes. The research team used the Index for Inclusion (Booth et al., 2000) to help guide school teams' documentation of school practices and outcomes. The index groups inclusive school practices in three dimensions: practices, policies, and cultures. The index is grounded in two research literatures: inclusive practices and school improvement (Ainscow et al., 2004b). School teams were assisted by university teams to create success criteria regarding learning outcomes and monitor the effect of efforts to transform their schools. Therefore, it was reported that schools created quantitative profiles to monitor the effect of the project. Evidence included test scores, student attendance, suspensions and other forms of exclusion, number of staff, etc. for the whole school, as well as for groups of students "that are known to be statistically 'at risk' of marginalization in schools" (Ainscow et al., 2004b, p. 129). Unfortunately, we could not locate reports and analyses of these data.

In addition, the research team invited participating practitioners to identify the student outcomes generated by the work done in the project. The task was framed consistent with the national standards movement (e.g., academic achievement and student attendance). Interestingly, teachers were not inclined to engage in such task because "they did not see their work as a mere technical exercise in raising levels of attainment" (Ainscow et al., 2000a, p. 14). Teachers argued that the project's agenda compelled them to question the relevance and usefulness of the mandated practices for the lives of students served in their schools. Rather, their work focused on reconfiguring practices to be responsive to the lives and needs of the student population; ultimately, these efforts led to a concern for "students' engagement with learning and their sense of themselves as learners" (p. 15). Therefore, Ainscow et al. (2004a) argue that participating teachers became involved in a sort of a transformative project in which the collaborative nature of practice called for in an inclusive education model made visible the limits and problems of the traditional schooling practices that underlie the current standards reforms. A by-product of dealing with this tension was that participants critiqued mainstream schooling practices and the requirements of current national reforms that reproduce them and embraced a more inclusive stance toward their labor. It was further explained that "soft measures" (e.g., student and teacher interviews and classroom observations) are better suited to monitor these outcomes.

In summary, Ainscow and his colleagues put forward a situated model of learning in inclusive education models. In such paradigm, although characteristics of locales and communities mediate what gets accomplished, a significant influence comes from the social spaces created when practitioner communities grapple with anomalies and contradictions that arise from the examination of routine practices in the midst of multiple contradictory reform demands (Dyson, Gallannaugh, et al., 2002). Although it was not articulated this way, the research team argued that (to borrow from Wertsch), *the process is the product.* However, as they explain, the presence of contradictions is not a sufficient ingredient for organizational learning; it depends on how analytic processes are enacted to create productive dynamics that encourage change. Hence, "the development of inclusive practices, particularly on a wide, national basis, might best be achieved not by seeking an improbable *transformation* of schools, but by an *incremental enhancement* of the processes which make the existing dynamic productive in an inclusive sense" (Ainscow et al., 2004a, p. 16, emphases in original). Finally, we identified unique tensions related to how learning is framed (practice change and problem solving) or underexamined (i.e., identity processes), and the units of analysis (community vs. individual) used in this program of research. We now turn to a discussion of inclusive education research that focuses on classroom contexts.

Classroom-Based Studies of Inclusive Education

The majority of research on inclusive education at the classroom and student levels has focused on processes of instruction that produce specific outcomes designated by the researchers. Questions are dominated by technique issues, such as what kinds of approaches to teaching students to problem solve in mathematics produce the most robust results, including knowledge production and transfer? Or, researchers might ask how should students be grouped to ensure that skill development is acquired by all students? The assumption is that once these techniques are uncovered, practitioners, particularly teachers, will adopt and use these techniques in their own teaching. What is missing in this work is the analysis of the complex labor students and teachers jointly create as they build identities as learners engaged in the production of schooling. Furthermore, this inclusive education research also needs to situate the analysis of identity production processes in the contemporary contexts of ongoing assessments imposed on teachers and students by both external measures, such as standardized and standards-based assessment, and classroom-anchored measures of academic progress that examine changes in learners, learners participation, and learner leadership, as well as context. In other words, what is missing in this work is the theoretical lens on complexity used in whole school-based inclusion research. The prevailing assumption in classroom-based research is that technique is the essential and most critical variable in producing learning for students. Furthermore, the research assumes that learning is measured by knowledge and skill acquisition. In much of inclusive classroom research, the interaction between student ethnicities, languages, cultures, and background experiences and classroom experiences and accomplishments remains unexplored (Klingner et al., 2005).

Research on inclusive classroom practices has generally revolved around two themes. One theme has focused on the experience of inclusive classrooms for students with and without disabilities, as well as their general and special education teachers (e.g., Giangreco, Dennis, Cloninger, Edelman, & Schattman, 1993; Kozleski & Jackson, 1993). This theme also encompasses instructional processes, such as peer-assisted teaching and cooperative learning (e.g., Greenwood & Delquadri, 1995; McMaster, Fuchs, & Fuchs, 2006) and how special and general educators work together in the same classroom (e. g., Magiera, Smith, Zigmond, & Gebauer, 2006; Pugach & Johnson, 1995). A second theme encompasses studies about what and how to assess and teach in specific content areas, including literacy, mathematics, science, and social studies (e.g., Fuchs & Fuchs, 2005; Swanson, 2006). Although these two themes have addressed different aspects of classroom research, they have both essentialized classroom practice. For example, neither theme foregrounds the complex interactions within classroom contexts, such as those among students, their teachers, and the ongoing construction of classroom cultures and individual identities. Instead, research focuses on one variable, such as how students with learning disabilities like inclusive classrooms (Klingner, Vaughn, Schumm, Cohen, & Forgan, 1998) or how grouping affects reading achievement (i.e., Schumm, Moody, & Vaughn, 2000). Nevertheless, interdisciplinary scholarship on teaching and learning suggests classroom contexts include such features as teacher and student activity for explicit and implicit purposes, the effect of classroom materials on the dynamics of learning, the interaction among home and school cultures, teacher and student experiences, tools for instruction, routines, roles, and expectations (Gallego, Cole, & Laboratory of Comparative Human Cognition, 2001). These multiple dimensions of the classroom context flavor and complicate the process of teaching and learning. Research that fails to account for these and other complex dynamics in classrooms runs the risk of shaping practice with unintended yet pernicious consequences. Instead, much of the research on inclusive practices focuses on one-dimensional aspects of instruction within the classroom.

Experiences in Inclusive Classrooms

The trajectory of research on the social benefits of inclusive classrooms provides one example of this one-dimensional exploration of learning in classrooms. As late as the 1970s, researchers were only beginning to learn how to teach students with severe disabilities. Primarily relegated to living in institutional, congregate care settings throughout the United States, children and youths with severe disabilities did not attend schools or receive educational services. Parents were counseled by their physicians and encouraged by their families to institutionalize their children. In the early seventies, institutions for children with severe disabilities were found in every state in the United States. For the most part, institutionalized children were considered to be uneducable until the work of Charles Ferster and B. F. Skinner (1957), Foxx and Azrin (e.g., Azrin, Besales, & Wisotzek, 1982), and others who applied the principles of classical conditioning and stimulus-response learning to teach children with severe disabilities to communicate (e.g., Kozleski, 1991), to reduce problem behavior (e.g., Axelrod, 1987), to build functional reading skills (e.g., Gast, Ault, Wolery, & Doyle, 1988), and to engage in leisure activities (e.g., Nietupski et al., 1986).

An advocacy framework grounded this work. By learning how to instruct students with severe disabilities, advocates for persons with severe disabilities demonstrated that it was possible to develop skill sets that would help them leave institutions and have opportunities for living in communities. By the 1980s, teaching procedures researched in institutional settings were brought into classrooms, first in separate schools, and later, in neighborhood schools to teach students with severe disabilities to manage their own care (e.g., brush their teeth), to develop functional skills for transportation (e.g., riding the bus), unskilled labor (e.g., sorting mail), leisure activities (e.g., visiting the mall and renting a video), and home life (e.g., keeping an apartment). Because initial research focused on how to teach in an institutional setting, much of what was taught reflected what was available in institutions and perceived as beneficial for the students (Smith & Kozleski, 2005). What was being taught reflected the movement from institutional- to community-based placements.

However, as students with severe disabilities were brought into neighborhood schools, the content of what was considered to be state-of-the-art curricula became a barrier for their inclusion in general education classrooms. The paradox was that the functional curricula that provided the impetus for institutional emancipation became a barrier for inclusion in general education classrooms. Special educators who taught students with severe disabilities were ill prepared to generalize their teaching strategies to the school curriculum. General educators felt ill prepared to teach functional skills in addition to their classroom curricula.

On the one hand, behaviorism helped to establish that students who were viewed as expendable were, in fact, capable of learning and developing functional behavior and communication. The methods that uncovered these processes were empirically derived and followed tightly focused systematic methodologies in which one variable at a time was introduced after a baseline was established. Because there were few participants available to involve in these studies, most of the researchers followed a single subject design model in which baseline and treatment conditions were proxies for control and experimental groups in large group experimental design. The detailed studies that documented these breakthroughs helped to establish a mandate for the right to education. Yet, the content of what was taught operated in pernicious ways to limit the view of what was possible or appropriate to teach students with severe disabilities. For instance, one of the deeply held tenets of instruction at this time was that instruction needed to occur in environments that were authentic or as nearly authentic as possible. Therefore, if a researcher was exploring methods for teaching individuals with severe intellectual disabilities to ride public transportation, then the best environment for instruction was public transportation. This approach was developed to solve issues that revolved around generalization of learning from familiar to novel situations. Not until the early 1990s did a group of researchers begin to examine the constraints that such a view of human behavior placed on individuals with severe disabilities.

Two studies published in 1993 explored the effects of placing students with severe disabilities into general education classrooms (Giangreco et al., 1993; Kozleski & Jackson, 1993). Socially and behaviorally, the students in each of these studies were able to participate in general education classrooms, although they were described as having severe sensory and intellectual disabilities. Students in both studies were able to learn alongside their classmates, although their participation may have been limited, and, according to classroom observation, interviews with their classmates or their teachers, were seen as members of the classroom community. Each of these studies provided a snapshot of what classrooms might look like when students with severe disabilities were added to the classroom mix. Data in one study focused on the social benefits of inclusion in general education classrooms for the students with disabilities and their classmates without disabilities, as well as evidence of learning for the student with severe disabilities (Kozleski & Jackson, 1993). In the other study, the experiences of general education teachers were explored.

Unlike the earlier studies that focused on counting the number of times students produced particular kinds of behaviors, these studies combined classroom observation, field notes, student and teacher interviews in a yearlong study (Kozleski & Jackson, 1993), and in a retrospective study (Giangreco et al., 1993). Kozleski and

Jackson observed over a full year the evolution of relationships, taking time to interview and survey children and teachers periodically about their experience of the social and learning environments in the classroom. However, even in this study, the focus was on an individual student rather than on the social activities of the group. Learning was defined as knowledge and behavior acquisition. The role of the teacher in mediating the relationship between students remained unexplored although attitudes and feelings of the students without disabilities were tracked over time as students became more familiar and interactive with the student with severe disabilities. Missing in this study and others like it was an understanding of the construction of identity in response to new challenges that existed in the classroom because of the student with disabilities.

In the Giangreco study, which relied on semistructured teacher interviews and a follow-up teacher survey, the focus was the changes in behavior that teachers made during the course of the year in which they had a student with severe disabilities in their general education classroom. Interviews revealed that teachers began the year feeling resistance to being asked to have a student with a disability in the classroom. Teachers were also anxious about their responsibility and their ability to teach a student with disability. The researchers chronicled substantial changes in teachers' attitudes over time. For instance, teachers reported at the beginning of the year that they would report on the number of students in their class as 20 plus the child with a disability. Over time, they stopped singling out the child with a disability from the count. The teachers reported realizing that the child with a disability had become a member of the class, not an outsider. Clusters of these types of changes signaled a transformational change in the teachers in which they reframed their identities as teachers of all the students, not only the general education students. Giangreco and his colleagues noted that these kinds of changes occurred as the teacher became more likely to use cooperative learning groupings, observe how his or her students interacted among each other and adopted those techniques, and used learning methods that were more discovery or inquiry oriented rather than teacher directed. The researchers explored the variables that led to these favorable outcomes for 17 out of the 19 teachers they studied. They concluded that teacher characteristics were responsible for teacher transformation rather than exploring the interactive nature of the students, the curriculum, the external supports, and the teachers' identities. This study, like the Kozleski and Jackson study, focused more on isolated variables rather than on the complexity of interactions occurring simultaneously in the classroom.

Both studies were products of a cognitive-behavioral orientation to understanding complex human interaction. From this viewpoint, the variables of interest remain those observable elements of classroom practice that can be defined and observed throughout researchers. Key to this approach is a research methodology that seeks to achieve interrater reliability to *collect* valid data rather than the collection of multiple sets of data that are available for multiple interpretations from researchers who seek common ground after discussion of various plausible explanations. Thus, observation itself is purposefully focused on a tightly constrained set of behaviors to the exclusion of other activity or events that may be occurring simultaneously in the environment. Researchers refrain from using additional information from the environment to inform the research question. This research methodology means that complexity within activity arenas is minimized as a premise for conducting research.

As researchers in this tradition moved from observable behavior to understanding how cognition mediates behavior, they developed methods that help to link internal decision making to explicit and observed behaviors. Thus, Giangreco's research team sought explanations for changes in how teachers discussed their students by linking interview data to observed behavior. By focusing early on identifying causal patterns, researchers may inadvertently omit important and complex variables that may shape their findings. This approach was repeated in a set of studies conducted later in the 1990s and early in 2000 and 2001.

This set of studies examined the social and academic experiences of students with learning disabilities in inclusive classrooms (i.e., Klingner, Vaughn, Schumm, et al., 1998; Klingner & Vaughn, 2002; Schumm et al., 2000). Some of these studies examined how coteaching and collaborative/consultative teaching models influenced student academic achievement, whereas others examined how students with learning disabilities fared socially in inclusive settings. One study followed a single special education teacher for a 7-year period as she changed her role from being a resource-room teacher to a collaborative/consultative special education teacher.

During the first year in which the special educator's role changed, teacher time in the school was organized in ways that supported joint planning time, shared unit, and lesson planning. The special educator had enough time with her colleagues to align her teaching strategies to those of the classroom teachers and to consult with her general education colleagues during times where they were not scheduled to be teaching. As the special educator navigated changes in her role, she also kept a reflective diary throughout the year in which she noted her challenges and successes. The diary was used as a communication tool between one of the researchers who was also serving as a mentor as the school underwent the change in service delivery model. The researcher wrote comments or suggestions in the diary for the special educator. Interviews with the special educator, her general education colleagues, and her building administrators were also conducted each of the 7 years of the study. Focus groups were conducted twice, in years 2 and 6. Classroom observations were conducted each year. Researchers kept field notes throughout each year of the study. In the last year, the special educator reviewed her diary from the first year and made oral comments into a tape recorder after passages, interrogating her own thinking, and adding to the comments that she had made originally.

What the researchers found was that the special educator's role was complex and multifaceted. Her ability to support students with learning disabilities in the general education classroom rested on her communication skills, her knowledge of special education services and supports, her ability to co-plan with general educators, her dedication and persistence, and her ability to accommodate whole-class instruction for students with learning disabilities.

An interesting but somewhat unexplored aspect of this study is the special educator's construction of her own identity. Over time, as the institution in which she worked expected changes in how she achieved institution goals (i.e., be an inclusive school), her identity as a teacher shifted dramatically. From being a teacher who worked directly with students whom she perceived as her own, she became a support to other teachers and the work of other teachers' classrooms. The article mentions her sense of loss as a teacher but the construction, deconstruction, and reconstruction of this identity and how it occurred were not the focus of the study. Instead, views of what occurred were emphasized, such as which roles the teacher liked and how well she did them. The researchers focused on what activities the special educator performed, how often those activities were performed, and how they were perceived by colleagues and administrators. Although this detail should inform readers about changes in role, the more complex challenges of identity construction, teachers' views of learning, and how they were negotiated, the tools that shaped their discourse and created opportunities for responding to specific challenges in specific classrooms remained unexplored.

Vaughn, Elbaum, and Schumm (1996) looked at how students with learning disabilities fared socially in inclusive classrooms. Students with learning disabilities in Grades 2 through 4 were enrolled in a school that was moving to an inclusive school model for the first time. They were in classrooms where teachers had volunteered to serve their students inclusively. Students were assessed in the spring and fall on three measures: (1) peer nominations of liking and nonliking, (2) a measure of self-concept, and (3) loneliness and social dissatisfaction scale. Together, these measures produced seven dimensions that were analyzed from social acceptance to perceptions of academic competence. The results suggested that the students with learning disabilities experienced less social acceptance than their peers who were not identified for disabilities. However, they did not fare any worse than students with learning disabilities in previous studies where social competence was measured for students receiving educational support in resource rooms. Complexities introduced by the ethnicities, backgrounds, socioeconomic status, and languages of teachers and students were not addressed in the study. Furthermore, because the only measure of social functioning was sociometric, students' voices and perceptions were not present in the study. One interesting perspective of this study is the degree to which learning and social adjustment were perceived as separate constructs. Conceptually, learning was a function of academic performance rather than a complex phenomenon that encompasses social, cognitive, cultural, aesthetic, and spatial dimensions.

Another study conducted in the same time frame by Klingner et al. (1998) questioned students with and without learning disabilities about their preferences for services delivered in the general education or resource classroom. In this study, 32 students were interviewed. Questions included such items as (1) what does the learning disability (LD) teacher do; (2) who does she work with; (3) why do you have two teachers in your class; (4) how do you like having two teachers; (5) which do you like best, pull-out or inclusion; (6) which way helps kids learn better; (7) which way helps kids have more friends; (8) what grouping helps you learn best: working alone, with a partner, in a small group, or with the whole class; and (9) do you like to teach other students; and do you like it when they teach you? Frequency counts of student responses were cataloged and organized by responses of students with and without disabilities. Researchers found that students with and without disabilities slightly preferred a resource room delivery model. However, the students who preferred it do so for the opportunities it gave them to (1) do easier work and (2) have a bit of free time on the way to and from class. Students in both categories preferred small-group instruction followed by pairs. They also enjoyed being taught by peers for reasons that included knowing one another for a long time and that there was focused time spent on learning. The information from the interviews was rich and varied, but the researchers were cautious in their conclusions, particularly regarding the importance of students' feedback on how schools might organize for instruction:

Should student preference affect placement decisions? We believe that students' views do provide insights into their learning needs and should be considered. However, their preferences should be just one of many relevant factors considered when making a placement decision or when evaluating the appropriateness of an ongoing program. (Klingner, Vaughn, Schumm, et al., 1998, p. 156)

Although students were the focus of this study, the research question—"Which do students prefer, pull-out or general class instruction?"—constrained the researchers' exploration of the data they collected. Indeed, the approach to reporting results (frequency counts) limited more robust analyses of the data. The researchers offered three student profiles from their study that represented the types of student responses they received. These profiles briefly described the students in terms of their academic proficiencies and then reported their responses to specific questions. Because the questions constrained student responses, ideas that students may have had about how they best learned, how teachers could best help them, and what they needed to learn were not explored. Although the researchers wanted to know what students thought about a particular practice, they missed students' perceptions about their learning context in general, including what they perceived to be of value to the teachers and how this informed students' participation in specific activities.

The studies reviewed are representative of a series of studies during the last 15 years that examined how inclusive education affects students and teachers (e.g., Baker, 1995; Dieker, 2001; Klingner, Vaughn, Hughes, Schumm, Elbaum, 1998; Walther-Thomas, 1997). Most of the research questions focus on technical dimensions of practices, such as is inclusive education a good practice or how should special and general educators work together. Because the questions were narrowly focused and had one-dimensional views of learning as measured by standardized academic and/or cognitive assessments, the research itself provides one-dimensional responses to the questions posed. Bransford et al. (2000) suggest that the goals for learning impose a kind of architecture for learning that incorporates multidimensional features, such as learner-, knowledge-, assessment-, and community-centered approaches. A learner-centered approach to learning would capitalize on what students bring to the learning situation (e.g., personal knowledge, beliefs about content or cultural/linguistic practices) and use those assets to develop shared learning goals. Culturally responsive instruction is an example of learner-centered models. In contrast, inclusive education researchers spend little time on defining learning or what is to be learned. One study provides more information about whether students prefer one kind of instruction or another but little about the personal and social contexts that influence their perceptions and opinions (e.g., Klingner, Vaughn, Schumm, et al., 1998). Another study focuses on the techniques that lead to including one child in a general education classroom but little about the institutional, professional, or familial histories that created the context (e.g., Kozleski & Jackson, 1993). Some studies focus on teachers and their responses to dealing with students with disabilities in their classroom (e.g., Giangreco et al., 1993) or how one special educator negotiates new roles (e.g., Klingner & Vaughn, 2002). In these studies, narrow views of learning are informed by narrowing research methods that fail to capitalize on the complex environment of classroom work. The problem in simplifying complex realities is that researchers risk engaging in essentialism that makes teachers the omniscient focus of all classroom activity and makes the role of learner passive and procedural. What classroom research on inclusive practices needs is complex views of learning and the roles that learners play in constructing learning over time.

Instructional Approaches for Content Acquisition

Although changes in how teachers organize the curriculum and their instructional practices have been at the heart of classroom research on inclusive practices, why teachers are unlikely to make these adaptations is a critical question for creating and sustaining inclusive classrooms (Boardman, Arguelles, Vaughn, Hughes, & Klingner, 2005). One possible explanation may lie within the assumptions made about teaching and the importance given to technique as the salient variable in good teaching. Behavioral views of human learning and single-subject methodologies produced evidence that students with severe intellectual disabilities could learn under carefully controlled situations in which the teachers' actions were critical in prompting, shaping, and reinforcing specific behaviors. However, conceptions of learning as directed and external diluted the possibility that the rich environments of classrooms provided incidental and informal opportunities for observation, participation, and the development of increasingly complex skill sets not anticipated by early researchers. In fact, some of the original tenets of instruction and curriculum, defined by professionals, inhibited opportunities to participate and learn in general education classrooms. Thus, context as a critical feature of opportunities to learn was subordinated to specific procedural knowledge that teachers need to ensure that learning occurs.

Research on special education instructional approaches has focused particularly on the following aspects of knowledge and skill development: (1) assessment for determining learning progress, (2) curriculum-based instruction, (3) strategy instruction vs. direct instruction, (4) literacy development vs. direct instruction of reading skills, (5) math skills development, (6) study skills, (7) social and emotional skills learning (such as aggression replacement training), and (8) positive behavior supports (including the functional analysis of behavior, whole school, classroom, and individual student behavioral interventions). Unlike research on instructional organization and delivery, this research focuses on specific procedures for teaching skill development. This research most often takes an experimental approach. Students in experimental and control conditions in which teachers are asked to vary only one or two aspects of their teaching approach are assessed before and after an intervention. Changes in performance on a measure of academic proficiency are used to measure effects of treatment and control procedures.

Using these inquiry techniques, two approaches to improving academic performance have shown particular promise. The first is strategy instruction. Strategy instruction assumes that students with disabilities fail to learn adequately because they lack the cognitive strategies or mental schemas for organizing themselves to learn. From this perspective, students need to develop skills in identifying what is to be learned, what is to be produced, select an appropriate process for accomplishing the task, manage their focus, attend to the task, self-reflect, and shift performance effort on the basis of the self-reflection. Research on both generic strategies for learning and task-specific strategies for learning, such as comprehension strategies, improve student performance (Bulgren & Schumaker, 2006). Early research on strategic instruction (e.g., Palincsar & Brown, 1984) drew on sociocultural theorists such as Vygotsky (1978) focusing specifically on aspects of learner self-regulation seemingly omitting other aspects of his work, including apprenticeship, modes of discourses, and the notion of a social collective. Englert and Mariage (1996) extended work on strategy instruction to incorporate student participation in communities of learners characterized by a focus on holistic activities, collaborative problem solving and skill building, and scaffolds meant to bridge knowledge gaps while students build their skills.

A second, well-researched approach to learning is direct instruction in which a specific set of teaching procedures is assembled for teaching a complex skill, such as reading. In this approach, students receive direct instruction from a teacher who introduces a subskill by modeling the skill, describing the components of the subskill, having the student practice each step of the subskill, chaining the elements of the subskill together, practicing the subskill with careful reinforcement from the teacher, and then practicing the skill in novel situations until the student is able to produce the skill without error. Once this occurs, the next subskill is introduced until a set of subskills can be linked together to produce a performance (Swanson, 2001).

Most of the research on strategy and direct instruction has been done in one-on-one settings and small groups rather than with whole classrooms. Furthermore, where classrooms have served as experimental and control groups as in Fuchs and Fuchs (2005), the focus has been on assessing the results of particular procedures on task attainment as the learning outcome. Bransford et al. (2000) suggest that knowledge-centered approaches to learning focus on promoting learners' understanding of a subject (e.g., math and history), not a mere memorization of information. Bransford also stresses the development of learners' metacognition and their ability to transfer such understanding to new situations and tasks. Ultimately, the goal is to support learners' understanding of a discipline's constructs and procedures, or as Greeno (1991) suggests, "learning the landscape" (p. 175) of a discipline. Intersections with learner-centered models are readily apparent because both build on what students bring to the learning environment. Knowledge-centered models have significant implications for the construction of meaningfully integrated curricula in the disciplines. As Bransford et al. (2000) explain, many approaches to curriculum produce disjointed knowledge and skills that lack coherence and a sense of wholeness. Although an individual learning objective might be reasonable, it must be seen as part of a larger network because expertise is characterized by knowledge networks, not disconnected knowledge chunks. Within knowledge-centered models the challenge becomes developing balanced learning designs that both promote understanding *and* develop skill automaticity. The result is smooth engagement in learning tasks without basic fluency issues. This issue of balance is crucial for the design of learning environments for students with intellectual, learning, and behavioral disabilities as they struggle to acquire automaticity of literacy and numeric skills.

Although ensuring that the field develops a better understanding of how students can learn specific cognitive strategies to master skill development, studies of classroom research on students with disabilities suggest that the prevailing special education paradigm for learning is the development and application of procedural knowledge to specific kinds of problem solving, a technical rather than critical view of what constitutes learning and its end uses. Connections to neo-liberal notions of education for globalization can be drawn. Because learning comprises sets of increasing complex skill acquisition and application, it suggests that the outcomes of a globalized view of education are also conceptualized as the reproduction of complex sets of skills for a knowledge economy. By focusing on technical knowledge acquisition determined by people and organizations distal to the learning environment, the relationships between teacher and students and among students are not well understood. Their role is crucial developing, practicing, using, and constructing knowledge in less structured situations where opportunities to learn might be advantaged by shared aspirations, supportive relationships between and among students and teachers, a community focus on local complexities, the development of tools for inquiry, and other features of a community linked together in purposeful learning.

IMPLICATIONS: RE-MEDIATING THEORY AND METHODS WITH A TRANSFORMATIVE AGENDA

Inclusion research has grown significantly in the last 30 years. We argued at the beginning of this chapter that a historical perspective is critical to understand the development of inclusion research, and we hope our brief historical discussion helped contextualize the meaning and development of inclusion in different eras. In addition, we identified several important shortcomings in this literature; we outline the five most visible:

1. Inclusive education theory has outpaced its practice. Although the conceptualization of inclusive education has become increasingly sophisticated, the research

focus has been on students with disabilities rather than on the complete composition of what is theorized to be an inclusive school.

2. Although inclusive education has been increasingly theorized, conceptual clarity is urgently needed. Because multiple definitions of inclusive education coexist in this literature, the design and implementation of studies and the accumulation of empirical facts and insights is compromised.

3. Although educational systems are influenced by globalization forces, research on inclusive education ignores this phenomenon. It is not yet clear that globalization will embrace a deterministic perspective. In a world made more fluid by the latest wave of globalization, it is critical that future research on inclusive education makes visible the struggles and transformations that are shaped and defined by globalizing forces.

4. Disparate conceptualizations of learning inform classroom- and school-based inclusion studies. The former tends to have a strong behavioral or cognitive (i.e., psychological) theoretical basis, whereas the latter is grounded in a practice-based (i.e., interdisciplinary) perspective. We discuss below several implications of this situation.

5. The research methods used have not produced thick descriptions of the complexities associated with the development of inclusive education programs. Additional gaps that result from methodological issues include the lack of detailed documentation of change processes and clear implications for the transferability of research findings.

Before we conclude, we reflect on two substantive issues that have significant relevance for future inclusive education research. These issues are historical and theoretical considerations around learning itself and the links between learning theories and research methods.

Theoretical Stipulations and History in Learning: A Transformative Agenda for Future Research

As we examined the literature on inclusive education, a somewhat fragmented picture of views of learning emerged. This is not surprising because tensions and contentious debates have always surrounded the evolution of learning theories (Phillips & Soltis, 2004). Nonetheless, it is important to reflect on the ways theoretical stipulations and assumptions about time (history) shape the divergent perspectives of learning in inclusive education research.

We explained at the beginning of this chapter that learning theories comprise three stipulations, namely a telos (the direction of movement of learning), subject-world relation, and learning mechanisms (Lave, 1996). Our review suggests the views of learning in classroom-based studies rely on different theoretical stipulations from the school-based work. The telos in classroom-based research is the acquisition of basic literacy and behavioral knowledge and skills. This work aims to equip students with disabilities with thinking and acting strategies and skills to engage effectively in mainstream tasks and activities. Implicit in this perspective is the assumption that reality lies in the world and thus, subjects must acquire the sanctioned tools to know it.

In turn, school-based research is purportedly grounded in a practice-based model of learning. Consequently, the telos is to become competent members of communities (i.e., schools) in which *all* students (i.e., students with disabilities) participate and achieve. The subject-world relation in school-based research is concerned with how inclusive schools are socially constituted through inclusive practices. In this model, learning is theorized as participation and its evolution. Nevertheless, as we indicated, the bulk of the evidence on learning addresses participating teachers with a preponderance of self-reported data on change. Interestingly, the evidence on student learning is purportedly grounded in more traditional indices, like the ones used in classroom-based research (e.g., achievement scores).

Time is a key dimension in the study of learning. Indeed, investigators need to trace the history of learning to assess changes. Scribner (1985) built on Vygotsky's work by exploring how history enters learning and developmental processes. She explained that learning processes can be traced along a microgenetic time scale to gauge the history of moment-to-moment processes. The next time scale is called ontogenetic, and it allows us to examine learning processes throughout the life history of an individual or during stages in biographical trajectories. Special education and developmental psychology researchers have favored this time scale. Above this timeline is the cultural historical scale, which accounts for the history of groups, communities, or institutions.

Classroom-based research has relied on an ontogenetic time scale to conduct studies. Although few studies report longitudinal analyses of learners' trajectories, this research has documented learning within specified ontogenetic time periods. In contrast, school-based inquiries focus on the cultural historical scale through the documentation of change processes for the entire school community (Artiles, 2003). It should be noted that perhaps the most powerful analytical models combine at least two time scales (Lemke, 2000). This means that future inclusive education research could examine the local instantiation of learning processes in classroom groups (microgenetic analyses) while changes in the ontogenetic trajectories of subgroups of learners are tracked over time. For instance, this kind of study could address such questions as: How do immigrant students in inclusive schools develop biliteracy while working in multilingual small groups? How do face-to-face and remote access to multiple linguistic communities (in the United States and abroad) mediate the emergence of biliteracy for immigrant students in inclusive classrooms in the early primary grades? Similarly, changes in teacher (and/or student) participation structures of inclusive schools could be investigated (cultural historical analyses) and combined with the study of the learning trajectories of individual or distinct groups of students. Possible research questions would include: How do the evolving discussion and problem solving among school personnel of racial discrimination in behavioral support practices mediate the social and academic performance of various racial groups of students?

These are highly consequential and timely questions for students and teachers living in the globalization age. These questions suggest that one of the most important challenges for inclusive education researchers is the need to recognize the role that power plays in schools and teacher and student lives. Although inclusive education analysts have been concerned about the exclusion of students with disabilities, there is little attention paid in this work to issues of power (Ferri & Connor, 2005). For instance, considering that racial minority and poor students comprise the majority in special education programs in many regions of the United States, how do race and social class mediate inclusion work? Is inclusion defined differently in programs that serve racial minority students? Why are racial minority students with disabilities placed in more segregated programs than their white counterparts? How are equity concerns for racial minority students addressed in inclusive education programs? This literature is surprisingly silent about this issue (Artiles, 2003). This is unfortunate, particularly for the work done from a whole-school perspective because the practice-based theory that informs this research is clearly mindful of these issues. As Lave (1996) explains, "racialization, gender-, social class-, and sexual-orientation making are aspects of American adulthood that kids are deeply engaged in constituting among themselves. Like the tailors' apprentices in Liberia they are learning in practice the salient social divisions and identities of the social formation in which they live their lives" (p. 159). Indeed, the stratification of American society is created and reproduced in schools every day and globalization is complicating these processes while it threatens to deepen longstanding structural inequities (Burbules & Torres, 2000). Critical questions that come to mind include: How is inclusive education contributing to the preparation of racial minority students with disabilities for technologically rich work environments? Is inclusive education enabling immigrant students to learn these new skills? Do special education student groups have differential access to the technological and literacy resources demanded by globalization changes? How do the unique struggles and tensions experienced by immigrant students mediate the work done to build inclusive classroom and schools? How do inclusion interventions to equip students with disabilities with certain types of skills consider historical legacies of discrimination and limited access to leaning experienced by girls and low-income students? An important challenge for future research is to understand how inclusive "schools *in particular ways,* ways not identical with the xenophobia, racism, sexism, and homophobia structuring other social institutions, make the learning of these divisions in practice ubiquitous" (Lave, 1996, p. 162).

As we imbue inclusion research with a critical lens to address power issues that affect school routines and people's lives, we are compelled to ask, "inclusion into what?" (Erickson, 1996). In other words, to what extent do inclusive education advocates question the nature of the mainstream into which we aim to include students with disabilities and its concomitant inequitable conditions? What counts as community in these contexts, and to what extent do we need to reimagine the communities from which students from marginalized groups come? (Gutiérrez & Arzubiaga, in press). This adds another layer in the definition of future inclusive education work, namely an attention to equity and social justice. Although we see attention to these issues in the justification for inclusive models (i.e., exclusion from mainstream practices and institutions), it is imperative to discuss what it means to be included and the nature of spaces in which students will be included (Artiles, Harris-Murri, & Rostenberg, 2006). Otherwise, inclusive education might just become a push for assimilation, particularly for those students who have been historically marginalized and who constitute the majority in many special education programs throughout the nation (Artiles, Trent, & Palmer, 2004).

Re-mediating Theory and Methods

We learned that inclusive education research is informed by diverse theoretical paradigms and methods. In a way, it is useful to build a knowledge base with multiple perspectives, though the risk is that, unless deliberate efforts are made to build cohesion and pursue programmatic efforts, conceptual confusion and dispersion of findings might occur. One problem we found in the literature is the lack of cross-fertilization between the classroom- and school-based inclusion research. Even if these inquiry strands use different learning views, we see the potential for enriching this emerging knowledge base. It will be important to pursue programs of research at the classroom and school levels within the same theoretical paradigms; at the same time, it is crucial to define overarching questions for a program of research that draws from the various theoretical paradigms represented in this literature.

Moreover, we underlined the need to coordinate various time scales that can be used to study inclusive education and the significant need to infuse a critical perspective to acknowledge power issues. We argue that researchers mediate their work (i.e., regulate their decisions and practices) through theories and research methods (Cole & Griffin, 1983). We discussed how researchers mediate inclusive education work at the classroom and school levels. We noted the strengths and limits of these efforts. One missing piece in this work is a systematic understanding of the role of culture in learning. In a sense, what we need is to *re-mediate* researchers' work as they design and carry out future inclusion research. "Re-mediation means a *shift in the way that mediating devices regulate coordination with the environment*" (Cole & Griffin, 1983, p. 69) (emphasis in original). There have been systematic efforts implemented, particularly in the last 30 years, to re-mediate an understanding of human development and its associated constructs (e.g., learning) as cultural phenomena (Cole, 1996; Rogoff, 2003). Therefore, a central challenge for future research is to re-mediate the design and implementation of inclusive educational environments with theories that offer a systematic understanding of the cultural and political nature of learning (Arzubiaga, Artiles, King, & Harris-Murri, 2006).

The strength of community-centered models is that they rely on a practice-based model of learning, which considers the role of culture. However, it will be important to develop multidimensional inclusive models that incorporate attention to learner-, assessment-, and content-centered models (Bransford et al., 2000). The unit of analysis in the next inclusion research will have to transcend the individual and focus on individuals acting in activity systems (Gutiérrez & Rogoff, 2003). This will open new and exciting possibilities to understanding the processes and outcomes of inclusion from an intercontextual angle; that is, researchers will examine inclusion-related questions throughout schools, communities, and homes. An important implication is that learning will not be construed solely as an outcome. Practice-based views of learning emphasize the transformation of identities over time as a key indicator of learning. From this perspective, learning is construed as becoming new types of persons (Lave & Wenger, 1991). This means that the *process is the product* (Wertsch, 1985), and thus future research must transcend the documentation of outcomes as the only legitimate proof of effect.

CONCLUSION

An analysis of views of learning in inclusive education requires understanding of the changing nature of education, the transforming communities served by schools, and the rapid economic and technological changes underway in a global scale. Inclusive education cannot ignore the demographic imperative of the new millennium. Because a sizable proportion of students have been historically marginalized, social justice must be a focal consideration of any inclusive program. By ignoring and failing to document how the politics of inclusive schools affect and interact with the construction of participation, this research runs the risk of simplifying and/or romanticizing a complex construct that has the potential to emancipate. Inclusive education, in a time of globalization, has the potential to offer places for teachers and students to explore their individual and collective identities as learners. By doing so, the opportunities to cross the boundaries of location, voice, knowledge, and learning are vast. This potential is the best of what a world in which space and time have been compressed can offer. Yet such a process requires the use of carefully considered definitions of what is being studied, nuanced ways of collecting and interpreting the data, and ongoing discourse within communities to purposefully explore and understand the nature of what an inclusive education can be.

ACKNOWLEDGMENTS

The first two authors acknowledge the support of the National Center for Culturally Responsive Educational Systems (NCCRESt) (www.nccrest.org) under grant H326E020003 awarded by the U.S. Department of Education's Office of Special Education Programs. Endorsement of the ideas presented in this chapter by the funding agency should not be inferred. We are grateful to the editors and consulting editors for their invaluable feedback on drafts of this chapter that helped us refine our thinking and writing. We also acknowledge Kathleen King's contributions for her editorial assistance during the preparation of this chapter. Address correspondence to alfredo.artiles@asu.edu.

NOTES

[1]There are instances in which the researchers describe participants in terms of "outsiders" and "insiders," although these terms tend to be defined categorically, for example, from outside local sites (e.g., staff from other schools in the LEA) or outside of the professional community (researcher vs. practitioner). See Howes et al. (2005) for a related discussion on social boundaries within schools.

[2]Hodges (1998) describes disidentification as when a "person may be rejecting the identity connected with the practice and yet is reconstructing an identification within the context of conflict and exclusion" (p. 273).

REFERENCES

Abe, Y. (1998). Special education reform in Japan. *European Journal of Special Needs Education, 13,* 86–97.

Ainscow, M., Booth, T., & Dyson, A. (2004a, October). Standards and inclusive education: Schools squaring the circle. Paper presented at the Teaching and Learning Research Programme annual conference, Cardiff, UK.

Ainscow, M., Booth, T., & Dyson, A. (2004b). Understanding and developing inclusive practices in schools: A collaborative action research network. *International Journal of Inclusive Education, 8,* 125–139.

Ainscow, M., Booth, T., & Dyson, A. (2006). *Improving school, developing inclusion.* London: Routledge.

Ainscow, M., Hargreaves, D., & Hopkins, D. (1995). Mapping the process of change in school. *Evaluation and Research in Education, 9,* 75–90.

Ainscow, M., Howes, A., Farrell, P., & Frankham, J. (2003). Making sense of the development of inclusive practices. *European Journal of Special Needs Education, 18,* 227–242.

Alpert, B. (1996, May 25). Schools request right to remove discipline cases. *Cleveland Plain Dealer* [LexisAcademic Universe database].

Arrendondo, G., & Ryan-Arrendondo, K. (1999). Special education in Mexico. In C. R. Reynolds & E. Fletcher-Janzen (Eds.), *Encyclopedia of special education* (pp. 1182–1184). New York: Wiley.

Artiles, A. J. (2003). Special education's changing identity: Paradoxes and dilemmas in views of culture and space. *Harvard Educational Review, 73,* 164–202.

Artiles, A. J., & Dyson, A. (2005). Inclusive education in the globalization age. In D. Mitchell (Ed.), *Contextualizing inclusive education* (pp. 37–62). London: Routledge.

Artiles, A. J., Harris-Murri, N., & Rostenberg, D. (2006). Inclusion as social justice: Critical notes on discourses, assumptions, and the road ahead. *Theory into Practice, 45,* 260–268.

Artiles, A. J., Rueda, R., Salazar, J., & Higareda, I. (2005). Within-group diversity in minority disproportionate representation. *Exceptional Children, 71,* 283–300.

Artiles, A. J., Trent, S. C., & Palmer, J. (2004). Culturally diverse students in special education. In J. A. Banks & C. M. Banks (Eds.), *Handbook of research on multicultural education* (2nd ed.) (pp. 716–735). San Francisco: Jossey Bass.

Arzubiaga, A., Artiles, A. J., King, K., & Harris-Murri, N. (2006). *Beyond culturally responsive research: Challenges and implications of research as cultural practice.* Manuscript submitted for publication.

Axelrod, S. (1987). Functional and structural analyses of behavior: Approaches leading to reduced use of punishment procedures? *Research in Developmental Disabilities, 8,* 165–178.

Azrin, N. H., Besales, V. A., & Wisotzek, I. E. (1982). Treatment of self-injury by a reinforcement plus interruption procedure. *Analysis and Intervention in Developmental Disabilities, 2,* 105–113.

Baker, J. M. (1995). Inclusion in Minnesota: Educational experiences of students with learning disabilities in two elementary schools. *Journal of Special Education, 56,* 515–526.

Blackorby, J., Wagner, M., Cameto, R., Davies, E., Levine, P., Newman, L., et al. (2005). *Engagement, academics, social adjustment, and independence.* Palo Alto, CA: SRI.

Board of Education v. Rowley, 458 U.S. 176 (1982).

Boardman, A., Arguelles, M., Vaughn, S., Hughes, M., & Klingner, J. (2005). Special education teachers' views of research-based practices. *Journal of Special Education, 39,* 168–180.

Booth, T., Ainscow, M., Black-Hawkins, K., Vaughn, M., & Shaw, L. (2000). *Index for inclusion: Developing learning and participation in schools.* Bristol, England: Centre for Studies on Inclusive Education.

Bransford, J., Brown, A. L., & Cocking, R. (2000). *How people learn: Brain, mind, experience, and school.* Washington, DC: National Academy Press.

Braswell, D. (1999). Special education in France. In C. R. Reynolds & E. Fletcher-Janzen (Eds.), *Encyclopedia of special education* (pp. 765–770). New York: Wiley.

Burbules, N., & Torres, C. A. (Eds.). (2000). *Globalization and education: Critical perspectives.* New York: Routledge.

Bulgren, J., & Schumaker, (2006). Teacher practices that optimize curriculum access. In D. Deshler & J. Schumaker, J. B. (Eds.), *Teaching adolescents with disabilities: Accessing the general education curriculum* (pp. 79–156). Thousand Oaks, CA: Corwin Press.

Castells, M. (1996). *The rise of the Networked Society.* Oxford: Blackwell Publishers.

Cobb-Roberts, D., Dorn, S., & Shircliffe, B. J. (2005). *Schools as imagined communities: The creation of identity, meaning, and conflict in U.S. history.* New York: Palgrave Macmillan.

Cocchi, R., Larocca, F., & Crivelli, C. (1999). Special education in Italy. In C. R. Reynolds & E. Fletcher-Janzen (Eds.), *Encyclopedia of special education* (pp. 998–1000). New York: Wiley.

Cole, M. (1996). *Cultural psychology: A once and future discipline.* Cambridge, MA: Harvard University Press.

Cole, M., & Griffin, P. (1983). A socio-historical approach to re-mediation. *The Quarterly Newsletter of the Laboratory of Comparative Human Cognition. 5*(4), 69–74.

Csányi, Y. (2001). Steps toward inclusion in Hungary. *European Journal of Special Needs Education, 16*(3), 301–308.

Cuban, L. (1996). Myths about changing schools and the case of special education. *Remedial and Special Education, 17*(2), 75–82.

Deng, M., Poon-McBrayer, K. F., Farnsworth, E. B. (2001). The development of special education in China—A sociocultural review. *Remedial and Special Education, 22,* 288–298.

Dieker, L. A. (2001). What are the characteristics of "effective" middle and high school co-taught teams for students with disabilities? *Preventing School Failure, 46,* 14–23.

Diniz, F. A. (1999). Race and special educational needs in the 1990s. *British Journal of Special Education, 26,* 213–217.

Dyson, A. (1999). Inclusion and inclusions. In H. Daniels & P. Garner (Eds.), *World yearbook of education 1999* (pp. 36–53). London: Kogan Page.

Dyson, A., Gallannaugh, F., & Millward, A. (2002, September). *Making space in the standards agenda: Developing inclusive practices in schools.* Paper presented at the European Conference on Educational Research. Lisbon, Portugal.

Dyson, A., Howes, A., & Roberts, B. (2002). A systematic review of the effectiveness of school-level action for promoting participation by all students (EPPI-Centre Review, version 1.1*). *In Research Evidence in Education Library.* London: EPPI-Centre, Social Science Research Unit, Institute of Education.

Eglér Mantoan, M. T., & Valente, J. A. (1998). Special education reform in Brazil. *European Journal of Special Needs Education, 13,* 10–28.

Engestrom, Y., Miettinen, R., & Punamaki, R. (Eds.). (1999). *Perspectives on activity theory.* New York: Cambridge University Press.

Englert, C. S., & Mariage, T. V. (1996). A sociocultural perspective: Teaching ways of thinking and ways of talking in a literacy community. *Learning Disabilities Research and Practice, 11,* 157–167.

Erickson, F. (1996). Inclusion into what? Thoughts on the construction of learning, identity, and affiliation in the general education classroom. In D. L. Speece & B. K. Keogh (Eds.), *Research on classroom ecologies* (pp. 91–105). Mahwah, NJ: Lawrence Erlbaum.

Ferguson, D. L., Kozleski, E. B., Smith, A. (2003). Transformed, inclusive schools: A framework to guide fundamental change in urban schools. *Effective Education for Learners with Exceptionalities, 15,* 43–74.

Ferri, B., & Connor, D. (2005). Tools of exclusions: Race, disability, and (re)segregated education. *Teachers College Record, 107,* 453–474.

Ferster, C., & Skinner, B. F. (1957). *Schedules of reinforcement.* New York: Appleton-Century Crofts.

Floriani, A. (1993). Negotiating what counts: Roles and relationships, texts and contexts, content and meaning. *Linguistics and Education, 5*(3–4), 241–274.

Friedman, T. (2000). *Lexus and the olive tree: Understanding globalization.* New York: Farrer, Straus & Giroux.

Fuchs, D., & Fuchs, L. S. (1994). Inclusive schools movement and the radicalization of special-education reform. *Exceptional Children, 60*(4), 294–309.

Fuchs, L. S., & Fuchs, D. (2005). Enhancing mathematical problem solving for students with disabilities. *Journal of Special Education, 39,* 45–57.

Gallagher, D. J. (2001). Neutrality as a moral standpoint, conceptual confusion and the full inclusion debate. *Disability & Society, 16,* 637–654.

Gallannaugh, F., & Dyson, A. (2003, September). *Schools understanding inclusion: Issues in inclusion and social class.* Paper presented at the British Educational Research Association annual conference. Hariot-Watt University.

Gallego, M. A., Cole, M., & Laboratory of Comparative Human Cognition. (2001). Classroom cultures and cultures in the classroom. In V. Richardson (Ed.), *Handbook of research on teaching* (4th ed) (pp. 951–997). Washington, DC: American Educational Research Association.

Garcia Canclini, E. (1995). *Hybrid cultures.* Minneapolis, MN: University of Minnesota Press.

Gast, D. L., Ault, M. J., Wolery, M., & Doyle, P. M. (1988). Comparison of constant time delay and the system of least prompts in teaching sigh word reading to students with moderate retardation. *Education and Training in Mental Retardation, 25,* 117–128.

Giangreco, M. F., Dennis, R., Cloninger, C., Edelman, S., & Schattman, R. (1993). "I've counted Jon": Transformational experiences of teachers educating students with disabilities. *Exceptional Children, 59,* 359–372.

Greeno, J. (1991). Number sense as situated knowing in a conceptual domain. *Journal for Research in Mathematics Education, 22,* 170–218.

Greenwood, C. R., & Delquadri, J. (1995). Class-wide peer tutoring and the prevention of school failure. *Preventing School Failure, 39,* 21–29.

Gutiérrez, K., & Arzubiaga, A. (in press). Re-imagining community. *International Journal of Educational Research.*

Gutiérrez, K. D., & Rogoff, B. (2003). Cultural ways of learning: Individual traits or repertoires of practice. *Educational Researcher, 32*(5), 19–25.

Gwalla-Ogisi, N., Nkabinde, Z. P., & Rodriguez, L. (1998). The social context of the special education debate in South Africa. *European Journal of Special Needs Education, 13*(1), 72–85.

Harrower, J. K. (1999). Educational inclusion of children with severe disabilities. *Journal of Positive Behaviour Interventions, 1,* 215–230.

Healey, F. H., & De Stefano, J. (1997). *Education reform support: A framework for scaling up school reform.* Washington, DC: Abel 2 Clearinghouse for Basic Education.

Hodges, D. C. (1998). Participation as dis-identification with/in a community of practice. *Mind, Culture, and Activity, 5,* 272–290.

Howes, A., Booth, T., Dyson, A., & Frankham, J. (2005). Teacher learning and the development of inclusive practices and policies. *Research Papers in Education, 20,* 133–148.

Kalambouka, A., Farrell, P., Dyson, A., & Kaplan, I. (2005). The impact of population inclusivity in schools on student outcomes. In *Research Evidence in Education Library.* London: EPPI-Centre, Social Science Research Unit, Institute of Education, University of London.

Khan, F. (1998). Case study on special needs education in Pakistan. *European Journal of Special Needs Education, 13*(1), 98–101.

Klingner, J., Artiles, A., Kozleski, E. B., Harry, B., Zion, S., Tate, W., et al. (2005). Conceptual framework for addressing the disproportionate representation of culturally and linguistically diverse students in special education. *Educational Policy Analysis Archives, 13*(38). Retrieved September 9, 2005, from http://epaa.asu.edu/epaa/v13n38/

Klingner, J. K., & Vaughn, S. (2002). The changing roles and responsibilities of an LD Specialist. *Learning Disability Quarterly, 25,* 19–31.

Klingner, J. K., Vaughn, S., Hughes, M. T., Schumm, J. S., & Elbaum, B. (1998). Outcomes for students with and without learning disabilities in inclusive classrooms. *Learning Disabilities Research and Practice, 13,* 153–161.

Klingner, J. K., Vaughn, S., Schumm, J. S., Cohen, P., & Forgan, J. W. (1998). Inclusion or pull-out: Which do students prefer? *Journal of Learning Disabilities, 31,* 148–158.

Kozleski, E. B. (1991). An expectant delay procedure for teaching requests. *Augmentative and Alternative Communication, 7,* 11–19.

Kozleski, E. B., & Jackson, L. (1993). Taylor's story: Full inclusion in her neighborhood elementary school. *Exceptionality, 4,* 153–175.

Labaree, D. F. (1997). *How to succeed in school without really learning.* New Haven, CT: Yale University Press.

Lave, J. (1996). Teaching, as learning, in practice. *Mind, Culture, and Activity, 3,* 149–164.

Lave, J., & Wenger, E. (1991). *Situated learning: Legitimate peripheral participation.* New York: Cambridge University Press.

Lemke, J. L. (2000). Across the scales of time: Artifacts, activities, and meanings in ecosocial systems. *Mind, Culture, and Activity, 7,* 273–290.

Lipsky, D. K., & Gartner, A. (1996). Inclusion, school restructuring, and the remaking of American society. *Harvard Educational Review, 66,* 762–796.

Little, J. W. (2002). Locating learning in teachers' communities of practice. *Teaching and Teacher Education, 18,* 917–946.

MacMillan, D. L., Gresham, F. M., & Forness, S. R. (1996). Full inclusion: An empirical perspective. *Behavioral Disorders, 21*(2), 145–159.

Magiera, K., Smith, C., Zigmond, N., & Gebauer, K. (2006). Benefits of co-teaching in secondary mathematics classes. *Teaching Exceptional Children, 37,* 20–24.

Magiera, K., & Zigmond, N. (2005). Co-teaching in middle school classrooms under routine conditions: Does the instructional experience differ for students with disabilities in co-taught and solo-taught classes? *Learning Disabilities Research & Practice, 20,* 79–85.

Manset, G., & Semmel, M. (1997). Are inclusive programs for students with mild disabilities effective? A comparative review of model programs. *The Journal of Special Education, 31,* 155–180.

McMaster, K. L., Fuchs, D., & Fuchs, L. S. (2006). Research on peer-assisted learning strategies: The promise and limitation of peer-mediated instruction. *Reading & Writing Quarterly, 22,* 5–25.

Misra, A. (1999). Special education in India. In C. R. Reynolds & E. Fletcher-Janzen (Eds.), *Encyclopedia of special education* (pp. 934–938). New York: Wiley.

Nietupski, J., Hamre-Nietupski, S., Green, K., Varnum-Teeter, K., Twedt, B., LePara, D., et al. (1986). Self-initiated and sustained leisure activity participation by students with moderate/severe handicaps. *Education and Training of the Mentally Retarded, 21,* 259–264.

Nutbrough, C., & Clough, P. (2004). Inclusion and exclusion in the early years: Conversations with European educators. *European Journal of Special Needs Education, 19,* 301–315.

Orfield, G., & Eaton, S. E. (1996). *Dismantling desegregation: The quiet reversal of Brown v. Board of Education.* New York: New Press

Osgood, R. L. (2005). *The history of inclusion in the United States.* Washington, DC: Gallaudet University Press.

Palincsar, A. S., & Brown, A. L. (1984). Reciprocal teaching of comprehension fostering and comprehension monitoring activities. *Cognition and Instruction, 1,* 117–175.

Phillips, D. C., & Soltis, J. F. (2004). *Perspectives on learning.* New York: Teachers College Press.

Pugach, M. C., & Johnson, L. J. (1995). *Collaborative practitioners: Collaborative schools.* Denver, CO: Love Publishing Company.

Putnam, R. W. (1979). Special education-Some cross-national comparisons. *Comparative Education, 15*(1), 83–98.

Richardson, V., & Placier, P. (2001). Teacher change. In V. Richardson (Ed.), *Handbook of research on teaching* (4th ed.) (pp. 905–947). Washington, DC: AERA.

Rizvi, F., Engel, L., Nandyala, A., Ruthowski, D., & Sparks, J. (2005). *Globalization and recent shifts in educational policy in the Asia Pacific.* Paper prepared for UNESCO Asia Pacific Regional Bureau for Education, Bangkok, Thailand. Urbana-Champaign, IL: University of Illinois at Urbana-Champaign.

Rogoff, B. (2003). *The cultural nature of human development.* New York: Oxford University Press.

Salend, S. J., & Duhaney, L. M. (1999). The impact of inclusion on students with and without disabilities and their educators. *Remedial and Special Education, 20,* 114–126.

Sarason, S., & Doris, J. (1979). *Educational handicap, public policy, and social history: A broadened perspective on mental retardation.* New York: The Free Press.

Schumm, J. S., Moody, S. W., & Vaughn, S. (2000). Grouping for reading instruction: Does one size fit all? *Journal of Learning Disabilities, 33,* 477–488.

Scribner, S. (1985). Vygotsky's uses of history. In J. V. Wertsch (Ed.), *Culture, communication, and cognition* (pp. 119–145). New York: Cambridge University Press.

Scruggs, T. E., & Mastropieri, M. A. (1996). Teacher perceptions of mainstreaming/inclusion, 1958–1995: A research synthesis. *Exceptional Children 63,* 59–74.

Shanker, A. (1994–1995, December-January). Full inclusion is neither free nor appropriate. *Educational Leadership, 52,* 18–21.

Shipitsina, L., & Wallenberg, R. (1999). Special education in Russia. In C. R. Reynolds & E. Fletcher-Janzen (Eds.), *Encyclopedia of special education* (pp. 1575–1579). New York: Wiley.

Sigmon, S. B. (1983). The history and future of educational segregation. *Journal for Special Educators, 19*(4), 1–15.

Smith, A., & Kozleski, E. B. (2005). Witnessing Brown: Pursuit of an equity agenda in American education. *Remedial and Special Education, 26,* 270–280.

Smith, S. W. (1991). Individualized education programs (IEPs) in special education—from intent to acquiescence. *Exceptional Children, 57,* 6–14.

Stainback, S. B., & Stainback, W. C. (Eds.). (1996). *Inclusion: A guide for educators.* Baltimore, MD: Paul H. Brookes Publishing Co.

Strange, S. (1996). *The retreat of the state.* Cambridge, MA: Cambridge University Press.

Suárez-Orozco, M. M. (2001). Globalization, immigration, and education. *Harvard Educational Review, 71,* 345–364.

Swanson, H. L. (2001). Searching for the best model for instructing students with learning disabilities. *Focus on Exceptional Children, 34,* 1–15.

Swanson, H. L. (2006). Cross-sectional and incremental changes in working memory and mathematical problem-solving. *Journal of Educational Psychology, 98,* 265–281.

Tomlinson, S. (1982). *A sociology of special education.* London: Routledge Kegan Paul.

Tyack, D., & Cuban, L. (1995). *Tinkering toward utopia.* Cambridge, MA: Harvard University Press.

Tyack, D., & Hansot, E. (1990). *Learning together.* New Haven, CT: Yale University Press.

U.S. Office of Special Education and Rehabilitative Services. (2002). *Twenty-fourth annual report to Congress on the implementation of the Individuals with Disabilities Education Act.* Washington, DC: Author. Retrieved July 2, 2004, from http://www.ed.gov/about/reports/annual/osep/2002/index.html

United Nations Educational, Scientific, and Cultural Organization (UNESCO). (1994). *The Salamanca Statement and Framework for Action on Special Needs Education.* New York: Author. Retrieved August 26, 2006, from http://www.unesco.org/education/pdf/SALAMA_E.PDF

Vaughn, S., Elbaum, B. E., & Schumm, J. S. (1996). The effects of inclusion on the social functioning of students with learning disabilities. *Journal of Learning Disabilities, 29,* 598–608.

Vygotsky, L. S. (1978). *Mind in society.* Cambridge, MA: Harvard University Press.

Wagner, M., Newman, L., Cameto, R., & Levine, P. (2003). *Changes over time in the early postschool outcomes of youth with disabilities. A report from the National Longitudinal Transition Study-2 (NLTS2).* Menlo Park, CA: SRI International. Retrieved September 6, 2006, from www.nlts2.org/pdfs/str6_execsum.pdf

Walther-Thomas, C. (1997). Co-teaching experiences: The benefits and problems that teachers and principals report over time. *Journal of Learning Disabilities, 30,* 395–407.

Weatherley, R., & Lipsky, M. (1977). *Street-level bureaucrats and institutional innovation: Implementing special education reform in Massachusetts.* Cambridge, MA: Joint Center for Urban Studies of the Massachusetts Institute of Technology and Harvard University.

Weick, K. E. (1976). Educational organizations as loosely coupled systems. *Administrative Science Quarterly, 21*(1), 1–19.

Wenger, E. (1998). *Communities of practice.* New York: Cambridge University Press.

Wertsch, J. V. (1985). *Vygotsky and the social formation of mind.* Cambridge, MA: Harvard University Press.

Wilson, S., & Berne, J. (1999). Teacher learning and the acquisition of professional knowledge. *Review of Research in Education, 24,* 173–209.

Woll, B. (1999). Special education in the United Kingdom. In C. R. Reynolds & E. Fletcher-Janzen (Eds.), *Encyclopedia of special education* (pp. 1861–1864). New York: Wiley.

Yell, M. L., Rozalski, M. E., & Drasgow, E. (2001). Disciplining students with disabilities. *Focus on Exceptional Children, 33,* 1–20.

Zigmond, N., Jenkins, J., Fuchs, D., Deno, S., & Fuchs, L. (1995). When students fail to achieve satisfactorily—reply. *Phi Delta Kappan, 77,* 303–306.

Chapter 4

Validity in Educational Assessment

PAMELA A. MOSS
University of Michigan

BRIAN J. GIRARD
University of Michigan

LAURA C. HANIFORD
California State University, Fullerton

Teachers and other education professionals use assessments in different contexts: in classrooms, subject-matter departments, committees, and informal learning groups; in schools; in district, state, and federal education offices; on school boards, commissions, and legislatures; and so on. Professionals working in different contexts have different decisions to make, different sources of evidence, different resources for interpreting the available evidence, and different administrative constraints on their practice. Educational assessment should be able to support these professionals in developing interpretations, decisions, and actions that enhance students' learning. Validity refers to the soundness of those interpretations, decisions, or actions. A validity theory provides guidance about what it means to say that an interpretation, decision, or action is more or less sound; about the sorts of evidence, reasoning, and criteria by which soundness might be judged; and about how to develop more sound interpretations, decisions, and actions. In this chapter, we review three distinct theoretical discourses—educational measurement, hermeneutics, and sociocultural studies—to support the development of validity theory for the routine use of assessment by professionals working in complex, dynamic, and always partially unique educational environments.[1,2]

Like any theory, a validity theory can be construed as an intellectual framework or set of conceptual tools that shapes both our understanding and our actions. It illuminates some aspects of social phenomena for consideration and leaves others in the background. As Mislevy (2006) notes, different theories:

are . . . marked by what is attended to and how it is thought about; . . . by the kinds of problems they address, the solutions they can conceive, and the methods by which they proceed; by the "generative principles" (Greeno, 1989) through which experts come to reason in a domain. They are also marked by what is not emphasized, indeed what is ignored. (p. 269)

We represent different validity theories as conceptual tools that enable and constrain what we can understand about the social world and that shape and are shaped by the contexts in which they are used.

A validity theory can also be construed as the representation of an epistemology— a philosophical stance on the nature and justification of knowledge claims—which entails a philosophy of science. The most sustained, explicit effort to develop validity theory about learning assessment has occurred within the field of educational measurement. Validity theory in educational measurement has been, for the most part, grounded in the epistemological understandings of a naturalist or unified conception of social science, which "maintains that the social sciences should approach the study of social phenomena in the same ways that the natural sciences have approached the study of natural phenomena" (Martin & McIntyre, 1994, pp. xv–xvi). From this perspective, the primary goals of social science are nomological (law-like) or generalizable explanation or prediction. In contrast, those who take what is often called an "interpretive" approach to social science (Bohman, Hiley, & Shusterman, 1991; Flyvbjerg, 2001; Rabinow & Sullivan, 1987) argue that social phenomena differ from natural phenomena because they are meaningful to the actors involved.[3] Furthermore, meanings are seen as embedded in complex social contexts that shape (enable and constrain) what can be understood in ways that the actors involved may not perceive. From this perspective, a primary aim of social science is to understand what people mean and intend by what they say and do and to locate those understandings within the historical, cultural, institutional, and immediate situational contexts that shape them. We turn to interpretive social science for two additional sets of theoretical resources—hermeneutics and sociocultural studies—to complement, extend, and reframe validity theory in educational measurement, thus situating it within a broader field of epistemological possibilities.

In educational measurement, validity theories have been developed around the use of tests and other standardized forms of assessment.[4] Although validity has focused on interpretations or uses of test scores rather than on the test itself—and scores from a particular test can be interpreted and used in multiple ways—the conceptual architecture is tied to a particular standardized assessment and the circumscribed evidence it provides about student learning. The questions that can be addressed and the interpretations, decisions, and actions that can be supported by the validity evidence provided are similarly circumscribed.[5]

Yet, the problems, issues, and questions that education professionals face and the types of evidence they need to address them are not similarly circumscribed. In describing the "problems of teaching," Lampert (2001) uses the productive metaphor of a camera lens shifting focus and zooming in and out. This allows her to address: "the problems of practice that a teacher needs to work on in a particular moment . . . [along with] the problems of practice that are addressed in teaching a lesson or a unit or a year" (pp. 2–3). An analogy may be easily drawn to the problems or issues facing professionals in other contexts. Many of the problems are of the "what do I/we do next?" variety, albeit at different levels of scale.

What's needed is a flexible approach to validity that begins with the questions that are being asked; that can develop, analyze, and integrate multiple types of evidence at different levels of scale; that is dynamic so that questions, available evidence, and interpretations can evolve dialectically as inquirers learn from their inquiry; *and* that allows attention to the antecedents and anticipated and actual consequents of their interpretations, decisions and actions. [From here on, we will refer to interpretations, decisions, and action, which frequently entail each other in practice, as IDAs, unless we need to refer to them separately.]

We also need to recognize that not all IDAs should or can be subjected to an explicit reflection on or documentation of their validity; in fact, most IDAs fall into this category. Much that might be called assessment is simply a routine part of social interaction in a learning environment. Therefore, we need a set of conceptual tools that can be applied, explicitly when needed, but that can also provide actors with adequate information and rules of thumb to shape their daily practice. Validity theory should also speak to the meta-issue of how learning environments are resourced— with knowledgeable people, material and conceptual tools, norms and routines, and evolving information about learning—to support sound evidence-based IDAs when explicit inquiry is not possible. It should speak to the issues of how assessment supports the professionals' learning to support students' learning and one another's learning (Moss & Greeno, in press).

Finally, we must recognize that assessment practices do far more than provide information, they also shape people's understanding about what is important to learn, what learning is, and who learners are (Engeström, 2001; Lave, 1993). Thus, any validity theory needs to consider how assessment functions as part of—shaping and shaped by—the local learning environment and its learners. We draw on hermeneutics to suggest practices for warranting IDAs that integrate multiple types of evidence, that evolve as new evidence is brought to bear, and that illuminate the social forces that shape them. We draw on sociocultural studies to suggest types of evidence that might be considered in developing an IDA and to provide resources for analyzing complex and dynamic learning environments in which assessment practices function.

In the following sections, we review validity theories in educational measurement, paying particular attention to how the needs of and expectations for the local user of standardized assessments are considered in this literature. Next, we expand the conception of assessment, pointing to studies of assessment in use and to the implications for assessment in evolving conceptions of learning. Then, we turn to theoretical resources for validity theory that can be located within an interpretive approach to social science and that support the development of situated interpretations. We turn to hermeneutics and its potential for supporting/inquiring into the validity of IDAs in response to a range of educational issues, problems, or questions. We also turn to sociocultural studies and their potential for analyzing complex and dynamic learning environments and the interactions between them (such as when evidence and people cross boundaries between levels of the educational system). We use extended examples as transitions between sections to demonstrate the need for alternative theoretical resources and to illustrate the theoretical resources that precede or follow. The examples illuminate some of the issues involved in developing validity theory to support assessment (1) as it might be used *within* a focal learning environment (e.g., a classroom) by those faced with the decision of "what do we do next?"; (2) as it might be used *outside* the focal learning environment by others (e.g., administrators, other teachers, and policy makers) who are responsible for monitoring, supporting, or evaluating the focal learning environment; and (3) as it might be used by those who are seeking to learn about the design and support of learning environments and the assessment practices enacted within them. We close with an analytic overview of the sets of theories on which we have drawn and suggest next steps for research and practice.[6]

VALIDITY IN EDUCATIONAL MEASUREMENT

Validity theories in educational measurement have been developed, primarily, to evaluate *intended* interpretations and uses of scores on tests or other standardized forms of assessment. Scores summarize patterns or consistencies in performance.[7] The scores and their aggregates are interpreted and used to inform decisions and actions. Standardization allows a common validity inquiry to be developed and used across individuals and contexts for which the assessment was developed. Validity theories in educational measurement offer principles, practices, and types of evidence through which interpretations associated with scores (and their implications for decision and action) should be evaluated. Much of the evidence and rationale supporting the validity of the intended interpretation is developed before the first operational use of a test (although validity inquiry often continues) and assumptions are made about the meaningfulness and appropriateness of this validity evidence in similar contexts with similar individuals. Educational measurement validity theorists also routinely caution that assessment developers and users have the obligation to identify those cases where the common interpretation and validity inquiry do not hold.

In this section, we first provide a brief history of the validity concept in educational measurement as traced in seminal documents to set what follows in context and to provide background for readers new to the field.[8] Then, we present descriptions of two more current approaches to validity theory/practice: one we call validity theory as scientific inquiry (e.g., Cronbach, 1988, 1989; Messick, 1989) and one we call validity theory as practical argument (e.g., Kane, 2006; Mislevy, Almond, & Steinberg, 2003)—labels taken from language used by the theorists. Although these approaches can be seen as largely complementary from an epistemological perspective, with the latter evolving from the former, viewed from the perspective of conceptual tools there are differences that potentially hold substantial implications for shaping understanding and practice. Finally, we consider the relevance of validity theories in educational measurement for teachers, administrators, and other education professionals.

Developments in validity theory in educational measurement can be traced to successive editions of two seminal publications: (1) the *Standards for Educational and Psychological Testing* (Testing Standards) (as it is now called), jointly sponsored by the American Educational Research Association, the American Psychological Association, and the National Council on Measurement in Education (Testing Standards, for short), and (2) the "Validity Chapter" in *Educational Measurement,* sponsored by the National Council on Measurement in Education and the American Council on Education (Validity Chapter, for short).[9]

Each edition of the Testing Standards is drafted by a committee of measurement scholars jointly appointed by the sponsoring organizations. The Testing Standards are intended to provide specific guidelines to test developers and users about "criteria for the evaluation of tests, testing practices, and the effects of test use" (1999, p. 2) and to represent a current "consensus" about best practice within the measurement field.[10] The process of developing an edition generally takes multiple years as developing drafts are submitted to the sponsoring organizations and the field for review and comment. Five editions of the standards have been published—in 1954/1955, 1966, 1974, 1985, and 1999—under slightly different names.[11]

The Validity Chapters have served a somewhat different purpose. These chapters provide historical overviews of validity theories, typically situating them within the philosophies of social science from which they are derived, and provide elaborated statements of the authors' views about how validity should be represented and practiced. The authors are typically selected for their sustained and seminal contributions to validity theory by an editorial board. Although multiple drafts of the chapters are peer reviewed by selected scholars in the field, the chapters are expected to represent the individual authors' perspectives on validity. There have been four Validity Chapters written since 1950, by Edward E. Cureton (1951), Lee J. Cronbach (1971), Samuel Messick (1989), and Michael J. Kane (2006).

Educational Measurement Validity Theories: 1950–1989

In the first Validity Chapter, Cureton (1951) characterized validity as indicating "how well the test serves the purpose for which it is used" (p. 621). He operationalized validity in terms of the relationship between test scores and "criterion" scores, which reflected performance "on the actual task" (p. 622) the test is used to measure. He argued that "[s]ince a test can be used as an indicator or predictor of performance in any number of situations, it can have as many validities . . . as the number of different criteria with which it is correlated" (p. 625). The chapter is rich with largely hypothetical examples of how one might develop criterion measures for concepts as varied as generosity, kindness, typing, proficiency in flying, and success in medical practice or engineering, along with various educational aims, such as artistic appreciation, reasoning ability, and effective use of the English language.[12]

By the time the first edition of the Testing Standards was published in 1954, the concept of validity had been conceptualized in terms of different "aims" of testing, each associated with a different "type" of validity investigation (of which Cureton's criterion-related validity was only one). This conception of validity persisted in similar form through the first three editions of the Testing Standards (1954/1955,[13]

1966, and 1974). The authors of the 1966 Testing Standards characterized three aims: (1) determining "how an individual performs at present in a universe of situations the test situation is claimed to represent" (e.g., an achievement test), where "*content validity*" demonstrates "how well the test samples the class situations or subject matter about which conclusions are to be drawn"; (2) "forecasting an individual future standing or estimating an individual's present standing on some variable of particular significance" (as when a test of academic aptitude is used to predict grades) where "*criterion-related validity*" compares test scores with "one or more external variables considered to provide a direct measure of the characteristic or behavior in question"[14]; and (3) inferring "the degree to which the individual possess some hypothetical trait or quality (construct) . . . that cannot be observed directly" (such as intelligence or creativity) (p. 13), where "*construct validity*" involved "a combination of logical and empirical attack" to investigate what qualities a test measures (pp. 12–13).

The concept of construct validity, elaborated by Cronbach and Meehl (1955), was viewed at the time as an "indirect" method of validation to be used when no criterion variable or content domain could indicate the degree to which a test measured what it was intended to measure, although this conception of validity soon became central. As fleshed out in the 1966 Standards:

Essentially, studies of construct validity check on the theory underlying the test. The procedure involves three steps. First, the investigator inquires (sic): From this theory, what hypotheses may we make regarding the behavior of persons with high and low scores? Second, he gathers data to test these hypotheses. Third, in light of the evidence, he makes an inference as to whether the theory is adequate to explain the data collected. If the theory fails to account for the data, he should revise the test interpretation, reformulate the theory, or reject the theory altogether (American Psychological Association [APA], 1966, pp. 12–13).

In his 1971 Validity Chapter, Cronbach gave "construct validity" far more centrality in his general conception of validity than had the Standards. Although he maintained the relevance of the now-familiar three types of validity inquiry (content, construct, and criterion-related) as aspects of a validity inquiry, he likened validity research to the evaluation of a scientific theory as characterized in "construct validity," and he argued that most educational tests entailed constructs: "whenever one classifies situations, persons, or responses, he uses constructs" (p. 462).

The 1985 Testing Standards moved in this direction, articulating more prominently a unified conception of validity that draws on multiple types of evidence to evaluate the inferences and uses of test scores. The authors renamed the traditional three categories to emphasize their role as types of evidence (construct-, content-, and criterion-related *evidence*) rather than types of validity: "An ideal validation includes several types of evidence, which spans all three of the traditional categories" (p. 9).

The third Validity Chapter (Messick, 1989) represented the completion of the move to a unified conception of validity as scientific inquiry into score meaning as articulated in the description of construct validity. It also drew on Messick's earlier work to highlight the importance of understanding the value implications of score meaning and the consequences of test use as part of this research effort. Thus one can trace across the seminal documents an evolution in the consensus understanding of validity within the measurement field and the implications for what sort of evidence should be made available to enable sound interpretations and uses. Messick characterized this as a: "shift in emphasis from numerous specific criterion validities to a small number of validity types and finally to a unitary validity conception" (p. 18), which privileged the explanation of score meaning as the fundamental focus of validity.

Validity Theory as Scientific Inquiry

In the third edition of the Validity Chapter, Messick (1989) argued that validation "embraces all of the experimental, statistical, and philosophical means by which hypotheses and scientific theories are evaluated" (p. 14). He defined validity as: "an integrated evaluative judgment of the degree to which empirical evidence and theoretical rationales support the adequacy and appropriateness of inferences and actions based on test scores or other modes of assessment" (p. 14). Validation entails ascertaining: "the degree to which multiple lines of evidence are consonant with the inference, while establishing that alternative inferences are less well supported" (p. 13). It also entails: "appraisals of the relevance and utility of test scores for particular applied purposes and of the social consequences of using the scores for applied decision making" (p. 13).[15]

Drawing on accumulated scholarship in the field, Messick articulated general guiding principles and categories of evidence that he argued should be considered in validity inquiry: "Convergent" evidence indicates test scores are related to other measures of the same construct and to other variables they should relate to as predicted by the conceptual framework; "discriminant" evidence indicates that test scores are not unduly related to measures of other constructs. For instance,[16] within some conceptual frameworks, scores on a multiple-choice reading comprehension test might be expected to relate more closely (convergent evidence) to other measures of reading comprehension, perhaps using other more extended texts or response formats (e.g., retelling or thinking aloud). Conversely, test scores might be expected to relate less closely (discriminant evidence) to measures of the specific subject matter knowledge reflected in the reading passages on the test, indicating it is not primarily a measure of topic knowledge.

Construct validation is most efficiently guided by the testing of "plausible rival hypotheses," which suggest credible alternative explanations or meanings for the test score that are challenged and refuted by the evidence collected. Prominent rival hypotheses or threats to construct validity include "construct underrepresentation" and "construct-irrelevant variance." "Construct underrepresentation" refers to a test that is too narrow in that it fails to capture important aspects of the construct. "Construct-irrelevant variance" refers to a test that is too broad in that it requires capabilities irrelevant or extraneous to the proposed construct. Continuing with the previous example, a potential rival hypothesis to the claim that a test measures reading comprehension is that it depends unduly on knowledge of specialized vocabulary, thus reflecting "construct irrelevant variance." Another rival hypothesis might be that the test "underrepresents" the construct by focusing on literal recall to the exclusion of interpretation or by using only short reading passages that are not typical of those students encounter in or out of school. These rival hypotheses suggest studies that might be conducted as part of the construct validation effort.

Messick (1989) also offered readers a list of *sources of evidence* that he argued should be gathered in the process of validity research, acknowledging that different types of inferences may require different emphases in evidence:

We can [a] look at the content of the test in relation to the domain [about which inferences are to be drawn] . . . , [b] probe the ways in which individuals respond to items or tasks . . . , [c] examine relationships among responses to the tasks, items, or parts of the test, that is the internal structure of test responses . . . , [d] survey relationships of the test scores with other measures and background variables, that is, the test's external structure . . . , [e] investigate differences in these test processes and structures over time, across groups and settings, and in response to experimental interventions, [and] [f] trace the social consequences of interpreting and using the test scores in particular ways, scrutinizing not only the intended outcomes but also unintended side effects. (p. 16)

To evaluate the potential consequences of a test use, Messick suggested pitting the proposed use against alternative assessment techniques and alternative means of serving the same purpose, including the generalized alternative of not assessing at all. This juxtaposition of alternatives exposes: "the value assumptions of a construct theory and its more subtle links to ideology" (p. 62). Messick also suggested contrasting "multiple value perspectives," citing the example of different value perspectives underlying various selection systems (e.g., according to abilities, efforts, accomplishments, and needs). These contrasts provide opportunities for well-informed debate.

As Messick (1989) noted, construct validation rarely results in a summative decision about whether a given interpretation is justified. More typically, the outcomes of a given study or line of research result in the modification of the test, the construct, the conceptual framework surrounding the construct, or all three. Thus, construct validity is as much an aspect of test development as it is of test evaluation. Almost any information gathered in the process of developing and using an assessment is relevant to construct validity when it is evaluated against the theoretical rationale underlying the proposed interpretation. Messick also acknowledged the need to balance the never-ending aspect of this approach to validity inquiry alongside the need to make "the most responsible case to guide . . . current use of the test" (p. 13).

In her 1993 *Review of Research in Education* (RRE) review "Evaluating Testing Validity," Shepard raised two interrelated concerns about Messick's conception of validity as scientific inquiry. First, she worried about the implication that research into score meaning *precedes* consideration of test use, misdirecting the conceptualization of theoretical frameworks intended to guide validity evaluations. Second, she worried that this approach, taken together with the conceptualization of validity as a never-ending process, may give "the sense that the task is insurmountable" and allow "practitioners to think that a little bit of evidence of whatever type will suffice" (p. 429). She argued, "measurement specialists need a more straightforward means to prioritize validity questions. If a test is proposed for a particular use, a specific network of interrelations should be drawn focused on the proposed use" (p. 429). She proposed that validity evaluations be organized in response to the question "What does the testing practice claim to do?" She raised additional questions: "What are the arguments for and against the intended aims of the test? And, what does the test do in the system other than what it claims, for good or bad?" (p. 429). A major contribution of her chapter is the construction of extended validity cases to illustrate her theoretical perspective. She pointed to Cronbach's (1988, 1989) conception of validity as evaluation argument, with its ties to program evaluation, and to a seminal article by Michael Kane (1992) that fleshed out this perspective of validity as interpretive or practical argument. Although Kane's approach is consistent with Messick's, it draws our attention more explicitly to the chain of inferences needed to move from the specific performances on a particular test to the "target domain" about which we want to draw conclusions and the decisions those conclusions inform.

Validity as Practical Argument[17]

In his 2006 Validity Chapter, Kane criticized validity theory as being "quite abstract" and called for a more pragmatic approach to validation. He defined validation "as the process of evaluating the plausibility of proposed interpretations and uses" and validity "as the extent to which the evidence supports or refutes the proposed interpretations and uses" (p. 17). The same test score "may have several legitimate interpretations and may be used to make different kinds of decisions" (p. 29), each of which requires validation.

He conceptualized validation as employing *two kinds of argument:* (1) An *interpretive argument* lays out "the network of inferences and assumptions leading from the observed performances to the conclusions and decisions based on the performances" (p. 23). It provides the framework for the validity argument. (2) The *validity argument* draws on logical and empirical evidence to provide an evaluation of the overall coherence of the interpretive argument and the plausibility of each of its assumptions. Importantly, he noted that specifying an interpretive argument helps protect against inappropriate interpretations and uses by making gaps in the evidence harder to ignore. He noted, for instance:

The target domains of most interest in education are not restricted to test items or test-like tasks, although they may include this kind of formal performance as a subset. A person's level of literacy in a language depends on his or her ability to perform a variety of tasks in a variety of contexts, ranging from the casual reading of a magazine to the careful study of a textbook or technical manual. These performances can occur in a variety of locations and social situations . . . The match between the target domain and the measure of a trait is a central issue in developing a trait measure and in validating a trait interpretation. (2006, p. 31)

Kane (1992) described categories of inferences that appear regularly in interpretive arguments. The first three (scoring, generalization, and extrapolation) are involved in almost all interpretive arguments.[18]

- The scoring inference involves the assignment of a score to each person's performance. This might entail scoring a student's responses to individual problems and then combining them into a total score.
- The generalization inference extends the interpretation from the performances actually observed to the "universe of generalization" composed of performances on similar test-like tasks under similar circumstances.
- The extrapolation inference extends the interpretation again from the universe of generalization to the much broader "target domain" (trait) about which the test user wants to draw inferences.
- An implication inference extends the interpretation to include any claims or suggestions that might be associated with verbal descriptions of the test score.
- A decision inference links the test scores to any decisions or actions and the potential (intended and unintended) consequences associated with them.
- A theory-based inference extends the interpretations to the underlying mechanisms or relationships that account for the observed phenomena.
- Technical inferences involve the appropriateness of assumptions regarding technical issues, such as equating forms, scaling, and the fit of statistical models.

The details of the interpretive argument depend on "the specific interpretation being proposed, the population to which the interpretation is applied, the specific data collection procedures being used, and the context in which measurement occurs" (1992, p. 529). Interpretive arguments can involve a number of inferences, some of which can be taken for granted "unless special circumstances suggest otherwise" (e.g., that students can read the question) and some of which will need to be evaluated (e.g., that an achievement test covers a content domain, which, he notes, is almost always questionable) (2006, p. 23).

The validity argument provides an evaluation of the interpretive argument. It would: "begin with a review of the argument as a whole to determine if it makes sense" (2006, p. 25). Then it would proceed through an evaluation of each of the inferences, each one involving multiple types of evidence, "including expert judgment, empirical studies, the results of previous research, and value judgments" (2006, p. 25). He divided the process of validation into two stages, one that occurs during the development of a test (the development stage), where any weaknesses identified can lead to modification of the test or the interpretive argument, and one that occurs after a test is developed (the appraisal stage), which is intended to be far more critical. Although low-stakes tests may only entail evidence gathered during the development stage; high-stakes tests appropriately require a more extensive evaluation of the fully developed test in use.

Kane argued that interpretive arguments tend to rely on informal or "presumptive" reasoning (citing Toulmin, 1958): their claims "are always somewhat tentative, and often include explicit indications of their uncertainty" (2006, p. 27) (e.g., standard errors). If the interpretive argument survives all reasonable challenges, it can be accepted as provisionally valid with the understanding that new evidence may later undermine its credibility. He noted further that: "the generic form of the interpretive argument represents the proposed interpretations and uses of test scores. It is applied every time test results are used to draw conclusions or make decisions" (2006, p. 25), such that it does not have to be developed anew for each person. However, "even if the interpretive argument works well in most cases, it may fail in situations in which one or more of its assumptions fails to hold" (p. 25).[19] Thus, it falls on local interpreters/users of test-based information to determine the validity of the intended interpretation and use in the local circumstances.

Validity Inquiry and Local Users/Interpreters of Externally Developed Tests

The approaches to validity inquiry/argument described all focus on the *intended* interpretations and uses of test scores—the interpretations and uses that are "presumptively" valid across individuals and contexts. As Cronbach notes, however:

In the end, the responsibility for valid use of a test rests on the person who interprets it. The published research merely provides the interpreter with some facts and concepts. He has to combine these with his other knowledge about the persons he tests and the assignments or adjustment problems that confront them, to decide what interpretations are warranted. (1971, p. 445)

Those who develop and evaluate assessments "meet [their] responsibility through activities that clarify for a relevant community what a measurement means and the limitations of each interpretation" (Cronbach, 1988, p. 3). The Testing Standards have spoken directly to the issue of what test developers should provide in Technical and Users manuals to enable sound judgments by users. Although generally acknowledging the never-ending nature of validity research, they have spoken about what should be available before the first operational use of a test. The 1999 Testing Standards, drafted just after the publication of Kane's 1992 article and Messick's Validity Chapter, walked a middle ground between validity as scientific inquiry and validity as practical argument with the concept of "scientific argument": "Validation can be viewed as developing a scientifically sound validity argument to support the intended interpretation of test scores and their relevance to the proposed use" (p. 9).[20] Similar to Messick, the authors listed five sources of evidence that might inform validity arguments; these were evidence based on "test content," "response processes," "internal structure," "relations to other variables," and "consequences of testing" (pp. 11–16). The authors of the Testing Standards acknowledged the role of "professional judgment" in deciding what constellation of validity evidence is necessary for a particular interpretation and use, and the document is, consequently, less prescriptive than some would prefer (e.g., Messick, 1989) about what should be included in a scientifically sound validity argument.[21]

Numerous measurement theorists have noted the disjunction between the scholarly literature and the practice of validity research, at least as reflected in technical and interpretive manuals made available to users. Cronbach (1989) criticized test manuals for providing readers with a "do-it-yourself kit of disjoint facts" (p. 156)—where "validation consists not so much in questioning the proposed interpretation as in accumulating results consistent with it" (p. 152)—rather than incisive challenges to score meaning integrated into an overall validity argument. Messick (1989) and Shepard (1993) echoed similar concerns. Shepard (2006) pointed to the unfortunate tendency of test developers to match test items to standards without illuminating the ways in which tests do and do not cover the depth and breadth of learning implied in the standards, an issue that Kane's (2006) conception of validity directly confronts.

Since the 1974 edition, the Standards have also included one or more additional chapters aimed at uses of tests, including chapters on educational uses in 1985 and 1999. These chapters offer relevant elaborations on the general concepts in earlier chapters, sometimes specifying additional obligations for users. They also provide some limited guidelines about appropriate practice for users of assessment.

With respect to the expectation that users will interpret test scores in light of additional evidence about the individual case or context, the approaches to validity described have less to offer about how to warrant local interpretations. Advice provided in the 1999 Testing Standards is somewhat ad hoc (and circular):

When interpreting and using scores about individuals or groups of students, consideration of relevant collateral information can enhance the validity of the interpretations, by providing corroborating evidence or evidence that helps explain student performance. Test results can be influenced by multiple factors including institutional and individual factors such as the quality of education provided, students' exposure to education (e.g., through regular school attendance), and students' motivation to perform well on the test. (p. 141)

The only "standard"—or explicit obligation—offered with respect to the use of collateral information in the education chapter involves the situation when consequential decisions are made: "In educational settings, a decision or characterization that will have major impact on a student should not be made on the basis of a single test score. Other relevant information should be taken into account if it will enhance the overall validity of the decision" (p. 146).[22] Examples cited include school records, classroom observations, and parent input. Yet, approaches to validity described so far have little to offer about how to combine such situated evidence into a well-warranted interpretation or decision.

Validity Inquiry and the Local Assessment Developer

The approaches to validity research we described have also been assumed to be relevant to the local assessment developer, including classroom teachers, albeit with somewhat less relevance. The authors of the 1999 Testing Standards assert:

Although the Standards applies most directly to standardized measures generally recognized as "tests," . . . it may also be usefully applied in varying degrees to a broad range of less formal assessment techniques. Admittedly, it will generally not be possible to apply the Standards rigorously to . . . instructor-made tests that are used to evaluate student performance in education and training (p. 3).

The authors of the Standards assert further that the standards may have some relevance for even less formal and less standardized "aids to day-to-day evaluative decisions" (p. 3), although they acknowledge that "it would be overreaching to expect that the standards of educational and psychological testing be followed by those making such decisions" (p. 4).

In an extensive historical review of measurement textbooks intended for teachers from the 1940s through the 1990s and of the research literature in measurement on the preparation of teachers, Shepard (2006) concluded: "Measurement theorists, responsible for 'Tests and Measurements' courses for teachers, believed that teachers should be taught how to emulate the construction of standardized achievement tests as well as how to use a variety of standardized measures" (p. 625). She noted that there was little guidance "about how teachers were to make sense of assessment data so as to redesign instruction" (p. 625).[23] As we demonstrate in the next sections, the issues teachers, administrators, and other local users of assessment face are considerably broader that what that can be easily addressed within the conventional conceptions of validity and standardized forms of assessment.

Contributions of Educational Measurement Validity Theory to Educational Assessment

Our primary focus is on the conceptualization of validity theory for the routine use of assessment by professionals working within their own educational contexts. Validity theory in educational measurement contributes in numerous ways to this goal. Consistent with its heritage in a naturalist or unified approach to social science, validity theory in educational measurement supports the development and evaluation of interpretations based on standardized forms of assessment that are intended to be generalizable—meaningful and useful—across relevant individuals and contexts. Validity research is conducted, in part, to ascertain the extent to which such generalizations may be warranted. However, validity theory in educational measurement also acknowledges the presumptive nature of the intended interpretations, the importance of illuminating those cases where the intended interpretation is not viable, and the role of the local interpreter in deciding what interpretation is warranted in a particular case.[24]

For the developer or evaluator of assessments intended for large scale use, validity theory in educational measurement suggests what evidence and rationale should be made available to support local interpretations and uses (although several theorists have raised concerns about the disjunction between theory and practice). With validity as scientific inquiry, we see a primary emphasis on explaining what scores mean by situating them in a larger theoretical framework. Validity questions about the relevance of the test for serving particular purposes in particular types of contexts are seen to build on this base. With validity as practical argument, we see a pragmatic move to focus validity inquiry directly on the purposes for which a test is used (and, we would argue, the meaning implied in that use). The conceptual architecture provided by Kane (1992, 2006) illuminates the inferential steps an interpreter must take in moving from particular observations permitted by the test through the domain of test-like items to the target domain about which one wants to draw inferences (advice which echoes Cureton, 1951).[25] Although consistent with Messick's approach to validity, it draws our attention to a particular aspect of validity work and a kind of evidence that seems particularly crucial in drawing sound interpretations based on test scores.

Although validity theory in educational measurement has much less to say about the how one might support situated interpretations of test scores, it does point to some general principles that we will see reflected, as well, in interpretive approaches to social science, including the value of challenges to developing interpretations, multiple sources of evidence, attention to consequences, and, increasingly, extended cases of practice that both illustrate, and, as Mislevy noted (personal communication), contribute to validity theory.

EXPANDING CONCEPTIONS OF ASSESSMENT

Evolving conceptions of learning and studies of how evidence of learning is actually used are pushing our conceptions of what assessment is and what validity theory needs to accomplish. In this section, we illuminate a range of purposes and practices regarding the use of evidence of student learning that can or have been considered "assessment" to substantiate the need for an expanded conception of validity. To illustrate what validity theory needs to accomplish, we point to studies of assessment in use in schools, districts, and classrooms; then we consider, briefly, conceptions of learning and assessment from cognitive and sociocultural theorists; we close with an extended example of how evidence is used by one teacher to inform her practice (Lampert, 2001). These practices and perspectives point to the importance of being able to routinely address the validity of IDAs that draw on multiple types of evidence from the local environment and the importance of understanding how assessment functions in the social systems of which it is a part.

Use of Assessment in Context

A small but growing body of policy research on how evidence, including standardized assessment, is used to inform educational practice suggests a range of purposes and practices (e.g., Diamond & Spillane, 2004; Honig & Coburn, 2005; Kerr, Marsh, Ikemoto, Darilek, & Barney, 2006; Massel & Goertz, 2002; Young, 2006). Questions to which assessment information is put include those about professional development planning, curriculum and text-book adoption, targeting topics in need of improved instruction, developing more specific instructional plans for struggling students (as well as identifying them and monitoring their progress), setting new instructional goals and targets, and as a way to communicate with the community in general and parents in particular (Diamond & Spillane, 2004; Heritage & Yeagley, 2005; Kerr et al., 2006; Massel & Goertz, 2002; Supovitz & Klein, 2003). Serving these purposes frequently requires multiple types of evidence.

Ikemoto and Marsh (in press), reviewing evidence from surveys and interviews of teachers and administrators in 10 districts throughout four states, characterize both data types and data-driven analyses along a continuum from basic to complex (and they are careful to note that complex forms are not always better than basic forms). Data can vary along this axis, depending on several characteristics, including the time frame it represents (single point vs. trends), the amount and sources of data (single score or source vs. multiple types and sources), and whether it is readily available or collected for inquiry purposes. Similarly, data analysis and decision-making practices range from "basic" (e.g., decisions based directly on reported test scores, with minimal additional evidence or analyses) to somewhat more complex analyses of multiple types of evidence to what they call "inquiry focused" analysis, which involves the development of questions and evidence to address them. Other variations along this axis include whether the process is individual or collective, one-time or iterative, based on assumptions or empirical evidence, and using basic or expert knowledge.

Coburn and Talbert (2006), drawing on surveys, interviews, and observations within a single district, uncovered a range of beliefs about what constitutes high-quality evidence (from the range of assessments employed by the district) and how it should be used. For example, some teachers and administrators privileged the alignment of the test with the standards when considering the validity of the tests, whereas others believed that only instruments that allowed them to "see" the students' cognitive processes were warranted as valid. Some used summative assessment in the service of accountability practices (both internal and external), and others used formative assessments to aid in the placement of students in educational programs and to inform instructional design. As Coburn and Talbert explained, "Individuals' conceptions of valid evidence, of evidence use, and of high-quality research differed in part according to their location in the local education hierarchy. This pattern appears to stem from the fact that different positions carry different kinds of responsibilities that shape individuals' conceptions" (p. 482). These differences in practices of data use and conceptions of validity suggest that interpretations and uses are always, ultimately, situated in local contexts that influence their meaning and the consequences of their use.

Shepard (2006) provided a brief review of a limited literature within educational measurement on assessment use at the classroom level:

Several studies, focused initially on how standardized tests were used in classrooms, revealed the much greater importance for teachers' day-to-day decision-making of teacher-made tests, curriculum-embedded tests, and informal interactions and observations (Dorr-Bremme, 1983; Salmon-Cox, 1981; Yeh, Herman, & Rudner, 1981). From interview data, Dorr-Bremme (1983) concluded that teachers act as practical reasoners and as clinicians, orienting their assessment activities to the practical tasks they have to accomplish in everyday routines, such as 'deciding what to teach and how to teach it to students of different achievement levels; keeping track of how students are progressing and how they (the teachers) can appropriately adjust their teaching; and evaluating and grading students on their performance' (p. 3) [quotes in original]. (Shepard, 2006, pp. 625–626)

A multiyear, multiclassroom ethnographic study by Stiggins and Conklin (1992) (Stiggins 2001b, also cited by Shepard, 2006) revealed a similarly wide range of practices and purposes.

Teachers . . . must detect the needs of individual students and various groups of students, not just at one moment, but continuously, and not for just a few students, but for as many as 150. They use classroom assessments to clarify achievement expectations for their students. Teachers must compile evidence to inform such decisions as the assignment of grades and the identification (with justification) of students with special needs. They use assessment as a behavior control system or motivator, and to evaluate the effectiveness of their instructional interventions, among other uses. (Stiggins, 2001b, p. 9)

Stiggins noted that teachers used various formal and informal assessment methods, including those that relied on personal interaction with students, and many different means of communicating with students about their achievement that were more or less specific (e.g., descriptive or judgmental, narratives, or grades). He noted several variables that related to the "assessment environments" teachers created, including their knowledge of the subject matter, needs for structure and control and willingness to take risks, beliefs about their own role as teachers, and perceptions of their students' willingness and ability to learn.[26] Again we see the importance of being able to address the validity of IDAs that draw on multiple types of evidence, the complex ways in which assessment practices (and hence validity issues) can differ, and the importance of understanding how any assessment is situated in the local context.

Evolving Conceptions of Learning and the Implications for Assessment

Evolving conceptions of learning, especially those based in cognitive and sociocultural studies, have substantial implications for the practice of educational assessment. Although these two research discourses privilege different conceptions of learning, they also share much in common in their visions about the role assessment can and should play in a learning environment.

For instance, in "Knowing What Students Know," the National Research Council (NRC) (2001) called for an approach to assessment that would "be largely determined by a model of cognition and learning that describes how people represent knowledge and develop competence in the domain" (p. 178). They called for assessments that address learners' knowledge structures, metacognition, problem-solving strategies, progress along a domain specific developmental continuum, transfer of knowledge and skills to problems in multiple contexts, and communicative practices in the domain. Assessments, they argued, make students' thinking visible to teachers and themselves, allow timely and informative feedback to enable learning, and show students' progress along a domain-specific developmental continuum (pp. 3–5).[27]

Sociocultural studies of learning construe learning in the interaction between learners and their environments, including all the conceptual tools (such as languages), physical tools (such as computers or dictionaries), and other people, all of which serve as resources and constraints on learning (Gee, forthcoming).[28] Whereas the emphasis in cognitive studies of learning is on "the way knowledge is represented, organized, and processed in the mind" (NRC, 2001, p. 3), the emphasis in sociocultural studies of learning is on *participation* in a practice where the knowledge is meaningful and useful (Greeno, 2002; Greeno and Gresalfi, forthcoming).

Learning also entails becoming a person for whom—and a member of a community in which—such knowledge is meaningful and useful. Thus, as Lave and Wenger (1991) put it, "learning involves the construction of identities" (p. 53). One can take on different identities in different communities that offer different resources for learning. Focusing on classroom identities, Greeno (2002) articulated an important distinction between conceptual and interpersonal relations and the different positions afforded individuals. Interpersonal relations "involve attention to the ways individuals are entitled, expected, and obligated to act toward each other" (p. 3). Conceptual relations involve "attention to the ways that individuals, the class, and groups within the class are entitled, expected, and obligated to act in and toward the subject matter content of the class" (Greeno, 2002, pp. 3–4). Again, this suggests that evidence of learning entails evidence of the interaction between learners and their environment.

Caroline Gipps, in her 1999 RRE chapter on sociocultural perspectives on assessment, highlighted the implications sociocultural theories of learning have for the practice of assessment: ". . . the requirement is to assess process as well as product; the conception must be dynamic rather than static; and attention must be paid to the social and cultural context of both learning and assessment" (p. 375). This includes the local context, as well as the larger institutional and social contexts in which it is embedded which shape the IDAs of local actors. These are themes which, in somewhat different language, appear throughout multiple articulations of sociocultural and sociological approaches to assessment (Broadfoot, 1996; Delandshere, 2002; Filer, 2000; Gipps, 2002; Hickey & Zuiker, 2003; Lee, forthcoming; Mehan, forthcoming; Moss & Greeno, forthcoming; Moss, Pullin, Haertel, & Gee, 2005).[29] Put more simply, the goal is to assess what, why, and how students are learning (Engeström, 2001; National Academy of Education [NAE], 2005). This entails understanding the relationship between learners and their learning environment and the larger social systems within which learning is occurring.

The importance of "formative assessment," or "assessment for learning"[30] is prominently represented in both cognitive and sociocultural approaches to learning. Shepard (2006), drawing on both discourses, defined formative assessment as "assessment carried out during the instructional process for the purpose of improving teaching or learning" (p. 627). She included the following as examples of assessment tools: oral questioning of students, observation, written work products, oral presentations, interviews, projects, portfolios, tests, and quizzes. She noted that the strategies could be either formal, where students know they are being assessed, or informal, where assessment is done in the ongoing context of instruction (Shepard, 2006; Shepard et al., 2005). She argued that an equally important role for classroom assessment is evaluation of teaching, where teachers consider "which . . . practices are working and which are not, and what new strategies are needed" (2006, p. 634). The evaluation of teaching, she noted, asks about the adequacy of students' opportunities to learn. While acknowledging the institutional role of summative assessment for documenting achievement, she described some of the ways it can pose threats to the type of learning that formative assessment supports. She offered suggestions for using summative assessment in a way that is coherent and that supports the developing competence of students toward valued learning goals. These arguments point us to the importance of integrating multiple types of evidence about interactions among learners, teachers, and resources, including evidence of how assessment is shaping learning.

Delandshere (2002) and Moss and Greeno (forthcoming; Moss, 2003) suggested that a sociocultural approach to assessment challenges our conception of assessment as a distinct component of a learning environment.

> We are moving here from an educational practice of assessment where we have defined a priori what we are looking for, to an educational practice where we are participating in activities in which we formulate representations to better understand and transform the world around us. If our purpose is to understand and support learning and knowing and to make inferences about these phenomena, then it seems that the idea of inquiry—open, critical, and dialogic—rather than of assessment (as currently understood) would be more helpful. (Delandshere, 2002, p. 1475)

Further Expanding Our Conception of Assessment

Although traditional distinctions between formative and summative assessment, or between assessment and learning activities, can be useful, it is important to remember that they conglomerate features and reify the resulting practices in arbitrary ways. To illustrate the complexities of how evidence is used in classroom learning environments, we turn to the case of Magdalene Lampert's teaching practice. We draw on Lampert's (2001) book, *Teaching Problems and the Problems of Teaching*, in which she analyzes her practice throughout 1 year of teaching mathematics to a diverse group of fifth graders. Given the goals of this chapter, we read Lampert's work with the question of how she uses evidence of students' learning to inform her practice.[31]

Lampert's conception of learning mathematics involves a particular understanding of the content—what it means to do mathematics—and of the identities and positions this entails. Lampert's curriculum was organized around mathematical problems, both practical ones—"like figuring out prices and schedules," and intellectual ones, "like identifying the conditions that make it necessary to conclude that all of the numbers that are divisible by twenty-one are also divisible by seven" (p. 6). "In the course of working on problems," Lampert reports, "[students] investigated different solution strategies," "represented relationships graphically and symbolically," and "disagreed and defended their approaches and clarified their assumptions" (p. 5). A typical day in Lampert's classroom began with one or more problems on the board, which students copied into their notebooks, worked on alone or in small groups, and then presented and discussed their work as a whole class. "Learning in my class," she states, "was a matter of becoming convinced that your strategy and your answer are mathematically legitimate" (p. 6).

As Lampert notes, this conception of learning entails the development of an academic identity, of becoming someone "more inclined to study, to initiate the investigation of ideas, and to be identified as someone who will and can do what needs to be to done to learn in school" (p. 268). Her teaching thus involves "influencing students to be the kinds of persons who are academic resources for themselves and for one another" (p. 266). She notes how being able "to make a mistake [in front of ones peers], admit one has made it, and correct it" (p. 266) is an essential part of an academic character.

Just like her curriculum, Lampert's representation of her teaching—and the evidence it entails—is similarly organized around problems. As noted in the introduction, Lampert uses the productive metaphor of a camera lens shifting focus and zooming in and out to represent the questions that shape her practice. She also notes that multiple problems—sometimes with conflicting solutions—must be solved at once.

Throughout her text, we see how she uses evidence to address different types of problems: getting to know her students at the beginning of the year, planning lessons, making decisions about what to do next in her interactions with students, and taking stock of their accomplishments. We also see how the ways in which she (and her students) use evidence shapes the nature of learning in that classroom.

Much of the evidence Lampert uses is a naturally occurring part of the (written and oral) discourse of the classroom. Some of it (quizzes and student notebooks) involves naturally occurring written records of students' work; much of it is simply present in the ongoing classroom dialogue. To learn about her students' learning from examples of their work, she examines their solutions and the strategies they used to reach them. Problem by problem, she considers the variations in students' performance, the types of errors they have made, keeps informal records of these in her journal, and designs her lessons accordingly. Lampert's journal—a routine part of her teaching practice—serves as an important space for jotting down evidence of interactions she wants to remember and for analyzing the evidence she has available. We also see how evaluation of work—by Lampert *and* her students—is a routine part of classroom interaction. Everyone participates in the assessment of the solutions proposed to problems. At the beginning of the year, we see the way in which she attends to students' performance on last year's standardized test. Instructively, she does not report (or seem to consider) their scores. Rather, she examines their work in solving the problems and considers, as she does with their notebooks, the approaches they took, the sorts of errors they made, and what these indicate about the meaning they make of mathematics. We see, as well, one example of how Lampert reports to parents about their student's progress—a prose description of what they have accomplished and what they have to work on—which is intended to represent the complexity of their mathematical performance in ways that grades cannot. It is important to note that Lampert routinely attends to evidence with a particular problem or question in mind about *what to do next*. Thus, evidence is always considered in light of the question or issue it is addressing: what problems to use in tomorrow's lesson, which mathematical concepts to illustrate with a given problem, what students' likely approaches to a problem will be, which student to call on, how to respond to students' misunderstandings, how to support students' willingness to "study" and to question their own solutions, how to support students in being a resource for other students, how to communicate progress to students and their parents, and so on. Although we listed questions that seem to differentially emphasize the social and intellectual aspects of Lampert's classroom, we note (as does she) that all teaching moves always entail both sorts of problems. And the evidence she records and uses is both about students' evolving participation and identities and about how they solve problems.

It is also important to note that her attention to evidence in solving a teaching "problem" was routinely *situated* in the ongoing interaction of which it was a part, *cumulative* in the sense of drawing on other available evidence (fitting this piece of evidence into her evolving understanding of students' learning), and *anticipatory* in the sense of considering how her next move was likely to affect students' learning. Even the more formal quiz was evaluated in light of how it fit with other evidence of students' progress, how the social situation and other affordances/ constraints of the quiz were different from the routine classroom interaction, and, equally important, how her response was likely to affect student's sense of themselves as learners, their understanding of accomplishment, and their progress in her class. As her work with the quiz illustrates, her use of evidence always involved consideration of *how her practice, including her assessment practice, shaped students learning.*

What Expanding Conceptions of Assessment and Learning Suggest Validity Theory Needs to Accomplish

The theoretical perspectives and practices represented in this section illuminate the need for an expanded conception of validity to support the interpretive work in which teachers and other education professionals routinely engage. They show how evidence of learning is used to address different types of questions at different levels of scale; how many of these questions are fundamentally about what does and does not work to support learning and thus require evidence of the interaction between learners and their environment (including its assessment practices); how different conceptions of learning (e.g., evolving mental representations; evolving ways of participating in practice and the identities they entail) require different kinds of evidence of learning and opportunities to learn; how assessment practices range from discrete activities designated as assessment to ongoing ways of looking at the evidence available in the environment; how assessment practices always entail multiple interacting elements and function in complex systems that shape and are shaped by them. In short, the practice of assessment, and the IDAs it informs, are unavoidably situated in always partially unique contexts; a robust validity theory must be able to take these features into account.

VALIDITY THEORY AS SITUATED INQUIRY:
RESOURCES FROM INTERPRETIVE SOCIAL SCIENCE

In this section, we describe and illustrate two sets of theoretical resources to support situated validity inquiry, both drawn from a constellation of perspectives that can be located within an interpretive approach to social science. Our goal is to develop an understanding of validity that begins with the *questions* that are being asked; that can develop, analyze, and integrate multiple types of evidence at different levels of scale; that is dynamic in the sense that questions, available evidence, and interpretations can evolve dialectically as inquirers learn from their inquiry; that allows attention to the antecedents and anticipated and actual consequents of their IDAs; and that situates the assessment in the broader context in which it is used.[32]

First, we draw on the tradition of *hermeneutics* to highlight general principles that might be considered in developing, investigating, documenting, and challenging the validity of situated IDAs in response to questions about educational practice. These tools are useful when validity claims, whether formal or informal, need to be made explicit. Second, we draw on the tradition of *sociocultural studies* to provide general guidelines for analyzing interactive, dynamic, and multidimensional educational environments. Analytical perspectives in sociocultural studies illuminate evidence relevant to the development and validity of situated IDAs and to the ways in which assessment shapes and is shaped by the education environments in which it is practiced. These sets of tools can be used both informally by actors within a system to reflect on their practice or formally by actors within and outside a system to better understand its resources and constraints for inquiry and learning.

It is important to note that these frameworks provide analytical perspectives (Lave & Wenger, 1991) that operate at a general level, much as the concepts provided by the educational measurement approach to validity do. We intend them to suggest types of questions that might be asked within any specific validity inquiry, but we argue that validity inquiries are always situated within a particular social context and guided by the problem, issue, or question one is trying to address and the available resources (evidence, conceptual tools) for addressing it. This illuminates the crucial role that concrete examples play in any representation of validity inquiry (much as they do in this chapter).[33]

Hermeneutics[34]

When the validity of an IDA in response to a question needs to be made explicit, whether formally or informally, the philosophical tradition of hermeneutics provides a useful set of analytic concepts. Like educational measurement, it provides a theory and practice of interpretation; it suggests validity questions, practices, and criteria that have important analogs in a range of approaches to interpretive social science or "qualitative" research methods[35]; and debates across fault lines within the tradition of hermeneutics (and between hermeneutics and educational measurement) pose instructive alternatives for validity inquirers to consider. Both educational measurement and hermeneutics provide means of combining information across multiple pieces of evidence, of dealing with disabling biases that readers may bring, and of bringing principles, criteria, or standards into contact with cases. Differences in how they address these problems can be framed, in part, in terms of the role that predetermined methods play in the development of an interpretation. Thus, hermeneutics provides a generative and theoretically coherent set of tools—coherent in the sense of creating a common language through which differences can be illuminated—to support multidisciplinary work.

We provide first a general overview of the tradition of hermeneutics, illuminating analytical concepts that can guide the development and evaluation of IDAs in response to questions. Then we turn to a more concrete example to illustrate the analytical perspectives.

An Introduction to Hermeneutics

Hermeneutics is about the theory and practice of interpretation, about the bringing of understanding into language. It was originally conceptualized as a practice for understanding written texts; however, the perceived relevance of hermeneutics has grown to include the interpretation of any meaningful social phenomenon, including complex (multitexted) social phenomena, such as historical traditions (see Bleicher, 1980, and Ormiston & Schrift, 1990, for introductions). Thus, hermeneutics suggests principles and issues relevant to the validity of IDAs based on "texts" or "text analogues" at quite different levels of scale, from a turn of talk or short answer essay to a recorded conversation or a portfolio of work to multimedia records of an implemented lesson or discussion of a test score report to compilations of multimedia records from a classroom or professional learning environment over time to accumulated scholarship in a field such as psychometrics or hermeneutics—all of which, of course, can be situated in larger social, cultural, and historical contexts. We will use the word "text" throughout this section to refer to this broad range of social phenomena of potential interest.

At the most general level, hermeneutics characterizes an integrative approach to combining sources of evidence in developing an interpretation. In this approach, readers seek to understand the "whole" body of evidence in light of its parts and the parts in light of the whole. Interpretations are repeatedly tested against the available evidence, until each of the parts can be accounted for in a coherent interpretation of the whole (Bleicher, 1980; Ormiston & Schrift, 1990; Schmidt, 1995). This iterative process is referred to as the *hermeneutic circle*. As new sources of evidence are encountered, developed, and brought to bear, the hermeneutic circle expands, thus allowing a dynamic approach to interpretation.[36]

Approaches to hermeneutics differ, however, in their representation of the role of the reader or interpreter. Here, we contrast "methodological hermeneutics" (as reflected, for instance, in the work of E. D. Hirsch) with the philosophical hermeneutics of H. G. Gadamer, on which we draw most heavily. In "methodological" hermeneutics, the goal of the interpreter is to produce objective knowledge by grasp-ing the "correct" meaning of text.[37] Although the correct interpretation is typically associated with the intended meaning of the author of the text—a problematic cri-terion in the evaluative context of educational measurement—E. D. Hirsch (1976) argued that this methodology could be extended to evaluation. Hirsch conceived of evaluation as the accurate application of explicit criteria, a process that also assumed the author's intended meaning was not distorted. The role of the interpreter, in both cases, was to bracket or control any prejudices they might bring to arrive at the correct interpretation or evaluation.

Viewed from the perspective of H. G. Gadamer's *"philosophical" hermeneutics* (1987, 1994), the notion that a text has a correct meaning misunderstands understanding. Against this vision, Gadamer argues (following Heidegger) that: "There is no such thing as a fully transparent text" (Gadamer, 1981, p. 106), rather we always approach a text with *fore-conceptions, presuppositions, or prejudices* that are shaped by our history and that shape our understanding. Interpretations are unavoidably shaped by the lin-guistic and cultural resources the interpreter already possesses and by the nature of the questions the interpreter brings to the text (by why it draws the interpreter's attention in the first place and by what the interpreter infers the text to be). In fact, without such preunderstandings, we would not be able to understand at all.

Thus, for Gadamer, the hermeneutic circle can be characterized as representing a dual dialectic: one between the parts of the text and the whole, and one between the text and the readers' foreknowledge, preconceptions, or prejudices. However, if "unacknowledged presuppositions are always at work in our understanding" (1981, p. 111), if we need them to understand at all, then we must acknowledge that there are "legitimate prejudices" and ask "what distinguishes legitimate prejudices from the countless others which it is the undeniable task of critical reason to overcome?" (1994, p. 277). It is that question which under girds Gadamer's advice on devel-oping interpretations.

For Gadamer, interpretation is most productively conceived as a *conversation* between two partners who are trying to come to an understanding about the subject matter in question. Gadamer (1987, 1994) offers some quite specific suggestions for the participants in a hermeneutic conversation that he characterizes as having a "hermeneutical attitude" (1987). He expects that all partners in the dialogue are will-ing to risk their own prejudgments, to look for the coherence in what others are say-ing, and to believe that they have something to learn from the others. The "art" of conversation this requires is not the art of arguing against the other person but the art of "questioning" to bring out the *strengths* in the other's argument (1994, p. 367). Thus, "reaching an understanding . . . means that a **common language** must first be worked out in the conversation" through which we can express our understanding of the other without distortion (p. 379, italics ours). "The important thing," Gadamer (1994) tells us, "is to be aware of one's own bias, so that the text can present itself in all its otherness and thus assert its own truth against one's own meaning" (p. 269). Taylor (2002) suggests, following Gadamer, that better interpretations are those that are less superficial, less ethnocentric and distortive, and more comprehensive. Taylor notes two important senses of the comprehensiveness of accounts: (1) "depending on how much detail and coverage they offer of the object studied" and (2) "on their taking in and *making mutually comprehensible a wider band of perspectives*" (p. 288, italics ours). Thus philosophical hermeneutic practices are productively conceived as a "conversation" (Gadamer, 1994) between an interpreter and a text and among interpreters about the subject matter in question.

This perspective has implications for the way criteria or principles should be brought into contact with texts. Given the importance of allowing what we are interpreting to challenge our preconceptions, Gadamer argues "*the object itself* must determine the method of its own access" (1987, p. 93). As Gadamer suggests (1987), the hermeneutic process used in making a legal judgment exemplifies the hermeneutic process as a whole. He argues that:

The judge does not simply 'apply' fixed, determinate laws to particular situations. Rather the judge must interpret and appropriate precedents and law to each new, particular situation. It is by virtue of such considered judgment that the meaning of the law and the meaning of the particular case are codetermined. (p. 148)

This does not deny the value of general principles or criteria. It does, however, change our understanding of their status and role. It suggests that the case plays a role in the criteria that are applied, it acknowledges that the criteria take on additional meaning when they are applied to a case, and that, rather than serving as "a guide for action," they become "a guide for reflection" (Gadamer, 1981, p. 82). Also it points to the importance of analyzed *precedents* (previously decided cases) in preparing interpreters to respond to new cases. When formal documentation is needed—as with consequential interpretations—the representation can take the form of an extended text. Interpreters can develop and represent interpretations that are appropriate to the available evidence and can situate the interpretations within descriptions of the evidence on which they are based and the process through which they were created. Remaining questions and insufficiencies in evidence can also be represented. This sort of representation allows others to evaluate the validity of the interpretation for themselves.

The discussion of hermeneutics, so far, suggests principles and raises issues about the development of interpretations that might inform validity theory. (1) The hermeneutic circle represents an integrative, dynamic process where questions, evidence, and interpretations are iteratively elaborated and revised. This allows the development of unique interpretations in response to unique configurations of evidence. (2) Different theoretical approaches to hermeneutics provide alternative and partially competing perspectives on the role of a priori criteria and the stance that readers might take. These include: (a) seeking to develop the correct interpretation or application of a priori criteria or (b) allowing the text to codetermine the criteria through which it is evaluated. (3) Seeking challenges to preliminary interpretations, from other interpreters and the text, is a crucial means through which sound interpretations are developed. (4) Learning from precedents—interpreted texts—as well as from abstract principles plays a crucial role in developing sound interpretations. (5) Agreement between interpreters and text, and among interpreters, who have actively sought challenges to their preconceptions in the others' perspectives, is a criterion of a good interpretation.

Scholars of Critical Theory criticize Gadamer's philosophical hermeneutics for failing to acknowledge and address the limits of hermeneutic understanding and point us to what is often called "critical" or "depth" hermeneutics. Habermas argued that hermeneutic consciousness is "inadequate in the face of systematically distorted communication" (1990b, p. 253), which occurs when participants in a dialogue are influenced by social, political or economic forces of which they are unaware. This can result in a "false consensus." His proposed corrective can be seen to involve two major components.

First, he offered us a regulative ideal (that he acknowledged is rarely achieved in practice): Interpretations are only valid if they are reached because of the power of good reasons, if they are unaffected by coercion or the effects of unequal power, and if everyone has an equal chance to contribute to the dialogue (see, e.g., 1990c, pp. 88–89; 1993, p. 164).[38] Habermas noted that when interpretations or decisions are intended to regulate people's actions or access to resources, interpreters have an added obligation: in addition to the observational evidence, they should consider the "consequences and the side effects . . . [that it] . . . can be anticipated to have for the satisfaction of everyone's interests" (1990c, p. 65).

Second, Habermas (1990b) argued that what is needed is a critically enlightened or depth hermeneutic "that differentiates between insight and delusion" (p. 267) in the process of discourse. Here, the goal is to *explain* the text and the interpretations of it in terms of the conditions that produced them. Studies that do this can range from large-scale studies to microanalytic studies of interaction that seek to connect meaning/interpretation to the social structures that shaped it.

Thus, critical or depth hermeneutics highlights the role that readers from outside the interpretive community can play—bringing an alternative perspective that illuminates the values and theories taken for granted by those within the interpretive community, so that they may be self-consciously considered. However, Habermas (1990b) noted, "there is no validation of depth-hermeneutical interpretation outside of the self-reflection of all participants that is successfully achieved in a dialogue" (p. 270).

Again, the discussion suggests principles and raises issues about the development and evaluation of interpretations that contribute to validity theory. (1) Again we see the privileging of agreement or consensus as a criterion of a sound interpretation, although Gadamer criticized Habermas's ideal of uncoerced agreement as "empty" (1990, p. 293).[39] (2) The difference between the third-person explanatory discourse of depth hermeneutics and the first- and second-person dialogue of philosophical hermeneutics offers interpreters productive alternatives that may be dialectically engaged. (3) The principle of depth interpretation—outside critical analysis of the interpretation and the process through which it was achieved—is useful in illuminating the social influences that may be operating beneath the interpreters' consciousness. (4) Consideration of consequences is important, especially for interpretations that control people's actions or limit their access to society's goods.

Scholars of more pluralist approaches to hermeneutics criticize both Habermas and Gadamer for seeming to privilege agreement or consensus among interpreters and the texts they are interpreting as an important criterion for a good interpretation. These theorists suggest that the goal of a successful hermeneutic conversation is to understand and learn from our differences. As Hoy (1994) described it: "The hermeneutic model calls for enlarging one's interpretations and enriching them by holding them open to other interpretations" (p. 264). Although agreement may be a welcome side effect: "interpreters can believe that their understanding is reasonable and right without also believing that everyone else will or even should agree with them" (1994, p. 182). The point, suggested Warnke (1994), is for participants "to be sure their own interpretations are as compelling and inclusive as they can be" (p. 133). From this perspective, a hermeneutic interpretive conversation becomes "a way to clarify our disagreements" (Bernstein, 1992, p. 338; see Moss & Schutz, 2001, for a fuller discussion), and it is an opportunity for the interpreters' learning.

That said, there are times when consequential decisions need to be made and actions taken. Consequential decisions and actions bring an arbitrary closure to the process of interpretation, which is otherwise open to new evidence and perspectives. Also, consequential decisions typically do not permit multiple resolutions; they require that a single best course of action be determined and justified. Sometimes there are a priori limitations on the available courses of action (e.g., a selection or placement decision; a decision about certification or licensure); sometimes unique and complex resolutions can be constructed (e.g., in the design of learning opportunities for students or professionals; in funding decisions).

Hermeneutics raises numerous productive questions relevant to validity that might be asked about the process and outcome of decision making: (1) What criteria and evidence can be used in making a decision, and when, how, and by whom they should be determined (e.g., do they remain open during the decision-making process, such that new sources of evidence and criteria can be considered, or are they specified before the process begins)? (2) Who participates in the decision-making process, what roles do they play, what affordances and constraints does each have for influencing the decision, and what stances does each take vis-à-vis the evidence and one another? (3) What role should anticipation and evaluation of the consequences of the decision play? and (4) Should (and how should) the process be evaluated to illuminate potential problems about (a) how ambiguous or insufficient evidence is handled, (b) how disagreements are resolved, (c) how differences in power and status shapes participation, (d) how experience and knowledge—in general and about the local context—shape participation, and (e) how preconceptions, biases or ideologies are illuminated and addressed? We note that these questions might equally well be asked about standardized decision-making processes as developed in educational measurement and that the questions illuminate important differences in the procedures. They point to the ways in which validity, or soundness of IDAs, cannot be separated from issues of ethics and power to shape them and their consequences.

An Illustration of an Interpretive Practice Informed by Hermeneutics

To illustrate the meaning and potential of the sometimes competing principles outlined previously, we offer the following concrete example based on our own work with the use of teaching portfolios to inform licensure decisions (Haniford & Girard, 2006; Moss & Schutz, 2001; Moss et al., 2004; Moss, Coggshall, & Schutz, 2006; Schutz & Moss, 2004). Although the assessment systems with which we have been working have been guided largely by the principles of educational measurement, our validity research has drawn on hermeneutic practices to illuminate assumptions and consequences and to highlight potential problems of the more conventional practices.

We focus here on a special study where small groups comprising experienced math teachers, math teacher educators, and mathematicians were asked to review portfolios submitted by beginning secondary mathematics teachers with the question of whether these teachers should be granted a renewable license. The portfolios had originally been submitted by beginning teachers to their state's department of education—passing this standards-based portfolio assessment is required to convert an initial license to a renewable license. Teachers are asked to include the following kinds of evidence in their portfolios: a description of the classroom context, descriptions of a series of lessons with instructional artifacts (e.g., handouts, assignments); videotapes, student work, and reflections on two featured lessons; a cumulative evaluation of student learning with accompanying reflection; a focus on two students throughout the featured lessons and cumulative evaluation of learning; and analysis of teaching and professional growth. We asked our readers to try to reach a similar decision but without the constraints and supports of the state's assessment system (which specified criteria and features of the portfolio to which readers were allowed to attend). Thus, our readers had a circumscribed evidence base but were asked to evaluate the portfolios in terms of their own criteria. First, they wrote independent narrative evaluations of the portfolio, along with a justification for the decision they had made; then they came together to debate the decision for those portfolios on which they had disagreed. Readers can find our extended analysis in Moss, Coggshall, and Schutz (2006).

In both the discussion and the independent written interpretations provided by the readers, we see a dialectical process of reference to pieces of evidence that raised questions that caused them to seek additional pieces of evidence and so on. This led to interpretations qualified in the available evidence (and the acknowledgment where evidence seemed to be insufficient or ambiguous) and the request for additional information where questions could not be addressed. Consider, for instance, their discussion of the quality of teaching in two portfolios and the cues they drew on to evaluate it. In a portfolio from an advanced mathematics teacher, they considered that the teacher had designed lessons that went beyond the mathematics in the text book, that she was willing to let her students struggle with a difficult problem, that the mathematical discourse showed good "sensibility" for mathematical issues, that she was sometimes sloppy in her mathematical language, that one of the lessons ultimately failed to find solutions to the difficult problem that had been set, and that she was not able to articulate connections between her teaching and what students were learning. With a portfolio from a teacher of introductory algebra, they observed a teacher who was communicating clearly about the mathematics but working directly from the textbook, in what appeared as a procedural approach. They also noted that the teacher's description of his practice did not match the videotape and other artifacts available in the portfolio and that his reflections illuminated an emotional response to the students and his own teaching that seemed problematic (in that it did not seem to allow him to explore productive solutions to the problems he perceived).

Central, as well, to their determination of an ethical decision was their estimate of the teacher's potential. One way they attempted to estimate a candidate's potential was by seeking to understand more about the context in which the candidate was working and the type of support he or she had received: for instance, with both portfolios, they wondered about what and how they were required to teach, what opportunities for learning their preparation program had provided, whether their choices were shaped by what they perceived were the needs of the portfolio readers, and so on. In many cases, these were questions that could not be resolved with the available evidence. With both portfolios, they argued about different possible explanations for the performance, which might imply more or less potential. In addition to context, they looked for other cues to help determine the teachers' potential: what they had contributed to the curriculum they were teaching, whether their subject matter knowledge provided a sufficient base on which to build, whether they could analyze their teaching in a way that would lead to productive changes, and so on. Again, the evidence in the portfolio was typically insufficient (and the portfolio was not designed) to answer these questions.

The readers uniformly resisted the limited interpretations and consequences that were available to them within the state's system. As one reader noted: "[E]ven though we may give two different people a two level, the reasons for the 'two' [pass] are highly differentiated. . . . These people each have quite specific and particular kinds of problems and they differ from one case to another." For each of the portfolios that were debated, the readers concluded that the teachers needed additional professional development of various sorts (consistent with what would happen for second-year teachers who failed) but were unwilling to arrive at a failing decision (in case these were third-year teachers who would not be allowed to continue) because there was either promising or insufficient evidence to determine the teachers' potential. They worried about various potential collateral consequences of providing teachers with a score—that low scores would have a negative psychological effect, that the system may not have a sufficient number of teachers to staff its schools, that a passing score would send the message that no additional work needed to be done, or that a high score would encourage wealthy districts to skim off the best teachers. They could not find a comfortable decision within the options that the state provided. Instead of distinguishing between more and less effective teachers and determining who would be licensed and who would not—while providing some limited professional development—the expert readers argued that the *main* focus of a portfolio assessment process should be on professional development. Of course, the actual consequences of the decisions in terms of the issues the readers have raised are empirical questions about how the assessment practice functions within the larger system, which sociocultural studies will help address.

Clearly, the given example does not illuminate all of the principles that might be considered in developing an interpretation. However, it does illustrate a dialectical, dialogical process of developing questions, evidence, and interpretations in attempting to reach an ethical decision. It also points to the deeply situated nature of interpretations and their consequences. It suggests the importance of understanding multiple elements of the activity systems (1) in which the evidence was produced (e.g., the readers' questions about the context of the teachers preparation and work), (2) in which it is being evaluated (what enabled and constrained the readers' interpretations), and (3) in which its consequences will be experienced as part of validity inquiry. Again, sociocultural studies provide theoretical resources that address these issues directly.

A SOCIOCULTURAL FRAMEWORK FOR ANALYZING LEARNING ENVIRONMENTS[40]

The practice of assessment always happens within a particular activity system, community of practice, or learning environment. As illustrated by our previous discussion, questions about learning and about how assessment documents and supports (or impedes) learning entail an understanding of the entire activity system. In an earlier section, we focused briefly on sociocultural understandings of learning and their implication for assessment. Here, we focus on the rich potential of sociocultural studies for guiding analysis of complex activity systems or learning environments. We refer here to any activity system in which evidence is produced and used and to all the actors (including education professionals) who work and learn within them. We focus first on providing conceptual tools that are useful in analyzing a single "focal" activity system or learning environment. Then we turn to the situation where information crosses boundaries to and from an external activity system that is responsible for supporting and monitoring the focal activity systems. Our goals are to suggest (1) the range of sources of evidence that might be considered in supporting/challenging IDAs about learning, (2) analytical perspectives through which we might examine how assessment practices function in a learning environment, and (3) an approach to validity inquiry that examines the learning of the professionals who are using the assessments.

We use the term "sociocultural" to encompass a range of theoretical perspectives, which, as Lave (1993) described, share an interest in "relations among the person, activity, and situation, as they are given in social practice" (p. 7). We draw in particular on three sets of resources: cultural-historical activity theory (activity theory or CHAT, for short) (Engeström, 1987; Engeström, Miettinen, & Punämaki, 1999), the sociocultural theory of mediated action (Wertsch, 1998; Wertsch, Del Rio, & Alvarez, 1995), and a situated theory of learning (Lave, 1988; Lave & Wenger, 1991; Wenger, 1998).[41]

Elements of a Learning Environment, Community of Practice, or Activity System

As Wertsch (1998) described, "The goal of a sociocultural approach is to explicate the relationships between human action, on the one hand, and the cultural, institution, and historical situations in which this action occurs, on the other" (p. 24). Human action includes human cognition and much more: "Action may be external as well as internal, and it may be carried out by groups, both small and large, or by individuals" (1998, p. 23). Wertsch (1998) argued that we need to treat "mediated action" (p. 17) or "individual-operating-with-mediational-means" (p. 26) as a primary unit of analysis. Mediational means are both physical (e.g., texts, calculators, and measuring instruments) and symbolic (e.g., concepts, language systems, representational schemes, and standards). They include the cultural tools that a community inherits and adapts, as well as those they produce and evolve. Cultural tools "provide the link or bridge between the concrete actions carried out by individuals and groups, on the one hand, and cultural, institutional, and historical settings, on the other" (Wertsch et al., 1995, p. 21).

Others foreground the entire community of practice (Lave & Wenger, 1991) or activity system (Engeström, 1987, 1993, 2001), including conceptual and physical tools and other people as the unit of analysis. For Lave and Wenger, "a community of practice is a set of relations among persons, activity, and world, over time and in relation with other tangential and overlapping communities of practice" (p. 98). With Wertsch, they noted that tools or "artifacts—physical, linguistic, and symbolic" (p. 57) are particularly important because they carry a community's heritage. Artifacts and social structures "leave a historical trace . . . which constitute and reconstitute the practice over time" (pp. 57–58).

Similarly, for Engeström, an *activity system* builds on the concept of mediated activity (or individual acting with mediational means) to "explicate the societal and collaborative nature" of actions (1999, p. 30). Engeström depicted the components of an activity system as follows.

In the model, the **subject** refers to the individual or subgroup whose agency is chosen as the point of view in the analysis. The **object** refers to the "raw material" or "problem space" at which the activity is directed and which is molded or transformed into **outcomes** with the help of physical and symbolic, external and internal **tools** (mediating instruments and signs). The **community** comprises multiple individuals and/or subgroups who share the same general object. The **division of labor** refers to both the horizontal division of tasks between the members of the community and the vertical division of power and status. Finally the **rules** refer to the explicit and implicit regulations, norms and conventions that constrain actions and interactions within the activity system. (Engeström, 1993, p. 67; see also, Engeström, 1987, for a fuller explication)

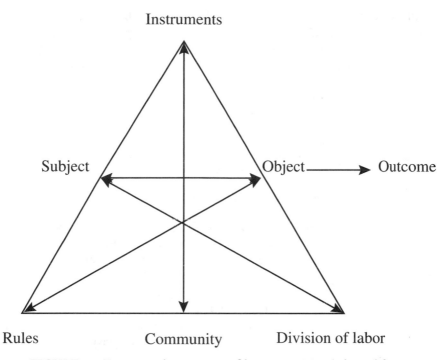

FIGURE 1   Engeström's structure of human activity (adapted from Engeström, 1993, p. 68).[42]

As Engeström noted, activity systems are neither static nor closed. They involve ongoing relationships among people and their world where the elements are continually reproduced and/or transformed. Thus, it is important to understand how an activity system has evolved over time, in terms of both its local history and the "global" history of the concepts, procedures, and tools it inherits (Engeström, 1999, p. 137). Indeed, from a sociocultural perspective, learning is perceived and understood in terms of evolving relationships among learners and the other elements of their learning environments (Lave & Wenger, 1991, p. 51). Transformations (or system-level learning) often happen when systems encounter contradictions, when new elements are introduced, or when alternative perspectives and practices are encountered. (The value of alternative perspectives and the challenges they raise is a theme encountered in educational measurement, as well as hermeneutic approaches to interpretation.)

A crucial element for our analysis is the understanding that *learning* is a central component of any activity system, whether or not explicitly intended to foster learning. Questions about what is being learned are equally relevant to activity systems where educational professionals work with one another as they are to classrooms. As Lave (1993) stated: "learning is an integral aspect of activity in and with the world at all times" (p. 8). It entails a dialectical relationship between experience and understanding. From this perspective, learning does not just happen as a response to teaching (where, they note what is learned may be quite different from what is intended to be taught); rather learning happens everywhere, all the time, as we participate in social (inter)action. A learning curriculum unfolds in opportunities for engagement in practice (Lave & Wenger, 1991, p. 57). Furthermore, learning always involves the "construction of identities":

In this view, learning only partly—and often incidentally—implies becoming able to be involved in new activities, to perform new tasks and functions, to master new understandings. Activities, tasks, functions, and understandings do not exist in isolation; they are part of broader systems of relations in which they have meaning. . . . Learning thus implies becoming a different person with respect to the possibilities enabled by these systems of relations. (Lave & Wenger, 1991, p. 53)

With respect to evidence use in *and outside* the classroom, this suggests we need to illuminate and analyze the "learning curriculum"—the opportunities for engagement in practice and the types of knowledgeable identities that different approaches to assessment afford teachers, administrators, policy makers, and other professionals, as well as students. Furthermore, we need to understand how people can learn when there is no explicit curriculum to point the way. Engeström's (1987, 2001) conception of "expansive learning," which characterizes the kind of learning that productive organizations engage in when "we must learn from new forms of activity that are not yet there" (2001, p. 138).

In analyzing an activity system, Engeström (1999) suggested, "it is fruitful to move from the analysis of individual actions to the analysis of their broader activity context and back again" (p. 32). Lave and Wenger (1991) suggested that the analysis of a community of practice would involve the following types of questions:

- about the sociocultural organization of space into places of activity and the circulation of knowledgeable skill;
- about the structure of access of learners to ongoing activity and the transparency of technology, social relations, and forms of activity;
- about the segmentation, distribution, and coordination of participation and the legitimacy of partial, increasing, changing participation within a community; [and]
- about its characteristic conflicts, interests, common meanings, and intersecting interpretations and the motivation of all persons vis-à-vis their changing participation and identities (pp. 55–56, paragraph marks and bullets inserted).

Lemke (2000), a frequent dialogue partner with our focal theorists, provided a useful elaboration for our conceptual toolkit, which focuses on levels of timescale in analyzing processes in dynamic "ecosocial" systems of interdependent processes. Lemke suggested that when analyzing ecosocial systems (of which the educational system is an example) there are two fundamental questions: "What processes, what kinds of change or doing, are characteristic of each relevant timescale of organization of the system/ network? and How are processes integrated across different timescales?" (p. 275). He suggested further that it is useful to analyze scale hierarchies in groups of three levels at once. For any given activity (happening or doing), this suggests the importance of looking at both what happens before and after and one level up and down in a hierarchical timescale.

For adjacent timescales it is also quite clear that the processes at the next lower timescale make possible the repeatable patternings of the next longer scale. . . . What is equally important, however, is that there is always also a higher level process already in place, already running on its own longer timescale, and this sets the context that constrains what is likely and what is socially appropriate at the next scale below. (p. 276)

For instance, the activity of the quiz in Lampert's classroom, which unfolds over a relatively short period of time, comprises a series of briefer interactions among the students, the instructions Lampert gives them to respond to, the responses they produce, the conceptual resources they use in responding, and Lampert's oral and written feedback on their responses. It is also situated in an implemented learning curriculum that gives students conceptual resources, roles, and responsibilities, and so on. It takes on meaning against this background.

These elements of an activity system are general analytic concepts that suggest questions to be asked about any group of people working together, with conceptual and physical tools, around an object. They are not intended, in and of themselves, as a description of a social reality. The full characterization of any particular activity system is typically constructed through empirical work involving observations, interviews, artifact analyses, and so on. It represents a generalized pattern that can be constructed, over time, from the study of particular (mediated) actions and interactions.

Thus, the conceptual tools we described call attention to people who take on different identities and positions (with respect to one another and the conceptual and physical tools); the conceptual and physical tools they inherit, adapt, or produce and use; the norms and routines in which they engage; the objects and intended outcomes that focus and motivate their actions; and the other communities of practice or activity systems with which they interact. They suggest that analysis of any happening must consider what happened before and after, the briefer happenings (e.g., actions and interactions) of which it is comprised, and the longer happenings of which it is a part.

Examples of Evidence Use in Different Activity Systems

To illustrate how tests and other sorts of evidence of learning and teaching have been incorporated into activity systems at the school level and how these practices might be analyzed with the types of resources described, we draw on examples from the work of James Spillane and colleagues with the Distributed Leadership Study. Although Spillane's focus was on "leadership practice," we can nevertheless read his work for how assessment and other evidence of teaching and learning function. The examples we cite involve the use of evidence from the classroom, of one sort or another, that crosses the classroom boundary to be used by teachers and administrators in school level activity systems (Diamond & Spillane, 2004; Spillane, 2006; Spillane, Halverson, & Diamond, 2001; Spillane, Diamond, & Halverson, 2004).

Distributed Leadership Study researchers examine how the relationship between leadership activities and teacher's classroom work is shaped by various institutional/ social structures in which they are embedded and by conceptual and material tools that mediate those relationships. *Material* resources or tools include artifacts such as students' tests and test scores, curriculum guides, text books, other printed materials, Internet and other technology resources, observation protocols, state and district standards, forms, and meeting agendas. These tools "mediate" (shape, enable, and constrain) leaders' actions; the sense leaders make of them in turn mediates the effect of the tool. Similarly, leadership practice is shaped by *conceptual* or *cultural* tools that leaders use to make sense of the ideas they encounter. These conceptual resources include "language, theories of action, and interpretive schema" that enable "intelligent social activity" (Spillane et al., 2001, p. 23): "even when a particular cognitive task is undertaken by an individual apparently *in solo,* the individual relies on various sociocultural artifacts, such as computational methods and language that are social in origin" (Spillane et al., 2001, p. 23, citing Wertsch).

Leadership activities occur within *institutional and social structures* that also shape them. These include structures (formal and informal relationships and routines) that have been developed within the school, such as subject matter or grade-level departments, faculty meetings or classroom observations, and time and space set aside for teachers to plan together or the lack of such opportunities. They also include the many external structures in which schools and their leaders are embedded, such as district and state education agencies, professional organizations, legislative requirements, school-community activities, and so on. These are all contexts and routines that bring people together in various configurations for various reasons. They shape the way leadership is practiced and how conceptual and material resources, such as tests and test scores, are used.

Distributed Leadership Study publications are rich with examples of how formal and informal evidence of teaching and learning is used by teachers and administrators in different social arrangements. Below we describe a series of vignettes, culled from this research agenda with 13 schools for 4 years, that draw on interviews, observations, and surveys.

Vignette 1: Teaching Observations

For instance, Spillane and colleagues (2004) describe how the instructional evaluation is carried out, interdependently, by the principal and assistant principal at one school:

The assistant principal, who maintains a friendly and supportive relationship with teachers, visits classrooms frequently and engages in formative evaluation by providing regular feedback to teachers on instructional issues. The principal, on the other hand, functions more as an authority figure and engages in summative evaluation. She visits the classrooms one to two times per year and makes final determinations on the quality of teachers' instructional practices. The assistant principal shares his learning with the principal, and the two use their collective observations to develop an understanding of teachers' instructional practices. (p. 17)

As the researchers noted, even though the two leaders appear to work separately, the evaluation practice at the school can only be understood by considering both practices. The same activities undertaken by either alone might amount to a different practice with different effects. To illustrate the importance of evaluation artifacts in the shaping of this activity, they invited readers to consider how the activity would differ based on two different protocols: focused on (1) a checklist of generic teaching processes (such as use of wait time and praise) or (2) questions about subject-specific practices, such as how mathematical tasks are represented or how students are required to justify their mathematical ideas. As they noted, these different forms draw observers' attention to different aspects of the teaching situation, and, thus, the leadership practice is likely to promote different kinds of teaching practice.

Vignette 2: Students' Writing as Evidence

For an example of how another source of evidence can shape leadership practice, the principal at one school engages in monthly reviews of writing folders from each classroom. The writing folders contain a sample of writing from each student in a teacher's classroom. The principal writes comments to the teacher on each folder and to each student. She keeps copies of her comments to the teachers in the file, monitors progress relevant to the comments in subsequent writing folders, and considers this in each teacher's summative evaluation at the end of the year. Interviews with teachers suggest how this leadership practice has shaped their teaching practice. One teacher reported, for instance, that she had switched her whole day around so her students got an hour for writing (Spillane, 2006). To illuminate the importance of different tools, Spillane asked his readers to consider what would have happened if the principal had decided to review teachers' lesson plans instead of their students' work.

In a contrasting example using students' written work (Spillane et al., 2004), a teacher leader and assistant principle held biweekly professional development meetings "to foster reflective dialogue" that would help teachers in facilitating writers' workshops in their reading classrooms. Teachers shared their accounts of how they enacted "Writer's Workshop," as well as examples of the stories their students had composed. Here the focus was on informal use of evidence to support collaborative learning among teachers to help improve their reading instruction. Again we see how differences in even one element of an activity system can shape the practice.

Vignette 3: External Test Scores as Evidence

Diamond and Spillane (2004) contrasted the use of test-based evidence in four schools, two that had been placed on probation and were at risk of being restructured and two that were relatively high performing on the district-mandated tests. They noted that leadership practices in all four schools showed evidence of attention to test scores, including prioritizing the subject areas and content covered and providing some form of explicit test-preparation activities for students. However, they observed important differences in how leaders from the different schools interpreted test-based information and used it to inform instruction. The high-performing schools used test results to both identify trends and focus attention on areas of specific need (p. 1164). At the probation schools, they saw less focus on instructional implications: "School leaders discussed the need to improve reading and mathematics and did speak in specific terms about subdimensions[43] of these subject areas but did not speak about specific instructional approaches and strategies as they did in the high performing schools" (p. 1165). Diamond and Spillane described probation school leaders working to manage the impression of outsiders, tending to focus more on the appearance of instructional innovation than substantive change. They also noted a tendency to "target" students and grade levels "to increase the number of students at or above cutoff points at benchmark grades" (p. 1155). They noted that in the higher performing schools: "the resources to enable data interpretation are higher" (p. 1165), staff work together to analyze the information provided to define specific instructional needs that provide a basis for instructional decisions, and they are, therefore, more likely to benefit from the information.

Thus, in the vignettes of leadership practices at these schools, we see examples of how formal and informal evidence of teaching and learning is used by teachers and administrators in different social arrangements. We see different types of evidence, different resources for interpreting them, different divisions of labor and positioning of adult learners, and different understandings of the appropriate outcome. Again, the vignettes point to the importance of understanding how assessment functions as part of a complex activity system.

Extending Our Analytic Framework to Include Assessments That Cross Boundaries

In this section, we focus on analytic questions that might be asked about evidence that crosses boundaries between activity systems either formally (systematically documented) or informally and with and without people to recontextualize it. Although this includes the large-scale student testing programs that states and districts use, it also includes the many (formal and informal) boundary crossings illustrated in the vignettes from the Distributed Leadership Project described previously. Thus, how evidence crosses boundaries varies on multiple dimensions, including the (1) types of evidence (narratives of practice, samples of student work, videotapes of classroom interaction, interviews and observations, and surveys, as well as standardized tests used by districts and states), (2) the extent to which the evidence is explicitly and systematically documented, (3) whether and how actors from the local context accompany the evidence into the new context and can thus recontextualize it, (4) the comprehensiveness of the representation of the local context (what is made visible and what remains in the background), (5) what norms and routines accompany the providing and interpretation of evidence, and (6) what roles the actors in the local and external contexts play in shaping the way in which practice is represented.

When evidence crosses boundaries, it brings far more than information: it entails sets of cultural tools, including artifacts, concepts, and often norms and routines, that mediate understanding and (inter)action in sending and receiving contexts. In the case of large-scale standardized assessments, for instance, the set of cultural tools includes artifacts, such as stated goals of the assessment, test forms, standards or domain descriptions, guidelines for evaluating performances, score reports, technical manuals, regulations for users; it includes concepts that represent what is important to learn and what counts as evidence of that learning; it includes expected practices (rules and norms), such as standardized administration formats, independent work; and it entails an implied division of labor (different roles for test developers, teachers, students, parents, administrators, policy makers, and others) in the construction and use of the information. In Greeno's terms (2002), it positions the different actors with differential authority, accountability, and agency for making decisions about how their practice is represented and how those representations should be interpreted and used. In short, it provides a partial vision of an activity system through which the assessment is enacted.

Therefore, it is important to remember that externally mandated tests are always interpreted and used in particular local contexts, which shape and are shaped by them. Depending on how they are implemented by the central authority—that is, what practices are required/expected to accompany them—and how they are taken up in the local context, they may involve more or less incentive to conform to their particular vision of learning. As Wertsch and colleagues (1995) note: "While cultural tools shape action, they do not determine it" (p. 22). Furthermore, when individuals use the tools in particular settings, both the tools and the setting [or activity system] are transformed (p. 26). Thus, "mediation is best thought of as a process involving the *potential* of cultural tools to shape action, on the one hand, and the unique use of these tools, on the other" (p. 22) (italics ours). As we have seen, the same tools can be taken up in different ways in different environments, to different effects. To the extent that externally mandated assessments are used across many local contexts, they can have a powerful and widespread effect, for better or worse (Bowker & Star, 1999; Jordan & Putz, 2004). Understanding this effect is an important element of validity inquiry, in no small part, because it shapes the learning that the assessments are intended to document.

The concept of a "boundary object" or "boundary infrastructure," developed by Star and colleagues (Bowker & Star, 1999; Star & Griesemer, 1989) provides additional theoretical resources for the analysis of assessments that cross boundaries. A boundary object is an object that inhabits multiple heterogeneous social worlds (or activity systems) and that enables communication and cooperation across these worlds. "Boundary infrastructures" involve "objects that cross larger levels of scale than boundary objects" (Bowker & Star, 1999, p. 287) as is typical with centrally mandated assessments. As they note, participants from different social worlds each "answers to a different set of audiences and pursues a different set of tasks" (p. 388) and "because . . . objects and methods mean different things in different worlds, actors are faced with the task of reconciling these meanings if they wish to cooperate" (p. 388). Furthermore, "unless they use coercion, each translator must maintain the integrity of the interests of the other audiences in order to retain them as allies" (Star & Griesemer, 1989, p. 389).

Thus, a boundary object is a particular kind of cultural tool that not only crosses boundaries of activity systems, such as mandated assessments, but also is plastic enough to adapt to local needs while maintaining a common identity across sites (Star & Griesemer, 1989, p. 393). It enables translation and, therefore, cooperation, but without coercion. A mandated assessment would function as a boundary object when actors in the local context are able to cooperate in providing necessary information to outsiders while maintaining a productive level of authority and agency over their own practice. Star and Griesemer note that the function of boundary objects cannot be understood from a single perspective. Rather, it requires an ecological analysis that examines both local (situated) and shared meanings, that traces the function of the boundary object across worlds and does not, therefore, privilege a single point of view:

> The major requirements, for such an ecological understanding of the path of rerepresentation, are thus: (1) How objects can inhabit multiple contexts at once, and have both local and shared meaning. (2) How people, who live in one community and draw their meanings from people and objects situated there, may communicate with those inhabiting another. (3) How relationships form between (1) and (2) above— how can we model the information ecology of people and things across multiple communities? (4) What range of solutions to these three questions is possible and what moral and political consequences attend each of them? (Bowker & Star, 1999, p. 293)

Thus, with externally mandated assessments, ideally and eventually, one would want to analyze (examples of) all the activity systems in which the assessment functions (how it shapes and is shaped by the local practice): this would include the activity systems through which the assessment was conceptualized, developed, mandated, and implemented; the school and classroom activity systems in which it is responded to, interpreted, and used; the activity systems involving administrators and policy makers at the district, state, and national levels; the activity systems of students' families and peer groups; the activity systems of professional organizations and teacher education institutions that attend to such information; and the "virtual" activity systems of members of the public who attend to evidence about how their educational systems are functioning.

Using Evidence That Crosses Boundaries: An Extended Example

The Data Wise inquiry model (Boudett, City, & Murnane, 2005), developed by researchers and graduate students at Harvard in conjunction with teachers and administrators in the Boston Public School system, provides a rich example of how externally mandated tests can be used as part of a local inquiry process. It illustrates, in our judgment, the potential for external tests to serve as boundary objects. The model consists of three basic phases (Prepare, Inquire, and Act), which are further subdivided into eight steps. In what follows, we summarize this process, highlighting the elements that represent concrete instantiations relevant to our argument.

The "Prepare" phase consists of building a foundation for data-driven inquiry in a school community by creating a community of adult learners. They note that school improvement efforts are likely to be more effective if responsibility for data interpretation is shared among school community members. Data Wise also suggests that the members must have "assessment literacy"—an understanding of how to read and interpret standardized test score reports. Although this can be initially supported by outsiders, such knowledge and capacity needs to become part of the larger community's repertoire.

As part of the initial phase, the Data Wise team suggested that schools create a "data inventory" of the types of data that are present in their system as a first step in the use of formal inquiry into school data. Examples of common data sources available in schools include standardized test results (including both state- and district-level tests), developmental reading assessments, observation surveys, running records, writing samples, unit assessments, other student background information (e.g., ethnicity and language proficiency), and attendance records. The inventory distinguishes between internal and external assessments (e.g., running records vs. state skill mastery tests), and then for each assessment suggests the following categories of information be included: content area, dates of collection, which students are assessed with it, who has access to the data, how it is currently used, and the potential for more effective uses (p. 15).

The next phase is "Inquire," which consists of three steps. First, schools must get a firm grip on the data that they have at their disposal already, which has been outlined in the data inventory discussed. Other types of data that might be developed include, for example, artifacts from classroom practice (such as class work and homework), student interviews, and teacher peer observations. Next is "Digging Into the Data," and it is at this interpretive phase that the advice provided becomes more clearly connected to our hermeneutic concepts. For example, Data Wise makes explicit the potential and value of data, like student work, to challenge teachers' assumptions, a key element of the hermeneutic process:

Examining student work helps to surface and challenge many assumptions—assumptions about what students can and cannot do, about which students can do what, and about why students are or are not able to do something. Challenging these assumptions is important for three reasons. First, you want the clearest understanding possible about the student learning problem, and assumptions often obscure this understanding by taking the place of evidence. Second, teachers fundamentally have to believe that students are capable of something different from the results of the current data. Otherwise, why bother putting any effort into helping students learn? And third, the solutions for the problem will require changes in what the faculty members do on a day-to-day basis. Making significant changes in what you do often requires changing what you believe. Opportunities for teachers to share their interpretations of student data provide occasions to address these fundamental beliefs about learning and teaching. (p. 88)

"Examining Instruction" is one of the explicit steps in the inquire phase, and attending to the particulars of the classroom is an important source of evidence for such inquiry. Accordingly, Data Wise places the examination of current practice at the heart of its investigation process.

Next, the Data Wise "Act" phase involves planning, action, and assessment. Of note is that in parallel with the development of an action plan is an emphasis on assessing the action, which creates a new corpus of data with which to start the inquiry cycle again. Furthermore, the criteria for success of the action plan may include both standardized assessments, as well as "home grown" measures determined by the inquiry team.

Like Data Wise, there are multiple projects that involve schools and districts in inquiry-based models of reform or organizational learning that combine many of the elements described above. Additional examples are listed in an endnote.[44] These models vary, instructively, in the types of evidence considered, the processes that surround its development and interpretation, the extent to which the evidence is comparable and aggregatable across contexts, the roles actors in local contexts play in representing their own practice to those to whom they are accountable, and so on.

We note that the focus of our examples has been on evidence use at the classroom, teacher community, and school level, although we argue that these analytical perspectives suggest categories of questions that might be asked of communities of practice or activity systems at different levels of the activity system.[45]

CONCLUSION

Our goal in this chapter has been to sketch and illustrate a constellation of theoretical perspectives that might be used to conceptualize the validity of evidence-based interpretations, decisions, and actions routinely made by teachers and other education professionals. We see this as a preliminary step in what we believe should be an ongoing multidisciplinary agenda of research and practice. The theoretical perspectives we have represented suggest categories of questions that might be asked about the use of evidence in any learning environment, including those in which education professionals are learning to support students' learning and one another's learning (Moss & Greeno, in press). We have pointed to examples of existing studies and representations of practice that might be situated within such an agenda. However, as these examples demonstrate, interpretations, decisions, and actions—even those based on standardized forms of assessment—are always situated in complex and partially unique learning environments, and judgments about their validity must be similarly situated. A robust validity theory and the research agenda through which it evolves must be able to consider the situated nature of IDAs.

The theoretical resources we have provided are intended to support formal inquiry, when the validity of an IDA is both explicit and documented; informal inquiry, when the validity of an IDA is explicitly considered; routine practice, when IDAs are enacted without explicit consideration of their validity (which draws attention to how the environment is resourced); and, of course, research into the practice of assessment in different learning environments. We have distinguished between routine inquiry, as it might be enacted within a focal learning environment (such as a classroom) and as it might be enacted in an external learning environment that is responsible to or for the focal learning environment (whether informally, as with a teacher study group, or formally, as with the accountability practices of school- or district-level adminis-trators). We have also considered questions that might be asked when evidence crosses boundaries between activity systems with and without people to recontextualize it.

We have drawn on three distinct theoretical discourses in conceptualizing valid-ity theory for these purposes: educational measurement, hermeneutics, and socio-cultural studies. These theoretical resources allow us to address (1) the soundness of particular IDAs about learning, (2) the resources of the activity systems in which they are developed and used, and (3) the opportunities for learning which different activity systems are providing their learners (students and professional educators). Within and across these theoretical discourses we see complementarities in serving the goals we have described, common understandings, and constructive disjunctions that illuminate taken-for-granted categories of thought and action for critical reflection (Bourdieu, 1991).

Educational measurement provides resources that are most directly useful when the goal is to develop a common validity argument, based on common sources of evidence and analyses, to support IDAs that are presumptively relevant across indi-viduals and contexts.[46] Hermeneutics provides resources that are crucial when unique, situated, and dynamic IDAs are developed based on multiple varied sources of evidence (including standardized assessments).[47] Sociocultural theories provide resources to assist in the analysis of complex activity systems, communities of practice, or learning environments. They suggest evidence that might be gathered in response to questions about learning and questions about how assessment (or any other aspect) functions interactively in a particular learning environment. They help illumi-nate the dialectical relationship between social structures (e.g., assessment and account-ability systems) and local practices (e.g., interactions among principals, teachers, and students or among school board members or legislators)—how each constructs, shapes, and/or challenges the other. Sociocultural studies provide a conception of educational assessment as inquiry (Delandshere, 2002) that focuses not just on what learners are learning, but also on how and why (Engeström, 2001), and that incorporates questions about what the inquirers—teachers and other education professionals—are themselves learning about supporting students' and one another's learning.

Common understandings about developing and evaluating sounder IDAs across these discourses include the importance of examining the processes through which IDAs are developed, seeking challenges to developing understandings in alterna-tive perspectives and practices, developing and studying concrete examples to both illustrate and extend current understandings, and examining the consequences of our decisions and actions as distinct from our intentions. Instructive disjunctions we have highlighted include different stances that inquirers might take (different relationships they might enact) with the people about whom they are inquiring and different perspectives on the appropriate role of methods or *a priori* decisions (about criteria, evidence, etc.) in inquiry. Although these discourses offer different conceptual tools—practices and perspectives—to inquirers, the alternatives, even when disjunctive, can be engaged dialectically to provide productive challenges to developing IDAs and conceptions of validity.

This constellation of theoretical perspectives relevant to validity theory holds important implications for actors who work in different communities of practice. Although we suggest sample implications here, we hope our arguments invite others who work in or with particular communities of practice to explore the implications in depth and to further develop and challenge the preliminary theoretical perspectives we have offered. For those who develop standards and curriculum frameworks intended to guide teaching, learning, and assessment, it is, perhaps, most important to provide rich descriptions and concrete examples that illustrate a full range of intended learning the standards or curriculum frameworks are intended to support. Furthermore, as an NAE panel suggested, providing access to multiple "coherent, professionally credible" standards discourages the assumption that there is "one best way to define and structure knowledge" (p. 24).

For developers of standardized assessments and those who mandate their use, it will be important to understand local users' needs and to provide them with information that will support them in making sound IDAs in their local contexts. This will include a well-specified content domain illustrated with concrete examples and, in the case where tests are intended to address standards or curriculum frameworks, explicit acknowledgment of what is not tested. Access to empirical studies that support and challenge these understandings of the tested domain will be important as well. This will allow users to consider what the mandated assessment makes visible, what is left in the background, and what the consequences of those choices are.

For teachers and those who support their preparation and development, it will be important to engage routinely in the kind of evidence-based inquiry described and to develop the norms and routines of professional practice that support critical, collaborative inquiry, and learning. For administrators, policy makers, and others who design educational environments, it will be important to consider as well how learning environments, including their own, are resourced and what opportunities they present for professional learning.

For researchers who are interested in assessment practice, there is important work to be done in studying the use of evidence by professionals working in particular contexts at all levels of the education system. What evidence do the education professionals working in these different learning environments need to know that students are learning and experiencing adequate opportunities to learn? What evidence do they need to know that the education professionals to/for whom they are responsible have the opportunities to learn and the resources necessary to support students' learning? How are the understandings and actions of education professionals shaped (enabled and constrained) by assessments and the routines that surround them? In short, the same types of questions that we have suggested should be asked of students' learning opportunities may equally well be asked of the learning opportunities available to educators. These will include questions about how assessment practices position them with varying authority, agency, and accountability (Greeno, 2002) and about the potential consequences of different choices. It is important to note that in raising these questions about analyzing learning environments, we have not directly addressed the question of the vision of learning that is guiding the learning environment. Our goals have been to raise questions that illuminate the "learning curriculum" (Lave & Wenger, 1991) and how the environment is functioning to support it and to highlight the critical importance of access to alternatives that illuminate the values and understandings that "we" in a given community take for granted.

The theoretical perspectives we have presented here suggest the importance of ongoing case study work to help in understanding how the always partially unique elements of any activity system interact to shape what is learned. To that end, it will be important to expand conceptions of generalizability (e.g., NRC, 2001), which support the application of generalized propositions to concrete situations, as educational measurement does, to incorporate the role that individual cases can play in developing useful knowledge. As we have argued (with theorists from each of the discourses we cite), general knowledge claims, when put to work, are always put to work in particular contexts, where evidence of how they shape and are shaped by local practice must be routinely considered. Expertise in complex professional domains does not develop only, or even primarily, through the acquisition of abstract concepts that can then be routinely applied (Beach, 1999; Bransford & Schwartz, 1999; NAE, 2005); rather, it develops through concrete experiences that allow us to develop increasingly sophisticated capabilities to respond to (learn from) the always partially unique features that each case represents.[48] Case studies not only illustrate general principles, but they also contribute to theory by expanding our experience and our ability to raise better questions about the next case.

A central principle of our approach to validity is that we learn by seeking out perspectives, practices, and social contexts that that are different from our own; such encounters make us aware of the categories of thought and actions we take for granted; allow us to imagine how things might be otherwise; and encourage us to reconsider our perspectives and practices in light of this knowledge. It is an approach that is intended as both critical and generative. We believe there is rich opportunity for dialogue, collaboration, and mutual learning across the discourses on which we've drawn. We hope that practitioners of other research discourses will find ways to bring their experience to bear in developing validity theory for the practice of educational assessment. It is through such encounters that we can "learn new forms of activity which are not yet there" (Engestrom, 2001, p. 138).

ACKNOWLEDGMENTS

One of the joys of working in the multidisciplinary field of educational research, and one of its greatest strengths, is the opportunity it provides to learn from colleagues who hold different perspectives. I (Pamela) have benefited from collaboration with scholars in each of the three research discourses on which we draw in this document. As we write, I am simultaneously working on a chapter with Jim Greeno on the implications of sociocultural theory for the practice assessment and opportunity to learn. The ideas in this chapter have been influenced in multiple ways by my conversations with Jim and the other members of Spencer's "Idea of Testing" Project: King Beach, Jim Gee, Carol Lee, Ed Haertel, Bob Mislevy, Bud Mehan, Fritz Mosher, Diana Pullin, and Lauren Young. Although the chapters serve somewhat different purposes, readers will find overlaps between them. Our section on hermeneutics is similarly influenced by my long-term collaboration with Aaron Schutz; readers will be able to trace many of the ideas presented here to Aaron's and my still-growing list of jointly authored publications. Jane Coggshall, Ray Pecheone, and Mark Wilson have contributed substantively to our work reported on the assessment of teaching. We are grateful to Judith Green, Jim Greeno, Allan Luke, Bob Mislevy, Annemarie Palincsar, Denis Phillips, and Aaron Schutz who generously provided comments on earlier drafts of this chapter. The Spencer Foundation has supported much of the work presented here, through an NAE/Spencer Fellowship, a major grant, and funds for the "Idea of Testing" conference series. We are deeply grateful for their support.

NOTES

[1] Although we distinguish among different theories of validity—different approaches to developing and evaluating interpretations, decisions, and actions—we also use the term "validity theory" to describe the conceptualization of such theories. Furthermore, we note that not all theorists on whose work we draw use the term "validity"; it is our description of the term, rather than the term itself, that guided our selection of theoretical resources.

[2] Our focus in this chapter is on education professionals and the communities of practice in which they work. We have not addressed equally important issues involving students and their parents/guardians as users of assessment.

[3] Readers should be cautioned that categories such as these always underrepresent or misrepresent the complexity of the issues involved. Within naturalist and interpretive conceptions of social science are diverse traditions, some of which represent distinct perspectives. Although the naturalist/interpretive cut foregrounds a particular set of issues—a particular set of commonalities within and differences across traditions—a different category scheme would rearrange allegiances among traditions.

[4] We will follow, initially, the *Standards for Educational and Psychological Testing's* (American Education Research Association [AERA], APA, National Council on Measurement in Education [NCME], 1999) distinction between tests and assessments. The authors of the Standards define a test as: "an evaluative device or procedure in which a sample of an examinee's behavior in a specified domain is obtained and subsequently evaluated and scored using a standardized process" (p. 3). They characterize "assessment" as a broader term, "commonly referring to a process that integrates test information with information from other sources (e.g., information from the individual's social, educational, employment, or psychological history)" (p. 3). Our definition of assessment, however, is broader still, and refers to process of inquiry that integrates multiple sources of evidence, whether or not test based, to support an interpretation, decision, or action.

[5] In understanding the potential relevance of validity theories in educational measurement for education professionals, it is important not to conflate standardization with multiple choice

tests. Essentially, standardization refers to the aspects of an assessment that are *common* across individuals and contexts. Although standardized assessments include multiple-choice tests, they can also include complex performance assessments, such as multimedia portfolios or observations systems, where features such as guidelines, criteria, and procedures for combining evidence are standardized.

[6] A chapter by Phillips (in press) productively addresses many of the same issues our RRE chapter addresses.

[7] The word "scores" is used generically to refer to both numbers and predetermined categories (such as diagnoses) assigned to individuals' performances.

[8] Extended historical overviews can be found in Kane (2001, 2006), Messick (1989), Moss (1992, 1995), and Shepard (1993).

[9] Both the Testing Standards and the *Educational Measurement* volume contain multiple chapters about aspects of test development and evaluation (such as sections on test development, reliability and errors of measurement, scaling and equating, and fairness or absence of bias), which are relevant to the overall judgment that validity entails.

[10] Earlier editions of the Standards framed the purpose somewhat differently. For instance, "the essential principle underlying this document is that a test manual should carry information sufficient to enable any qualified user to make sound judgments regarding the usefulness and interpretation of the test" (1966, p. 2).

[11] See APA, 1954; AERA & National Council on Measurements Used in Education (NCMUE), 1955; APA, 1966; APA, 1974; AERA, APA, & NCME, 1985; and AERA, APA, NCME, 1999. Although not apparent from the name of the copyright holder, AERA, APA, and NCME jointly sponsored all five editions.

[12] He cautioned that general concepts such as these must be specified in terms of observable acts or behaviors of persons. Cureton noted that that some criteria, frequently criteria involved in educational objectives, may not be directly observable, because they "refer to acts which will occur (or fail to occur) long after the end of formal schooling" (p. 653) and they are stated in terms of generalities that make it hard to specify observable acts. It becomes necessary, therefore, to define more immediate objectives and intermediate criteria. However, he cautioned: "All too often the immediate objectives are derived by backward reasoning from traditional elements of the curriculum:. . . . If the arbitrary immediate objectives lack ultimate relevance, such tests retard educational progress instead of stimulating it" (p. 654).

[13] Actually, two versions were published, one on "Technical Recommendations for Psychological Tests and Diagnostic Techniques" (APA, 1954) and one on "Technical Recommendations for Achievement Tests" (AERA and NCMUE, 1955), although the conception of validity was essentially the same in both documents, so we focus on the 1954 standards.

[14] The 1954 edition had listed predictive validity and concurrent validity as two distinct types of validity distinguished by whether the criterion measure was administered at the same time as the test in question or at some future time.

[15] Messick (1989) depicted his conception of validity by crossing two dimensions or "facets" of validity inquiry. One facet, focusing on the function or outcome of testing, distinguishes between interpretation and use. The other facet, focusing on the justification for testing, distinguishes between appraisal of evidence and appraisal of consequence.

	Test Interpretation	Test Use
Evidential basis	Construct validity	Construct validity + relevance/utility
Consequential basis	Value implications	Social consequences

Messick noted that this is a progressive matrix, with construct validity appearing in every cell. This highlights construct validity as the foundation or "integrating force" for validity inquiry (p. 20).

[16] The example we used to illustrate these concepts is not taken directly from Messick's text.

[17] Language of title is taken from Kane (1992).

[18] In 1992, he summarized categories of inferences in separate section of his article—and although not separately named as of general use in 2006, the same inferences appear repeatedly in different interpretative arguments: observation (or scoring), generalization, extrapolation, theory-based inferences, decisions, and technical inferences.

[19] Mislevy (2006; Mislevy, Almond, & Steinberg, 2003), who, like Kane, draws on Toulmin's (1958) argument analysis provides an alternative set of conceptual resources for validity theory within what we are calling validity inquiry as practical argument. We should note that both Kane and Mislevy argue that their general analysis of a validity argument, based in Toulmin's framework, is relevant to unique interpretations based on nonstandardized assessments as in a conversation between a teacher and a student. Kane characterizes Toulmin's general model for evaluating informal arguments as containing six elements. (1) a *claim* or conclusion, (2) data, (3) a warrant specifying the rule for going from the data to the claim, (4) backing or evidence to justify the warrant, (5) a qualifier that indicates the strength of the claim, and (6) conditions of rebuttal indicating the circumstances under which the warrant would not apply. Each inference in the overall interpretive argument becomes a claim that must be warranted. Mislevy's characterization varies slightly. Readers will see both themes and variations between these conceptions and those we draw from hermeneutics below.

[20] The senior author was a member of the committee that drafted the 1999 Testing Standards.

[21] Although the standards are somewhat more specific about evidence needed with respect to particular technical issues (reliability and errors of measurement, scaling and equating), they are less direct about validity evidence more directly related to score meaning. Of the 24 standards in the Validity Chapter, only a few are framed as general obligations for all test users; others are conditioned on the type of evidence the developer may have deemed necessary. For example, "When the validation rests in part on the appropriateness of test content, the procedures followed in specifying and generating test content should be described . . ." (p. 18).

[22] Of course, the import of this statement depends on your conception of validity.

[23] She cited two recent textbooks (Stiggins, 2001a, and Taylor & Nolen, 2005) and a recent issue of *Educational Measurement: Issues and Practice* edited by Susan Brookhart (Brookhart, 2003) as providing theory and practice that begin to address teachers' needs more directly.

[24] Of course, different policies of test use, as distinct from educational measurement validity theory, give differential attention to considering whether an individual case fits within the intended interpretation. For advice about appropriate uses of standardized tests, see AERA et al., 1999; Koretz & Hamilton, 2006; Herman & Haertel, 2005.

[25] Mislevy et al., 2003 accomplish a similar purpose and provide an extended example from the domain of second language testing.

[26] They cited, as well, purposes for which students and parents used assessment, including for students "deciding whether they were capable of learning" and whether it was worth trying, and for parents, "when to reward and punish, how to allocate family resources, and whether to seek additional help" (p. 9).

[27] The report contains multiple brief examples in every chapter to illustrate the committee's recommendations. Examples of assessments that were intended as at least partially consistent with the vision of assessment found in *Knowing What Students Know* can be found in two volumes edited by committee member Mark Wilson (2004, Wilson & Bertenthal, 2006), and a Web site developed by committee co-chair James Pellegrino is http://aim.psch.uic.edu/.

Subsequent articles by committee member Bob Mislevy and colleagues (e.g., Mislevy et al., 2003) offer extended advice for building a validity argument, within the practical argument framework, that can support assessment involving complex forms of evidence and dynamic interpretations and, Mislevy argues, multiple visions of learning.

[28] Many, but not all, sociocultural approaches to learning and assessment trace their roots in part to the work of Vygotsky and his arguments for the role of social interaction in learning and

the notion that social interaction precedes mental representations: "Every function in the child's cultural development appears twice: first, on the social level, and later, on the individual level; first, between people (interpsychological) and then inside the child (intrapsychological). This applies equally to voluntary attention, to logical memory, and to the formation of concepts. All the higher functions originate as actual relationships between individuals" (p. 57). Wertsch (1995) further notes that Vygotsky did not, himself, use the word, sociocultural.

[29] Examples of more standardized approaches to assessment have been proffered as consistent with a sociocultural approach to assessment. With dynamic assessment (e.g., Magnusson, Templin, & Boyle, 1997), the assessment is designed to scaffold the learner's performance, providing whatever social support is necessary to complete the task successfully. The performance is evaluated of the extent of social support the learner needs to be successful. Hickey and Zuiker (2003) provide multiple examples of group interactions, typically video recorded, that are evaluated for various criteria of participation. They argue that these studies of interaction might be used, dialectically, with more traditional approaches to assessment and with in depth ethnographic research into a learning environment. Mislevy (forthcoming), drawing on his Evidence Centered Design approach to large-scale assessment consistent with sociocultural perspective, points to the portfolio assessments used in AP Studio Art (see also Myford & Mislevy, 1995). The AP Studio Art examples allows substantial flexibility for students to present a coherent series of pieces that represents their own areas and themes of specialization, which are then centrally scored with a standardized rubric. As such, he argues, it takes context and students into account.

[30] As Shepard (2006) noted, "assessment for learning" was a term coined by the Assessment Reform Group of the British Educational Research Association.

[31] This description is excerpted from an extended case study based on Lampert (2001) in Moss and Greeno (forthcoming).

[32] Numerous scholars in educational measurement and assessment have pointed to interpretive research traditions for supporting the validity interpretations based on nonstandardized forms of evidence, especially in the context of classroom assessment (Delandshere, 2002; Gipps, 1999, 2002; Kane, 2006; Mislevy, 2006, in press; Moss et al., 2003; Shepard, 2001, 2006).

[33] The importance of concrete examples or cases of practice has been highlighted by theorists from each of the traditions on which we draw (e.g., Shepard, 1993; Gadamer, 1994; Lave & Wenger, 1991).

[34] This section draws on Moss, 2005; Moss and Schutz, 2001; Moss, Coggshall, and Schutz, 2006.

[35] It is beyond the scope of this review to draw the connections between hermeneutics and other characterization of validity within "interpretive" or "qualitative" research. Interested readers might consider, for instance, the chapters on qualitative research in the two recent editions of the *Handbook for Research on Teaching* (Erickson, 1986; Lather 2004) to see the extent to which it is possible to develop an interpretation of the differences in these approaches in the language developed here.

[36] Such interpretations can incorporate results from standardized tests and benefit from the research that presumptively supports them, contextualized, as educational measurement validity theory suggests, in locally relevant evidence.

[37] As characterized by Ormiston and Schrift (1990), the correct meaning was typically conceptualized as the original intent of the author (Schleiermacher) or as the events or objects experienced by the author (Dilthey). Betti (1990) and Hirsch (1976) provide more recent arguments for this approach to hermeneutics. (Note copyright dates do not reflect chronology.)

[38] In his earlier work, Habermas (1984) called this the "ideal speech situation," although he has since abandoned this label because of the misinterpretations it provoked (1993, pp. 163–164).

[39] The debate between Gadamer (1990) and Habermas (1990a) about the ideal speech situation and the role of explanatory discourse is instructive and offers interpreters alternative stances (see Ormiston & Schrift, 1990). Gadamer worried that Habermas's emphasis on rationally

motivated consensus is a "fantastic overestimation of reason by comparison to the affections that motivate the human mind" (1994, p. 567). Gadamer also worried that the move to explanatory discourse or depth hermeneutics, as Habermas framed it, signals a failure in conversation—instead of talking with the other person, we are talking about them, and we can no longer "be reached" by the text. That this may happen does not absolve us of the initial obligation to search for coherence and for what we can learn from what they have said. Although both Habermas and Gadamer believed that unconscious prejudices distort understanding and that they must be somehow "provoked" (Gadamer, 1987, p. 137) and made explicit, Gadamer believed that this could be accomplished through the encounter between an interpreter and a text, as long as the interpreter approaches the text with hermeneutic attitude—the willingness to acknowledge the coherence and truth in the text, and thereby risk his or her own prejudices. For additional discussions of philosophical and depth hermeneutics see Flyvbjerg (2001), Ricoeur (1990), and Thompson (1990).

[40] Our descriptions of sociocultural theories overlap substantially with those in Moss and Greeno (forthcoming).

[41] Seminal theoretical resources can also be found in the work of Bruner (1990), Cole (1996), Rogoff (1990), and of course, in the historically relevant texts of Leontiev (1978), Luria (1979), and Vygotsky (1978, 1986). Accessible introductions to newcomers can be found in Lave and Wenger (1991); Wertsch, Del Rio, and Alvarez (1995); and Wells and Claxton, (2002).

[42] Figure taken from Gee, forthcoming.

[43] As Mislevy (personal communication) noted, measurement theorists might well raise questions about the quality of diagnostic information at the subdimension level on large-scale standardized tests, in part because of questions about the reliability of subdimensions and in part because of questions about connection to the local curriculum.

[44] These include the Institute for Learning's Framework for effective management of school system performance (Resnick, Besterfield-Sacre, & Mehalik, in press), The Center for the Study of Teaching and Policy's Leading for Learning model (Knapp, Copland, & Talbert, 2003), the Center for Research in Evaluation, Standards, and Student Testing (CRESST) Quality School Portfolio, and the Center for Collaborative Education's (CCE) Turning Points School Reform Model (Jackson & Davis, 2000). More information can be found at depts.washington.edu/ctpmail/, qsp.cse.ucla.edu, www.instituteforlearning.org, and www.turningpoints.org.

[45] A forthcoming NSSE Yearbook on "Evidence and Decision Making" (Moss, in press) and a separate volume on "Opportunity to Learn" (Moss, Pullin, Gee, Haertel, and Young, forthcoming) provide additional illustrations that focus on evidence use at different levels of the educational system.

[46] Well-designed standardized assessments and the validity inquiry that supports them can serve numerous important purposes for educational professionals working in different contexts. For instance, they can provide carefully researched examples of sound assessment practice, they can permit economies of scale that make use with larger numbers of individuals or institutions feasible, they can raise hypotheses about or identify cases for further study, they can provide a synoptic view to support decision making by administrators and policy makers who work at centralized levels of the educational system, and they can enable comparisons across individuals and contexts that are crucial to addressing questions about equity.

[47] Although it is beyond the scope of this chapter to review, we note that activities involved in the development of standardized assessments frequently resemble these dynamic and integrative interpretive practices (Moss & Schutz, 1999; Mislevy, personal communication). These include the IDAs taken during development of tasks, scoring rubrics, strategies of aggregation and analysis, standard setting, and so on.

[48] Conversations with Fred Erickson, Jim Gee, and Bob Mislevy have influenced my (Moss) conceptions of generalizability.

REFERENCES

American Education Research Association, American Psychological Association, & National Council on Measurement in Education. (1999). *Standards for educational and psychological testing.* Washington, DC: American Educational Research Association.

American Education Research Association & National Council on Measurements Used in Education. (1955, January). *Technical recommendations for achievement tests.* Washington, DC: National Education Association.

American Education Research Association, American Psychological Association, & National Council on Measurement in Education. (1985). *Standards for educational and psychological testing.* Washington, DC: Authors.

American Psychological Association. (1954). Technical recommendations for psychological tests and diagnostic techniques [supplement]. *Psychological Bulletin, 51*(2, Pt.2), 201–238.

American Psychological Association. (1966). *Standards for educational and psychological tests and manuals.* Washington, DC: Author.

American Psychological Association. (1974). *Standards for educational and psychological tests.* Washington, DC: Author.

Beach, K. (1999). Consequential transitions. In A. Iran-Nejad & P. D. Pearso (Eds.), *Review of research in education* (Vol. 24) (pp. 101–139). Washington, DC: American Educational Research Association.

Bernstein, R. J. (1992). *The new constellation: The ethical-political horizons of modernity/postmodernity.* Cambridge: The MIT Press.

Betti, E. (1990). Hermeneutics as the general methodology of the *Geisteswissenschaften.* In G. L. Ormiston & A. D. Schrift (Eds.), *The hermeneutic tradition: From Ast to Ricoeur.* Albany: SUNY Press.

Bleicher, J. (1980). *Contemporary hermeneutics: Hermeneutics as method, philosophy, and critique.* London: Routledge and Kegan Paul.

Bohman, J. F., Hiley, D. R., & Shusterman, R. (1991). The interpretive turn. In D. Hiley, J. F. Bohman, & R. Shusterman (Eds.), *The interpretive turn* (pp. 1–16). Ithaca, NY: Cornell University Press.

Bourdieu, P. (1991). The peculiar history of scientific reason. *Sociological forum, 6*(1), 3–26.

Boudett, K. P., City, E. A., & Murnane, R. J. (Eds.). (2005). *Data wise: A step-by-step guide to using assessment results to improve teaching and learning.* Cambridge: Harvard Education Press.

Bowker, G. C., & Star, S. L., (1999). *Sorting things out: Classification and its consequences.* Cambridge: MIT Press.

Bransford, J. D., & Schwartz, D. L. (1999). Rethinking transfer: A simple proposal with multiple implications. In A. Iran-Nejad & P. D. Pearson (Eds.), *Review of research in education* (Vol. 24) (pp. 61–100). Washington, DC: American Educational Research Association.

Broadfoot, P. M. (1996). *Education, assessment and society.* Buckingham, UK: Open University Press.

Brookhart, S. M. (2003). Developing measurement theory for classroom assessment purposes and uses. *Educational measurement: Issues and practice, 22*(4), 5–12.

Bruner, J. (1990). *Acts of meaning.* Cambridge: Harvard University Press.

Coburn, C. E., & Talbert, J. E. (2006). Conceptions of evidence use in school districts: Mapping the terrain. *American Journal of Education, 112*(4), 469–495.

Cole, M. (1996). *Cultural psychology: A once a future discipline.* Cambridge: The Belknap Press of Harvard University Press.

Cronbach, L. J. (1971). Test validation. In R. L. Thorndike (Ed.), *Educational measurement* (2nd ed.). Washington, DC: American Council on Education.

Cronbach, L. J. (1988). Five perspectives on validity argument. In H. Wainer (Ed.), *Test validity.* Hillsdale, NJ: Lawrence Erlbaum Associates, Inc.

Cronbach, L. J. (1989). Construct validation after thirty years. In R. L. Linn (Ed.), *Intelligence: Measurement, theory and public policy* (pp. 147–171). Urbana, IL: University of Illinois Press.

Cronbach, L. J., & Meehl, P. E. (1955). Construct validity in psychological tests. *Psychological Bulletin, 52,* 281–302.

Cureton, E. E. (1951). Validity. In E. F. Lindquist (Ed.), *Educational measurement* (pp. 621–694). Washington, DC: American Council on Education.

Delandshere, G. (2002). Assessment as inquiry. *Teachers College Record, 104*(7), 1461–1484.

Diamond, J. B., & Spillane, J. P., (2004). High-stakes accountability in urban elementary schools: Challenging or reproducing inequality? *Teachers College Record, 106*(6), 1145–1176.

Dorr-Breme, D. W. (1983). Assessing students: Teachers' routine practices and reasoning. *Evaluation comment, 6*(4), 1–12.

Engeström, Y. (1987). *Learning by expanding: An activity-theoretical approach to developmental research.* Helsinki: Orienta-Konsultit.

Engeström, Y. (1993). Developmental studies of work as a testbench of activity theory: The case of primary care medical practice. In S. Chaiklin & J. Lave (Eds.), *Understanding practice: Perspectives on activity and context* (pp. 64–103). Cambridge, UK: Cambridge University Press.

Engeström, Y. (1999). Activity theory and individual and social transformation. In Y. Engeström, R. Miettinen, & R. Punämaki (Eds.), *Perspectives on activity theory* (pp. 19–38). Cambridge, UK: Cambridge University Press.

Engeström, Y. (2001). Expansive learning at work: Toward an activity theoretical reconceptualization. *Journal of Education and Work, 14*(1), 134–156.

Engeström, Y., Miettinen, R., & Punämaki, I (Eds.), (1999). *Perspectives on activity theory.* Cambridge, UK: Cambridge University Press.

Erickson, F. (1986). Qualitative methods in research on teaching. In M. C. Wittrock (Ed.), *Handbook of research on teaching* (pp. 119–161). New York: Macmillan.

Filer, A. (Ed.). (2000). *Assessment: Social practice and social product.* New York: Falmer Press.

Flyvberg, B. (2001). *Making social science matter: Why social inquiry fails and how it can succeed again.* New York: Cambridge University Press.

Gadamer, H. G. (1981). *Reason in the age of science* (F. G. Lawrence, Trans.). Cambridge: MIT Press.

Gadamer, H. G. (1987). The problem of historical consciousness. In P. Rabinow & W. M. Sullivan (Eds.), *Interpretive social science* (pp. 82–140). Berkeley: University of California Press.

Gadamer, H. G. (1990). Reply to my critics. In G. L. Ormiston & A. D. Schrift (Eds.), *The hermeneutic tradition: From Ast to Ricoeur.* Albany: SUNY Press.

Gadamer, G. H. (1994). *Truth and method.* (G. Barden & J. Cumming, Trans.) New York: Seabury (Original work published in 1975).

Gee, J. P. (forthcoming). A sociocultural perspective on opportunity to learn. In P. A. Moss, D. Pullin, E. H. Haertel, J. P. Gee, & L. J. Young (Eds.), *Opportunity to learn.* New York: Cambridge University Press.

Gipps, C. V. (1999). Socio-cultural aspects of assessment. In A. Iran-Nejad & P. D. Pearson (Eds.), *Review of Research in Education, 24,* 355–392. Washington, DC: American Educational Research Association.

Gipps, C. V. (2002). Sociocultural perspectives on assessment. In G. Wells & G. Claxton (Eds.), *Learning for life in the 21st century* (pp. 73–83). Malden, MA: Blackwell Publishing.

Greeno, J. G. (1989). A perspective on thinking. *American Psychologist, 44,* 134–141.

Greeno, J. G. (2002). *Students with competence, authority and accountability: Affording intellective identities in the classroom.* New York: The College Board.

Greeno, J., & Gresalfi, S. (forthcoming). Opportunity to learn in practice and identity. In P. A. Moss, D. Pullin, E. H. Haertel, J. P. Gee, & L. J. Young (Eds.), *Opportunity to learn.* New York: Cambridge University Press.

Habermas, J. (1984). *The theory of communicative action, Volume one: Reason and the rationalization of society* (T. McCarthy, Trans.). Boston: Beacon Press.

Habermas, J. (1990a). A review of Gadamer's *Truth and Method.* In G. L. Ormiston & A. D. Schrift (Eds.), *The hermeneutic tradition: From Ast to Ricoeur* (pp. 213–244). Albany: SUNY Press.

Habermas, J. (1990b). The hermeneutic claim to universality. In G. L. Ormiston & A. D. Schrift (Eds.), *The hermeneutic tradition: From Ast to Ricoeur* (pp. 245–272). Albany: SUNY Press.

Habermas, J. (1990c). *Moral consciousness and communicative action.* (C. Leinhardt & S. W. Nicholsen, Trans.). Cambridge, MA: MIT Press.

Habermas, J. (1993). *Justification and application.* (C. P. Cronin, Trans.). Cambridge, MA: MIT Press.

Haniford, L., & Girard, B. (2006, April). *Constructing difference: Teacher practice, portfolios and case studies.* Paper presented at the Annual Meeting of the American Educational Research Association, San Francisco, CA.

Heritage, M., & Yeagley, R. (2005). Data use and school improvement: Challenges and prospects. In J. L. Herman & E. H. Haertel (Eds.), *Uses and misuses of data for educational accountability and improvement. The 104th yearbook of the National Society for the Study of Education,* Part II (pp. 320–339). Malden, MA: Blackwell Publishing.

Herman, J. L., & Haertel, E. H. (Eds.) (2005). *Uses and misuses of data for educational accountability and improvement. The 104th yearbook of the National Society for the Study of Education,* Part II. Malden, MA: Blackwell Publishing.

Hickey, D. T., & Zuiker, S. J. (2003). A new perspective for evaluating innovative science programs. *Science Education, 87,* 539–563.

Hirsch, E. D. (1976). *The aims of interpretation.* Chicago: University of Chicago Press.

Honig, M. I., & Coburn, C. E. (2005). When districts use evidence to improve instruction: What do we know and where do we go from here? *Voices in Urban Education, 6*(Winter), 22–29.

Hoy, D. C. (1994). Critical theory and critical history. In D. C. Hoy & T. McCarthy (Eds.), *Critical theory* (pp. 101–214). Oxford: Blackwell.

Ikemoto, G. S., & Marsh, J. A. (In press). Cutting through the "data driven" mantra: Different conceptions of data-driven decision-making. In P. A. Moss (Ed.), *National Society for the Study of Education (NSSE) 2007 Yearbook: Evidence and decision making.* Malden, MA: Blackwell Publishing.

Jackson, A. W., & Davis, G. A. (2000). *Turning points 2000: Educating adolescents in the 21st century.* New York: Teachers College Press.

Jordan, B., & Putz, P. (2004). Assessment as practice: Notes on measures, tests, and targets. *Human organization, 63*(3), 346–358.

Kane, M. T. (1992). An argument-based approach to validity. *Psychological bulletin, 112,* 527–535.

Kane, M. T. (2001). Current concerns in validity theory. *Journal of Educational Measurement, 38*(4), 319–342.

Kane, M. T. (2006). Validation. In R. L. Brennan (Ed.), *Educational measurement* (4th ed.) (pp. 17–64). Westport, CT: American Council on Education/Praeger Publishers.

Kerr, K. A., Marsh, J. A., Ikemoto, G. S., Darilek, H., & Barney, H. (2006). Districtwide strategies to promote data use for instructional improvement. *American Journal of Education, 112*(4), 496–520.

Knapp, M. S., Copland, M. A., & Talbert, J. E. (2003). *Leading for learning: Reflective tools for school and district leaders.* Seattle, WA: University of Washington, Center for the Study of Teaching and Policy.

Koretz, D. M. & Hamilton, L. S. (2006). Testing for accountability in K-12. In R. L. Brennan (Ed.), *Educational measurement* (4th ed.) (pp. 531–578). Westport, CT: American Council on Education/Praeger Publishers.

Lampert, M. (2001). *Teaching problems and the problems of teaching.* New Haven, CT: Yale.

Lather, P. (2004). Validity as an incitement to discourse: Qualitative research and the crisis of legitimation. In V. Richardson (Ed.), *Handbook of research on teaching* (4th ed.) (pp. 241–250). Washington, DC: American Educational Research Association.

Lave, J. (1988). *Cognition in practice.* Cambridge, UK: Cambridge University Press.

Lave, J. (1993). The practice of learning. In S. Chaiklin & J. Lave (Eds.), *Understanding practice: Perspectives on activity and context* (pp. 3–32). Cambridge, UK: Cambridge University Press.

Lave, J., & Wenger, E. (1991). *Situated learning: Legitimate peripheral participation.* Cambridge: Cambridge University Press.

Lee, C. (forthcoming). A cultural modeling perspective on opportunity to learn. In P. A. Moss, D. Pullin, E. H. Haertel, J. P. Gee, & L. J. Young (Eds.). *Opportunity to learn.* New York: Cambridge University Press.

Lemke, J. L. (2000). Across scales of time: Artifacts, activities, and meanings in ecosocial systems. *Mind, Culture, and Activity, 7*(4), 273–290.

Leontiev, A. N. (1978). *Activity, consciousness, and personality.* Englewood Cliffs, NJ: Prentice-Hall.

Luria, A. R. (1979). *The making of mind.* Cambridge, MA: Harvard University Press.

Magnusson, S. J., Templin, M., & Boyle, R. A. (1997). Dynamic science assessment: A new approach for investigating conceptual change. *Journal of the Learning Sciences, 6*(1), 91–142.

Martin, M., & McIntyre, L. C. (1994) Introduction. In M. Martin & L. C. McIntyre (Eds.), *Readings in the philosophy of social science* (pp. xv–xxii). Cambridge: The MIT Press.

Massell, D., & Goertz, M. E. (2002). District strategies for building instructional capacity. In A. M. Hightower, M. S. Knapp, J. A. Marsh, & M. W. McLaughlin (Eds.), *School districts and instructional renewal* (pp.43–60). New York: Teachers College Press.

Mehan, H. (forthcoming). A sociological perspective on opportunity to learn and assessment. In P. A. Moss, D. Pullin, E. H. Haertel, J. P. Gee, & L. J. Young (Eds.), *Opportunity to learn.* New York: Cambridge University Press.

Messick, S. (1989). Validity. In R. L. Linn (Ed.), *Educational measurement* (3rd ed.) (pp. 13–103). New York: American Council on Education/Macmillan.

Mislevy, R. J. (2006). Cognitive psychology and educational assessment. In R. L. Brennan (Ed.), *Educational measurement* (4th ed.) (pp. 257–305). Westport, CT: American Council on Education/Praeger Publishers.

Mislevy, R. J. (forthcoming). Issues of structure and issues of scale in assessment from a situative/sociocultural perspective. In P. A. Moss, D. Pullin, E. H. Haertel, J. P. Gee, & L. J. Young (Eds.). *Opportunity to learn.* New York: Cambridge University Press.

Mislevy, R. J., Almond, R., & Steinberg, L. (2003). On the structure of educational assessment. *Measurement: Interdisciplinary Research and Perspectives, 1*(1), 3–62.

Moss, P. A. (1992). Shifting conceptions of validity in educational measurement: Implications for performance assessment. *Review of Educational Research, 62*(3), 229–258.

Moss, P. A. (1995). Themes and variations in validity theory. *Educational Measurement: Issues and Practice, 14*(2), 5–13.

Moss, P. A. (2003). Rethinking validity for classroom assessment. *Educational Measurement: Issues and Practice, 22*(4), 13–25.

Moss, P. A. (2005). Understanding the other/understanding ourselves: Towards a constructive dialogue about "principles" in educational research. *Educational Theory, 55*(3), pp. 263–283.

Moss, P. A. (Ed.). (in press). *National Society for the Study of Education (NSSE) 2007 Yearbook: Evidence and decision making.* Malden, MA: Blackwell Publishing.

Moss, P. A., Coggshall, J., & Schutz, A. (2006, April). *Reaching ethical decisions in portfolio assessment: Evaluating complex evidence of teaching.* Paper presented at the Annual Meeting of the American Educational Research Association, San Francisco, CA.

Moss, P. A., & Greeno, J. (forthcoming). Sociocultural implications for the practice of assessment. In P. A. Moss, D. Pullin, E. H. Haertel, J. P. Gee, & L. J. Young (Eds.), *Opportunity to learn.* New York: Cambridge University Press.

Moss, P. A., Pullin, D., Gee, J. P., Haertel, E. H., & Young, L. J. (Eds.). (forthcoming). *Opportunity to learn.* New York: Cambridge University Press.

Moss, P. A., Pullin, D. P., Haertel, E. H., & Gee, J. P. (2005). The idea of testing: Expanding the foundations of educational measurement. *Measurement: Interdisciplinary Research and Perspectives, 3*(2), 63–83.

Moss, P. A., & Schutz, A. (1999). Risking frankness in educational assessment. *Phi Delta Kappan, 80*(9), 680–687.

Moss, P. A., & Schutz, A. M. (2001). Educational standards, assessment, and the search for consensus. *American Educational Research Journal, 38*(1), 37–70.

Moss, P. A., Sutherland, L. M., Haniford, L., Miller, R., Johnson, D., Geist, P. K., Koziol, S. M., Star, J. R., & Pecheone, R. L. (2004, July 20). Interrogating the generalizability of portfolio assessments of beginning teachers: A qualitative study. *Educational Policy Analysis Archives, 12*(32). Retrieved June 1, 2006, from http://epaa.asu.edu/epaa/v12n32/

Myford, C. M., & Mislevy, R. J. (1995). *Monitoring and improving a portfolio assessment system* (Center for Performance Assessment Research Report). Princeton, NJ: Educational Testing Service.

National Academy of Education. (2005). *Preparing teachers for a changing world: What teachers should learn and be able to do* (L. Darling-Hammond, J. Bransford in collaboration with P. LePage, K. Hammerness, & H. Duffy, Eds.). San Francisco: Jossey-Bass.

National Research Council (NRC). (2001). *Knowing what students know* (J. W. Pellegrino, N. Chudowsky, & R. Glaser, Eds.). Washington, DC: National Academy Press.

Ormiston, G. L., & Schrift, A. D. (Eds.). (1990). *The hermeneutic tradition: From Ast to Ricoeur.* Albany: SUNY Press.

Phillips, D. C. (in press). Adding complexity: Philosophical perspectives on the relationship between evidence and policy. In P. A. Moss (Ed.) *National Society for the Study of Education (NSSE) 2007 Yearbook: Evidence and decision making.* Malden, MA: Blackwell Publishing.

Rabinow, P., & Sullivan, W. M. (Eds.). (1987). *Interpretive social science.* Berkeley: University of California Press.

Resnick, L., Besterfield-Sacre, M., & Mehalik, M. (in press). A framework for effective management of school system performance. In P. A. Moss (Ed.), *National Society for the Study of Education (NSSE) 2007 Yearbook: Evidence and decision making.* Malden, MA: Blackwell Publishing.

Ricoeur, P. (1990). Hermeneutics and the critique of ideology. In G. L. Ormiston & A. D. Schrift (Eds.), *The hermeneutic tradition: From Ast to Ricoeur* (pp. 298–334). Albany: SUNY Press.

Rogoff, B. (1990). *Apprenticeship in thinking: Cognitive development in social context.* New York: Oxford University Press.

Salmon-Cox, L. (1981). Teachers and standardized achievement tests: What's really happening? *Phi Delta Kappan, 69*(9), 631–634.

Schmidt, L. K. (Ed.). (1995). *The specter of relativism: Truth, dialogue, and phronesis in philosophical hermeneutics.* Evanston, IL: Northwestern University Press.

Schutz, A., & Moss, P. A. (2004). "Reasonable" decisions in portfolio assessment: Evaluating complex evidence of teaching [online]. *Educational Policy Analysis Archives, 12*(33). Retrieved June 1, 2006, from http://epaa.asu.edu/v12n33

Shepard, L. A. (1993). Evaluating test validity. *Review of Research in Education, 19,* 405–450.

Shepard, L. A. (2001). The role of classroom assessment in teaching and learning. In V. Richardson (Ed.), *Handbook of research on teaching* (4th ed.) (pp. 1066–1101). Washington, DC: AERA.

Shepard, L. A. (2006). Classroom assessment. In R. L. Brennan (Ed.), *Educational measurement* (4th ed.) (pp. 623–646). Westport, CT: American Council on Education/Praeger Publishers.

Shepard, L. A., Hammerness, K., Darling-Hammond, L., & Rust, F. (2005). Assessment. In L. Darling-Hammond, & J. Bransford (Eds.), *Preparing teachers for a changing world: What teachers should learn and be able to do* (pp. 275–326). San Francisco: Jossey-Bass.

Spillane, J. P. (2006). *Distributed leadership.* San Francisco: Jossey-Bass.

Spillane, J. P., Diamond, J. B., & Halverson, R. (2004). Towards a theory of leadership practice: A distributed perspective. *Journal of Curriculum Studies, 36*(1), 3–34.

Spillane, J. P., Halverson, R., & Diamond, J. B. (2001). Investigating school leadership practice: A distributed perspective. *Educational Researcher, 30*(3), 23–28.

Star, S. L., & Griesemer, J. R. (1989). Institutional ecology, 'translations' and boundary objects: Amateurs and professionals in Berkeley's Museum of Vertebrate Zoology, 1907–39. *Social Studies of Science, 19*(3), 387–420.

Stiggins, R. J. (2001a). *Student-involved classroom assessment* (3rd ed.). Upper Saddle River, NJ: Prentice-Hall.

Stiggins, R. J. (2001b). The unfulfilled promise of classroom assessment. *Educational Measurement: Issues and Practice, 20*(3), 5–15.

Stiggins, R. J., & Conklin, N. F. (1992). *In teachers' hands: Investigating the practices of classroom assessment.* Albany: State University of New York Press.

Supovitz, J. A., & Klein, V. (2003). *Mapping a course for improved student learning: How innovative schools systematically use student performance data to guide improvement.* Philadelphia: Consortium for Policy Research in Education, University of Pennsylvania Graduate School of Education.

Taylor, C. (2002). Understanding the other: A Gadamerian view on conceptual schemes. In J. Malpas, U. Arnswald, & J. Kertscher (Eds.), *Gadamer's century: Essays in honor of Hans-Georg Gadamer* (pp. 279–298). Cambridge: The MIT Press.

Taylor, C. S., & Nolen, S. B. (2005). *Classroom assessment: Supporting teaching and learning in real classrooms.* Upper Saddle River, NJ: Pearson Education.

Thompson, J. B. (1990). *Ideology and modern culture.* Stanford: Stanford University Press.

Toulmin, S. E. (1958). *The uses of argument.* Cambridge, UK: Cambridge University Press.

Vygotsky, L. S. (1978). *Mind in society: The development of higher psychological processes* (M. Cole, V. John-Steiner, S. Scribner, & E. Souberman, Eds.). Cambridge, MA: Harvard University Press.

Vygotsky, L. S. (1986). *Thought and language.* (A. Kozulin, Ed.). Cambridge, MA: MIT Press.

Warnke, G. (1994). *Justice and interpretation.* Cambridge: MIT Press.

Wells, G., & Claxton, G. (Eds.) (2002). *Learning for life in the 21st century.* Malden, MA: Blackwell Publishing.

Wenger, E. (1998). *Communities of practice: Learning, meaning, and identity.* Cambridge, UK: Cambridge University Press.

Wertsch, J. V. (1995). The need for action in sociocultural research. In J. V. Wertsch, P. del Rio, & A. Alvarez (Eds.), *Sociocultural studies of mind* (pp. 56–74). Cambridge, UK: Cambridge University Press.

Wertsch, J. V. (1998). *Mind as action.* Oxford: Oxford University Press.

Wertsch, J. V., Del Rio, P., & Alvarez, A. (1995). Sociocultural studies: History, action, and mediation. In J. V. Wertsch, P. Del Rio, and A. Alvarez (Eds.), *Sociocultural studies of mind* (pp. 1–36). Cambridge, UK: Cambridge University Press.

Wilson, M. (Ed.). (2004). *National Society for the Study of Education (NSSE) 2004 Yearbook: Towards coherence between classroom assessment and accountability.* Malden, MA: Blackwell Publishing.

Wilson, M. R., & Bertenthal, B. W. (Eds.). (2006). *Systems for state science assessment.* Washington, DC: National Academies Press.

Yeh, J. P., Herman, J. L., & Rudner, L. M. (1981). *Teachers and testing: A survey of test use.* (CSE Report No. 166). Los Angeles: UCLA, Center for the Study of Evaluation.

Young, V. M. (2006). Teachers' use of data: Loose coupling, agenda setting, and team norms. *American Journal of Education, 112*(4), 521–548.

Chapter 5

Social, Methodological, and Theoretical Issues Regarding Assessment: Lessons From a Secondary Analysis of PISA 2000 Literacy Tests

JEAN-YVES ROCHEX

University Paris 8 Saint-Denis

Over the last twenty years, one of the principal changes that has occurred in the educational system concerns the appraisal of the worth of school systems based on comparative analyses of their students' performance. . . . However, to assess the quality of a school based on its students' performance entails a new approach to thinking about and to implementing educational policies. In the past, political leaders acted upon their own political beliefs and opinions. Today, the trend is to rely upon facts. The most commonly used facts are those that present a school's efficiency and those that are used to promote educational reforms; both are meant to help a growing number of students. Recent models of assessment no longer promote evaluation of students on the same or equal footing, but rather support affirmative action policies in order to increase the performance of "less able students." (Orivel, 2005, pp. 11–12)

These words, from Francois Orivel's preface to *Monitoring Educational Achievement,* published by Neville Postlethwaite in the Principles on Planning Education series of the United Nations Educational, Scientific and Cultural Organization (UNESCO),[1] set the stage for this chapter and provide one of the most eloquent illustrations of the evolutions governing international surveys such as the Program for International Student Assessment (PISA; see http://www.pisa.oecd.org) and the issues that arise from them. Orivel's arguments are reminiscent of Dominique S. Rychen's (2001) in her introduction to the book *Defining and Selecting Key Competencies.* This book accounts for the first phase of DeSeCo (Definition and Selection of Competencies; see http://www.portal-stat.admin.ch/deseco/index.htm), led by the Swiss Federal Statistical Office under the auspices of the Organization for Economic Cooperation and Development (OECD) in collaboration with the National Center for Education Statistics. Rychen argued:

In line with a growing concern from governments and the general public about the adequacy and quality of education and training, and the actual return on public educational expenditure, there has been, since the mid-1980s, an increased policy interest in comparable outcomes indicators in the education field. In fact, assessing the quality of education outcomes, estimating economic and social returns on learning, and identifying key determinants to a successful life and full participation in society are ongoing discussion topics that stimulate keen interest around the world. (Rychen, 2001, p. 1)

The growing interest in assessing the quality of education outcomes can be seen in the ever-increasing frequency of use of international or national surveys (e.g., PISA, the Progress in Reading and Literacy Study [PIRLS], or the Third International Mathematics and Science Study [TIMSS]; http://timss.bc.edu). These surveys seek to assess students' academic achievement and to make comparisons between countries and national school systems or between different schools within countries. The scope of such surveys is expanding: While 32 countries were involved in the first phase of PISA 2000 (28 of them being members of OECD), 11 additional countries, none of them belonging to OECD, joined it 2 years later; PISA 2003 was implemented in 41 countries. In 2004, 30 OECD countries and 30 non-OECD countries were involved in PISA assessment surveys (OECD, 2004). Because of the situations with the national governments involved, international surveys such as PISA (or the Southern Africa Consortium for Monitoring Educational Quality in eastern and southern Africa) are, for many of these countries, the only ones that enable them to assess their school systems' outcomes; as a result, they depend on Western countries' tools, which they have no power to influence or modify.

Managers of national school systems or international organizations such as OECD or the European Commission that promote and implement such surveys aim at affecting the teaching policies of the countries concerned as well as policies affecting the schools thus evaluated and compared with one another. They assume that assessing and comparing school systems or school units on the basis of common indicators is the primary way to increase their effectiveness and, therefore, the economic competitiveness of a given country. This set of assumptions allows them to pay attention not only to international comparisons but also to "good practices" determined by these indicators. Furthermore, these policymakers view diffusion or prescription of good practices as necessary and sufficient to improve the effectiveness of their school systems and to reduce social inequalities.

Critical issues related to international assessment approaches are explored in depth in the next three sections of this chapter. The first section summarizes the main questions about, and criticisms of, the use of PISA-like surveys; more generally, it questions school effectiveness research and evidence-based policies that make use of such assessments as well as the relations between them. It focuses on work—technical and scientific, normative and reductive—that oversimplifies the field and problems of education and on the social uses and misuses of the results of such surveys. The second section examines issues related to the construction of PISA, including the development and administration schedule, the underpinning psychometric model, and the way in which skills—specifically literacy skills—are conceptualized. The third section is based on a secondary analysis of literacy tests from PISA 2000. It focuses on the results of French students and on the ways they deal with these literacy tests.

SUBSTITUTION OF GOALS AND ROLES AND SHIFTING OF MEANING
Knowledge and Policy

An analysis of numerous articles written on the topic shows that one of the most highly debated areas associated with international assessments concerns the relationship between research and the policies or politics that form a context in which to view such assessments. In this section, I review key debates and the evolutions that have shifted the relationship between research and policy and, now, between research and politics. At the center of these debates are contentious critiques and countercritiques between proponents and opponents of school effectiveness research as well as of evidence-based policies. Analysis of the development of the relations between school effectiveness research and evidence-based policies or practices shows a twofold shift in both the fields of politics and social sciences and the relationship of one field with the other. Politics has moved from policy to management and from government to governance. The problem of school efficiency, presented as being a technical question, has taken precedence over the political debate about educational values and goals. This substitution denies or underestimates the inherent conflicts of interest between the different social agents or social classes that exist in educational politics as in any other social issue. Those supporting these shifts tend to think of and to value educational politics by means of the single, unique barometer of economic competition within the different countries, greatly reducing the issues at hand. This direction can be clearly seen in a recent claim of Randy Bennet[2] (2006):

Accountability has become critical because today's globalized economy means that companies can invest anywhere that is politically stable and that has a skilled, productive, workforce. Anywhere. To beat their competitors, companies must go to those locations that afford the best mix of skills and productivity. To keep jobs and to maintain current living standards, governments need to constantly improve the skill levels and productivity of their existing workforce. But to guarantee that future living standards are maintained, those governments must also ensure that today's students are educated to the highest achievement standards possible. And schools must be held accountable for that achievement if those standards are to be met. (p. iii)

Bennet's position is a prime example of a top-down view—from the whole world to each school and each country—of social, cultural, or political life as being ruled mainly by economic competition and by an idea of "accountability" presented as natural and not open for discussion. The "rational" norms and constraints linked to this economic view are meant to be applied to students and their families, who are supposed to act, whatever their social, cultural, or ethnic background, as if they are rational economic agents whose decisions could build public (or general) interest if they are enlightened by and founded on public evaluations of evidence. The market economic model, in fact, leads to an evolution from an evaluation of "products" (students' knowledge and ability linked, to a certain extent, to the curriculum studied or to competencies judged necessary for a "successful life") to an evaluation of the "producers" (the different school systems and the different schools, teachers, and practices). Teachers are then often considered as service providers for their students-consumers and for financial backers and policymakers. Policies and practices (of producers and consumers of educational goods) are thought to be all the better because they are supported by facts and are evidence based. The technique of assessment and accountability is considered the main instrument in this new normative model. Annie Vinokur summed this up as follows:

> The first hypothesis is that a market must first be established, and in order to do this, be equipped with standard tools which allow normalization and measurement of the educational products' quality. The establishment of these work and teaching markets—now transnational—requires that, to assure their transparency, an initial technology of evaluation, of comparability and of certification is put in place. (2005a, p. 9; see also Vinokur, 2005b)

These arguments raise a series of questions: Is it possible to eliminate questions of values and social or cultural aims so easily? And at what price? Could there be only one way of defining the criteria for efficiency and competition by adopting, as Randy Bennet seems to do, those of the multinational companies and the international markets?

Dependent on this first evolution is a second one that concerns the relationship between, on one hand, research work and researchers, and, on the other hand, educational policies, policymakers, and international organizations' managers. For these managers and policymakers, the assessment tools and the results they produce are no longer considered essentially as a means, among many, of understanding and measuring the effects of political decisions or organizational methods. They are now increasingly used as technical tools of change to legitimize implementation of what is considered to be the way, even the only way, to improve school systems' efficiency. This approach represents a shift in the way indicators are used: from knowledge tools that can inform political decision-making processes to a normative use of these indicators as simple technical tools that allow such processes to be modified and legitimized (see, e.g., Normand, 2003, 2004).

A parallel evolution can be observed in educational research, especially in the sociology of education. In the past, the researcher's standpoint, at least in Europe, was one of criticism and even of denunciation of the institution of education and the social order. Researchers, through their research, did their best to reveal the underlying educational and noneducational mechanisms that were linked to the social domination and that led to social reproduction (see Bourdieu & Passeron, 1970). Today educational research seems to have become invested with the improvement of the educational system and each of its components and with the desire to reveal and increase their protagonists' room to maneuver. This explains the intensity of the criticism by researchers such as Martin Thrupp (2001, 2002) of colleagues who contributed to school effectiveness research and, especially, evidence-based policies. Thrupp charged them with adopting a narrow, pragmatic point of view. This point of view led them not only to want to undertake "useful" research that could help political decision makers and education practitioners resolve their own problems of efficiency[3] but also, in so doing, to adopt the normative presuppositions of these policymakers and practitioners. As such, to a certain extent, this would permit researchers to veer from their work and point of view as critics to take on the discourse and position of experts or "political advisers."

A third evolution deals with the relationship between research and politics in general. Not only has there been a shift from a critical stance to that of an expert, but also to increasingly technological instruments of measurement that are more and more sophisticated and less and less accessible to the critical minds of nonspecialists. This shift allows the expert to dominate the political debate and substitutes expert discourse and point of view for public political debate. Indeed, politics has become increasingly dominated by these experts, who have legitimized ways of determining problems in education and their solutions. Those in the political arena often attempt to use researchers who consider themselves experts to legitimize their politics and even to explain to those who are recalcitrant that they are wrong and that they have no right to participate in the debate, because science is seen as the only neutral arbitrator, above all conflicts of interest.

The link between the concerns and ideologies of researchers and those in the political arena is seen by some as a guarantee of beneficial effects of research on educational decision-making processes. For others, however, it is considered as a risk or a threat that weighs heavily on research and the capacity to provide in-depth theoretical results and analyses. Several examples of these positions follow. On one end of the spectrum is Postlethwaite (2005), who stated that "a tight collaboration between state educational planners and researchers is necessary. In certain countries, the responsibility of the studies is given to the planners themselves. This is an adequate approach that allows research to give way to action" (p. 104). Although he argued for this position, he also admitted that "things are not so simple and that to expect a direct relationship between research and political action is not realistic" (p. 104). At the opposite end of the spectrum is Martin Hammersley (2001), who rebelled against the "rhetorical coup de force," which is in itself the basis of evidence-based practice or policy:

There is an initial, and generic problem with the notion of evidence-based practice which needs to be dealt with. This is that its name is a slogan whose rhetorical effect is to discredit opposition. After all, who would argue that practice should not be based on evidence? So there is an implication built into the phrase "evidence-based practice" that opposition to it can only be irrational. (p. 1)

Hammersley did not dispute the fact that the contribution of research might be useful to practitioners and policymakers. He did, however, warn of the risk (already acknowledged as such) of research findings based on the hybrid mixture of effective research, governments, auditors and inspectors, or think-tanks' ideas and presuppositions and of researchers' affirmations in an area that is beyond their competence and the validity of their research evidence and conclusions. Moreover, he disputed with equal vehemence the importance given to research evidence to the detriment of other sources, especially professional experience:

Practice is [necessarily] a matter of judgment, in which information from various sources (not just research) must be combined. . . . In addition, there are problems concerning how one applies research evidence about aggregates to particular cases, and about how one weighs the implications of such evidence against information from other sources where the two conflict. . . . It is important to emphasize that research evidence cannot serve as a court of appeal for judging competing conceptions of best practice, in the way that Chalmers and most other advocates of evidence-based practice believe. (Hammersley, 2005, p. 88)

Although less critical than Thrupp or Hammersley, Goldstein and Woodhouse (2000) nonetheless inquired about the strain that exists between politically useful research and academically legitimate research; the tension this creates characterizes school effectiveness research, in which all work is not equal in quality (as is true in other fields). They called on researchers in school effectiveness to improve the quality of their work and, in order to do so, to reconsider their relationship ties with the political field and its presupposed norms. After pleading for renaming this field of research educational effectiveness research, a less restrictive and less oversimplified appellation than school effectiveness research, they concluded their review of the debate with the following warning:

The requirement for better data, for a concern with knowledge not driven by particular policy agendas and for attention to the possibility of whether and how to develop well-grounded theory, poses a considerable challenge to [educational effectiveness] researchers. Unless this challenge is met successfully [educational effectiveness research] will not establish itself as a reputable field of study. In particular, if it continues to exist as [school effectiveness research], if many of its proponents remain superficially defensive and if it ignores or fails to understand the warning of its critics, we have very little optimism that it will survive its present state of adolescent turmoil to emerge into a full maturity. (Goldstein & Woodhouse, 2000, p. 361)

In previous work, Goldstein and Myers (1997) wrote:

We believe that the future health of the area depends crucially on establishing [school effectiveness research] activity as an autonomous area of study rather than by always responding to immediate external requests. Whilst it should certainly be addressing policy concerns it should not be dependent on a too-cozy relationship with politicians. (p. 2)

Oversimplifications and Undesirable Effects

The second hotly debated points of discussion concern, on one hand, conceptions of the "educational product" and of social and scholastic processes that, more or less explicitly, underlie international surveys and interpretation of their results and, on the other hand, the possible undesirable social effects that publication of these results as ranking lists or league tables[4] can have on educational policies, the functioning of schools, and the practices of teachers.

On a scientific basis, critics often point out the insufficient theoretical foundation of school effectiveness research, for which the increasingly sophisticated statistical models cannot compensate. Both Thrupp (2001) and Goldstein and Woodhouse (2000), for instance, disputed the oversimplification induced by the theoretical and methodological given that individuals and schools can be considered as independent and unique entities and that social processes can be considered as the addition and combination of their actions and decisions. Such a given, built on the model of the market economy, neglects the relationships of interdependency of social structures and the constraints, contradictions, and conflicts of social relations and power fields. Goldstein and Woodhouse argued:

One of the enduring features of [school effectiveness] research is its conceptualisation of schools as discrete non-interacting entities which have characteristics derived from their student body and their staff as well as more permanent structures. These characteristics can, in principle, be measured and a study of the relationships among them, for example between intake and output achievements, is assumed to be capable of yielding insights into the processes of schooling, and possibly to indicate paths for positive change. . . . But there is a fundamental problem with the basic assumption mentioned at the start of this paragraph, namely that schools are assumed to be *non-interacting* entities. A cursory reflection on the way schools function, especially in England, reveals that the actions and characteristics of any one school are linked to those of other schools. Schools which, in one way or another select students on the basis of capabilities, influence the capacity of surrounding schools to do so. . . . Yet, there is very little attempt within [school effectiveness] research to take this into account. This failure underlines and gives credence to many of the critiques. . . . Perhaps the most important consequence is in its impact on School Improvement research and practice. Attempts to change the practices of each school considered as an independently functioning unit not only seem ill-conceived, but also likely to meet with limited success, however well-meaning the intention may be. (2000, p. 356)

This tendency to consider schools (or individuals and their practices) as individual entities is obviously linked (one influencing the other) to statistical models and modalities of data computing treatments that work with variables and measurements of effects rather than social and school processes and interpretation of the modes of production of these effects. Here again different authors dispute the weakness of these types of measurements and emphasize the need to create a dialogue between different types of approaches. According to Thrupp:

Most critics of [school effectiveness] research are probably much less worried about technical issues in statistical modeling than with whether this kind of modeling is really *at all* plausible in terms of being able to capture the school processes it is expected to measure. For instance, in investigating compositional or "school mix" effects, *hierarchical linear models* studies use an input/output formulation which fails to model how compositional influences act through school processes. (2001, p. 450)

Quoting Sayer (1992), Thrupp further argued:

The concept of a "variable" that is used in quantitative analysis is an indifferent one as regards causal explanation: variables can only register (quantifiable) change, not its cause. The vocabulary of mathematics may be useful for recording the effects associated with the exercise of causal powers but other "languages" are needed to show why objects possess them. (Sayer, 1992, pp. 179–180, cited by Thrupp, 2001, p. 450)

Delving deeper into the theoretical aspect is essential not only for the relationship between measurement and explanation or interpretation, but also for construction of variables, even before statistical treatment and interpretation. Furthermore, modes of characterization of facts and social and cultural processes and of the competencies grasped with the assistance of these variables also need greater theoretical reflection and debate. Questions for debate include the following: What are the most pertinent descriptive modes and categories of teaching? Of students' and families' literacy practices? Of social, ethnic, and gender characteristics of different schools? Of a school's climate or way those in charge run the school? Of the socioeconomic status of the students and their families? Of course, there are no answers to these questions that can be considered as worthy, independent of specific questions of research. And it seems to be a dialogue of the deaf between, on the one hand, researchers who use methods based on meta-categories taken out of their context (such as those used by the PISA designers and analysts or by most of those undertaking meta-analyses that attempt to assess the efficiency of different pedagogical approaches) and, on the other hand, researchers who use methods and categories that are extremely contextualized so that their findings and conclusions cannot be generalized. In addition, it is hard to disagree with Goldstein and Woodhouse (2000) when they claim that new foundations and greater theoretical work are needed to move beyond this dialogue of the deaf. This work is not only the responsibility of individuals or research teams, but also the collective responsibility of the entire community of research in education.[5] Yet, no noticeable changes have been produced in this direction.

The theoretical or methodological conceptions that underlie most of the school effectiveness studies, because they treat schools and their staff as independent entities or discrete variables to measure their statistical weight, can take into account neither the interdependent relationships between schools and between their protagonists nor the way in which different variables combine and interact. Neither can they take into account the constraints, the possibilities, and impossibilities that are dependent not on individuals' or schools' actions but on the different social context levels in which they work. These conceptions frequently lead school effectiveness researchers and, even more so, the policymakers who use their findings to overestimate school solutions and the importance of teachers' and school staffs' room to maneuver. Indeed, they present, implicitly or explicitly, professional practices as the first and even as the only possible means of action to improve school efficiency and students' performance or to reduce social, ethnic, and gender inequalities. This argument was captured succinctly by Thrupp (2001):

This overemphasis occurs not in the body of their analyses, where school effectiveness researchers are usually quite honest about the small size of school effects versus background effects, but in the sheer weight of discussion given over to the effects of schooling rather than broader social structures. (p. 448)

Such an overestimation leads to a logic of shaming or naming and of designating or even hunting for "failing" schools, teachers, and children. This impact is all the more so when the results of these studies are published as league tables. Schools, teachers, and even students and their families are held responsible both for weak levels of performance and for actions and efforts to improve them. Thus, after having deplored that "hunting failing schools has become an exciting and rewarding journalistic and political pastime" and stating that they were "particularly concerned by the way that school effectiveness research has been misused to 'shift the blame'," Myers and Goldstein (1998) insisted on the fact that

ironically, contextualizing performance, by using adjusted league tables of test scores, for example, may actually strengthen the belief that blame resides in the school by encouraging the view that *all* other factors have been accounted for, and that any residual variation *must* have its origin in the schools. (p. 184)[6]

Their criticisms converged with those of West and Pennel (2005):

The focus on results of tests and examinations and pupils' education progress . . . does appear to have resulted in a focus on internal school processes as the key means of improving learning and knowledge, rather than, for example, addressing structural issues [having] to do with pupil mix or structural inequalities within society. (p. 195)

One could object to these criticisms on the basis that the logic of blaming, shaming, or faming involves social and political misuse of the results produced by school effectiveness research and does not directly concern this field of research. But this objection does not take into account the frequent shifts or changes of position by individuals who move between the academic field and the administrative or political world. Criticism of the influence on or contamination of the scientific register by the political register is no longer limited to the social and political uses and misuses of research and its results. It must deal with the ways in which researchers conceptualize their objectives and questions for research, the ways they conceive and evaluate the production of academic performance, and the level of ease in which their research methodologies, issues, and results provide "a technology for the possibility of 'blaming' the school" (Ball, 1990, p. 161). This risk is all the more probable given that the modes of categorizing "good" and "bad" practices and judging their efficiency are often thought of and treated outside of any consideration of conflicts of interest or conflicts of habitus between social groups concerned by educational policies and practices. This way of working proceeds as if what were valid and efficient and appropriate to the middle and upper classes, which have preponderant weight on scholastic policies and are most at ease with pedagogical ideologies, were also valid for the lower classes, those who are the most disadvantaged and the least familiar with the middle-class scholastic culture and running of a school. It does not take into account the questions asked more than 30 years ago by Basil Bernstein or Pierre Bourdieu, who had investigated and conceptualized how the implicit features of school functioning and school practices are one of the most important means of (re)production of social inequalities in the education field (Bernstein, 1975a, 1975b; Bourdieu & Passeron, 1970).

The same criticism that has been made of the known risks of oversimplification, ranking, and "blaming or shaming" can also be made for comparisons of schools and the use of international assessment surveys that rank educational systems on a national level. According to the oversimplified underlying theory, a country's ability to compete on the world market is directly related to the level of its educational system. Myers and Goldstein (1998) challenged this underlying theory:

> To attribute the poor economic performance of a country to the organization or the performance of its education system is to make a logical and empirical blunder. It is just as easy to argue the reverse, namely that a poor economic performance in a nation has a direct effect on its education system in terms of motivation, resource provision or some other feed back mechanism. . . . Likewise it is not legitimate to argue that league tables of international educational performance reflect the quality of education systems. The attribution of cause and effect is fraught with difficulty in these circumstances, and the mere repetition of one interpretation does not strengthen its plausibility. (p. 185)

Following the example of Reynolds and Teddlie (2000), proponents of school effectiveness research and evidence-based policies often argue that only findings based on results can bring about real changes within school systems that are inequitable and immutable. At times, they even go so far as turning the argument of the critics, claiming that their opponents are the conservatives while they in fact are the radicals:

> Critics have always—implicitly if not explicitly—made it clear that they see a conservative orientation to effectiveness research. . . . One could ask what is the more conservative act? To research and discuss how children are determined by the wider society or to research and discuss how to change that society by generating children possessed of the intellects to change it? I would answer the latter of course. In its commitment to maximizing the educational quality of schools, both for its own merits and to generate wider social change, school effectiveness is the discipline in which radicals should situate themselves. With their pessimism, passivity and inability to do anything more than talk about change, it is the critics that are the true conservatives, now as in the 1960s. (Reynolds & Teddlie, 2000, p. 10)

Despite the overly simplified caricature that these two authors drew on critical sociology, whose researchers never restrict their work to "research and discussion about how children are determined by the wider society," and, despite their overly simplified analysis of the sociological fatalism of the 1960s, Reynolds and Teddlie asked an important question about which method best helps a school or school system be more efficient and less inequitable. Such a question, and the comparative analysis of social, political, and epistemological practices and issues needed to deal with it, goes beyond the topic of this chapter (on this issue, see, e.g., Slee, Weiner, & Tomlinson, 1998 or Matters, 2006). However, this limit does not cancel our doubts about the critical scope of school effectiveness research and its capacity to generate wider social change.

The hopes and affirmations of Reynolds and Teddlie (2000) have been countered by different studies. These studies have shown that the publication and political uses of surveys such as those used by school effectiveness researchers often lead to the opposite of their desired or claimed effect. Myers and Goldstein summed up the British policy of using and publishing standards and rankings:

> Publishing the average test scores of schools in the form of ranking or league tables has encouraged competition rather than collaboration and cooperation between schools and thereby undermines one of the prerequisites for school improvement—the opportunity and capacity of schools to learn from each other. . . . In England and Wales where schools' examination results have been published nationally in

rankings or league tables, some schools have responded by concentrating their efforts on those students they believe may improve their average examination results, while giving less attention to the rest. (1998, pp. 176, 182; see also Goldstein, 2001)

The same conclusions have been drawn by many other researchers (e.g., see Ball & Van Zanten, 1998; Gewirtz, Ball, & Bowe, 1995; Van Zanten, 2001). They have shown how, in school systems as different as those in France and Britain, the combination of educational market (or semimarket) ideologies and practices and of policies associated with publication of standards and league tables did not generally incite the most disadvantaged schools to help their weakest and most socially, economically, and culturally disadvantaged pupils. Instead, their efforts and the way they used their resources went into trying to attract or keep those students who do not need as much help to do well. This was done to increase their averages and allow them to streamline their students to make up "good" classes and to be attractive to middle-class students and families. Without wider governmental regulation, each school must deal with this combination of market economy and assessment practices on its own. This is a detriment to the most disadvantaged and furthers social and ethnic segregation in schools (Diamond & Spillane, 2004; Goldstein & Noden, 2003; Lauder & Hughes, 1999; Van Zanten, 2001).

Another undesirable effect also concerns teachers and school staff. Management and accountability policies depend on the idea that school effectiveness researchers can discover, locate, and measure "good methods" of teaching. In turn, these methods should be spread through efficient and pedagogical engineering, which would then lead to an increase in teachers' efficiency and, therefore, to an increase in students' efficiency as well. Paradoxically, instead of producing this desired effect, such a policy often deters teachers from veritable thought processes and collective analyses. Instead, they feel forced or encouraged to train and teach to the test. Researchers do not observe the teacher empowerment or student performance increases that the proponents of school effectiveness research and evidence-based policies hoped or claimed; rather, they see work processes leading to a restricted curriculum and a narrow form of pedagogy, especially where disadvantaged schools or pupils are concerned (e.g., see Gillborn & Youdell, 2000; Hargreaves, 2003; Kherroubi & Rochex, 2002, 2004; Normand, 2005; Van Zanten, 2001).

This challenging and complex state of affairs led Myers and Goldstein (1998) to draw a parallel between the medical and the educational world, as proponents of evidence-based policies are so keen to do (see Chalmers, 2003; Davies, 1999), but to draw it to warn of the negative consequences of publication of school performance rankings. According to them, the results should not be published and, if so, only with the most extreme caution:

In such circumstances, we would argue, information should not be made available publicly: or it should have warnings attached about the dangers of interpretation so that nobody would wish to take it seriously. This warning would be more than that which appears on tobacco advertisements. It would involve a proper explanation of why the information is suspect and a reassurance that those who publish the information fully accept its limitations. (Myers & Goldstein, 1998, p. 183)

One cannot help but notice that this warning has not been heeded, even years later.

It is still too early to know whether large-scope international assessment surveys such as PISA will produce the same social cultural effects as did earlier assessments on a national scale or whether they will have similar effects on those countries whose educational systems are deemed insufficient. There are no comparative international analyses of the effects of PISA on educational systems and policies. Nonetheless, certain articles dealing with European national systems (Gruber, 2006; Moreau, Nidegger & Soussi, forthcoming; Prenzel, forthcoming) show that a country's reaction to PISA is often related to its ranking on the scale. The use of PISA can reinforce educational policies and production of standards that contribute to normalizing, decontextualizing and impoverishing school curricula. Narrowing of curricula occurs when policymakers and school system managers rethink and redefine curricula in terms of basic skills, responding to PISA design principles and their focus on "real-life situations" rather than on curricular, cultural, and linguistic contexts.

Such a perspective is explicitly stated by the OECD, which promotes PISA and the DeSeCo project (see Rychen & Salganik, 2001), and by the European Commission (Rodrigues, 2002; for a critical analysis, see Dale, 2005). These international organizations do not seem to have taken into account Paulston's (1988) warnings about the results of previous international surveys. Paulston argued that these surveys have not brought to light links to cause and effect; rather, they have shown the importance of unintentional processes and components of teaching and the dangers represented by both an overabundant production of facts and an insufficient conceptual model. He further argued that, without conceptual models, policymakers and others cannot interpret these facts accurately and that, by making cursory comparisons of schools or school systems, they underestimate the impact of the different historical, social, political, cultural, and linguistic contexts in which schools and school systems are always embedded (Paulston, 1988).

The questions and critiques presented in this section, taken together, do not solely concern problems of comparison. There are also issues involving the theoretical and methodological concepts used to construct surveys and analyze their data. These questions are dealt with in the next two sections of this article. One section deals with the methods used in the PISA 2000 survey, especially the tests used to measure literacy competencies. The second section presents a secondary analysis of French students' results and the ways they coped with the PISA literacy tests. This research was requested and funded by the French Ministry of Education.[7]

CONSTRUCTION OF THE PISA TESTS

Perhaps more than any other assessment procedure, because of their size and their aims, international surveys such as PISA have been developed through disparate and complex decision-making processes in which different countries and participants can weigh unequally. These processes combine political, scientific, technical, and financial stakes and logics. In the end, the methods and tools of assessment selected are the result of diverse and sometimes contradictory needs. Obviously, the interested parties have an impact on the give and take of these surveys' requirements. This does not mean to say that these surveys are useless or that those who have worked to conceive and implement them do not do a rigorous job. However, it is necessary to take precautions because these types of surveys have frequently been overused, especially in politics and the media. It is important to understand what these surveys do and do not measure, what their results mean, and how to conduct additional research accordingly. Through what methodological and theoretical conceptions and hypotheses were the PISA 2000 tests, especially the survey's literacy tests, established?

A Rapid Development and Administration Schedule

PISA is different from most other international assessment surveys in that its program was determined by the Educational Committee of the OECD, which is an inter-governmental organization. This survey is reviewed every 3 years, and at each review point there is an emphasis on literacy, mathematics, or science. PISA benefited from the previous surveys conducted by the International Association for the Evaluation of Educational Achievement (IEA). The PISA project began in 1997. Most of the people who structured and managed PISA had worked previously to conceive and implement the IEA surveys. This fact is perhaps what enabled this program to be conducted "under rapid fire."[8] As Bottani and Vrignaud (2005) argued: "Considering the size of the project, the rapidity with which the project was directed is astonishing. This is probably due to other pre-existing work outside the official process described and presented by the OECD documents" (p. 75).

Indeed, Bottani and Vrignaud pointed out that it took only 7 or 8 months (from May 1997 to February 1998) to develop and put everything in place, including the initial political decision and preparation, international bids, selection of bids, choice of project managers and experts, and signing of contracts. This time frame is extremely short. It is hardly surprising therefore that, given the project's magnitude and tech-nicalities, those responsible for implementing PISA at the OECD sent out few bids (seven according to Bottani and Vrignaud). Even more curious is that the institutions to which the bids were sent had only 1 month to answer. They had obviously already been made aware of the project's content; if not, they would not have been able to respond in such a brief period. These institutions were, of course, expressly chosen for their established competence and technical abilities in dealing with large student assessment surveys. Nonetheless, this entire procedure lacks transparency, as does the way in which the functional experts in charge of working with the consortium were chosen. This has made it very difficult to distinguish between the scientific and the political parts of the process that led to the decisions determining what followed.

All in all, PISA took half the time—from its beginning to the publication of its first results—of the TIMSS survey conducted by the IEA in the 1990s. It goes without saying that the support of the OECD and national governments, as well as understandings gleaned from previous surveys, helped shorten the process. It is also a given that the governments' influence and political, administrative, and managerial decision-making processes were factors in this schedule as well as in the choice to renew the survey every 3 years. According to Bottani and Vrignaud (2005):

> We can suppose that such a rapid pace was a necessary price to pay to receive governmental financial backing. . . . We can question this tri-annual rhythm, not only because it is costly but also because the period is too brief to draw pertinent conclusions. . . . In one sense, the three year time frame creates pressure on the countries and forces the rather recalcitrant scientific body to sustain a high rhythm of production and analysis. The OECD undoubtedly knew that they would thus have political backing since the politicians wanted the most recent, available figures that would allow them to assess a school system almost instantaneously. (p. 17)[9]

Conceptualizations of "Key Competencies" and Literacy

Contrary to surveys conducted by the IEA, such as TIMSS, those established by the OECD (PISA as well as the International Adult Literacy Survey [IALS]) were not designed to assess students' knowledge or the competencies linked to their school curriculum—an aim that necessitates identifying the elements common to different school systems. Instead, the PISA assessment surveys were designed to assess "the aptitude to undertake tasks found in everyday life" (OECD, 2001, p. 20). A curriculum-free or a cross-curricular test is meant to measure the generic competencies of students that are considered to be indispensable to live a successful life in a democratic, market-based society. Such a perspective—justified and held in reference to the socioeconomic theories of human capital currently shared by international organizations and national governments—considers that "competency development should be viewed in terms of preparation of life rather than achievement in school" (Salganik, 2001, p. 19).

This point of view was also held in the DeSeCo project, which, as indicated previously, was conducted by the Swiss Federal Statistical Office under the auspices of the OECD in collaboration with the National Center for Education Statistics. This project recognized that the need to produce data and results quickly using surveys such as PISA or IALS had taken precedence over the need to deepen theoretical and conceptual aspects of these surveys. As a consequence, DeSeCo's goal was to establish and reinforce the theoretical aspects of such surveys and to redefine the competencies they aim to assess. This project therefore purported to answer the following two questions: "What competencies and skills are relevant for an individual to lead a successful and responsible life and for society to face the challenges of the present and the future? What are the normative, theoretical and conceptual foundations for defining and selecting a limited set of key competencies?" (Rychen, 2001, p. 2). It attempted to define these "key competencies for a successful life and a well-functioning society" (p. xx), in the words used by Rychen and Salganik (2003) in the title of the second book devoted to this project.

During the first phase of the DeSeCo project, various renowned scholars from different disciplines were solicited to give their points of view on this issue. A reading of some of these contributions (all of which can be found in Rychen & Salganik, 2001) provides evidence of the incredible difficulty (maybe the impossibility) and the socially dangerous nature of this type of project. Thus, German psychologist F. Weinert, whose chapter sought to clarify the concept of competency and its numerous uses, wrote the following:

It is not possible to discern or infer a coherent theory of these many uses. There is no basis for a theoretically grounded definition or classification from the seemingly endless inventory of the ways the term competence is used. (2001, p. 46)

This conclusion led him to plead for a more pragmatic definition and to state that such a concept can be useful only for its practical, not its theoretical, side. The authors in that volume raised other issues as well. Weinert questioned the notion of competence as used in the project, arguing that this notion faces a formidable paradox:

The more general a competency or strategy (i.e., the greater the range of different types of situations to which it applies), the smaller the contribution of this competency or strategy to the solution of demanding problems. (2001, p. 53)

Goody (2001) held the same discourse, although his conclusions on DeSeCo's objectives were much more radical. For one, he felt that the project was pointless and unworkable: "I think that such an outcome is only possible at a very general level, which I regard as rather useless" (p. 187). For another, he argued that the project seemed dangerous because it relied totally on the abstract notion of competencies and because it dismissed the heterogeneous and conflict-ridden nature of society:

There is no competency without an end. The end cannot be competence for "an individually and socially valuable life" in the abstract since such lives differ enormously both within and between cultures. . . . The notion that there should be any general competency for living in one country let alone across nations seems open to serious questions, not only questionable but dangerous. It is questionable because different countries have different life courses. And within countries there are clearly different expectations in terms of the lives that people are likely to lead and that are required to fill their social, cultural and economic needs. (pp. 184–186)

As a specialist in literacy, Goody was particularly critical of the idea that literacy could be evaluated outside its cultural, linguistic, and even "local" context. Yet, IALS and PISA have been built on such a supposition. Indeed, PISA defines literacy in these generic terms, which were criticized by Goody: "Reading literacy is understanding, using and reflecting on written texts in order to achieve one's goals, to develop one's knowledge and potential, and to participate in society" (OECD, 1999, p. 20). This definition is very close to the one on which the IALS based its survey, although the PISA assessment survey stresses the reader's thought processes on the content as well as the form of the written texts.

The use of such a generic definition means that extreme care must be taken concerning the issue of translating from one language to another. Thus, the designers of PISA worked to translate each test from the two sources, English and French; these translations were worked into a target third language until the two translations concurred. The design of the PISA assessment survey presupposes that as long as these precautions are taken, the various tests used as tools to assess students from different countries will be able to assess the same competencies in all countries and to rank them on a one-dimensional scale. However, this presupposition is far from being confirmed, as can be seen in the work showing the difficulties in translating PISA and other international surveys (see Adams & Wu, 2002; Goldstein, 1995; Rémond, 2001). Despite all precautions, certain items in PISA 2000 show the cultural bias that affected results on the literacy tests of various countries. Murat and Rocher (2004; see also Rocher, 2003) showed that, contrary to the PISA designers' conceptions or intentions, "the similarity of the performance profiles of countries generally coincides with the similarity in terms of geography, culture or language" (p. 205).

The general, and possibly ineffective, definition of literacy they used led the designers to subdivide this general competency into different subcompetencies. However, the number and types of such components has varied from one stage to another, as noted by Bonnet (2002; see also Salganik, 2001):

While one of the first PISA documents (OECD, 2000) was referring to the assessment of five skills— global understanding, locating a piece of information, developing interpretation, reflecting on the content of texts, reflecting on the form of texts—only three—retrieving information, interpreting texts, reflection and evaluation—are finally accounted in the international report. As is pointed out in a recent Italian book (Nardi, 2002), no table of conversion was ever supplied, thus making it impossible to conduct an independent comparison of what has been measured as opposed to what was originally intended. (p. 395)

The three competencies that were finally selected were assessed via either closed questions, multiple-choice questions in particular (approximately 55%), or open questions (approximately 45%), most of which asked for well-construed written answers. These questions, therefore, went beyond reading literacy and called for writing skills from a reflective point of view (I return to this point later). Such questions, which require writing skills as much as they require reading and writing comprehension, represented nearly 80% of the items focusing on assessment of reflection and evaluation. Yet, this went unnoticed in PISA's first international report. The results referring to each of the three competencies were presented by means of three scales, each with five hierarchical levels of competencies, and gathered on a unique combined scale, also with five levels. One can question the reduction of literacy subcompetencies from five to three given that this choice lacked both argument and theory; one can also question the conception of the literacy competency or subcompetencies as homogeneous and as independent and nonhierarchical. Mendelovits (2003) noted that the reflection and evaluation items cover at least four very different tasks (making hypotheses or explaining a text's contents, formulating personal opinions, identifying formal elements or features in a text, and conducting a critical analysis of a text).

These subscales are so intermixed that the decision to place an item in one category or another is at times extremely difficult and open to debate. One can wonder, therefore, as did Rémond (2001, 2006), whether the translation of a debatable item might result in it belonging to a category other than the one in which it was placed in the original language. What is more, Goldstein (1995) and Dickes and Flieller (1997) pointed out the contradiction that exists between constructing independent subscales and then grouping all of them together in a one-dimensional scale: "It might be incompatible to claim to use a one-dimensional scale of assessment and yet to present results that deal with separate elements" (Goldstein, 1995, p. 25). Finally, there are several examples in PISA 2000 in which the principle of theoretical functional independence required by the statistical model (Van Geert, 2002a, 2002b) was not followed (Bottani & Vrignaud, 2005). This is the case when several items deal with the same text but assess different competencies and when one question must be understood or one item must be successfully completed to complete the others.

Salganik emphasized that the conception of literacy underlying the IALS and PISA assessment surveys "represents a significant departure from earlier ideas because it proposes a multi-dimensional continuum of skills ranging from none at all to high-level literacy skills rather than a single cut-off between literacy and illiteracy, and in the emphasis on skills for everyday life" (2001, p. 20). As a result, the authors who publicized the first PISA 2000 results (OECD, 2001) wrote that "the concept of literacy was adopted to emphasize that PISA assesses a whole range of competencies that goes much further than the historical concept of literacy. Literacy is measured as a continuum, not as a set standard that is either present or absent" (p. 19). This desire to stay clear of all binary oversimplified dichotomies, or a "great divide" between literate and illiterate cultures, societies, or individuals, can be regarded positively. Nonetheless, this continuist conception of literacy could decrease the importance of literacy and writing skills' roles in modes of thought and in the transformation of thought and knowledge processes, which are at the heart of works by Goody (1977, 1993), Olson (1994), Vygotsky (1934/1985, 1978; see also Rochex, 1997), Scribner and Cole (1981), Detienne (1992), and many other researchers.

The work of these scholars is often disregarded by those who reduce language and, more globally, all semiotics into a mere tool of communication. The debate between continuist and discontinuist conceptions of the relations between orality and literacy, the different discursive genres, and the different linguistic and semiotic practices is of great complexity. It remains a highly discussed topic among specialists from various disciplines (anthropology, history, psychology, sociology). Although I do not address the details of the ongoing debate in this chapter, its existence raises questions relevant to the current discussion; in particular, it raises questions as to why the PISA designers favored the continuist approach and on what theoretical reasons this choice was grounded. Furthermore, these issues lead one to ask the following question: If this decision did not rely on theoretical grounds, on what did it rely?

One possible hypothesis, given the goal of assessment, is that this choice had more to do with psychometric reasons and necessities than with theoretical ones. Therefore, the choice made by the PISA designers in the final stage of its development appears to be debatable. At question are the meaning of the results of the literacy tests as well as the risk of minimizing or oversimplifying the discontinuity between discursive genres and the linguistic-cognitive activities required for pupils to succeed on these tests. This risk must be taken into account because it slants the possibility of using the PISA results to improve teaching methods and student performance.

In this section, I have presented conceptual challenges to PISA's conception of literacy, at the level of conception of tests as well as interpretation of results. Given the issues raised here, one overarching question must be asked: How can these results be both scientifically pertinent and pragmatically useful? Consequently, one must question how PISA results, analyses, and commentaries can help teachers and decision makers improve the performance of school systems and students, especially the most economically and scholastically underprivileged students. As a "didactician" of literacy,[10] Bain (2003) wrote, at the end of a critical discussion of PISA 2000, that

the absence of a deep grounded theory which organizes the different dimensions of written comprehension as a language practice, and which provides a decisive point of view on the steps in reading . . . is the first major obstacle to using these results pedagogically. (p. 62)

The apparent lack of deep, grounded theory raises questions about what the designers of PISA used to define literacy. One way to interpret this omission is view their definition of literacy as what is being measured by the test. This omission, therefore, raises serious questions about what counts as literacy when literacy counts, an issue raised by Magda Becker Soares (1992) in a literature review for UNESCO's measurement division. I explore this issue further in the next section.

From Substantialist Postulate to Psychometric Model, and Back

The PISA designers seem to have worked with two related suppositions that go hand in hand. The first supposition is that the generic competency or subcompetencies of literacy (or of numeracy) are universal, independent of cultural and linguistic contexts. The second is that these (sub)competencies are stable and consistent for a given individual, regardless of the situation and of the test in which they are measured. These two suppositions constitute a substantialist point of view and explain the methodological recourse of using item response theory modeling[11] (IRT). However, it is difficult to know whether IRT was really used because of these suppositions or because of its metric and ordinal qualities. IRT depends on validity conditions or on a hypothesis that assumes that the competencies to be measured are unidimensional and the different tests used to assess them are functionally independent (see, concerning this issue, the debate between Goldstein and Masters, 1995).

The aim of such a model is to assess people's performance in relation to different tasks rather than in comparison with other people, unlike other classically standardized procedures. Another aim is to ensure that individual performance assessment is independent of the difficulty evaluation of items; IRT presupposes that whatever items are passed by an individual, one could make the same assessment of his or her competencies, and that whatever the groups of individuals that pass a test, whatever the contexts in which these individuals live, and whatever the situations in which they are assessed, one could make the same evaluation of the test's difficulty (see Bottani & Vrignaud, 2005).

Although the metrical and ordinal virtues of this type of analysis are undeniably powerful, it appears to be simplistic and reductive in regard to the analyses and contributions of different scientific fields (e.g., history, psychology, sociology, educational studies) in dealing with the tasks, competencies, and cultural practices at stake in such surveys. In addition, it ignores or underestimates debates and questions between and within these different scientific fields, particularly concerning literacy. PISA 2000 also reduces these interdisciplinary issues and questions.

IRT presupposes that the difficulty or discriminative value of each item (or of the different levels of the subcompetency scales) is independent of any context. This explains the efforts to minimize, and even eliminate, all linguistic and cultural bias that could "favor" a country, a language, or a culture and then falsify the validity of ranking different students or different countries on performance scales. Such biases decreased substantially because of the considerable efforts made and the solution chosen by the PISA conceivers.

Nevertheless, such an aim (to minimize or eliminate all cultural or linguistic biases) is questionable, as I discuss later, and difficult (maybe even impossible) to accomplish. This argument was identified by Murat and Rocher (2004), who compared PISA 2000 results between French and American students. Using the Mantel-Haenszel statistic and the statistical index of bias, they showed that two thirds of the test items could be considered biased on the basis of their comparison. Furthermore, they showed that the different countries did not have the same performance profile; that is, item rankings based on student success rates were not the same from one country or one cultural or linguistic area to another, as would be the case if, in accordance with the statistical model, the level of difficulty and the discriminative value of the different items were independent of any context. Such variations or biases can also be found if one compares the level of difficulty of the three scales (retrieving information, interpreting texts, reflection and evaluation) or if one takes into account the level of difficulty or the frequency at which different types of items are left unanswered (multiple-choice questions, short-answer questions, and essay questions). This finding was, in fact, acknowledged in the OECD's (2003) secondary report devoted to literacy, which stated that "these variations seem to occur based on different linguistic groups." The report explained these variations by proposing a general hypothesis regarding a "linguistic, cultural or pedagogical effect" (OECD, 2003, p. 76).

Another problem arises from the fact that IRT also depends on a twofold hypothesis or validity condition. First, whatever items a person passes, he or she should obtain the same level of performance on the global scale or the three literacy subscales. Second, whatever the person's level of performance, the processes and ways of answering a question should be similar and could be organized on a continuum. This double hypothesis appears to be questionable on a theoretical level (Reuchlin, 1997; Van Geert, 2002a, 2002b) and much too simple in light of the PISA literacy test results. This issue is examined in depth later in the chapter in the analysis of the different ways French students dealt with PISA 2000 literacy tests. According to the PISA 2000 results of French students, the hypothesis that the competencies of a given student

remain stable regardless of the item answered is true only at each end of the performance scale, that is, for those with the highest or lowest performance. In contrast, the
performance and ways of coping with the tests among students in between appeared
extremely heterogeneous and therefore reveal neither univocal nor stable competencies
(Bautier, Crinon, Rayou, & Rochex, 2004, forthcoming).

Chatel (2005) obtained the same findings in her research on educational assessment.
She disputed that student performances could be evaluated on a continuum and criticized the supposedly linear training that would justify using such a continuum.[12] Test
scores (especially aggregate scores) possess only relative, not absolute, properties, or
they function as hypotheses about student knowledge and competencies, which are
always embedded in different contexts, rather than statements of fact representing
actual student competencies.

There is no doubt that this conceptualization of scores as representing fixed properties aids the shift from assessing to ranking, but this shift greatly narrows the range of
possibilities for interpretation of results and their possible uses in improving students'
and teachers' intellectual efficiency and empowering them in terms of ways of thinking
and working. Further along these lines, Van Geert (2002a, 2002b) argued that it is
also necessary to consider people's intra-individuality as well as their dynamic and
contextual nature, and he called for "a new approach in psychometry" (Van Geert,
2002a). Equally, Goldstein (1995) disputed unidimensional views of the meaning of
score rankings in the case of those aiming to assess competencies in fields as large and
heterogeneous as the sciences, mathematics, and literacy.

Reequilibrating Psychometric Constraints and Heuristic Perspectives

In summary, the choices made in the conception and application of the PISA assessment survey and in the analysis of its results seemed to be motivated more by psychometric and political concerns than by theoretical reasons or research results in the
different disciplines involved (history, psychology, sociology, and the science of
education). Thus, the goal of the designers of PISA and other similar international
surveys was to build measurement instruments that would permit a more trustworthy
and equitable ranking of student performance, one that would neither favor nor
disfavor a particular country or group of countries. Postlethwaite (2005) expressed
this concern succinctly when he argued that "ideal conditions for comparison will never
exist, but what is important is to try to come as close to it as possible in order for the
public to perceive them as sufficiently equitable" (p. 102). Such a wish clearly shows
the shift from scientific concerns and norms (which would require interpretations of
results that involve pertinence and validity for a scientific community) to political ones
(which involve equity for the public). It also shows the shift from assessment and
comparative approaches to the primary goal of ranking, a move consistent with the
political goal of equity.

The primacy of psychometric concerns is clearly visible in the response by Masters
(2005), president of IEA's technical advisory board, to Goldstein's (2005) criticisms
of the conceptions and methodologies in international comparisons of students' per-

formances. Masters claimed that the one-dimensional conception of competencies that was criticized by Goldstein is not a hypothesis but an explicit intention (although he was referring to IEA, the same could be said of PISA):

> As regards education, the tests are built to measure only one particular dimension of a student's knowledge acquisition. This does not occur unfortunately. This is fully intentional since it is exactly the reason for creating the instrument. . . . Those who designed the IEA instruments do not submit "hypotheses" but create intentions. They do not try to summarize complex facts; they try to establish measurements of variables. (2005, pp. 34, 36)

Masters held that it is impossible to proceed otherwise and believed that Goldstein's criticisms were "such that it is difficult to ascertain whether he is favourable to the conception of any sort of scale of measurements" (p. 36). This conceptualization of the debate is overly simplistic. Therefore, to avoid choosing between these two seemingly opposing positions—refusing any measurement scale (which is, of course, neither Goldstein's position nor mine) and fully accepting IEA's or PISA's methodologies and tools as the only ones possible—I return to the alternative propositions formulated by other assessment specialists about the potential goals and uses of such surveys.

Before that, I would emphasize that the combined effect of the three stances taken by PISA's developers—substantialist postulate, psychometric model, and comparative, or ranking, perspective—leads logically to attempts to reduce or eliminate any potential source of cultural bias in favor of particular countries or particular linguistic or cultural groups. The goal of these designers is then to hunt for anything that might blemish the objectivity and accuracy of the survey's comparative scales on which different countries and school systems could be ranked. The belief that it is absolutely necessary to minimize cultural and linguistic biases is shared by people who attempt to do so and who claim that surveys such as PISA are almost unbiased as well as by people who consider such a project as illusory and such a claim as deceptive. Therefore, those who conceptualized PISA and other similar surveys must consider eventual cultural and linguistic biases as a potential technical and methodological dysfunction. As a result, they attempt to erase any element linked to specificity that was not taken into consideration when they designed the "model" of competency they aimed to assess.

What this position failed to consider is how to deepen the analysis and interpretation of data (that include biases) rather than comment on rankings. According to this aim, the biases could be seen not as psychometric nuisances but, rather, as a heuristic call and an opportunity to analyze in depth the specificities of different countries and different cultural and linguistic groups (Bottani & Vrignaud, 2005; Murat & Rocher, 2004). This does not necessarily imply that one must renounce the use of any scale of measurement, as Masters (2005) seemed to believe (or tried to make us believe). However, this does suggest that designers of surveys need to develop ways of combining quantitative and qualitative modes of investigation so as not to reduce comparison to ranking. This approach would permit development of ways of complementing assessment of students' performance (through common criteria and common scales) with deep analysis of differences between countries or cultural or linguistic areas, beyond their different ranks on score scales.

The conceptual analysis presented here argues that different projects and different conceptualizations lead to particular (and different) understandings of performance. To explore this alternative further, I mention the C-BAR (Culturally Balanced Assessment of Reading) Project. This project is administered by the European Network of Policy Makers for the Evaluation of Educational Systems, in which eight European countries are involved. The aim of this project is for comparative evaluations of competencies and literacy to be based on tests written by each country in its own language, without the use of a standard test that has been translated in different languages, or on the use of a standard test only as an anchoring tool.[13] The feasibility of such a project seems promising (see Bonnet et al., 2003), and there are undoubtedly fruitful perspectives to promote the dialogue between psychometric approaches and heuristic or hermeneutic ones, as called for by Gipps (1998) and Moss (1994; see also Moss, Girard, & Haniford in this volume).

Another possibility is to develop secondary analyses of results from international surveys. Yet, as Goldstein (1995) clearly deplored, the interests, financial means, and methodological sophistication of the heuristic approach are of much less importance (this is a euphemism) than those of the psychometric method and ranking goals. Indeed, the heuristic approach seems to be limited to secondary analyses of data from international surveys. And when these secondary analyses exist, the limited budgets allocated to them are not of the scale of PISA-type surveys, thus limiting or prohibiting their use on a comparative, international scale. In the next part of the chapter, I present a heuristic approach to analysis of the results of the PISA 2000 literacy tests that focuses on French students as an illustrative or telling case (Mitchell, 1984).[14]

SECONDARY AND COMPLEMENTARY ANALYSES OF PISA 2000 LITERACY TESTS

This section of the chapter presents the results of secondary and complementary analyses of literacy tests from PISA 2000 (Bautier et al., 2004, 2006). Although we[15] would have liked to analyze cross-cultural differences between countries or groups of countries, such a study was out of reach for a single team and would have required international collaboration. Thus, this study can be viewed as a first step in framing a larger issue for future international collaboration and exploration. Our goal was to better describe and better understand the sociocultural differences that have been observed among pupils attending school in France. To do so, we focused our attention on the methods students used to answer the questions in literacy tests from PISA 2000, on the different backgrounds they mobilized to cope with these different questions, and on their scores and achievements or failures as defined by the PISA designers. Furthermore, our data led us to question the ways PISA instructions treat, assess, and reduce students' answers on some of the tests. The project progressed through three stages that we labeled exploratory, secondary, and complementary studies of PISA 2000 literacy tests and of students' ways of coping with them.

Theoretical Frame and Research Methods

The first exploratory study, undertaken without the use of statistical tools, consisted of examining approximately 150 student folders to scrutinize and analyze students' answers and their coherence (or lack of coherence) as well as the construction of the PISA tests, the work required of students, and the ways in which correcting and coding instructions assessed and sometimes reduced this work. This first analysis of students' answers revealed that it was often difficult to predict how pupils would answer a particular item on the basis of their response to another item. A heterogeneous range of answers was identified not only between different students but also between the answers of the same student on different parts of a test or on different tests. This observed pattern of heterogeneity led us to conclude that for many pupils who participated in the tests, the competencies were neither univocal nor stabilized, contrary to the hypothesis of the PISA designers.

This conclusion, hypothetical at this first stage, guided our deliberations about how to conceptualize the problem and what research methods to select to address our questions during the second and third stages of the research. Moreover, we were perplexed about the fact that PISA's grading instructions demanded that some answers be identically rated even though they appeared to be produced through very different ways of coping with tests and texts. For example, identical ratings were required when the expected answer could be provided by spotting and selecting only one word or one narrow part from the text, by taking into account and thinking about a greater and more significant part of the text, or by referring to its syntactic or linguistic features and constraints. To illustrate this state of affairs further, I provide some examples later in a section devoted to the analysis of a particular literacy test from PISA 2000.

This first exploratory study, as well as our previous research concerning reading and writing activities of secondary school pupils (Bautier & Goigoux, 2004; Bautier & Rochex, 1998, 2004; Rayou, 2002; Rochex, 2002), was based on a conception of literacy inspired by the work of Goody (1977, 1993), Olson (1994), and Bakhtin (1994). This body of work led us to consider that what students had to do to answer PISA items, particularly those requiring interpretations of and comments on the given texts and documents, was, by nature, extremely heterogeneous. Many of the PISA literacy tests required students to mobilize various fields of reference and various registers of resources and to combine and organize the elements that they could draw from these fields and registers into a hierarchy. The issue of hierarchy was all the more the case given that the goal of the PISA designers was to assess "the skill to carry out tasks that belong to real-life situations," rather than specific knowledge, and that their themes were often close to the social and cultural references and experiences of the young people taking the test. More than traditional tests in the French secondary school, the work required to take the PISA literacy tests not only involved dealing with the given texts and questions; it also involved, depending on the different tests, students' ability (or inability) to mobilize the following five registers or to distance themselves from some of them:

1. The register of school knowledge, of general knowledge about the world, and of cultural references necessary to understand all or parts of the texts and to be able to build hypotheses from them. For instance, on some of the PISA 2000 tests,[16] students were asked about the motives that lead people from a particular South American village to behave the way they do in regard to movies; in another, they were asked about the reasons for the weakness of the humanitarian aid of a non-governmental organization in Ethiopia.
2. The register of individual or collective experience that teenagers have about social and cultural events, topics, or practices evoked in the texts of the tests (e.g., the beach, the movies, graffiti, linguistic exchanges).
3. The register of values, opinions and prejudices, and beliefs associated with youth or social backgrounds from which personal experience is woven, which in turn shapes students' views of the world and different social practices, values, and beliefs. On some tests, the examples could appear to be contradictory or counterintuitive to some of the assumptions students held about the world.[17]
4. The register of habits or ways of interpreting school or near-school situations or tasks. For example, some students might use an approach to answering the questions by focusing on each task, treating the questions separately to find and provide the "good" answer as soon as possible versus taking into account the entire problem, its relation with other problems or with knowledge fields, and the intellectual work required by the tasks (i.e., in Piaget's [1974] words, focusing on succeeding rather than on understanding what is necessary to succeed).
5. The field of cognitive skills and attitudes unique to literacy and linked to acculturation, which give students the possibility and ability to reconfigure and rethink their experience of the world and their uses of language by creating a secondary register of discourse and experience of thought, work that is seldom taught explicitly.

Central to our analysis of these five registers was the concept of creating a secondary register. This concept enabled us create a way to better understand students' oral or written and academic or nonacademic language practices. It originated in the distinction Bakhtin (1994) made in the area of literary production between different genres of discourse, the primary genres and the secondary genres. The primary genres can be described as dealing with a spontaneous, immediate production linked to the context wherein they are produced, and they exist only through this context, ignoring any underlying work or learning. Born from spontaneous oral exchanges, these primary speech genres are strongly related to people's personal experiences.

The secondary genres are founded on primary ones. Secondary speech genres take the primary genres, work them out, and reconfigure them in a way that releases them from the circumstances of their production. Secondary speech genres presuppose discursive work, which represents its own purpose and its own object and whose meaning goes far beyond the interaction in which it can circumstantially fit (on this topic, see Bautier, 2005; Bautier & Rochex, 2004; Schneuwly, 1994). Such secondary genres, or rather the work of creating secondary genres, seems to be required by many PISA items. These items ask students to approach a given opinion not only from the angle of its content but also from the angle of its form, its style, and its argumentative method. These items are the ones that attracted our major interest in both the second and third stages of our research, described next.

The second stage of our work consisted of a secondary analysis of the responses of French students who had taken PISA 2000. PISA assessment surveys involve an approach called the "revolving folders" method. All of the survey's items are placed in nine evaluation folders, each with common groups of items from one folder to the other. These nine folders are randomly given to the tested students. This procedure allows the PISA designers to assess the equivalent of 7 hours of evaluation if students were to respond to all items, and it enables each student to work for 2 hours only. Our secondary analysis focused on two of these nine folders (Numbers 6 and 7 in the French survey) that we chose because they contained the greatest number of items related to the understanding of long texts and questions requiring argumentative answers. We began with a global recoding of the responses of nearly all students assessed with these two folders (842 students).[18]

This level of recoding involved a grid of different types of indicators[19] built to grasp the diversity of registers mobilized by students. Reading competency indicators were developed first. Two types of such indicators were used: The first one represented the cognitive competencies necessary to deal with, identify, and understand the content of the texts (see Van Dijk & Kintsch, 1983); the second one represented students' ability to consider a text as both a social and linguistic object, to identify its aim, and to consider its forms as an essential means of achieving this aim. To take into account the range of registers that, according to our conceptual framework, were at stake in the students' methods, we elaborated two other types of categories and indicators. The first represented the way students related to the world, to values and opinions, and to intellectual habits allowing them to interpret the world as well as the experiences they had of the world that might interfere with their reading of the texts they had been given. The second included transversal indicators coded across all of the folders rather than test after test. The goal of this aspect of the analysis was to capture students' relation with school knowledge and their competencies related to writing code (correct or faulty syntax, spelling gaps). This part of the analysis also included an assessment of the number and frequency of unanswered questions.

All of the answers were thus recoded through the use of this grid. The data from the grid were analyzed via two statistical methods: a principal-components analysis and a hierarchical clustering analysis. The aim of these statistical analyses was to construct student categories or profiles based on students' answers. The profiles we obtained are described subsequently.[20] To explore the variability or stability of the methods used by the students according to the topics of the different texts used and the different question formats (e.g., multiple-choice questions, yes/no questions, questions needing a written constructed response), we carried out (on one folder only) a qualitative analysis of the overall answers of nearly 50 students, each representing the different profiles identified through the statistical analyses.

In the third stage of our work, we collected new data in an attempt to describe and understand the different methods used by different students as well as by the same student. This approach enabled us to explore how students coped with the different items and the different texts. Furthermore, it enabled us to examine students' responses. To achieve this aim, we created a new folder containing six tests from the PISA 2000 survey.[21] We chose them for two reasons. First, they were tests that required students to read and sometimes compare long texts and to write constructed answers; consequently, they seemed more likely to show the diversity of postures, registers, and world references mobilized and combined in students' ways of coping with them.

We asked 40 students who were 15 years old (the same age of the students rated in the PISA 2000 survey) to complete these six tests, and immediately afterward we conducted interviews with the students. During these interviews, we asked students to try to tell us how they worked to answer the different questions on the tests, to explain why and how they chose one answer rather than another, to describe their doubts and hesitations, and to talk about their thoughts regarding the tests and the texts' topics.

Given that the French educational system retains students across grades and offers different academic and technical programs, 15-year-old students, and therefore all students assessed by PISA, may attend many different schools or courses. Given these differences, we chose to survey two categories of students. The first group included students attending the fourth and final class of junior high school ("college" in French, which includes the four classes of the first level of secondary school); these students had repeated one class along their school course, most often because of learning difficulties or school failure. The second group included students attending the first class of senior high school ("lycée" in French, which includes the three classes of the second level of secondary school, leading to the baccalaureate). These two categories of students, referred to subsequently as junior high students and senior high students, make up more than 79% of the French student population assessed by PISA 2000. Furthermore, because we were particularly interested in the situations of students from working-class and underprivileged backgrounds, we mainly interviewed students in schools in which a majority of students were from low socioeconomic backgrounds (two of these schools were identified according to French policy as "educational priority areas," a form of affirmative action involving school policies).

To summarize, the three stages of our work included the following components:

- An exploratory study of nearly 150 student folders that allowed us to improve the way we conceptualized the problem and to choose and construct research methods to address it;

- A secondary statistical analysis of 842 French students' responses to PISA 2000 tests that enabled us to construct student categories or profiles and to reexamine the coherence or incoherence among the responses of a set of 50 students, each representing the different profiles; and
- A complementary study that consisted of interviews of 40 students 15 years of age immediately after they had completed six of the literacy tests from PISA 2000.

The analyses and discussion that follow are based on these studies. In the next three sections, I raise questions about the construction and grading instructions of a PISA test relating to the range of answers and words we analyzed from folders and interviews, present the student categories that we constructed using the statistical analyses and show that some of them can be considered stable and others unstable, and present case studies of four students' different ways of coping with the PISA literacy tests based on analyses of interviews.

Results and Ways of Coping, Performance, and Competencies: Example of a PISA Test

The complex relationship between PISA grading instructions, on the one hand, and students' ways of coping with tests, on the other hand, can be illustrated through an analysis of one of the specific tests on which our research has focused. On the test selected, students had to read a long text in which the opinions and arguments of some individuals or some groups of individuals who favored or opposed the mechanical cleaning of beaches were presented. The test required that students answer four questions about this extended passage. The following analysis comprises both an a priori examination (i.e., an analysis of the text and of the tasks before their presentation to students) of this test and an examination of student interviews after administration of the test. The two analyses are presented in an interactive approach that illustrates how each contributed particular information about students' performance and perceptions.

Analysis of the interviews showed that what puzzled students was essentially the irrelevant or counterintuitive nature of some of the viewpoints and arguments developed by environmental experts and activists who argued against the mechanical cleaning of beaches because it aggravates seashore erosion and contributes to the destruction of animals and plants. These positions were summarized by the paradoxical title given to the text: "Save a beach: keep it dirty." This title and related positions were viewed not only as surprising but as absurd by a majority of the students that we interviewed, according to their own experience and common opinion.

The complexity of the relationship between the grading of answers and ways of coping was further visible in the response pattern to the two multiple-choice questions proposed for this text. The first asked students to indicate why mechanical cleaning of beaches caused a drastic decrease in the bird population; it was successfully answered by 73% of French students. But the students' interviews indicated that such success could have been due to extremely different ways of coping with the question. Successful students described different approaches that were supported either by a genuine understanding of the issue (allowing them to overcome their lack of knowledge concerning some words in the text or the question) or by the mere spotting of limited elements from the text, allowing them to choose between the different answers without the requirement of a full understanding of the text or even a nearly complete misunderstanding of the passage involved.

The second multiple-choice question was apparently more difficult: 52% of French students answered it successfully. Students were asked to indicate the consequences of leaving waste on the beach, as argued by the people opposed to the mechanical cleaning of beaches. But the way in which the question was phrased led some students, who did not pay enough attention to the words, to explain the consequences of cleaning the beaches instead of explaining the consequences of leaving the waste. However, those who did read the question accurately responded in two distinctly different ways, indicating further the complexity of assessing the meaning of the response. The students who were not trapped by the phrasing of the question could find the expected answer nearly word for word in the text itself. Yet an important subgroup of these students, ones who possessed a good overall understanding of the text, chose a different answer. Their answer claimed that leaving waste on the beach could raise tourists' awareness and consequently make them adopt a more responsible attitude toward the environment. This answer fit the context and endorsed the institutional discourse of campaigns calling for each individual's responsibility in preserving nature and defending our living environment. The practice used by these students supported their choice of an answer that was both likely and intelligent, providing proof of a good understanding of the text's meaning. However, this answer was invalidated by the PISA grading instructions, whereas the choice of the expected answer did not guarantee a good understanding of the overall meaning of the passage or of the text.

Examination of a third question for this text further illustrates the complexity involved in interpreting competence from test performance. This question asked students to respond by circling the correct word indicating whether the different people or groups of people referred to in the text were favorable or opposed to mechanical cleaning of beaches. Slightly more than 50% of French students answered this question correctly; further analysis showed that neither this percentage nor the instructions seemed to point out the different kinds of work necessary to find the different correct answers. All of the correct answers were considered equivalent according to the scoring guide, whereas the preanalysis of the task as well as the students' comments about their answers proved they were far from equivalent.

Students were asked to indicate the opinions of two groups of individuals referred to as "tourism executives" or "residents defending the environment." Many students told us that they did not even need the text to know that tourism executives had no choice but to be in favor of the cleaning of beaches (forgetting in the process that the issue involved *mechanical* cleaning, which did not matter for this question). One way of interpreting this comment was that, in this case, common knowledge and experience helped students select the correct answer. This was not the case with "residents defending the environment," because to assume that residents would be against the cleaning of their beaches would be in full contradiction with common experience and opinion. Thus, to choose the correct answer, students had to keep common experience and opinion at a distance and focus on the phrase *residents defending the environment* (instead of *residents* only). Moreover, they had to pay attention to the way the statements in the text followed one another, in that the question could not be answered correctly by spotting only one of the elements.

Students were also asked to indicate the opinions of three individuals, referred to by their family names in both the text and questions, about whom they could not possibly mobilize any knowledge or any preconceived idea outside the text. A simple spotting of only one semantic clue was sufficient to answer the same question correctly for two of these three individuals, and this question was not a problem for the students. However, the quoted words of the third person were difficult for the students to understand, barely allowing them to infer this person's opinion about the mechanical cleaning of beaches. Our analysis of the text and the students' comments about the processes they used in working with it showed that, to infer this third person's opinion, it was necessary to focus less on the local semantic meaning of these quoted words than on textual and modal clues, for example the linguistic devices by means of which the text presented (and not only quoted) the different protagonists' opinions. Analysis of students' comments showed that most of those interviewed did not use or identify such textual cues, even when we asked them explicitly to focus on the way the sentences followed one another in the passage. Only good students paid attention to textual clues and not only to semantic ones; all of these students were attending senior high school. However, neither the students who focused only on the semantic meaning of the quoted words nor those who did not understand them were prevented from answering this question correctly because, as in the question about the other protagonists involved, a correct response could be obtained through selecting one out of two possible answers.

Analysis of these questions revealed two issues related to interpretation of the results for students. On the one hand, as illustrated earlier, we identified the need to consider how the choice of the expected answer can conceal dramatically different and intellectually unequal working methods, both from one student to another and from one question to the other for the same student. On the other hand, the study also revealed how the question format (correct/incorrect) and the treatment of the answers tended to overshadow the varying levels of difficulty of different questions that were considered equivalent by the PISA designers and interpreters.

One final example brings this issue into sharp relief. The final task, a written one related to the text about beaches, required the students to write a statement about whether they thought the paradoxical title of the text was a "correct summary of the issue debated in the text" and then explain their answer. All of the answers, whether positive or negative, were to be considered correct, according to the scoring instructions, as long as students indicated that the article developed two opposite points of views, whereas the title took up only one point of view. No special credit was given to the answers of students who wondered and pondered, in a secondary posture, upon the aim of such a title or what was (or must be) a debate (e.g., students who suggested that the author had used a form of irony or that he or she had wanted to catch readers' attention by puzzling them). Rates of correct scores on this item were very low among both French (23%) and international (17%) students.

Analyses of answers and interviews showed a broad range of patterns of work in relating the text to the title. Most students seemed to be unable to keep at bay their own opinions on the views and arguments presented in the text or to consider the relevance of the title given to the text independently of their opinion about its contents. They tended to comment more on the text, their own attitude about the title, and the counterintuitive position in regard to their common opinion than on the title, which they did not take into consideration. Less numerous were those who paid attention to the title but forgot that it concerned a debate. Some of these students stated that they found the title relevant because it reflected the idea they thought was expressed by the majority of the protagonists of the debate; other students, even less numerous, suggested another title summing up the same idea (e.g., "another solution for a clean beach"). Important to note is the fact that all of these answers, which obviously did not originate from the same type of interpretation of or working methods for the text and title and one's experience of the world, were considered nonvalid according to PISA's grading instructions. This fact confirmed our earlier analyses: as with the previous example of the multiple-choice response, the work of students to construct or provide an answer was ignored, raising further questions about what competencies were being assessed.

Student Categories and Profiles: Stabilities and Instabilities

The following analyses and discussion are based both on our statistical treatment of French students' responses in the two PISA assessment survey folders and on our examination of the homogeneity or heterogeneity of the overall answers of nearly 50 students representing the different profiles that the statistical treatment enabled us to construct (see the earlier description of the second stage of our research). Because there were differences in the tasks proposed in the two folders, our statistical treatments were applied separately to the body of answers specific to each folder. The procedure used allowed us to create five categories of students for each folder, which were comparable from one folder to the other.

From these five categories, three "stable" categories of students were identified in the analysis across the folders. The first category of students we were able to define represented 16% of the entire corpus (19.5% and 13% for the two different folders). We labeled this category "abstainers" given that these students were characterized by a high occurrence of questions left unanswered, as though they had given up as a result of the difficulties encountered. For example, Maryse answered only multiple-choice questions or questions that required her to pick up details of the texts; she failed to respond when construction of the global meaning of the text was involved. This pattern led us to think that she focused on only one detail of the text. Given this pattern and the high occurrence of unanswered questions, we were unable to explore further the methods used by students such as Maryse or the knowledge, experience, or values they mobilized, limiting what we could say about the practices or competencies of this group (which was 62% male). However, the students in this category had weak scores on the PISA tests, and 80% were in junior high school.

A second category, defined as students in "global failure," represented 20% of the corpus (19% and 22% for the two different folders). The main characteristic of the students in this group was their inability to mobilize the knowledge, know-how, or strategy necessary for interpreting the texts of the PISA tests. The practices identified for these students showed that, in answering, they awkwardly tried to pick up and copy certain passages of the text they read or repeat the terms of the question asked, or they answered with information or opinions beyond the text without regard to its contents or style. Thus, they appeared to have relied on ready-made statements and to have replaced what the text actually stated with personal conformist or relativist statements. Some of their answers appeared completely devoid of logic. Nonetheless, in contrast to the first category of students, the students in this group attempted to answer the questions, and their scores were not as low as those of students in the first group (51% of these students were boys, and 74% were in junior high school).

Analyses of the overall pattern of answers and of characteristics of students considered to be most clearly representative of this category enabled us to go beyond the simple facts of test scores. By examining the quality of these students' answers, we were able to show that they did not deal with the text as a text (a given object) but, rather, viewed the text as a means or an opportunity to express themselves. They essentially referred to their own selves, their own feelings, and their own experiences in answering, and they were unable to build another text by crossing their own voice with the voice proposed in the text. One way of understanding this practice is that they were using a primary genre of discourse approach and were faced with the challenge of carrying out the work of constructing a secondary genre for their own speech, experience, or thought, as required by the text and the test. They were unable to weave their own voice with the secondary voices of the text; most of the time, their answers were overwhelmingly based on an emotional or doxological (or commonsense) point of view. They did not appear to mobilize any knowledge beyond experience or common opinion, and they did not engage in any modal use of language. Their reading of the texts as represented in their written responses showed that they did not consider these texts in their materiality.

Furthermore, some of these students were able to produce the correct answer for many of the easy items by spotting certain elements of the text and reproducing them without demonstrating that they really understood the text. In their answers, they used limited pieces of information from a text that related to the question and thus were capable of producing correct answers more frequently than the students in our first category.

A third category (21% of the corpus; 22% and 20% for the two different folders) unsurprisingly contrasted with the two previous ones. We labeled the students in this category the "good understanders." When confronted with texts, they were able to mobilize the entire panel of cognitive competencies and postures to construct correct answers and take into account both the contents and forms of the texts. These students demonstrated good spelling and grammatical competencies. They did not mobilize conformist points of view, and when they referred to a relativist viewpoint, it did not hinder their understanding of the text. To understand a text, they knew how to question it, how to propose hypotheses, and how to draw inferences from the different statements of the text and from what was said and what was not (e.g., reading between the lines). They were particularly apt at distancing themselves from the literal meaning of the words to grasp the essential meaning of the text and rephrase it in their own words as well as apt at expressing and confronting their own viewpoint. They knew how to find the most important information and to focus their interest on the author's intention and on the way the author chose to convey this information.

Of these students, who obtained far higher scores than average on the PISA tests, 53% were girls, and unsurprisingly all attended senior high school. Analysis of the answers of these students revealed that they almost systematically provided the correct answers to the tests. Their performance indicated their capacity to mobilize simultaneously their academic knowledge, cultural knowledge, or personal experience; a method of approaching the documents relying on real and stable literacy competencies; and larger cognitive competencies. Analyses across items showed that throughout the different items in the folder, these students could be considered as able to reshape the different sources they mobilized and then to adopt the posture required by the test. These students were able to mobilize themselves in ways that went beyond their subjective experience to take up a position as authors of a thought, of a work, of a secondary written discourse that itself went beyond personal experience or opinion.

Whereas these three categories or profiles of students appeared nearly stable, the two other categories we established from our statistical analysis of each folder (four additional categories) were much less stable. These four categories contained more than 42% of the students in the two folders analyzed. In the first folder, we established two categories that we labeled "information spotters" and "meaning makers hindered by a conformist attitude." They constituted, respectively, 21% and 19% of the students assessed in this folder. We chose to label the two additional categories of students assessed in the second folder "readers restricting themselves to the explicit meaning of the text" and "minimalist students" (21% and 24% of these students, respectively). Success rates among the students belonging to these categories were equal or superior to the PISA average; 54% were girls, and almost 62% were in senior high school.

Their answers were much less homogeneous than those of students in the three previously described categories and revealed much more unstable competencies (or gaps) and postures. Their answers seemed more linked to methods and mobilization processes that differed according to the texts and questions. They depended more on the texts' topics, on the question format (multiple-choice questions or open-ended questions requiring a more complex written answer), and on the nature of the expected tasks (spotting explicit information in the text, overall comprehension, comments on or analysis of arguments or style).

The students in the "information spotters" category had relatively good scores on the simplest reading tasks, those that required picking up a piece of information, recognizing it when it was being paraphrased in a multiple-choice question, or giving one's personal opinion. Conversely, in addition to important grammatical and spelling gaps, they appeared to have difficulties reasoning from the text and organizing its information into a hierarchy. The texts seemed to be transparent for them, and they did not seem familiar at all with the methods allowing the texts to become an object of reflection, analysis, and comments. Some of their features brought them close to the category of "readers restricting themselves to the explicit." As indicated previously, the latter were students whose answers from the second folder revealed that they mainly worked with the text they were able to understand, when all of the necessary data were present, but that they had a hard time mobilizing beyond its content to carry out the necessary inferences. The observed pattern raises a series of questions: How can we interpret this pattern? Is it due to a sense of caution and exactness? Or is it due to these students' lack of knowledge of the need to link the content of a text to elements outside the text to understand it? Our data did not allow us to answer these questions.

The group that we called "minimalist" students had an even more heterogeneous profile. They had assimilated some competencies, cognitive and linguistic, and were able to answer many of the PISA questions better than other students, but these competencies were hardly stable and seemed hardly reliable. The ability to use secondary postures or genres was sometimes present and sometimes absent. These student' achievements, however, stopped when they needed to use written language as a cognitive or semiotic tool that would allow them to go further in their reflections about the text.

Our final category brought together students involved in their work and in the texts they wrote. These students were able to comment on the texts and to reason so that they could understand them. However, their reference to a conformist view frequently hindered their reflection. Their answers were often longer than those of the other students, but they were not necessarily pertinent. These students talked extensively about themselves while interpreting the text. Most of their written responses suggested that they dealt with the texts and the questions as an opportunity to express themselves about certain topics; therefore, their answers and their ways of coping with the tests appeared very heterogeneous and depended on the degree of interest they showed in the issues in the different texts. Their arguments seemed to be based on moral values of justice and truth. Such a self-commitment to certain items allowed them to produce correct answers because of shared values or experience with the positions in the text or to one of its protagonists. But this commitment also led to incorrect assertions, answers beyond the point of the text, or questions left unanswered when the conformist point of view they invoked did not allow them to understand the intention of the text or the question. In such instances, they were unable to construct a proper form of reasoning. The students in this category were those with the most unstable response patterns and the most irregular performance.

To conclude our quantitative analysis, we systematically studied how the scores obtained for PISA and the occurrences observed for each indicator we defined in our coding grid were related. This study, as well as the study of the joint occurrences of the indicators that led to the categories characterizing students' performance patterns from the hierarchical analysis, allowed us to examine the indicators that best discriminated among the students. This analysis revealed two facts. On the one hand, the most statistically significant indicators were those that referred to cognitive competencies (e.g., the ability to understand the relationships between the different parts of a text and their causal links and the ability to infer implicit from explicit elements). One reason for this result may have been that these competencies were the ones most frequently involved in the tests. On the other hand, indicators of contrasts between "good" and "bad" students were less frequent.[22] These indicators referred to the ability to relate to knowledge, experience, and language in what we called secondary genres and postures. They were those we defined to estimate whether, as we hypothesized, the genres and postures required by PISA were related to students' capacity to consider the linguistic and rhetorical aspects of a text as a topic of reflection, to consider the world and their experience of the world as an object of knowledge and analysis, and to use language, especially writing, as a device for further thinking. Conversely, we also found that our hypothesis about the mobilization of different social, juvenile, or personal experiences and common opinions could be observed in the different categories of students but did not enable us to discriminate between students. This mobilization did appear to be a resource for the good students, who readily used any material at hand to concentrate on the texts and questions. Furthermore, as previously noted, such mobilization constituted either a help or a hindrance for students whose competencies and postures were much less stable and less reliable.

Performances and Mobilized Registers: Four Students' Differentiated Profiles

Our analysis focusing on the student folders, which were actually submitted to PISA 2000, was completed through an examination of the observation and interview data we collected 2 years after the OECD survey. As mentioned earlier, we submitted our own folder containing six tests from the original survey to 40 students 15 years of age. We also collected different types of information concerning their schooling and their social and family backgrounds. In this section, I present our analysis of the methods and statements of four of these students, all attending school in one of the most underprivileged areas in the suburbs of Paris (the Seine Saint Denis department). We selected these students because we thought they fit closely with some of the student categories identified through our statistical analysis. In the following, quotations from interviews with the students are included, as well as excerpts from their written test answers.

Hawa: A Reflective Posture in Any Circumstance

Hawa (student names are pseudonyms) was representative of the category of students defined as good readers and "good understanders" in our previous analysis; she constantly demonstrated—in her work on the tests as well as in her interview—a secondary posture and important cognitive mobilization; and she constantly reflected on the texts and the tests as well as on the world and herself. A top student in her first year of senior high school, she was to be accepted in the scientific syllabus at the end of the school year.[23] The eldest of three girls born in the Congo from Congolese parents, she came to France at 2½ years of age. Her father is a technical agent and her mother a catering employee. She is considering becoming an engineer, after having considered becoming a doctor, but she said in her interview that she wants "to let time go by [in order to] decide the job . . . I'll do." A prolific reader, she said that she has a "passion" for writing and that she has written "stories which come out of my head [and that one of them] has turned into a 100-page novel." She described the change from junior high to senior high in terms of "a new independence [that] fits in with our capacity to express ourselves."

Whatever the question, Hawa seized all of the themes evoked by the tests or during the interview to put them at a distance and turn them into reflection topics, sources of lessons, and generic considerations. She asserted herself as the author of this reflection and of these considerations to establish a dialogue or to debate with the authors of the texts she had been asked to think about. The PISA tests, their topics, and the examples suggested by her own experiences or interests were quickly boosted into generalities. She located and commented on them in relation to general principles as much as with reflection on herself. For example, concerning the test involving graffiti, she stated:

As for Sophie's text, I understand her arguments, but it somewhat follows the guidelines I have established for myself. . . . We think, OK, advertising pays off and graffiti doesn't pay off. In this society, what comes first are the things which pay off. As if we compared it to smoking, they tell us everywhere that it's bad for our health but they continue to sell tobacco because it has long-term effects, unlike drugs, and it generates a lot of money for the state.

A similar pattern was identified for her experience with movies, a topic of another test:

I like films which project us into the future like *Matrix*, for instance. . . . I'm also fond of films about real life, to keep from dreaming too much. Because we enjoy dreaming, but we mustn't forget our two feet are standing on the earth, that we walk on concrete and that anything can happen. [She used these words in an exchange about a film, *Elephant*, directed by Gus Van Sant, that Hawa wanted to see.]

She told us that she was irregularly interested in the themes submitted to her for reflection on the tests and that she paid varying amounts of attention to them. However, her lack of interest and what she described to us as a superficial overall reading of the text about the cleaning of beaches did not prevent her from succeeding in correctly answering all of the questions with the exception of the most difficult one. In contrast, both her declared interest in some of the topics proposed by other tests and the reflective posture she showed led her to become involved at times and to think about an issue raised by a text or test rather than dealing with the precise questions asked. This attitude did not cause any problems when her comments actually led to the correct answers to the questions. However, her agreement with the views expressed in a particular text resulted in her failing to give a correct answer on a test that required students to read a text about space research and indicate, from among four other texts about the same topic, the one most opposite to the point of view of the first text. Despite this error, she did not only take up the argument of the text she chose incorrectly; rather, she rephrased it and put it at a distance to get a better grasp of it, although in so doing she reflected less on space research than on the world's disorder:

It is true that the exploration and the exploitation of space make us ponder. But I think it would be preferable to focus our attention on current issues. And the billions spent for space research are not the only obstacles to the solving of these problems.

Moreover, she qualified this point of view by taking into account another author's viewpoint and then starting a virtual discussion with him:

Felix is also right when he says we must not only care about our generation but also about the generations to come. This argument, I make mine. I'd like to tell him that if some young people don't exist today, well, there won't be any tomorrow. To have a tomorrow you must have a today. . . . So we had better think about improving our living conditions today before thinking about tomorrow.

This virtual discussion, in which Hawa acknowledged the legitimacy of arguments she did not share, revealed a genuine capacity to be flexible in her judgments, a flexibility she also showed about the topic of graffiti:

I like it only when it's nice to look at. But when it's insulting or for instance in the metro, when we see window panes with a lot of things written on them, it's true that it's not really a pretty sight, and it also shows a lack of respect for people.

Yet, in her test answer, it is from her own relationship to language and from her own commitments that she was able to judge, between two letters about graffiti, the one that was best written: "As for me, Sophie has written the best letter. Her tone, as well as her arguments, strike home. The fact of asking questions to the readers the way she does conveys a true conviction." She commented on this answer in her interview just before telling us that she writes a lot. Her comments about Sophie's letter revealed that she recognized herself in Sophie's way of writing: "It's much more convincing because we've got the impression that she is standing in front of us, and that she is yelling her questions at us."

In the overall PISA tests we asked her to do, Hawa appeared perfectly capable of mobilizing relevant school and cultural knowledge to understand the texts and rephrase their themes, as well as to grasp their paradoxical aspects and express explanatory hypotheses about them. Thus, she was able to speak of "developing countries or the ones under the poverty level" by using a specific vocabulary that appeared neither in the text nor in the questions about humanitarian aid, before presenting the hypothesis about how a war in Ethiopia could explain the feeble amount of aid granted to this country. In the same way, she explained the attitude of South American villagers discovering the cinema for the first time by writing that they give too much importance to what is only fiction before expressing in her interview, in a spontaneous comment on the text, the hypothesis that "it's certainly the first time they go in a movie theater, fiction doesn't directly come to their minds."

Cindy: Looking for the Answers to the Questions or Thinking the Texts Over?

Cindy, a 10th grader from a senior high school in the suburbs of Paris, was representative of the group of students we qualified as "information spotters," whose school competencies allowed them to spot information in a text and provide good answers to questions requiring retrieval of information but who had problems reasoning about the global text. Cindy seemed to be perfectly aware of this weakness ("My problem is that I don't read the text"). She told us that she rushes over the questions and reads the text mostly to find the answers. She told us that she knew the proper method is to understand the overall meaning of the text to be able to answer to specific questions. Yet, she was too worried about the grading prospect, and she could think about the text only from a point of view that was neither the author's nor hers but the one she thought to be the examiner's. She realized that this was not effective but remained unable to adopt another attitude: "I throw myself right into the questions, I feel like answering them; I don't know, I don't even know why I do like that."

The daughter of a father who drives metros and a mother who works at a chemist's store, Cindy had attained good grades in junior high school. But in senior high school, she was starting to find herself overwhelmed, especially in literacy subjects. When exercises began to be less guided and to require personal resource and knowledge to take into account the issues presented in the text and organize them, her "localistic" method was no longer effective. This is the reason why she found particularly helpful the PISA items that asked precise questions on very distinct elements of the text. An example is an item concerning a list of 14 pieces of advice for students who were preparing for a linguistic school journey: "First they give us a little information, they tell us 'read number 13 of the list, or number 1.' So they give us precisely the sentence which corresponds to the question." During the interview, she revealed that another advantage for her was that some of the texts asserted viewpoints she thought she shared. This agreement allowed her to reach a degree of comprehension she did not usually have or authorize herself to reach.

She had a difficult time with the test about the cleaning of beaches. Her difficulties arose from two sources. On the one hand, because of the number of protagonists in the debate and the diversity of their views on a topic she apparently knew very little about, she was limited in her ability to build the text as a whole rather than as a succession of elements. On the other hand, she was unable to understand or embrace some of the environmental viewpoints expressed in the text arguing that it is better, under certain circumstances, to leave the beaches dirty: "I don't go to the beach when it's dirty." Very ill at ease among all of these arguments she often found absurd, she said she underlined all of the grammatical subjects in the text, hoping to be able to answer the questions she had yet to read more easily. Thus, she wasted a great amount of time in doing that and found herself unable to mobilize the relevant elements of the text when she was required to do so. Her actions were not due to her lack of commitment to the task; indeed, her permanent misgivings led her to constantly reread passages from the text, which did not allow her to answer the last items of the folder within the given time. Rather, her actions resulted from the general approach she used to deal with such texts.

On another PISA text, she was unable to infer that South American villagers could discover cinema for the first time and then be unable to understand that the story and characters of a movie are fictional, not real. On still another test involving a humanitarian aid project, she was unable to phrase any hypothesis on the paradoxical aspect of the lack of help given to one of the poorest countries on earth: "Ethiopia? We never talked about it in geography; no, we never did." Her responses proceeded as if she needed to base herself on a well-identified school reference and, without such a reference, she was unable to take the text and her own stance on the text as a topic of reflection, as the most difficult PISA tests (and senior high school curricula) required her to do. Beyond the stress due to the test, the PISA assessment survey, by loosening its ties with academic methods, calls upon an intellectual autonomy, an autonomy that students such as Cindy have not been able to build even though they painstakingly carried out their scholarly tasks as junior high students.

Hachem: When Too Much Sense Destroys Meaning

Hachem, a ninth grader, did not have the exact profile of the students we qualified as "meaning makers hindered by a conformist attitude." However, like the representative students in this category, he could not prevent himself from forgetting his own capacity to rationally understand what he read; instead, he considered the written lines submitted to him as signals requiring him to project his own vision of the world.

Analysis of his interview and folder showed that he lacked the necessary vocabulary to make his access to the texts easier. For example, he did not know the meaning of the words *damage* and *residents* (in French, *préjudice* and *residents*), and he said that he did not understand the word *trivial* or the meaning of the phrase *governing idea* (in French, *négligeable* and *idée maîtresse*). He revealed some further gaps concerning school knowledge that he should have assimilated (he confused "coastal erosion" with the rising level of water due to global warming). He also had a hard time imagining situations he had never experienced as a linguistic school journey.

This simple lack of competencies did not appear to be at the origin of the shifts of meaning he made on some topics, nor did it explain why he managed quite well on others that did not seem to be easier cognitively. Paradoxically, it was often his connection to the topic, and the sense that resulted, that drove him to make mistakes, because he gave up the emotional distance necessary to pay attention to the text itself. In such instances, he became immersed in reacting to the text's topic; in other instances, he was able to use this emotional distance if the themes did not affect him to the same degree. The interview we conducted with him uncovered a few keys, although not enough to be certain of this interpretation because of the short time we had. These clues allowed us to have a limited access to the moments when the texts' contents reminded him of his daily environment and made adopting an objective posture complex and difficult for him.

From Algerian origins, Hachem told us he had difficulty with the French language. His ambition was to follow advanced studies because he wanted to work in aeronautics and become a pilot. He sometimes hesitated when asked about which country he would like to live in, but he thought he was luckier than his cousins who had remained in Algeria: "It's normal, there are a lot of problems over there. It's not easy to work, to learn." The tension between the two countries and two cultures seemed strong, but he said in different ways that he was looking forward to his integration in his adoptive homeland. Thus, the items that generated tensions between conformist positions and positions more centered on one's own opinions put him particularly ill at ease.

This response pattern was typically the case on a PISA test that presented two short texts (about 20 lines) in which opposite opinions about graffiti were argued. For example, in the first text, a student named Helga claimed her anger at seeing graffiti damage the city walls and the "criminal artists" who spoil the environment, thus tarnishing young people's reputation. In the second text, a student named Sophie highlighted the creative sense of graffiti writers as inventors of shapes and regretted that those who disapprove of them readily accept the advertisements that invade our streets.

Hachem partially included Helga's arguments in his initial response. When he was asked to find in the text other damages she pointed to, however, he could see only the social cost generated by the necessity of erasing the graffiti over and over again. He did not refer to the argument used in Helga's text about destruction of the ozone layer stemming from the compressed gas used by graffiti makers, although his interview showed clearly that he was perfectly aware of this phenomenon. One interpretation of his response, then, is to view Hachem as apparently too centered on his own experience as a junior high school student of immigrant origins eagerly looking for integration. He was proud to work in a school in a good state of repair, unlike "the ones we see all the time on TV where there are always troubles." This asserted hypermoralistic posture did not help him enter the overall argument of the first text and forbade him access to the second opinion. He did not understand Sophie's attempt at considering the similarities between urban graffiti signs and advertisements, at claiming the influence of the former on the latter, or at thinking of the difference between graffiti artists and advertisers regarding the law as unimportant. For him, the argument was only "Graffiti, it represents nothing, [and worse] it's writing your name with a weird handwriting to show that the person who wrote that is tough or that he/she knows people." The interview did not make him change his mind: "I didn't understand nothing about Sophie's adverts. . . . Anyway, it's dirty." For him, the debate over the common good was essentially related to lawfulness. Other questions in the same folder, based on the tension between opportunities to give his own opinion and concerns about social integration, triggered in him a similar type of cognitive blindness that, together with his hypermoralistic posture, seemed to not allow him (or at least to make it very difficult for him) to depart from a moral and rigid judgment.

Mehmet: Low Performance and Submissive Relationship With the Text and the World

Mehmet, a ninth grader in a particularly tough priority educational area school, was representative of the students we labeled as in "global failure." The fourth of five children, he was born in France from Turkish parents. His father was retired, and his mother did not work. Always admitted in the upper class "because of his age" and in spite of poor school results, he reported having had tremendous difficulty since his first year of junior high school (sixth grade), which he entered after he had repeated one class in primary school. Mehmet reported great difficulty in understanding the meaning of the different texts of the PISA tests, about which we questioned him and asked him to put his mind to work. His interview showed that his difficulties, which led him to abstain only once from giving an answer to a test question he had been asked, were not related to the degree of interest he said he had in the contents of the texts or in the topics mentioned. Rather, they led him more frequently to provide apparently random answers, for example answers to questions dealing with different opinions for or against mechanical cleaning of beaches, to which he had one chance of two of giving the correct answer. In other instances, his answers seemed to treat only one element of limited and local interest without taking into account the overall meaning of the text. This method led him at times to propose seemingly absurd answers that we could not understand until we realized that he blended into his answers different expressions he had selected from the sentences of the text that were semantically closest to one of the words used in the phrasing of the question. Furthermore, he appeared to do this without considering grammatical or semantic coherence.

His difficulty in understanding the text reached a peak when the text argued a position that was in opposition to common sense. At such points, his difficulty could be seen as leading him to find an exit in common sense. An example of this occurred when he was asked about the relevance of the title of the article dealing with the cleaning of beaches: "I had a hard time understanding. . . . There are more words I don't understand than words I understand. So . . . I answered that it's better to keep it clean." He could not or did not achieve the "secondary genre" posture that would have allowed him to take the title of a text, or the arguments being developed, into account without falling back on the text's content (or, rather, on one extremely limited element of the content) or on his own opinion and his agreement or disagreement with this content or element of the content. This type of response and way of dealing with texts can be viewed from our theoretical perspective as coming more from a submissive relationship to the world or to others than from a real questioning of the world and others. This interpretation is supported by the fact that the way in which Mehmet nearly always supported his agreement with a statement of a text or an author was to indicate that what they said is "true," without giving any basis whatsoever to which this "truth" could refer.

Such a relationship of submission and adherence to the world's and language's "truth" was further revealed in the interview through his hyperdependence on, or subordination to, adults; this frequently led him to interpret any question asked by the interviewer as a form of disapproval or refutation of his answers. In such instances, he gave up his own point of view and instead adopted the one he thought he detected in what the interviewer was saying or expecting him to say. For example, several times during the interview, he said "if you say that it is another answer" when the analysis of the interview showed that the interviewer said nothing of the kind. His responses were the same when the dialogue was about the reasons that motivated his agreement with a particular opinion rather than another one (about space conquest, for example), and he seemed to think that the interviewer must know better than he did what he thought or preferred. One reason for this behavior may have been the formal setting of the interview, which was perceived by Mehmet as unsafe. But beyond this aspect, it was the overall words Mehmet used that revealed his submissive relationship to adults, whose different institutional roles were most frequently embraced in the word "they" (e.g., when he evoked the decisions to come at the end of the academic year about his potential future schooling).

Analysis of his interview and folder showed that his relationship to the texts and to literacy and his relationship to the world were closely linked. This link, which cannot be disconnected from a dominated position within social power and social relationships, prevented us from considering Mehmet's score on the PISA tests that we submitted to him as originating solely from the cognitive competencies of written comprehension.

CONCLUSION

The preceding analyses confirmed most of our hypotheses about the heterogeneity of methods and registers or universes of reference mobilized by students in coping with the PISA literacy tests and the impossibility of reducing them to sole reading and written comprehension competencies. Indeed, one of our most concrete findings involved the heterogeneity and diversity revealed, not only in the comparisons we made between students or between the student categories we established but also for the same student from one test to another. Such heterogeneity and diversity was also related to the themes involved and to the nature of the expected task. This affected a significant number of students and raises questions not only about the literacy concept that underlies the PISA assessment survey but also about the project or the possibility of assessing literacy competencies as if they are stable or can be mobilized in a systematic way for a category of tasks considered as equivalent by test designers. The study of students' methods showed that, for a great number, these methods varied more in relation to the texts and contexts, topics, and type of tasks or question formats than to their sole text treatment and reading and writing competencies. The task of forecasting the successes and failures of students in this type of testing situation is thus rendered much more difficult and complex, which in turn adds more difficulty and complexity to the process of developing possible remedies at the institutional, academic, and educational levels.

Furthermore, our overall analyses of the PISA tests and the patterns of answers for each student category and in the student interviews reinforced our hypothesis that the competencies required for the PISA literacy tests are, in fact, much more complex and heterogeneous than the designers claimed. Our analyses showed that a large number of the items not only require students to have good comprehension of the texts and questions they have to work on but also require written competencies based on reshaping or reconfiguring one's experience of the world and of language on secondary genres. In addition, our analyses showed that these tests not only require students to shape meaning and to be able to mobilize written comprehension and production, they also require them to be able to carry out a method that allows them to "know" (know in doing rather than knowing in an explicit way) what is necessary and meaningful to mobilize or reject. These requirements often further require students to reshape each of the reference registers potentially requested and their ways of dealing with these registers and with academic tasks. Our (re)analysis of the PISA literacy tests, despite the intentions of their designers and promoters, shed light on the crucial importance on the literate habitus and on the set of dispositions and postures linked to what students do on the test. More generally, it shed light on the broad cultural capital incorporated by individuals on the basis of their social and educational backgrounds and histories (Bernstein, 1975b; Bourdieu, 2001) rather than on the sole weight of specific reading skill acquisition per se.

The preceding analyses do not lead to dismissal of the idea of an international assessment survey project that seeks to assess what students have acquired through schooling or social experiences. However, they raise a series of issues about such assessment surveys and their uses or misuses. The first issue concerns what counts as knowledge or as competencies being assessed—for example, in our study on PISA what counts as literacy and consequently what kinds of assessment surveys and tests enable researchers to "capture" what counts as literacy. The second issue concerns the risk of shifting, or the temptation to shift, from assessment and comparison to ranking. This shift is consequential in that it gives primacy to psychometric constraints and political concerns to the detriment of theoretical reasons and concerns as well as to the potential of the results of assessment surveys to increase the power of thought and action of all of the protagonists involved in the processes of schooling. The third issue concerns requirements to assess "processes as well as products" (Gipps, 1998), that is, ways of coping with tests as well as scores. We need to better understand what shapes (i.e., supports, constrains, enables, or impedes) the work of the students assessed to help both teachers and education practitioners make sense of assessment data and interpretation. Furthermore, such understandings are necessary to improve teachers' and education practitioners' ability to support students' learning and to increase each country's and school system's capacity to better diagnose its own educational difficulties and better cope with them. The fourth issue concerns the necessity of taking social and cultural specificities into account rather than considering them as biases to be reduced or eliminated. Also of concern is the ability to use multidimensional statistical tools and models that retain rather than eliminate social, linguistic, or cultural differences between groups or countries (Goldstein, 2004).

I hope the work presented in this chapter provides a possible direction for research on assessments and their relationship to policy. My colleagues and I, in our secondary and complementary analyses of the PISA tests, sought to demonstrate how research can critique while simultaneously offering alternative directions to policymakers, test designers, and educators. Our study may provide a way in which educational effectiveness research can be rethought and reshaped and forms of assessment made more responsible in regard to student performance. By demonstrating how a reanalysis of student performance in one country raised questions about the meanings of the current practices and claims of international assessments, we hoped to promote a new dialogue about the validity of such assessments and how to make them more responsive to local as well as global needs and to school constraints and practices as well as to social ones. Finally, we sought to propose a different approach that can form the basis of new international collaborations designed to test the results of our analyses in other countries and strengthen the value of such assessments across national boundaries.

ACKNOWLEDGMENTS

I am most grateful to Jean-Claude Emin, Jacqueline Levasseur, and Thierry Rocher (Direction of Assessment, French Ministry of Education) for the opportunity and the help they gave to me in my work on the PISA; to Élisabeth Bautier, Jacques Crinon, and Patrick Rayou for the collaborative work reported in the third section of this chapter; to Richard Durán, Judith Green, Allan Luke, and Gabrielle Matters for their comments on drafts of the chapter; to Marie-Hélène Fougeron, Judith Green, and Célia Roques for their help with English translation; and to Vincent Charbonnier and Thierry Rocher for their help in accessing documentation.

NOTES

[1]Gudmund Hernes of UNESCO described this collection as "intended mainly for education managers, state administrators and policy makers." Neville Postlethwaite was, with Torsten Husén, the primary foundation on which the IEA was founded and developed. He

was IEA's president from 1978 to 1986. François Orivel, an economist, was one of the founders of the Institut de Recherche sur l'Économie de l'Éducation (IREDU), the main French research team in the field of school efficiency and student performance evaluation surveys. He was IREDU's manager from 1985 to 1994.

[2]Randy Bennet was described in this article as a "distinguished presidential appointee in the Research and Development Division of the Educational Testing Service, Princeton, New Jersey."

[3]Such a pragmatic point of view was explicitly claimed by C. Teddlie in answering the critics of school effectiveness research:

> *The first author of this paper, being a native of the USA, has a natural inclination towards pragmatism which is a debunking philosophy that eschews the more armchair philosophical orientation of the European philosophies. The orientation of many in the USA is to do rather than to reflect. . . . In reality many practitioners are currently interested in what could work at their school [rather] than in ruminations about social inequalities associated with different socio-economic classes. Redistribution of resources is about the last thing on their minds.* (Teddlie & Reynolds, 2000, p. 27)

[4]League tables is primarily a U.K. term that refers to (a) a table in which people or clubs are placed according to their performances or (b) any grouping in which relative success or importance is compared or monitored. It is also used to refer to rankings of higher education institutions or programs of study.

[5]"It is not incumbent upon every research endeavour to provide a strong theoretical basis of the kind that allows interesting predictions and shapes our interpretation of the world being studied" (Goldstein & Woodhouse, 2000, p. 360).

[6]In an earlier paper, these authors wrote:

> *Worst of all, the school effectiveness research base is used to justify blaming schools for "failing" on the assumption that because some schools succeed in difficult circumstances the reason others do not must be their own fault. In this scenario complexity and context are ignored. Furthermore some politicians and policy makers have found it possible to deny their role in "failure" by shifting all the blame onto individual schools.* (Goldstein & Myers, 1997, p. 1; see also Gewirtz, 1998)

[7]The Direction of Assessment of the French Ministry of Education realized or funded other works about PISA: Bourny, Braxmeyer, Dupé, Rémond, Robin, & Rocher, 2002; Duru-Bellat, Mons, & Suchaut, 2004; Robin, 2002.

[8]The French words used by Bottani and Vrignaud were "au pas de charge."

[9]In addition, Goldstein (1995) noted that governments and decision makers put pressure on assessment survey designers to complete simple and quick comparative analyses.

[10]"Didactics" is a term used in Europe to refer to the study of teaching and learning processes from a point of view that focuses essentially on content of knowledge.

[11]IRT is referred to in France as IRM (item response model).

[12]These statements echo the questions mentioned earlier concerning the debate between continuist and discontinuist approaches to the relations between orality and literacy, between the different discursive genres, and between different linguistic and semiotic practices.

[13]Other anchoring means can be conceived if one uses standardized tests that have already been adapted to each culture and language or if bilingual students take the tests in both of their languages.

[14]Mitchell argued that telling cases make visible what cannot be theoretically described or inferred. Such cases do not depend on representativeness, nor are they simply illustrative.

[15]Although I am responsible for the current chapter, in this section I draw on collaborative research conducted in France. Therefore, for this section, I shift the referent to "we" to represent the collaborative work reported.

[16]I am unable to quote verbatim examples of texts or questions from the PISA tests because these tests may be used again. The PISA consortium and the French agency asked that the questions not be published. Thus, I can only evoke them here at the risk of being too allusive.

[17]It is difficult, for example, for young people aware of world starvation issues or environmental issues to accept that space conquest could be a major purpose for a society or that environmentally aware inhabitants would be opposed to the mechanical cleaning of beaches.

[18]According to the PISA designers, the nine folders could be considered equivalent; however, our research hypotheses and the analyses they enabled us to carry out showed that this was not really the case. Thus, it was not possible to deal simultaneously with the two folders we had selected. Furthermore, the number of students within each folder was similar (415 and 427), making it easy to compare the quantitative results.

[19]These categories were developed with a reduced corpus of nearly 100 folders that enabled us to be more accurate and precise in applying them to the 842 folders.

[20]Given the topic of this chapter, which is essentially focused on qualitative analyses, I cannot present here all of the details of our statistical treatments and primary results. They can be found in Bautier et al. (2004).

[21]These tests (in French) were *Graffiti* (Items R081Q01, R081Q02, R081Q05, R081Q06A, and R081Q06B), *Guide de conduite* (Items R228Q02, R228Q03, and R228Q04), *Macondo* (Items R061Q01, R061Q03, R061Q04, and R061Q05), *Plage* (Items R070Q07, R070Q03, R070Q04, and R070Q02), *Plan international* (Items R099Q02, R099Q04A, R099Q04B, and R099Q03), and *Avis d'élèves* (Items R120Q01, R120Q03, and R120Q06). Three of the six tests were common to the two folders on which we focused our secondary statistical analyses.

[22]Their lower frequency was due to the fact that the PISA tests were designed on the basis of a different conception of literacy than the ones used to frame our analyses. The PISA indicators were not designed to highlight the methods and postures that our indicators sought to apprehend. The fact that they were made visible is therefore all the more revealing of their importance in the differentiation process between students.

[23]In France, the scientific syllabus is the most elective one in senior high school; it takes in the students with the best grades, even when they do not wish to follow scientific studies after the baccalaureate.

REFERENCES

Adams, R., & Wu, M. (Eds.). (2002). *PISA 2000 technical report.* Paris: Organization for Economic Cooperation and Development.

Bain, D. (2003). PISA et la lecture: un point de vue de didacticien [PISA and reading: A point of view of a didactician]. *Revue suisse des sciences de l'éducation, 25,* 59–78.

Bakhtin, M. (1994). *Esthétique de la création verbale* [Aesthetics of verbal creation]. Paris: Gallimard.

Ball, S. J. (1990). Management as moral technology: A Luddite analysis. In S. J. Ball (Ed.), *Foucault and education: Disciplines and knowledge* (pp. 153–166). London: Routledge.

Ball, S. J., & Van Zanten, A. (1998). Logiques de marché et éthiques contextualisées dans les systèmes scolaires français et britanniques [Logics of market and ethics contextualized in the French and British school systems]. *Éducation et sociétés, 1,* 47–71.

Bautier, É. (2005). Formes et activités scolaires, secondarisation, reconfiguration, différenciation sociale [School forms and activities, secondarization, reconfiguration, social differentiation]. In N. Ramognino & P. Vergès (Eds.), *Le français hier et aujourd'hui: Politiques de la langue et apprentissages scolaires. Études offertes à Viviane Isambert-Jamati* (pp. 49–67). Aix, France: Publications de l'Université de Provence.

Bautier, É., Crinon, J., Rayou, P., & Rochex, J.-Y. (2004). *Socialisation scolaire et non scolaire des élèves: Présupposés et mobilisés chez les jeunes évalués. Analyse secondaire de l'enquête PISA 2000* [School and nonschool socialization of pupils: Secondary analysis of PISA 2000]. Paris: Université Paris VIII.

Bautier, É., Crinon, J., Rayou, P., & Rochex, J.-Y. (forthcoming). Performances en littéracie, modes de faire et univers mobilisés par les élèves: Analyses secondaires de l'enquête PISA 2000," [Performances in literacy, ways of coping and universes mobilized by pupils: Secondary analysis of PISA 2000]. *Revue française de pédagogie, 157.*

Bautier, É., & Goigoux, R. (2004). Difficultés d'apprentissage, processus de secondarisation et pratiques enseignantes: Une hypothèse relationnelle [Difficulties of training, secondary processes, and teachers practices: A relational assumption]. *Revue française de pédagogie, 148,* 89–100.

Bautier, É., & Rochex, J.-Y. (1998). *L'expérience scolaire des "nouveaux lycéens": Démocratisation ou massification?* [The school experience of "new high-school pupils": Democratization or massification?]. Paris: Armand Colin.

Bautier, É., & Rochex, J.-Y. (2004). Activité conjointe ne signifie pas signification partagée [Joint activity does not mean shared significance]. *Raisons éducatives, 9,* 199–220.

Bennet, R. (2006). Foreword. In G. Matters, *Using data to support learning in schools: Students, teachers, systems.* Victoria: Australian Council for Educational Research Press.

Bernstein, B. (1975a). *Classes et pédagogies: visibles et invisibles* [Classes and pedagogies: Visible and invisible]. Paris: CERI-OCDE.

Bernstein, B. (1975b). *Langage et classes sociales* [Language and social classes]. Paris: Éditions de Minuit.

Bonnet, G. (2002). Reflection in the critical eye: On the pitfalls of international assessment. *Assessment in Education, 9,* 387–399.

Bonnet, G., Daems, F., De Glopper, C., Hopper, S., Lappalainen, H. P., Nardi, E., et al. (2003). *Culturally Balanced Assessment of Reading.* Paris: DPD Édition.

Bottani, N., & Vrignaud, P. (2005), *La France et les évaluations internationales* [France and international evaluation surveys]. Paris: Ministère de l'Éducation Nationale.

Bourdieu, P. (2001). *Language and symbolic power.* Palo Alto, CA: Stanford University Press.

Bourdieu, P., & Passeron, J.-C. (1970). *La reproduction: Éléments pour une théorie du système d'enseignement* [Reproduction: Elements for a theory of the educational system]. Paris: Éditions de Minuit.

Bourny, G., Braxmeyer, N., Dupé, C., Rémond, M., Robin, I., & Rocher, T. (2002). *Les compétences des élèves français à l'épreuve d'une évaluation internationale. Premiers résultats de l'enquête PISA 2000* [Competencies of French pupils on an international evaluation: First results of PISA 2000]. Paris: Direction de la Programmation et du Développement.

Chalmers, I. (2003). Trying to do more good than harm in policy and practice: The role of rigorous, transparent, up-to-date evaluations. *Annals of the American Academy of Political and Social Science, 589,* 22–40.

Chatel, É. (2005). *L'évaluation de l'éducation et l'enjeu des savoirs* [Evaluation of education and stakes of knowledge]. Paris: Université Paris VIII.

Dale, R. (2005). The potentialities of *La mesure en éducation:* The European Union's open method of coordination and the construction of a European education space. *Cahiers de la Recherche sur l'Éducation et les Savoirs, 1,* 49–65.

Davies, P. (1999). What is evidence-based education? *British Journal of Educational Studies, 47,* 108–121.

Detienne, M. (Ed.). (1992). *Les savoirs de l'écriture en Grèce ancienne* [Knowledge of writing in ancient Greece]. Lille, France: Presses Universitaires de Lille.

Diamond, J. B., & Spillane, J. P. (2004). High-stakes accountability in urban elementary schools: Challenging or reproducing inequality? *Teachers College Record, 106,* 1145–1176.

Dickes, P., & Flieller, A. (1997). *Analyse secondaire des données françaises de la première enquête internationale sur la littéracie des adultes (enquête IALS).* [Analysis of secondary French data from the first international investigation into adult literacy]. Rapport pour le Ministère de l'Éducation nationale, France: Laboratoire de Psychologie—Université de Nancy 2.

Duru-Bellat, M., Mons, N., & Suchaut, B. (2004). *Caractéristiques des systèmes éducatifs et compétences des jeunes de 15 ans: L'éclairage des comparaisons entre pays* [Characteristics of education systems and competences of 15-year-old young people: Comparisons between countries]. Cahiers de l'IREDU, Dijon, France: University of Burgundy.

Gewirtz, S. (1998). Can all schools be successful? An exploration of the determinants of school success. *Oxford Review of Education, 24,* 439–457.

Gewirtz, S., Ball, S. J., & Bowe, R. (1995). *Markets, choice and equity in education.* Buckingham, England: Open University Press.

Gillborn, D., & Youdell, D. (2000). *Rationing education: Policy, practice, reform and equity.* London: Routledge.

Gipps, C. (1998). Socio-cultural aspects of assessment. In P. D. Pearson & A. Iran-Nejad (Eds.), *Review of research in education* (Vol. 24, pp. 355–392). Washington, DC: American Educational Research Association.

Gipps, C., & Murphy, P. (1994). *A fair test? Assessment, achievement and equity.* London: Open University Press.

Goldstein, H. (1995). *Interprétation des comparaisons internationales des résultats scolaires* [Interpretation of international comparisons of school results]. Paris: United Nations Educational, Scientific and Cultural Organization.

Goldstein, H. (2001). Using pupil performance data for judging schools and teachers: Scope and limitations. *British Educational Research Journal, 27,* 433–442.

Goldstein, H. (2004). International comparisons of students' attainment: Some issues arising from the PISA study. *Assessment in Education, 11,* 319–330.

Goldstein, H., & Myers, K. (1997, September). *School effectiveness research: A bandwagon, a hijack or a journey towards enlightenment?* Paper presented at the annual meeting of the British Educational Research Association, York, England.

Goldstein, H., & Noden, P. (2003). Modelling social segregation. *Oxford Review of Education, 29,* 225–237.

Goldstein, H., & Woodhouse, G. (2000). School effectiveness research and educational policy. *Oxford Review of Education, 26,* 353–363.

Goody, J. (1977). *The domestication of the savage mind.* Cambridge, England: Cambridge University Press.

Goody, J. (1993). *The interface between the written and the oral.* Cambridge, England: Cambridge University Press.

Goody, J. (2001). Competencies and education: Contextual diversity. In D. S. Rychen & L. S. Salganik (Eds.), *Defining and selecting key competencies* (pp. 175–190). Bern: Hogrefe & Huber.

Gruber K. H. (2006). The German "pisa-shock": some aspects of the extraordinary impact of the OECD's PISA study on the German education system. In H. Ertl (Ed.) *Cross-national Attraction in Education. Accounts from England and Germany* (pp. 195–208). Oxford, England: Symposium Books.

Hammersley, M. (2001, September). *Some questions about evidence-based practice in education.* Paper presented at the annual meeting of the British Educational Research Association, Leeds, England.

Hammersley, M. (2005). Is the evidence-based practice movement doing more good than harm? Reflections on Ian Chalmers' case for research-based policy making and practice. *Evidence and Policy, 1,* 85–100.

Hargreaves, A. (2003). *Teaching in the knowledge society: Education in the age of insecurity.* Philadelphia: Open University Press.

Kherroubi, M., & Rochex, J.-Y. (2002). La recherche en éducation et les zones d'éducation prioritaires en France: Première partie. Politique ZEP, objets, postures et orientations de recherche [Research in education and educational priority areas in France: First part. ZEP policy, objects, postures and orientations of research]. *Revue française de pédagogie, 140,* 103–131.

Kherroubi, M., & Rochex, J.-Y. (2004). La recherche en éducation et les zones d'éducation prioritaires en France: Deuxième partie. Apprentissages et exercice professionnel en ZEP: résultats, analyses, interprétations [Research in education and educational priority areas in France: Second part. Training and professional exercises in ZEPs: results, analyses, interpretations]. *Revue française de pédagogie, 146,* 115–190.

Lauder, H., & Hughes, D. (1999). *Trading in futures: Why education markets don't work.* Buckingham, England: Open University Press.

Masters, G. N. (1995). *Élaboration d'échelles de mesure et agrégation dans les études de l'IEA: Critique du rapport du Professeur Goldstein* [Development of scales of measurement and aggregation in the studies of the IEA: Critique of the report of Professor Goldstein]. Paris: United Nations Educational, Scientific and Cultural Organization.

Matters, G. (2006). *Using data to support learning in schools: Students, teachers, systems.* Victoria: Australian Council for Educational Research Press.

Mendelovits, J. (2003, August). *Patterns of performance on the reading literacy subscales.* Paper presented at the European Conference for Research on Learning and Instruction, Padova, Italy.

Mitchell, C. (1984). Case studies. In R. Ellen (Ed.), *Ethnography: A guide to general conduct* (pp. 151–153). London: Academic Press.

Moreau, J., Niddeger, C., & Soussi, A. (forthcoming). PISA: Définition des compétences, choix méthodologiques et retombées sur la politique scolaire en Suisse [PISA: Definition of competences, methodological choices and repercussions on school policy in Switzerland]. *Revue française de pédagogie, 157.*

Moss, P. A. (1994). Can there be validity without reliability? *Educational Researcher, 23*(2), 5–12.

Murat, F., & Rocher T. (2004). On the methods used for international assessments of educational competencies. In J. H. Moskowitz & M. Stephens (Eds.), *Comparing learning outcomes* (pp. 190–214). London: Routledge Farmer.

Myers, K., & Goldstein, H. (1998). Who's failing? In L. Stoll & K. Myers (Eds.), *No quick fixes: Perspectives on schools in difficulty* (pp. 175–188). London: Falmer Press.

Nardi, E. (2002). *Leggere a quindiceni anni: Riflessionni sulla ricerca PISA* [Reading when 15 years old: Reflections about PISA survey]. Milan: Franco Angelli.

Normand, R. (2003). *Le mouvement de la school effectiveness et sa critique dans le monde anglo-saxon* [The school effectiveness movement and its critique in the Anglo-Saxon world]. Brussels: Université libre de Bruxelles.

Normand, R. (2004). Les comparaisons internationales de résultats: Problèmes épistémologiques et questions de justice [International comparisons of results: Epistemological problems and questions of justice]. *Éducation et Sociétés, 12,* 73–89.

Normand, R. (2005). La mesure de l'école: politique des standards et management par la qualité [Measurement of schools: Policy standards and management by quality]. *Cahiers de la Recherche sur l'Éducation et les Savoirs, 1,* 67–82.

Olson, D. (1994). *The world on paper: The conceptual and cognitive implications of writing and reading.* Cambridge, England: Cambridge University Press.

Organization for Economic Cooperation and Development. (1999). *Mesurer les connaissances et compétences des élèves: Un nouveau cadre d'évaluation* [Measuring knowledge and competencies of pupils: A new framework of evaluation]. Paris: Author.

Organization for Economic Cooperation and Development. (2001). *Knowledge and skills for life: First results from PISA 2000.* Paris: Author.

Organization for Economic Cooperation and Development. (2003). *La lecture, moteur de changement: Performances et engagement d'un pays à l'autre. Résultats de PISA 2000* [Performances and engagement from one country to another: Results of PISA 2000]. Paris: Author.

Organization for Economic Cooperation and Development. (2004). *Learning for tomorrow's world: First results from PISA 2003.* Paris: Author.

Orivel, F. (2005). Foreword. In N. Postlethwaite, *Monitoring educational achievement.* Paris: United Nations Educational, Scientific and Cultural Organization.

Paulston, R. G. (1988). Comparative and international education: Paradigms, theories and debates. In *Education: The complete encyclopedia 1.1*. New York: Elsevier.

Piaget, J. (1974). *Réussir et comprendre* [Succeeding and understanding]. Paris: Presses Universitaires de France.

Postlethwaite, N. (2005). *Monitoring educational achievement*. Paris: United Nations Educational, Scientific and Cultural Organization.

Prenzel, M. (forthcoming). Les prolongements de PISA 2003 en Allemagne: Principaux résultats et avantages [Prolongment of PISA 2003 in Germany: Principal results and advantages]. *Revue française de pédagogie, 157*.

Rayou, P. (2002). *La dissertation de philosophie. Sociologie d'une épreuve scolaire* [The philosophy dissertation in high school. Sociology of a school work]. Rennes, France: Presses Universitaires de Rennes.

Rémond, M. (2001). Adapter n'est pas traduire: Adaptation dans différents contextes culturels d'épreuves d'évaluation de la littéracie [To adapt is not to translate: Adaptation in various cultural contexts of tests of evaluation of literacy]. In C. Sabatier & P. Dasen (Eds.), *Cultures, développement et éducation: Autres enfants, autres écoles* (pp. 171–184). Paris: L'Harmattan.

Rémond, M. (2006). Regards croisés sur les évaluations institutionnelles [Translations crossed on international evaluations]. *Repères, 31,* 113–140.

Reuchlin, M. (1997). *La psychologie différentielle* [The psychology of difference]. Paris: Presses Universitaires de France.

Reynolds, D., & Teddlie, C. (2000, April). *Reflections on the critics and beyond them*. Paper presented at the annual meeting of the American Educational Research Association, New Orleans, LA.

Robin, I. (2002). L'enquête PISA sur les compétences de lecture des élèves de 15 ans: Trois biais culturels en question [The PISA investigation on reading competencies of 15-year-old pupils: Three cultural biases in question]. *VEI Enjeux, 129,* 65–91.

Rocher, T. (2003). La méthodologie des évaluations internationales de compétences [On methodology used for international assessments of educational competencies]. *Psychologie et psychométrie, 24,* 117–147.

Rochex, J.-Y. (1997). L'œuvre de Vygostki: fondements pour une psychologie historico-culturelle [The work of Vygotsky: Basis for a historico-cultural psychology]. *Revue française de pédagogie, 120,* 105–147.

Rochex, J.-Y. (2002, May). *Misunderstandings and unequal participation in knowledge practices in the classroom*. Paper presented at the Qualitative Classroom Research seminar, Mexico City.

Rodrigues, M. J. (Ed.) (2002). *The new knowledge economy in Europe: a strategy for international competitiveness and social cohesion*. Aldershot: Elgar.

Rychen D. S. (2001). Introduction. In D. S. Rychen & L. S. Salganik (Eds.), *Defining and selecting key competencies* (pp. 1–15). Bern: Hogrefe & Huber.

Rychen, D. S., & Salganik, L. S. (Eds.). (2001). *Defining and selecting key competencies*. Bern: Hogrefe & Huber.

Rychen, D. S., & Salganik, L. S. (2003). *Key competencies for a successful life and a well-functioning society*. Bern: Hogrefe & Huber.

Salganik, L. S. (2001). Competencies for life: A conceptual and empirical challenge. In D. S. Rychen & L. S. Salganik (Eds.), *Defining and selecting key competencies* (pp. 17–32). Bern: Hogrefe & Huber.

Sayer, A. (1992). *Method in social science: A realist approach*. London: Routledge.

Schneuwly, B. (1994). Genres et types de discours: considérations ontogénétiques et psychogénétiques [Genres and types of speech: Ontogenetic and psychogenetic considerations]. In Y. Reuter (Ed.), *Les interactions lecture-écriture* (pp. 155–173). Bern: Peter Lang.

Scribner, S., & Cole, M. (1981). *The psychology of literacy*. Cambridge, MA: Harvard University Press.

Slee, R., Weiner, G., & Tomlinson S. (Eds.). *School effectiveness for whom? Challenges to the school effectiveness and school improvement movement.* London: Falmer Press.

Soares, M. B. (1992). *Literacy assessment and its implication for statistical measurement.* Paris: United Nations Educational, Scientific and Cultural Organization.

Teddlie, C., & Reynolds, D. (2000, April). *Responses to the criticisms of school effectiveness research contained in Slee, Weiner & Tomlinson (1998) and Thrupp (1999).* Paper presented at the annual meeting of the American Educational Research Association, New Orleans, LA.

Thrupp, M. (2001). Recent school effectiveness counter-critiques: Problems and possibilities. *British Educational Research Journal, 27,* 443–457.

Thrupp, M. (2002). Why meddling is necessary: A response to Teddlie, Reynolds, Townsend, Scheerens, Bosker and Creemers. *School Effectiveness and School Improvement, 13,* 1–14.

Van Dijk, T. A., & Kintsch, W. (1983). *Strategies of discourse comprehension.* New York: Academic Press.

Van Geert, P. (2002a). Variabilité intra-individuelle et recherche d'une approche nouvelle en psychométrie [Intra-individual variability and the search for a new approach to psychometry]. In J. Lautrey, B. Mazoyer, & P. van Geert (Eds.), *Invariants et variabilités dans les sciences cognitives* (pp. 335–354). Paris: Éditions de la Maison des Sciences de l'Homme.

Van Geert, P. (2002b). Measuring intelligence of dynamic systems and contextualist frameworks. In R. J. Sternberg, J. Lautrey, & T. I. Lubart (Eds.), *Models of intelligence: International perspective* (pp. 195–212). Washington, DC: American Psychological Association.

Van Zanten, A. (2001). *L'école de la périphérie: Scolarité et ségrégation en banlieue* [The school of the periphery: Schooling and segregation in the suburbs]. Paris: Presses Universitaires de France.

Vinokur, A. (2005a). Foreword. *Cahiers de la Recherche sur l'Éducation et les Savoirs, 1,* 7–13.

Vinokur, A. (2005b). Mesure de la qualité des services d'enseignement et restructuration des secteurs éducatifs [Measure of the quality of teaching services and reorganization of the educational sectors]. *Cahiers de la Recherche sur l'Éducation et les Savoirs, 1,* 83–108.

Vygotsky, L. S. (1985). *Pensée et langage* [Thought and language]. Paris: Messidor. (Original work published 1934)

Vygotsky, L. S. (1978). *Mind in society: The development of higher psychological processes.* Cambridge, MA: Harvard University Press.

Weinert, F. E. (2001). Concept of competence: A conceptual clarification. In D. S. Rychen & L. S. Salganik (Eds.), *Defining and selecting key competencies* (pp. 45–65). Bern: Hogrefe & Huber.

West, A., & Pennel, H. (2005). Market-oriented reforms and "high stakes" testing: Incentives and consequences. *Cahiers de la Recherche sur l'Éducation et les Savoirs, 1,* 181–199.

Chapter 6

Culture and Learning in the Context of Globalization: Research Directions

WAN SHUN EVA LAM
Northwestern University

The United States has found itself again roiled in an immigration debate over the past year as the massive migration of labor, fueled by global economic restructuring, seemed to suddenly hit a red button in the public consciousness. A more substantive policy discussion of the economic basis of the influx of labor across the southern border was elided by get-tough policy initiatives that proposed criminalization of undocumented immigrants, heightened policing of the U.S.-Mexico border, and fermented a symbolic legislative amendment to make English the "national language" of the United States with the aim to reaffirm "the preeminence of English" (Hulse, 2006). Debates in the public arena across the political spectrum abounded as to the relative cost and benefit of immigration, debates that reflected deeper anxiety and uncertainty about the changing demographics of the labor pool and the cultural transformation it is bringing to the country.

While the anti-immigration discourse on undocumented immigrants is "alien"-ating Hispanics, by far the largest immigrant and minority group in the country, U.S. corporations and media companies have embraced the Hispanic population as "ideal customers" and are targeting this group with customized advertising campaigns across the country (Nightly Business Report, 2006; Richtel & Belson, 2006). In these corporate advertising maneuvers, multilingualism becomes less of a threat than a resource and leverage to garner the trust and buying power of this fastest-growing demographic group. Cell-phone companies, such as Verizon and Sprint, are sponsoring concert tours of Latin American pop singers and promoting multimedia functions on their phones that include viewing television and downloading songs in Spanish. The fact that Hispanics often have families that span international borders becomes the rallying point of transnational companies such as Sprint-Nextel, which is mining this market with its push-to-talk walkie-talkie service that allows subscribers in the United States to communicate instantly with other Sprint-Nextel customers in Mexico, Argentina, Brazil, and Peru.

On the other side of the Atlantic, a similar commercial and media embrace of migrant and minority populations can be found in, among other places, Germany, where ethno-marketing is targeting German Turks and thereby contributing to a redefinition of their cultural and social space across national boundaries (Caglar, 2002). As noted by Caglar (2002, pp. 180–181):

> Nowadays in Berlin, Turkish is in the air. After almost 40 years of a Turkish immigrant presence in the city, suddenly the Turkish language became respectable in big companies like the *Deutsche Telekom*, *Bundespost* and *Mercedes*. Plastic bags containing "Turkish bread" are covered with *Telekom* ads in Turkish and the *Döner Kebabs* are also wrapped in paper covered with *Telekom* ads in Turkish. The German Turks receive mail in Turkish from *Bundespost* informing them about what services they offer in Turkish. Similarly, the *Telekom* distributes postcards with pictures of famous Turkish pop or *arabesk* singers in Turkey to Turks, along with information (in Turkish) about *Telekom* facilities that give access to private Turkish channels through cable operators like the *Kanal D* or *Artif Television (ATV)*—broadcast from Turkey.

In addition to the proliferation of Turkish in corporate and media companies' marketing strategies intended to connect with this significant and growing consumer base, a new crossover language between German and Turkish, which is widespread among German Turks, is becoming increasingly adopted in advertising and media broadcasting, serving to institutionalize this new hybrid language.

These three scenarios of contemporary movement of capital, labor, media, technologies, images, ideas, and symbolic mediums such as language across geographical and social spaces are meant to illustrate some of the new realities and paradoxes of what has come to be called *globalization*. Globalization has become an umbrella term for what is taking place around the world in association with global integration of economies, rapid media and information flow facilitated by new communication technologies, international migration of labor, the rise of transnational and pan-regional organizations, and resultant cultural transformations challenging traditional social structures. As pointed out by Rizvi (2005a, p. 188), globalization is about "the restructuring and extension of networks of money, technologies, people and ideas and of their articulations with real spaces at different scales."

In the scenarios of the U.S. Hispanic and Turkish German populations, we see the coming together of transnational capital, multicultural demographics, and media and communication technologies in the creation of new transcultural spaces within and across societies. Whereas diverse languages, even one in which the national anthem is sung,[1] are silenced in the legislative debates over migration in the United States, the presence of these languages is galvanized for economic productivity and market expansion by media companies and business corporations alike. Meanwhile, multicultural citizenries in different parts of the world are forging new diaspora and hybrid spaces of social and cultural activities through their growing economic and demographic presence and the use of instantaneous forms of communication. These sociocultural changes taking place in the context of globalization are affecting how young people grow up, learn, play, work, and interact with the world around them.

The goal of this chapter is to lay out some new conceptualizations and research directions for understanding the relation of culture and learning in the shifting terrains of globalized economies and media flows, youth cultures, and transnational migration. In a time when young people's experiences and life pathways are increasingly forged in the overlapping social and cultural spaces between economies and societies, we need to develop new approaches to working with issues of diversity that go beyond static, territorial, and state-bound categories to address the multiple kinds of intercultural transactions that characterize our collective lives in the contemporary era. To this end, I identify the limitations of current formulations of cultural diversity that have restricted it to a "minority" issue within the locality of the nation-state. I draw on a social practice and transcultural perspective to discuss promising research directions for studying new formations of culture, community, identity, and processes of learning as young people interact with diverse others in the globalized spaces of media and migration. This discussion highlights the need to reconsider notions of culture and identity, of agency and learning, and of societal engagement and education of our multicultural youth population. In closing, I propose some conceptual frames for developing an educational research agenda that engages with the new openings for cosmopolitanism and intercultural learning engendered by our global conditions.

DIVERSITY IN EDUCATION: LOOKING WITHIN AND BEYOND THE MULTICULTURAL STATE

As many researchers have noted (e.g., Banks & Banks, 1995; Fisher, Jackson, & Villarruel, 1998; Gonzáles, 2004; Lee, 2003; Valdez, 1996), for a long time approaches to cultural and linguistic diversity in education have centered around a deficit-difference paradigm whereby the life ways of nondominant groups (e.g., members of racialized ethnic minority groups, migrant and multilingual populations, the working class and working poor, and stigmatized religious groups) are understood as a set of cultural traits that are ascribed moral and economic values. The notion of culture, as it became a major explanatory variable for the poor academic achievement of nondominant groups, is considered to be a holistic set of attitudes, values, and behaviors that characterize particular groups in society and differentially predispose them to success or failure in school. Cultural markers considered to be salient, such as kinship patterns, child-rearing practices, language use, time and space orientations, and communication patterns, have been variously characterized, stereotyped, studied, and used to explain why students exhibit different degrees of readiness for and receptivity to formal schooling (Baratz & Baratz, 1970; Spindler, 2000; Ybarra, 1983). In other words, the degree to which a student's primary group socialization aligns and matches with the expectations and practices of the educational institution becomes the linchpin in the likelihood of success or failure in school.

In the cultural deficit model, difference is construed as an aberration of mainstream norms, and the explanatory logic of low achievement is that of negation, whereby the cultural patterns of nondominant groups are viewed as lacking in the social and cognitive resources deemed necessary for moral living and economic mobility (Bereiter & Englemann, 1966; Deutsch et al., 1967; Hess, Shipman, Brophy, &

Bear, 1968; Hunt, 1969; Lewis, 1966). Although the deficit model has been refuted many times over in the educational field, it is still insidious in the ideologies and practices pervasive in society, as manifested, for example, in the racial connotations of terminologies such as "inner-city" and "at-risk" children (Lee, 2003), the perception even by well-meaning educators of the exorbitant needs and demands of urban minority children (Rogers, Marshall, & Tyson, 2006), the model minority myth that homogenizes students of Asian origin and pits them against other minority groups (Lee, 2005), and the devaluation of students' native languages in the overall education of multilingual children (Gutiérrez, Baquedano-Lopez, & Asato, 2000).

In contrast to the deficit view, difference is reinterpreted as legitimate in what can be called a cultural affirmation model, a model that offers validation of the integrity of the diverse cultural practices of minority groups along with acknowledgment that these practices diverge from what educational institutions expect and value (Au & Jordan, 1981; Delpit, 1989; Deschenes, Cuban, & Tyack, 2001; Heath, 1983; Phillips, 1972; Scollon & Scollon, 1981; Valdez, 1996). To bridge the gap between home and school and provide cultural congruence to students' academic experience, educators have sought out ways to incorporate into classroom instruction specific community practices familiar to the children, in the form of narrative styles, communication patterns, discussion and participation modes, and so forth. It is believed that, while the cultural backgrounds of minority students should be valued and respected, these students also need to be made aware of the *language of power*— the dominant codes and discourses in society—if they are to succeed both inside and outside of the classroom (Cope & Kalantzis, 1993; Delpit, 1996).

As observed by Lee (2003), prevailing understandings of group differences in education are mostly predicated on hegemonic opposition, with the dominant culture serving as the arbitrating standard to which other people's children are being understood and evaluated. Consequently, the notion of culture becomes "something we need to understand about the 'other folks' (those who are not identified as White)" (Lee, 2003, p. 3).

We find the following in these approaches to diversity. First, culture is turned into a minoritized concept in educational research and used primarily as an explanatory variable for educational and developmental issues among minority children. Second, culture is characterized as a distinct, holistic, and autonomous set of dispositions (composed of values, beliefs, attitudes, and behaviors) shared by members of a particular population (often read in racial and ethnic terms), with some forms of culture being ascribed more power than others. Finally, culture is perceived and demarcated in a majority-minority binary opposition within the boundaries of a multicultural nation-state, as if cultural practices automatically stop at the majority-minority junction and come to a halt at state borders.

A current promising research direction on issues of diversity in education takes a social practice and cultural-historical approach to look at how individuals develop and assume particular cultural practices and affiliations through their history of engagement in multiple, changing, overlapping, and conflicting communities (Erickson,

2002; González, 2004; Gutiérrez & Rogoff, 2003; Moll & González, 2004; Rogoff, 2003; Rogoff & Angelillo, 2002). This approach shifts our understanding of culture from stable identities, categorical memberships, and holistic traits to ways of *acting and participating* in diverse social groups and the heterogeneous sets of cultural knowledge, skills, and competence that are acquired in the process. As noted by Rogoff and Angelillo (2002, pp. 222–223) in regard to a participation view of culture:

The idea is to focus on the involvement of people in community practices rather than their inclusion "in" (or exclusion "out") of bounded entities. People are often participants in the practices of more than one community (e.g., participating in national as well as religious, political, ethnic, and economic groups' traditions); the cultural ways of the varying communities in which they participate may or may not conflict with each other. The distinction between participation and membership is intended to get beyond the either/or boundaries of being inside or outside of bounded communities, to allow examination of the forms of people's participation in communities (which may involve being excluded from some activities as well as being ratified participants).

This perspective on culture acknowledges the multiplicity of cultural forms and practices that people are exposed to and participate in with various roles and capacities in any given period and over time. As such, this perspective enables us to move beyond static or bounded notions of culture to explore the ways in which people's affiliations are dispersed across a variety of social practices, communities, and social geographies and how they develop repertoires of skills and competencies through their engagement in heterogeneous communities (Gutiérrez & Rogoff, 2003). By extension, it allows us to explore the porous boundaries between cultural practices as these practices travel with people and media channels across diverse communities and shifting social and spatial territories. In the following, I build on this perspective of culture and diversity to discuss the formation and flows of cultural practices in young people's participation in the transnational spaces of mass media, youth cultures, digital communication, and diaspora relations. I explore the relationships of culture, learning, and identity in these emerging social spaces and their implications for research on learning in globalized contexts.

YOUTH IDENTITIES AND TRANSCULTURAL FLOWS
Global Media and New Identities

Media theorists have observed that the notion of hybridity—how cultural forms and practices intermingle and traverse across social boundaries—is no longer a sequestered academic discourse of cultural theory but has become a driving engine of the corporate sector, media industries, and grassroots producers and consumers (e.g., Ito, in press; Jenkins, 2006; Kraidy, 2005; Tobin, 2004a). While the international flow of media has always been marked by asymmetrical power relations and remains a structured and uneven process, with some countries playing dominant roles in the global export of information and entertainment products, we are presently dealing with more complicated geometries of power in media production and imposition given the rise of transnational media financing, growing intraregional trade, and new kinds of communication technologies. Jenkins (2006), in particular, noted that media cultures in different parts of the world are undergoing forms of convergence supported by both corporate design and grassroots interest manifested in the flow and adaptation of cultural goods through multiple global and regional circuits. On the one hand, corporate mergers and concentration of media ownership have created strong vested interest in and the capacity to coordinate multiple platforms and distribution networks for promoting the flow of media content across national boundaries. On the other hand, digitally empowered consumers are increasingly transgressing the role of passive end user of media products and becoming active participants in reshaping these products and directing their distribution through amateur cultural production. The latter is especially true of grassroots consumers/producers who have developed cross-cultural and cross-border networks and creative techniques through digital communication technologies and global migration.

For example, the promotion of animation (animé) and manga (graphic novels) as one of Japan's major cultural exports has relied upon transnational media financing to promote and adapt mega-hits such as *Pokemon* to local markets around the globe. Corporate "glocalizers" work as cultural intermediaries to modify aspects of the original productions to suit local mores and expectations of the genre (Iwabuchi, 2004; Katsuno & Maret, 2004). Yet, animé fans stood as an instrumental force in facilitating the early flow of these Japanese products to the U.S. market and continue to mediate access to less commercialized and mainstream products through the use of alternative peer-to-peer networks, providing subtitles and translations into local languages and creating fanzines, digital search engines and Web sites, and amateur fan art, fan guides, and fan fiction (Black, in press; Tobin, 2004a). The growth of Bollywood (Hindi films) and bhangra music into global industries has ridden on the wings of the Indian diaspora and migrant networks (Maira, 2002). And while hip-hop has transformed from its early roots among disenfranchised African American youth in New York City in the 1970s into a transnational youth culture and music industry, its manifestations in different societal contexts are characterized by particular local and regional identities, grassroots concerns, and artistic styles that are simultaneously connected to a larger global affiliation with hip-hop culture (Mitchell, 2002).

Rather than belonging simply in the domain of media studies, these corporate- and grassroots-driven transcultural flows have significant effects on how young people develop their identities and affiliations, learn and work, and develop visions of the world in their everyday lives. Even among psychologists, who have traditionally considered identity development as a stage-wise process of interaction with one's primary and secondary socialization groups toward eventual stabilization of an integrated self, there is growing recognition that globalization is creating greater fluidity and multiplicity in the identity formation of young people (e.g., Arnett, 2002; Hermans & Kempen, 1998; Jensen, 2003; Suárez-Orozco, 2004). These scholars examining the psychological consequences of globalization have argued that media and popular cultures have emerged as particularly important sites in which young people interact with diverse cultural materials and images and develop social affiliations. Arnett (2002, p. 777), for example, noted that the concept of "bicultural identities," traditionally used by social psychologists for understanding the experiences of immigrants and members of ethnic minority groups within a given society, is no longer applicable only to minority groups but applies to many young people around the world who are exposed to multiple forms of local and global cultures. Arnett (2002, p. 778) further posited that, for young people who come from immigrant backgrounds, "bicultural" may even be a misnomer given that they "develop identities that combine their native culture, the local culture to which they have immigrated, and the global culture, thus leading to a multicultural identity or a complex hybrid identity."

In developing constructs of identity as analytical lenses for educational research, Gee (1999, 2004) contended that the contemporary global economy, popular culture, and youth sociality are promoting a kind of collective belonging that is better described as "affinity groups" wherein social relationships are created and sustained through coparticipation in a set of distinctive practices. An affinity group identity is developed through networking, collaborating, and affiliating, sometimes across distance, around common interests, joint endeavors, and shared causes. As explained by Gee (1999, p. 105): "What people in the group share, and must share to constitute an affinity group, *is allegiance to, access to, and participation in specific practices* that provide each of the group's members the requisite experiences." Because this kind of collective identity is centered around shared practices of various sorts, there is a tendency to cross traditional lines of "race"/ethnicity, class, gender, ability, and other institutional classifications. Understanding identity through an affinity group perspective provides educational researchers with an analytical tool to examine not only the ways in which learning and identity development take place within new forms of cultural practices and alignments but also how dominant notions of culture (as ethnic, class, and gender differences) are inflected, perpetuated, or given new meanings in these practices.

In the following, I turn to a number of research studies that have started to explore how young people in different parts of the world engage with the transcultural flows of global media in their local settings and how, through these engagements, they develop a facility with valued social practices and new forms of cultural identities. The research reviewed here includes studies focusing on youth practices surrounding Japanese-origin anime/manga and hip-hop/rap music, both of which have attained global significance as forms of popular youth culture. These studies have explored (a) how Western English-speaking fans of Japanese anime and manga participate in peer networks for sharing knowledge and producing media through amateur cultural production (and, in addition, how English-language learners develop multilingual literacy and transcultural identities in their engagement with these media) and (b) the kinds of "glocalized" identities, linguistic innovation, and ethnic realignments that are produced by young people in hip-hop/rap communities in East and Southeast Asia and French-speaking Canada.

Youth Practices and Learning in Convergence and Participatory Cultures

In recent years, a growing number of research inquiries into the new digital and media literacies practiced by today's youth in North America and the United Kingdom have, by design or default, revealed avid engagement with Japanese animé and manga and related franchised media, such as computer and card games, among these young people (e.g., Black, 2005, 2006; Buckingham & Sefton-Green, 2003; Chandler-Olcott & Mahar, 2003; Gee, 2004; Lam, 2000, in press; Tobin, 2004b; Vasquez, 2003). An important theme brought forth by this research is that young people's engagement with these media is seldom mere passive reception but involves a blending of receptive and productive activities encompassing both cultural and semiotic media materials and young people's personal experiences and familiarity with other forms of popular culture. Moreover, their productive activities often take place in affinity groups where they seek and give advice to each other, exchange media resources and know-how, and engage in collaborative endeavors, mentoring, and problem solving.

For example, in exploring adolescent girls' use of digital technologies in the United States, Chandler-Olcott and Mahar (2003) found that the digital literacy practices of their focal participants (of European-American and working-class backgrounds) revolved heavily around animé and manga. Their in-depth study of two girls' designs of animé-based Web sites, fan fiction writing, and artistic production of amateur manga showed that the girls were actively involved in online networks of animé fans and manga artist circles devoted to the exchange of knowledge, digital resources, and artistic skills and judgment. Although not the central focus of the study, the authors described how the girls' critical exchanges with their online communities included discussions of differences in how American and Japanese people deal with controversial topics in cartoons and the ways in which gender is represented in different artistic forms with Japanese and American influences.

Whereas studies of digital and media literacies among youth who are of European descent or "young people in general" tend not to examine the relation of learning and cultural identity, showing again how notions of "culture" and "identity" are marked categories for non-White populations, a series of recent studies with English-language learners and migrant students revealed the ways in which these students developed multicultural and multilingual identities in the global arena of popular cultural fandom (Black, 2005, 2006; Lam, 2000, in press). Black's innovative study of English-language learners' literate and social practices on Fanfiction.net, the largest English-based multifandom archive on the Web, showed how these young people and their English-speaking and multilingual peers around the world engaged in creative writing around animé that "refashion[ed] the preexisting media tales by infusing them with social and cultural themes, multiple literacies, various forms of expertise, and concerns from their daily lives" (2006, p. 173). The multiple literacies that these youth integrated into their writings included knowledge of the historical context of the fictional world of Japanese animé, allusion to pop culture from different countries familiar to readers, and peer review and critical feedback from their fellow fan fiction writers. Black provided a longitudinal analysis of how a Canadian adolescent girl who was of Chinese descent and was studying English as second language was able to draw on her knowledge of Asian cultures and languages to construct English texts with multilingual influences, express pride as an Asian-origin writer, and attain expert status in the transnational animé fan fiction community.

Similarly, Lam's (2000, in press) work with Chinese adolescent immigrants in the United States showed that these young people's digital networking and multimedia production in the international animé culture repositioned their acquisition and use of English beyond that of acculturation to an English-speaking nation. Through multisite research with the students in both their school environments and their online communities, Lam provided ethnographic and linguistic analyses of how, in contrast to their school experiences, their acquisition of English in the online context was less a matter of assimilation to a monolingual national (e.g., American) or racial-ethnic (Chinese American) identity than a matter of affiliation with a global animé youth culture crossing national boundaries.

The destabilizing of linguistic and cultural boundaries in young people's interactions with globalized youth cultures emerges again as a salient theme in recent sociolinguistic and educational research on international hip-hop/rap (e.g., Androutsopoulos & Scholz, 2002; Cutler, 2003; Mitchell, 2002; Pennycook, 2003, 2005; Sarkar & Allen, in press; Sarkar, Low, & Winer, in press; Sarkar & Winer, 2006). For example, Sarkar and her colleagues' collaborative research on the hip-hop community in Montreal, Canada, revealed multilingual code switching or language mixing in rap to be a fertile ground for the production of new identities across ethnic and national lines. Montreal rappers draw on standard and nonstandard Quebec French, European French, standard North American English, African American vernacular English, Haitian Creole, Jamaican Creole, and Spanish in their rap lyrics to signify the multiple cultural roots, influences, and attachments of the Montreal youth community. The researchers argued that "rap lyrics constitute a discursive space in which the juxtaposing of many different kinds of sources for identity claims and/or relational linking through kinship and affection enables a new idea of community to emerge" (Sarkar et al., in press). Through linguistic and semiotic analysis of the music produced by local Montreal rap artists and interviews of these artists as well as their fans and audience members (14 years old and older), the research showed that use of several different languages and varieties is common among both minority and majority (read: White) group artists, reflecting their cross-ethnic peer associations, and references in the lyrics to events and societal issues in North and South America and the Caribbean both signal and acknowledge the multiple national affiliations of these young people and their audience.

Pennycook's (2003, 2005) extensive study of glocalized varieties of rap music in urban centers of East and Southeast Asia (Malaysia, Japan, Korea) led him to argue for a new way of conceptualizing the teaching and learning of English as a global language in the context of young people's experiences of transcultural flows. Pennycook showed that the use of English in these diverse varieties of rap music, what he termed "raplishes," exists in creative blending and juxtaposition with local national and colloquial languages and exemplifies how "the flows of cultural forms produce new forms of localization, and the use of global Englishes produce[s] new forms of global identification" (2005, p. 32). The hybrid blending of linguistic, rhythmic, and referential content in these "raplishes" with ties to both the global hip-hop lexicon and local artistic forms and cultural references represents a kind of "semiotic reconstruction" that produces new identities through the act of performance (Pennycook, 2003). Taking inspiration from the uptake of rap and hip-hop among new generations of youth, Pennycook proposed a pedagogy of English that goes beyond the dichotomizing of international and indigenous standards and native and nonnative English to a critical engagement with students' "multilayered modes of identity at global, regional, national and local levels" (2005, p. 41).

While these studies are not meant to be representative of the various kinds of youth experiences around the world, they constitute a significant beginning in laying out a research vista for understanding how young people are participating in new cultural formations and modes of learning in the context of globalized economies. A number of implications can be drawn from the previous discussion for furthering our understanding of the notions of culture and identity, the nexus of power in globalization, and the sites of agency and learning.

First, these studies show that in the global transit of youth cultures, young people are developing affiliative identities and shared practices that cut across national, ethnic, and linguistic lines and simultaneously involve them in multiple attachments at the global and local levels. These identities and practices disrupt a one-to-one correspondence of culture and ethnicity and thrive on hybrid innovation to create new forms of competence and knowledge and to reach a wider audience. Sometimes such hybrid practices go beyond the making of personal and collective identities and new artistic forms to a strategy of repositioning oneself in the global economy. The latter is seen, for example, among young Montreal rappers of Latin American descent who aspire to use their multilingual and multiethnic music to communicate and market not only to the local youth communities in Canada but also to countries across Latin America where their music and message will strike a chord (Sarkar & Allen, 2006; Sarkar et al., in press). This kind of world consciousness transforms multicultural identities from a minoritized state-bound category to one that engages with transnational solidarities, audiences, and markets.

Second, these explorations of how young people participate in the transcultural flows of global media complicate our understanding of the nexus of power in globalization. Globalization has often been characterized as an objective reality of global market forces and new communication technologies that are changing the face of the earth. Such objectification turns global processes into something we have to respond to and fit our lives into—something that has power over the way we live, learn, and work. This ahistorical view assumes globalization to be "a set of naturalized economic processes operating in a reified fashion" (Rizvi, in press-a). Yet, what we see from these studies is that youth are not just recipients of the forces of globalization but are also playing the role of active cultural workers, reshaping and recontextualizing global materials in their particular communities and local settings. By producing manga with cross-cultural influences and critically reflecting on these artistic sources, by crafting multilingual texts with a transnational network of youth, by developing cross-ethnic solidarity and realignment, and by reinventing English in glocalized forms of rap, these young people are acting on the forces of globalization to create new spaces of knowledge and collective identities.

Through these practices of crossing ethnic, linguistic, and national lines of division, the youth are claiming interculturality—the ability to act through heterogeneity and differences—as the site of agency and the site of learning. Surely, these practices are both facilitated and constrained by what kinds of media, products, images, and ideas are promoted around the world via corporate capitalism. But what we also see is that young people are using these corporate-sponsored materials in conjunction with their local and cross-cultural experiences to create new forms of communities and creative practices. Here developing knowledge, defining oneself, and producing symbolic goods and materials take place through active engagement with heterogeneous cultural sources and multilayered identifications. Power is not unilaterally ascribed to particular forms of culture but resides in navigating the tension and redefining the relationships between diverse cultural forms and practices. I revisit this notion of intercultural learning and related issues of identity and agency in the final section; in the following, I turn to how new forms of societal engagement and learning figure in the shifting contexts of transnational and diaspora relations.

TRANSNATIONAL REFRAMING OF MIGRANT AND MULTILINGUAL POPULATIONS

In the introduction, I highlighted the ways in which media developments, supported by global capital, and the growing demographic and economic presence of multicultural citizenries are working in concert to create new transnational cultural spaces. By involving multiple and nonexclusive affiliations, these transnational spaces challenge conventional notions of locality, community, and belonging. As Caglar (2002, p. 186) noted with the Turkish-German population in this regard, "In the emergent discourses centred on these spaces, heterogeneity and being cosmopolitan seem to have replaced the ethnic closure of the common representations of Turkey and Turkishness that conflate the public and scholarly discourses on the German Turks in Germany."

The need to rethink societal engagement beyond the bounded framework of the nation-state has been taken up in international migration research. Specifically, the coupling effect of electronically mediated communication and global migration on the creation of diaspora consciousness and transnational identities has been developed into a growing line of research in diaspora studies. In this section, I discuss these works and their significance for expanding education research and models for understanding societal participation and learning of migrant and multilingual student populations.

Transnationalism and Diaspora Youth

In the past decade, research on international migration and immigrant incorporation in multicultural societies has increasingly turned to the notion of *transnationalism* to understand the various kinds of global or cross-border connections that are sustained or created in the process of migration and how the identities of individuals and groups of people are negotiated within social worlds that span more than one place (e.g., Castles, 2005; Conradson & Latham, 2005; Kennedy & Roudometof, 2002; Levitt & Glick Schiller, 2004; Levitt & Waters, 2002; Orellana, Thorne, Chee, & Lam, 2001; Vertovec, 2003). This body of work has successfully highlighted the need to understand immigrant adaptation and the developmental trajectories of children of immigrants beyond a straightforward notion of assimilation or acculturation within the confines of the receiving country. While some migrants may participate regularly in the economic, political, and cultural activities of both their country of origin and their country of settlement, others (including children of migrants) may not participate directly but are integrally involved with the flow of economic resources, ideas, images, and contact with people from far away. Within these "transnational social fields" (Levitt & Glick Schiller, 2004, p. 1009) in which ideas, practices, and resources are structured and exchanged through a set of multiple interlocking networks of social relationships across nations, people are exposed to social expectations, cultural values, and patterns of human interaction that are not confined to a single socioeconomic and political system.

A significant arena for the development of transnational social fields that has been taken up with great fervor by young people is digital and computer-mediated communication (e.g., Ignacio, 2005; Kitalong & Kitalong, 2000; Lam, 2004; Landzelius, 2006; H. M. Lee, 2003; Miller & Slater, 2000; Mitra, 2001; Valverde, 2002). This body of research that looks at the creation of diaspora and transnational online networks shows how individuals and groups at the grassroots level are capitalizing on the global reach of Internet communications to build social, cultural, and political connections or exchanges and multilingual practices and learning across national borders.

For example, Miller and Slater's (2000) in-depth ethnographic study of Trinidadians' use of Internet communications revealed a "natural affinity" between the everyday, mundane networking possibilities of the Internet and Trinidadians' intensely diasporic relations. Miller and Slater provided ample evidence that young Trinidadians in diaspora have appropriated the Internet to facilitate sustained contact and mutual support with their extended families, educate people of other nationalities about Trinidad through personal Web pages to counter the global positioning of Trinidad as marginal or unknown, and re-create through the chat medium unique forms of Trinidadian verbal expressions, including the mixing of English and patois, to create an Internet space that is specifically Trinidadian but Trinidadian defined in global terms.

In Helen Lee's (2006) research on the digital communications of Pacifican Tongan young people with their peers at "home" and around the world, she found active organizing and debate around the notion of global or diaspora Tongan identity. The use of the Tongan language is promoted in some digital forums as a means to revitalize the language among young Tongans who are growing up in Western countries and to represent their identity and pride in their heritage. However, equivocation of the Tongan language and heritage is challenged by some who see it as a form of exclusion that discourages the participation of their fellow overseas Tongans who do not speak or read and write the language. For many of these youth who are fluent in English, "Tonglish," in which English and Tongan are combined within sentences, is adopted to signify their hybrid and pan-Polynesian identity. In addition, a range of studies have explored the voicing of diverse perspectives in diaspora online environments—whether involving criticism and defense of traditional Tongan practices (Lee, 2006) and notions of Filipino cultural identity (Ignacio, 2005), debate among Indians around the world on the West's intervention in Indian policies (Mitra, 2001), or exchange of political opinions between Vietnamese Americans and Vietnamese nationals outside of the political pressure and fear of reprisal they would experience in their respective societies (Valverde, 2002), to name just a few examples.

In my work with adolescent immigrants in the United States, I have looked at the kinds of language and literacy learning that are fostered as these young people develop transnational relationships and communities through the use of networked digital media (Lam, 2004, in press; Lam & Rosario, 2006). In a recent survey and interview study (Lam & Rosario, 2006) with a broad segment of adolescent immigrants of diverse national and regional origins (including Hispanic, Korean, Polish, and South Asian),[2] we found that a majority of the students use networked digital media to conduct relationships spanning more than one country, in most cases involving both the United States and the students' countries of origin. Within their online fields of communication, students draw on multiple languages, informational sources, and cultural input from different countries and perceive an increase in their ability to connect with friends and family, obtain news and information, learn about other countries, and read and write in their native languages, English, and, in some cases, other languages learned in their country of origin. These students' digital literacy practices situate them in a transnational circuit of news and ideas in which they are exposed to political narratives, social expectations, cultural values, and societal experiences that are not confined to a single sociopolitical system. We argued that these digital practices seem to foster a kind of multifocality—the inclination to see things from multiple perspectives—that is part of growing up in transnational networks.

The ways in which media and migration have created multilayered transnational social fields have prompted some social scientists (Beck, 2000; Faist, 2000; Levitt & Glick Schiller, 2004; Urry, 2000) to propose a reformulation of the concept of society that goes beyond the view that takes "rootedness and incorporation in the nation-state as the norm and social identities and practices enacted across state boundaries as out of the ordinary" (Levitt & Glick Schiller, 2004, p. 1007). In view of the shifting boundaries of social life propelled by global cultural flows and migration, it is incumbent upon educational researchers to start asking new questions about possible forms of societal participation and learning among our growing populations of migrant and multilingual students. Such questions would ultimately involve how we understand and value the cross-border connections, perspectives, and cultural, economic, and linguistic resources that immigrant students may develop and contribute as part of society in an interdependent world.

Rethinking Models of Societal Participation and Learning

In most liberal democratic countries on the receiving end of global migration, the mode of incorporation for migrant populations tends to oscillate between the dichotomy of assimilation and cultural pluralism, with each side of the binary taking a stronger hold at different points in history (see, e.g., Kivisto, 2005; Kymlicka, 1995; Rumbaut, 1999). Whereas assimilation takes the dominant culture of society as the center and goal of immigrant incorporation and participation in society, pluralism sees incorporation and participation as legitimately dispersed among a diversity of cultures that together make up the fabric of a modern multicultural society.

In the assimilation model, immigrant students and their "foreignness" are often construed as a problem to be solved or a deficit to be remediated. Historically, the fear and stigmatization of "un-Americanness" in this country have been expressed in both inclusionary and exclusionary forms of educational policies and practices used to incorporate new immigrants into the social and economic structure of American society (Crawford, 2000; Moreno, 1999; Olsen, 1997). As Olsen (1997) commented in regard to immigrant experiences in the context of U.S. schooling, integral elements in the Americanization process include (a) the requirement to become English speaking at the expense of one's native language; (b) academic marginalization and the disproportional tracking of immigrant students into remedial, special education, and vocational classes; and (c) the exorbitant pressure to find and take one's place in the racial hierarchy of this country.

Yet, the past several decades have seen the ascendancy of the concept of cultural pluralism and its translation into official state policies that recognize the rights of members of ethnic minority groups to cultural maintenance and community formation. Cultural pluralism resists the myth of homogeneous and monocultural nation-states and envisions a society based on democratic values of equity and social justice. Hence, the freedom to maintain one's ethnic and linguistic heritage becomes linked to an overall guarantee of social equality and protection from discrimination. The concept of cultural pluralism serves as a foundational principle of the multifaceted movement of multicultural education in the United States, a major tenet of which is that "every child's home culture must be affirmed and respected and opportunities must be provided for all children to reach their fullest potential" (Bennett, 2001, p. 173). It was within this milieu of cultural rights and democratic justice that bilingual educational programs became imaginable as a way to guarantee immigrant students' access to comprehensible and meaningful learning by providing literacy and content area instruction in their primary language while they develop proficiency in English (Crawford, 1995; *Lau v. Nichols,* 1974). However, since their inception, bilingual and multicultural programs have been the target of intense political contention in the United States (Gutiérrez et al., 2000; Olneck, 2000; Ovando, 2003), illustrating the persistent binary opposition of assimilationist and pluralist discourses in this country.

While cultural pluralism has contributed significantly to social equity in the civic and political life of society, its primary focus on ethnic distinctions of communities of descent and general subscription to the territorial principle of society do not account for migrant transnational relations and diaspora cultures that traverse state boundaries (Castles, 2005). New global conditions of intensified population movement, trans-border media flows, and the growth of communication technologies have facilitated a new *pluralism of space* (Faist, 2000) in which practices that foster multiple, uneven, and nonexclusive affiliations across national borders are becoming more prevalent and viable. It was in this context that Faist (2000) proposed the concept of "border-crossing expansion of social space" as an additional model for understanding societal participation that takes into account the myriad forms of cross-border transactions and cultural circulation that accompany mobility in the contemporary world. In differentiating this model from the assimilationist and pluralist views, Faist (2000, p. 211) noted:

At the root of these phenomena lies the mobility not only of persons but also of cultural practices, meanings and symbols (Hannerz, 1996, p. 64). Hence the need to supplement the two canonical views to take into account diffusion and syncretism. The concept of border-crossing expansion of social space tries to capture how immigrant cultural syncretism connects to ongoing transnationalization.

In my research exploring the transnational relationships and cultural practices of adolescent migrants in the United States, I have suggested the need to shift from a unilinear view of *acculturation* that focuses on adaptation to the structural and cultural conditions of the host society to a more multidimensional view of *transculturation* that looks at the multilayered modes of belonging and participation within, across, and at the intersections of societies (Lam, in press).

A shift or expansion of perspective as described would allow educational researchers to begin to address a lacuna in our understanding of socialization, identity formation, and the development of cultural, linguistic, and cognitive orientation and competence at the intersocietal level. As a number of educational scholars have pointed out, in a world of deepening interdependence and penetration in almost all areas of collective life—economic, cultural, political, environmental, and so forth—it is no longer necessary or advisable to subscribe to an anachronistic view of immigrant identity as an achievement that involves overcoming the baggage of other cultural identifications (Maira, 2004; McCarthy, Giardina, Harewood, & Park, 2003; Suárez-Orozco & Qin-Hilliard, 2004; Suárez-Orozco & Suárez-Orozco, 2001). According to immigration and education scholars Suárez-Orozco and Qin-Hilliard (2004, p. 22):

Youth who are players in a global stage must cultivate the multiple identities that are required to function in diverse, often incommensurable cultural realities. Rather than theorizing identity as oriented toward "either" the home culture "or" the host culture, many immigrant youth today are articulating and performing complex multiple identifications that involve bringing together disparate cultural streams.

Exploring the processes, resources, tensions, and challenges of young people's socialization and learning in transnational contexts, such as family networks, the flow of
diaspora media and popular culture, digitally mediated communities, and organized
religion and other cultural institutions, would allow us to begin to understand what
it means to learn and grow up in today's contiguous and overlapping cultural spaces
between societies. It would enable us to uncover the kinds of competencies, skills,
and knowledge that are developed as young people negotiate multiple cultural representations and societal perspectives and realities. A transnational reframing of the
cultural and linguistic resources of migrant and multilingual youth would lead us
beyond approaching diversity with tolerance and respect within a multicultural society to looking at how diversity can be leveraged as a global resource to enhance
young people's future contributions as workers, citizens, and intercultural bridges in
an interdependent world.

TOWARD COSMOPOLITAN AND INTERCULTURAL LEARNING

By laying out two broad lines of research issues around how young people are
interacting with global youth cultures, transnational social networks, and mass electronic and digital media, I have sought to identify the location or dislocation of culture beyond a majority-minority state-bound category to forms of transcultural flows
propelled by globalized economies, youth participatory practices, and multicultural
and migrant communities. At the same time, I have proposed that learning takes
place within this globalized context in the form of intercultural practices wherein
young people draw upon and reshape diverse cultural materials, develop multisite
and multilayered identifications, and navigate the overlapping and dividing lines
among cultures, ethnicities, languages, and nations. These forms of learning deviate
from the historical construction of education and schooling as "technologies of nation,
nationality, and nationalism" (Luke, 2004, p. 1437) and suggest new kinds of knowledge and subject formation. In this concluding section, I highlight three conceptual
frames that may help guide our research endeavors in generating questions and understanding the new formations of knowledge, identity, and community—the new forms
of learning—that are occurring in contemporary cultural contexts. The frames that
I discuss locate learning in the production of intercultural capital, cosmopolitan
identities, and sites of digital transcultures.

The ways in which diverse images, ideas, material, and semiotic products are circulated in globalized economic exchanges and the transnational circuits of social relations and diaspora cultures involve young people in forms of intercultural navigation
that require them to work with and define their relationships to multiple cultural
practices at the global and local levels and across differently positioned subjectivities
and histories. These glocalized spaces of cultural and economic exchange are redefining the forms of cultural capital—embodied ways of knowing and reasoning, schemes
of perception and appreciation (Bourdieu, 1986)—that some young people are developing and many will need to engage critically and creatively with the many kinds of
intercultural transactions that will mark their life pathways. As noted by Suárez-Orozco

and Qin-Hilliard (2004, p. 3), the challenge of learning and of education here involves developing "the cognitive skills, interpersonal sensibilities, and cultural sophistication of children and youth whose lives will be both engaged in local contexts and responsive to larger transnational processes."

It is in this context that Luke and his colleagues (Luke, 2004; Luke & Goldstein, 2006) have argued for a reconceptualization of agency and learning in globalized cultures and economies as the formation of *intercultural capital,* the knowledge and dispositions that allow one to negotiate understanding across multiple lines of difference in the intrinsically intercultural and glocalized forms of exchanges that penetrate our collective and personal lives. Intercultural capital involves "the capacity to engage in acts of knowledge, power and exchange across time/space divides and social geographies, across diverse communities, populations and epistemic stances" (Luke, 2004, p. 1429). This formulation of capital or human capacity reorients our notion of power from particular stabilized cultural practices that confer distinction and status on individuals to an agentive form of power that enables one to mediate across cultural and societal differences in pursuit of equitable relations, common purposes, and mutual understanding.

As we have seen, in their engagement with popular culture, digital media, affinity groups, and transnational networks, young people are already active players in shaping these new transcultural contexts of exchange and knowledge production. Questions to pursue in this regard include what kinds of intercultural knowledge and dispositions young people develop as they navigate across lines of difference in their participation in glocalized affiliative and transnational networks. We also want to know what sorts of conditions and processes in these affiliative and transnational networks (including the specific types of interactions and nature of the practices involved) are related to the development of different kinds of cultural perspectives, orientations, and social alignments. In addition, how might the perspectives, knowledge, and dispositions that are cultivated in these glocalized and transnational exchanges affect the developmental trajectories of young people in their approaches to formal schooling, career and other life choices, relation to diverse communities, and functioning in different societal contexts? In other words, do the kinds of intercultural capital developed in one setting come to be used in other settings to enhance young people's life pathways? And what might we learn from all of these questions that could be used to redesign educational practices to leverage the intercultural experiences, skills, and competence of young people and further build their critical and creative capacities to analyze different forms of global interconnections and dialogue across epistemic and ideological positions.

As discussed earlier, the multilayered forms of affiliations, allegiances, and identifications that are fostered in global youth cultures and diaspora relations are undermining or at least disrupting the boundedness of traditional notions of identity at the local, communal, and national levels and along lines of distinction according to ethnicity, culture, and language. As pointed out by Caglar (2002), with the development of cross-border media and relational spaces, a new sense of cosmopolitan or transnational consciousness is infiltrating the typical representation of migrants and minorities as ethnic populations within a multicultural state. As young people forge new affinity groups that involve them in interactions with diverse others and multiple attachments across global and local terrains, what are we to make of the new kinds of identities that are being formed and their relation to young people's learning and developmental trajectories?

The recent revitalization of the notion of *cosmopolitanism* has sought to conceptualize the complexity of new global subjectivities involving the experience of mediating one's relation to people, events, and practices in multiple localities and sustaining pluralized and nonexclusive affiliations (e.g., Appiah, 2006; Cheah & Robbins, 1998; Hollinger, 2000; Vertovec & Cohen, 2002; Waldron, 1992). This formulation of cosmopolitan identity seeks to displace the elitist, globe-trotting, frequent-flyer image of cosmopolitanism and signal the many kinds of cosmopolitan experiences on the ground practiced by ordinary people who have developed various kinds of globalized visions as a result of conditions such as forced or voluntary migration of labor; exposure to transnational media; border-crossing exchanges of an educational, corporate, or bureaucratic nature; and contact with cultural "others" in historically insular locales (Chua, 2004, cited in Luke & Goldstein, 2006). While cosmopolitanism emphasizes the multiplicity and overlapping identifications an individual may hold, "it is *the ability to stand outside of a singular location (the location of one's birth, land, upbringing, conversion) and to mediate traditions* that lies at its core" (Held, 2002, p. 58).

In a period in which the predominant educational response to globalization in the United States is cast as a growing anxiety to preserve the country's competitive edge in ever-spiraling economic competition and rivalry among nations, we are overlooking other equally important educational responsibilities of fostering in young people the cosmopolitan vision to see the world in more complex and interdependent ways, pursue translocal forms of solidarities in addressing global issues and problems, and understand cultures "in relation to each other, historically formed and globally interconnected through cultural mobility, exchange and hybridization" (Rizvi, in press-b). Given that today's youth are to some extent already developing multiple and dynamic identities and embracing local, global, and transnational perspectives, an education that focuses on more of the same (in the form of academic basics, content-area factual knowledge, and standardized testing and pedagogies) to increase national competitiveness is unlikely to provide a sufficiently comprehensive context for young people to draw upon and integrate their experiences and identities in productive ways. We need an educational research agenda that examines the processes for developing cosmopolitan sensibilities in a variety of learning and educational contexts. This includes exploring what kinds of conditions and practices are conducive to the cultivation of multiple global/local perspectives and identifications and what conditions and practices would lead beyond a consumerist logic of strategic positioning in the global market to a critical and moral sense of global solidarity (Kraidy, 2005; Rizvi, 2005b). This research agenda needs to take place in a societal milieu in which the transnational ties of ordinary people and minority populations are viewed not with suspicion but as resources to forge bridges across cultures, traditions, and societies.

Lastly, the salience of popular culture, media, and digital technologies in young people's lives is indisputable (Alvermann, 2002; Hagood, Leander, Luke, Mackey, & Nixon, 2003; Ito, in press; McCarthy et al., 2003; Sefton-Green, 1998) and is illustrated in the range of studies discussed in this chapter that reveal how youth in various parts of the world use digital media to exchange ideas and cultural products, engage in multimedia authoring and collaborative activities, develop transnational ties, and create new kinds of glocalized identities. It is important to note that people living in affluent countries and urban centers around the world have access to very different kinds of informational and media landscapes than those residing in poor and rural areas of developing regions. And research on digital literacy and learning needs to rigorously account for the effects of economic and political structure, race, gender, socioeconomic status, urban-rural disparity, and other social variables on young people's media use and practices. Yet, as today's youth stand at the forefront in the adoption of Internet and digital technologies (Lenhart, Madden, & Hitlin, 2005; Luke & Luke, 2001), and as these new technologies are mediating the variegated flow of ideas, images, cultural products, and human connectivity through both corporate and grassroots designs, digital media provide a fertile ground for the study of learning in globalized transcultural contexts.

In a comprehensive survey of digital literacy practices around animé, manga, and fan fiction, Black (in press) commented on how these media practices have coalesced into a kind of heterogeneous "third space" (Bhabha, 1994, cited in Black, in press) where meaningful participation and learning are less dependent on common geographical and historical backgrounds than on the creation of shared discourse and semiotic repertoires that are glocalized in nature and linked to popular youth media. With respect to this "third space" of digital media use and production, Black (in press) noted:

> Such a paradigm is crucial to understanding key issues . . . including: 1) the fact that media such as Japanese animé and manga carry with them certain generic, ideological, cultural, and literate conventions; 2) how, as these media become part of global flows of information and spectacle, they are taken up by fans and are revised and recontextualized through local literate and social interactions; and 3) how these reworked texts in turn are shared and re-disseminated into global networks via new ICTs [information and communication technologies].

Such processes of transcultural learning and production wherein texts, images, graphics, sounds, and other kinds of semiotic representation are appropriated, rearticulated, produced, and projected in glocalized digital spaces apply not only to youth involvement in popular cultures but also to various transnational linkages in diaspora media and online networks in which migrant and minority youth are forging diverse perspectives and self-definitions in relation to people, events, and practices across geographical locales.

Researching practices of learning in digital transcultures would require us to explore how uses of new information and communication technologies constitute a "field of relations" (Olwig & Hastrup, 1997, cited in Leander, 2003) wherein knowledge and subjectivities are developed in the porous boundaries among culturally configured ideas and images, semiotic resources and materials, and collective histories and imaginations. It would look at the possibilities and limitations of such contexts to facilitate the development of intercultural perspectives and understanding and new forms of social alignment and solidarity. This kind of exploration compels us to move beyond viewing technology as information access/processing/production to looking at how learning in digital networked spaces is about relationality and movement and about different types of mobility (Luke, 2003). Following the relational logic of digital spaces, we would look at the different forms of mobility (across social, cultural, and knowledge domains, with respect to cognitive horizons and self-imagining) that are facilitated or forestalled for different populations in these contexts. Studying how social practices are developed, how relationships are formed, and indeed how learning and teaching take place in new digital landscapes and other translocal contexts would allow us to uncover the human processes behind our global conditions and the real opportunities and challenges of working with and for diversity in the contemporary era.

ACKNOWLEDGMENTS

I wish to thank the editors for their bold vision for this volume and my consulting editors for this chapter, Kris Gutiérrez and Fazal Rizvi, for very helpful and supportive comments.

NOTES

[1] The release of a Spanish-language version of the U.S. national anthem recorded by a group of well-known Latino artists coincided with Congress's debate on immigration legislation and was seen as a high-profile case that helped to instigate the proposal of a legislative amendment to make English the "national language" of the United States.

[2] This research involved a survey of 271 foreign-born students and interviews with a subset of 40 students from a mixed-income and ethnically/linguistically diverse public school located on the border of a metropolitan midwestern city. While the survey included students from a variety of national origins, we recruited for the interviews participants from four major national/regional groups—Hispanic, Korean, Polish, and South Asian—for the purpose of comparative analysis.

REFERENCES

Alvermann, D. E. (Ed.). (2002). *Adolescents and literacies in a digital world.* New York: Peter Lang.
Androutsopoulos, J., & Scholz, A. (2002) On the recontextualization of hip-hop in European speech communities: A contrastive analysis of rap lyrics. *Philologie im Netz, 19.* Retrieved May 2, 2006, from http://www.fuberlin.de/phin/phin19/p19tl.htm
Appiah, K. A. (2006). *Cosmopolitanism: Ethics in a world of strangers.* New York: Norton.
Arnett, J. J. (2002). The psychology of globalization. *American Psychologist, 57,* 774–783.
Au, K. H., & Jordan, C. (1981). Teaching reading to Hawaiian children: Finding a culturally appropriate solution. In H. T. Trueba, G. P. Guthrie, & K. H. Au (Eds.), *Culture and the bilingual classroom: Studies in classroom ethnography* (pp. 139–152). New York: Newbury House.
Banks, J., & Banks, C. (Eds.). (1995). *Handbook of research on multicultural education.* New York: Macmillan.

Baratz, J., & Baratz, S. (1970). Early childhood intervention: The social scientific basis of institutionalized racism. *Harvard Educational Review, 39,* 29–50.

Beck, U. (2000). The cosmopolitan perspective: Sociology in the second age of modernity. *British Journal of Sociology, 5,* 79–107.

Bennett, C. (2001). Genres of research in multicultural education. *Review of Educational Research, 71,* 171–217.

Bereiter, C., & Englemann, S. (1966). *Teaching disadvantaged children in preschool.* Englewood Cliffs, NJ: Prentice Hall.

Black, R. (2005). Access and affiliation: The literacy and composition practices of English language learners in an online fanfiction community. *Journal of Adolescent and Adult Literacy, 49,* 118–128.

Black, R. W. (2006). Language, culture, and identity in online fanfiction. *E-learning, 3,* 170–184.

Black, R. W. (in press). Just don't call them cartoons: The new literacy spaces of animé, manga, and fanfiction. In D. Leu, J. Coiro, C. Lankshear, & M. Knobel (Eds.), *Handbook of research on new literacies.* Mahwah, NJ: Erlbaum.

Bourdieu, P. (1986). The forms of capital. In J. Richardson (Ed.), *The handbook of theory and research in the sociology of education* (pp. 241–258). New York: Greenwood Press.

Buckingham, D., & Sefton-Green, J. (2003). Gotta catch 'em all: Structure, agency and pedagogy in children's media culture. *Media, Culture, and Society, 25,* 379–399.

Caglar, A. (2002). Media corporatism and cosmopolitanism. In S. Vertovec & R. Cohen (Eds.), *Conceiving cosmopolitanism: Theory, context, and practice* (pp. 180–190). New York: Oxford University Press.

Castles, S. (2005). Migration and community formation under conditions of globalization. In P. Kivisto (Ed.), *Incorporating diversity: Rethinking assimilation in a multicultural age* (pp. 277–298). Boulder, CO: Paradigm.

Chandler-Olcott, K., & Mahar, D. (2003). Tech-savviness meets multiliteracies: Exploring adolescent girls' technology-mediated literacy practices. *Reading Research Quarterly, 38,* 356–385.

Cheah, B., & Robbins, B. (1998). *Cosmopolitics: Thinking and feeling beyond the nation.* Minneapolis: University of Minnesota Press.

Conradson, D., & Latham, A. (Eds.). (2005). Transnational urbanism [special issue]. *Journal of Ethnic and Migration Studies, 31*(2).

Cope, B., & Kalantzis, M. (1993). *The powers of literacy: A genre approach to teaching writing.* Pittsburgh, PA: University of Pittsburgh Press.

Crawford, J. (1995). *Bilingual education: History, politics, theory, and practice.* Los Angeles: Bilingual Education Services.

Crawford, J. (2000). *At war with diversity: US language policy in an age of anxiety.* Clevedon, England: Multilingual Matters.

Cutler, C. (2003) "Keepin' it real": White hip-hoppers' discourses of language, race, and authenticity. *Journal of Linguistic Anthropology, 13,* 211–233.

Delpit, L. (1989). The silenced dialogue: Power and pedagogy in educating other people's children. *Harvard Educational Review, 58,* 280–298.

Delpit, L. (1996). *Other people's children: Cultural conflict in the classroom.* New York: New Press.

Deschenes, S., Cuban. L., & Tyack, D. (2001). Mismatch: Historical perspectives on schools and students who don't fit them. *Teachers College Record, 103,* 525–547.

Deutsch, M., Bloom, R. D., Brown, B. R., Deutsch, C. P., Goldstein, L. S., John, V. P., Katz, P. A., Levinson, A., Peisach, E. C., & Whiteman, M. (1967). *The disadvantaged child.* New York: Basic Books.

Erickson, F. (2002). Culture and human development. *Human Development, 45,* 299–306.

Faist, T. (2000). Transnationalization in international migration: Implications for the study of citizenship and culture. *Ethnic and Racial Studies, 23,* 189–222.

Fisher, C., Jackson, F., & Villarruel, F. (1998). The study of African American and Latin American children and youth. In R. Lerner (Ed.), *Handbook of child psychology* (5th ed., pp. 1145–1207. New York: Wiley.

Gee, J. P. (1999). Identity as an analytic lens for research in education. In W. G. Secada (Ed.), *Review of research in education* (Vol. 25, pp. 99–125). Washington, DC: American Educational Research Association.

Gee, J. P. (2004). *Situated language and learning: A critique of traditional schooling.* New York: Routledge.

González, N. (2004). Disciplining the discipline: Anthropology and the pursuit of quality education. *Educational Researcher, 33*(5), 17–25.

Gutiérrez, K., Baquedano-Lopez, P., & Asato, J. (2000). "English for the children:" The new literacy of the old world order, language policy and educational reform. *Bilingual Research Journal, 24,* 87–112.

Gutiérrez, K., & Rogoff, B. (2003). Cultural ways of learning: Individual traits or repertoires of practice. *Educational Researcher, 32*(5), 19–25.

Hagood, M. C., Leander, K. M., Luke, C., Mackey, M., & Nixon, H. (2003). Media and online literacy studies. *Reading Research Quarterly, 38,* 386–413.

Heath, S. B. (1983). *Ways with words.* Cambridge, England: Cambridge University Press.

Held, D. (2002). Culture and political community: National, global, and cosmopolitan. In S. Vertovec & R. Cohen (Eds.), *Conceiving cosmopolitanism: Theory, context, and practice* (pp. 48–58). New York: Oxford University Press.

Hermans, H. J. M., & Kempen, H. J. G. (1998). Moving cultures: The perilous problems of cultural dichotomies in a globalizing society. *American Psychologist, 53,* 1111–1120.

Hess, R., Shipman, V., Brophy, J., & Bear, R. (1968). *The cognitive environments of urban preschool children.* Chicago: University of Chicago Press.

Hollinger, D. A. (2000). *Postethnic America: Beyond multiculturalism.* New York: Perseus Books.

Hulse, C. (2006, May 19). Senate passes a bill that favors English. *New York Times,* p. A4.

Hunt, J. M. (1969). *The challenge of incompetence and poverty: Papers on the role of early education.* Urbana: University of Illinois Press.

Ignacio, E. (2005). *Building diaspora: Filipino cultural community formation on the Internet.* New Brunswick, NJ: Rutgers University Press.

Ito, M. (in press). Technologies of the childhood imagination: Yugioh, media mixes, and everyday cultural production. In J. Karaganis & N. Jeremijenko (Eds.), *Structures of participation in digital culture.* Durham, NC: Duke University Press.

Iwabuchi, K. (2004). How Japanese is Pokémon? In J. Tobin (Ed.), *Pikachu's global adventure: The rise and fall of Pokémon* (pp. 53–79). Durham, NC: Duke University Press.

Jenkins, H. (2006). *Convergence culture: Where old and new media collide.* New York: New York University Press.

Jensen, L. A. (2003). Coming of age in a multicultural world: Globalization and adolescent cultural identity formation. *Applied Developmental Science, 7,* 189–196.

Katsuno, H., & Maret, J. (2004). Localizing the Pokémon TV series for the American market. In J. Tobin (Ed.), *Pikachu's global adventure: The rise and fall of Pokémon* (pp. 80–107). Durham, NC: Duke University Press.

Kennedy, P., & Roudometof, V. (2002). *Communities across borders: New immigrants and transnational cultures.* London: Routledge.

Kitalong, K. S., & Kitalong, T. (2000). Complicating the tourist gaze: Literacy and the Internet as catalysts for articulating a postcolonial Palauan identity. In G. E. Hawisher & C. L. Selfe (Eds.), *Global literacies and the World-Wide Web* (pp. 95–113). London: Routledge.

Kivisto, K. (Ed.). (2005). *Incorporating diversity: Rethinking assimilation in a multicultural age.* Boulder, CO: Paradigm.

Kraidy, M. (2005). *Hybridity or the cultural logic of globalization.* Philadelphia: Temple University Press.

Kymlicka, W. (1995). *Multicultural citizenship: A liberal theory of minority rights.* Oxford, England: Oxford University Press.

Lam, W. S. E. (2000). Literacy and the design of the self: A case study of a teenager writing on the internet. *TESOL Quarterly, 34,* 457–482.

Lam, W. S. E. (2004). Second language socialization in a bilingual chatroom: Global and local considerations. *Language Learning and Technology, 8*(3), 44–65.

Lam, W. S. E. (in press). Re-envisioning language, literacy, and the immigrant subject in new mediascapes. *Pedagogies: An International Journal.*

Lam, W. S. E., & Rosario, E. M. (2006, April). *Digital literacy and transnationalism among adolescent immigrants in the U.S.* Paper presented at the annual meeting of the American Educational Research Association, San Francisco, CA.

Landzelius, K. M. (Ed.). (2006). *Native on the Net: Indigenous and diasporic peoples in the virtual age.* London: Routledge.

Lau v. Nichols, 414 U.S. 563. (1974).

Leander, K. (2003). Writing travelers' tales on new literacyscapes. *Reading Research Quarterly, 38,* 392–397.

Lee, C. D. (2003). Reconceptualizing race and ethnicity in educational research. *Educational Researcher, 32*(5), 3–5.

Lee, H. M. (2003). *Tongans overseas: Between two shores.* Honolulu: University of Hawaii Press.

Lee, H. M. (2006). Debating language and identity online: Tongans on the Net. In K. M. Landzelius (Ed.), *Native on the Net: Indigenous and diasporic peoples in the virtual age.* London: Routledge.

Lee, S. J. (2005). *Up against whiteness: Race, school and immigrant youth.* New York: Teachers College Press.

Lenhart, A., Madden, M., & Hitlin, P. (2005). *Teens and technology: Youth are leading the transition to a fully wired and mobile nation.* Washington, DC: Pew Internet and American Life Project.

Levitt, P., & Glick Schiller, N. (2004). Conceptualizing simultaneity: A transnational social field perspective on society. *International Migration Review, 38,* 1002–1039.

Levitt, P., & Waters, M. (2002). *The changing face of home: The transnational lives of the second generation.* New York: Russell Sage Foundation.

Lewis, O. (1966). The culture of poverty. *Scientific American, 215,* 19–25.

Luke, A. (2004). Teaching after the marketplace: From commodity to cosmopolitanism. *Teachers College Record, 106,* 1422–1443.

Luke, A., & Goldstein, T. (2006). *Building intercultural capital: A response to Rogers, Marshall, and Tyson.* Retrieved October 22, 2006, from http://dx.doi.org/10.1598/RRQ.41.2.3

Luke, A., & Luke, C. (2001). Adolescence lost/childhood regained: On early intervention and the emergence of the techno-subject. *Journal of Early Childhood Literacy, 1,* 91–120.

Luke, C. (2003). Pedagogy, connectivity, multimodality, and interdisciplinarity. *Reading Research Quarterly, 38,* 397–403.

Maira, S. (2002). *Desis in the house: Indian American youth culture in New York City.* Philadelphia: Temple University Press.

Maira, S. (2004). Imperial feelings: Youth culture, citizenship, and globalization. In M. M. Suárez-Orozco & D. B. Qin-Hilliard (Eds.), *Globalization: Culture and education in the new millennium* (pp. 203–234). Berkeley: University of California Press.

McCarthy, C., Giardina, M., Harewood, S., & Park, J. K. (2003). Contesting culture: Identity and curriculum dilemmas in the age of globalization, postcolonialism, and multiplicity. *Harvard Educational Review, 73,* 449–465.

Miller, D., & Slater, D. (2000). *The Internet: An ethnographic approach.* Oxford, England: Berg.

Mitchell, T. (Ed.). (2002). *Global noise: Rap and hip-hop outside the USA.* Middletown, CT: Wesleyan University Press.

Mitra, A. (2001). Marginal voices in cyberspace. *New Media and Society, 3,* 29–48.

Moll, L., & González, N. (2004). Engaging life: A funds of knowledge approach to multi-cultural education. In J. Banks & C. McGee Banks (Eds.), *Handbook of research on multicultural education* (2nd ed., pp. 699–715). New York: Jossey-Bass.

Moreno, J. F. (1999). *The elusive quest for equality: 150 years of Chicano/Chicana education.* Cambridge, MA: Harvard Educational Press.

Nightly Business Report. (2006, April 17). *Businesses are logging on to Hispanic buying party on line.* Retrieved October 22, 2006, from http://www.pbs.org/nbr/site/onair/transcripts/060417b/

Olneck, M. (2000). Can multicultural education change what counts as cultural capital? *American Educational Research Journal, 37,* 317–348.

Olsen, L. (1997). *Made in America: Immigrant students in our public schools.* New York: New Press.

Orellana, M. F., Thorne, B., Chee, A. E., & Lam, W. S. E. (2001). Transnational child-hoods: The participation of children in the processes of family migration. *Social Problems, 48,* 572–591.

Ovando, C. J. (2003). Bilingual education in the United States: Historical development and current issues. *Bilingual Research Journal, 27,* 1–26.

Pennycook, A. (2003). Global Englishes, Rip Slyme, and performativity. *Journal of Sociolinguistics, 7,* 513–533.

Pennycook, A. (2005). Teaching with the flow: Fixity and fluidity in education. *Asia Pacific Journal of Education, 25,* 29–43.

Philips, S. (1972). Participant structure and communicative competence. In C. Cazden, V. John, & D. Hymes (Eds.), *Functions of language in the classroom* (pp. 370–394). New York: Teachers College Press.

Richtel, M., & Belson, K. (2006, May 30). Cell carriers seek growth by catering to Hispanics. *New York Times,* p. C1.

Rizvi, F. (2005a). Rethinking brain drain in the era of globalization. *Asia Pacific Journal of Education, 25,* 175–193.

Rizvi, F. (2005b). International education and the production of cosmopolitan identities. *RJHE International Publication Series, 9,* 77–92.

Rizvi, F. (in press-a). Internationalization of curriculum: A critical perspective. In M. Hayden, J. Levy, & J. Thompson (Eds.), *Handbook of research in international education.* London: Sage.

Rizvi, F. (in press-b). Postcolonial perspectives on globalization and education. *Cultural Studies-Critical Methodologies.*

Rogers, T., Marshall, E., & Tyson, C. A. (2006). Dialogic narratives of literacy, teaching, and schooling: Preparing literacy teachers for diverse settings. *Reading Research Quarterly, 41,* 202–224.

Rogoff, B. (2003). *The cultural nature of human development.* New York: Oxford University Press.

Rogoff, B., & Angelillo, C. (2002). Investigating the coordinated functioning of multifaceted cultural practices in human development. *Human Development, 45,* 211–225.

Rumbaut, R. (1999). Assimilation and its discontents: Ironies and paradoxes. In C. Hirschman, P. Kasinitz, & J. DeWind (Eds.), *The handbook of international migration* (pp. 172–195). New York: Russell Sage Foundation.

Sarkar, M., & Allen, D. (in press). Identity in Quebec hip-hop: Language, territory and ethnicity in the mix. *Journal of Language, Identity and Education.*

Sarkar, M., Low, B., & Winer, L. (in press). "Pour connecter avec le peeps": Québéquicité and the Quebec hip-hop community. In M. Mantero (Ed.), *Identity and second language learning: Culture, inquiry, and dialogic activity in educational contexts.* Greenwich, CT: Information Age.

Sarkar, M., & Winer, L. (2006). Multilingual code-switching in Quebec rap: Poetry, pragmatics and performativity. *International Journal of Multilingualism, 3,* 173–192.

Scollon, R., & Scollon, S. (1981). *Narrative, literacy and face in interethnic communication.* Norwood, NJ: Ablex.

Sefton-Green, J. (Ed.). (1998). *Digital diversions: Youth culture in the age of multimedia.* London: UCL Press.

Spindler, G. D. (Ed.). (2000). *Fifty years of anthropology and education: 1950–2000.* Mahwah, NJ: Erlbaum.

Suárez-Orozco, C. (2004). Formulating identity in a globalized world. In M. M. Suárez-Orozco & D. B. Qin-Hilliard (Eds.), *Globalization: Culture and education in the new millennium* (pp. 173–202). Berkeley: University of California Press.

Suárez-Orozco, C., & Suárez-Orozco, M. (Ed.). (2001). *Children of immigration.* Cambridge, MA: Harvard University Press.

Suárez-Orozco, M. M., & Qin-Hilliard, D. B. (Eds.). (2004). *Globalization: Culture and education in the new millennium.* Berkeley: University of California Press.

Tobin, J. (2004a). The rise and fall of the Pokémon empire. In J. Tobin (Ed.), *Pikachu's global adventure: The rise and fall of Pokémon* (pp. 257–292). Durham, NC: Duke University Press.

Tobin, J. (Ed.). (2004b). *Pikachu's global adventure: The rise and fall of Pokémon.* Durham, NC: Duke University Press.

Urry, J. (2000, June). *The global media and cosmopolitanism.* Paper presented at the Transnational America Conference, Munich, Germany.

Valdez, G. (1996). *Con respeto: Bridging the distances between culturally diverse families and schools.* New York: Teachers College Press.

Valverde, C. K. L. (2002). *Making transnational Viet Nam: Vietnamese American community-Viet Nam linkages through money, music and modems.* Unpublished doctoral dissertation, University of California, Berkeley.

Vasquez, V. (2003). What Pokémon can teach us about learning and literacy. *Language Arts, 81,* 118–125.

Vertovec, S. (Ed.). (2003). International perspectives on transnational migration: An introduction [special issue]. *International Migration Review, 37*(3).

Vertovec, S., & Cohen, R. (Eds.). (2002). *Conceiving cosmopolitanism: Theory, context, and practice.* New York: Oxford University Press.

Waldron, J. (1992). Minority cultures and the cosmopolitan alternative. *University of Michigan Journal of Law Reform, 25,* 751–793.

Ybarra, L. (1983). Empirical and theoretical developments in the study of Chicano families. In A. Valdez, A. Camarillo, & T. Almaguer (Eds.), *The state of Chicano research in family, labor and migration studies: Proceedings of the First Stanford Symposium on Chicano Research and Public Policy* (pp. 91–110). Stanford, CA: Stanford University Press.

Chapter 7

Engaging Young People: Learning in Informal Contexts

JENNIFER A. VADEBONCOEUR
University of British Columbia

Over the past decade, "out-of-school time" and "after-school programs" have been identified as objects of research, funding, and policy initiatives across federal and state agencies (e.g., de Kanter, Williams, Cohen, & Stonehill, 2000; Miller, 2003; Perry, Teague, & Frey, 2002) as well as public, private, and nonprofit foundations such as the Charles Stewart Mott Foundation, the Robert Bowne Foundation, the Harvard Family Research Project, and the Afterschool Alliance. In the United States, this interest was fueled, in particular, by direct federal funding from the Clinton administration, with bipartisan support in Congress, that expanded the Jeffords-Gunderson legislation from $25 million in 1994 to $800 million in 1999, the most rapid increase in funding for any federal program in history (Bartko, 2005). This increase continued until recently, reaching $2.5 billion at the federal government level. However, as noted by the Afterschool Alliance (2006), at the time of this review, the budget proposal of the Bush administration had reduced the authorized funding from the No Child Left Behind Act for the 21st Century Community Learning Centers initiative from $2.5 billion to $981 million. Although the amount of financial support has been cut, the current level of federal funding represents an increase of $181 million since 1999.

The increasing attention to and funding of programs that engage youth outside of the formal institution of schooling was motivated by a number of overlapping concerns, including a desire to improve school achievement, a commitment to youth safety, and an interest in enrichment programs that offer opportunities to explore and study in the arts or sciences, coupled with occasions for social and emotional development. The field of informal contexts for learning generally reflects a goal of learning "writ large," that is, learning that is not designed in many instances to meet the formal institutional structures and demands of schooling.

During this social era of public and private investment, the present review of research was conducted to understand and conceptualize what counts as *learning in informal contexts*. Given the scope of research incorporating these terms, I needed to examine how they were used and what different authors meant when they were used. Both *learning* and *contexts* were frequently qualified by the terms formal, nonformal,

239

and informal, often with little definition. I began with the following question: What makes learning formal, nonformal, or informal? What I found was that learning was viewed as informal simply by virtue of it occurring in programs outside of school. The "informal" category was claimed not by virtue of an analysis of learning but by virtue of the location being "other than school."

As my exploration moved to contexts, the questions became more complex: What features of a context make it "informal"? Does informal characterize the *location?* Does informal refer to the *relationships* between participants? Does informal denote that what is to be learned, the *content,* is informal or that the method used for instruction, the *pedagogy,* is informal? Or perhaps the informality surfaces because participants are assessed via formative, dynamic, or performative *assessments* rather than standardized tests? The question of how to define terms such as learning and informal contexts, along with related issues of conceptual grounding, is examined in the review to follow.

The focus of this chapter is on *structured* informal contexts that engage young people between 12 and 18 years old in the United States, for example, those found in after-school programs and community-based youth organizations, which represent the bulk of the research in the field. The first section describes the method used to conduct the review. The second section provides a historical perspective for the chapter, along with a discussion of terms and categories and a framework. The third section examines theoretical and methodological issues that have surfaced in the field of learning in informal contexts. Promising programs of research and promising informal programs based on research are highlighted in the fourth section. In the fifth section, social and discursive practices are described, with an emphasis on how contexts for learning are constituted through participation. In the sixth section, gaps in the research and additional questions are coupled in an attempt to identify directions for future research.

One caveat needs to be acknowledged. This chapter is by necessity a partial representation of educational research on learning in informal contexts. The literature base is vast by virtue of the range of contexts for learning outside of schools, as well as the recent increase in research undertaken from the perspective of program evaluation. For example, research conducted on learning that occurs outside of structured programs, such as learning in homes, shopping malls, friendship groups, or other everyday settings, is beyond the scope of this review. In addition, studies that follow participants into particular informal contexts created through the use of technology (e.g., chat rooms or video gaming) are included elsewhere (see Sefton-Green's chapter in this volume), as are cross-national explorations of learning more generally (Vásquez's chapter). Perhaps most important, however, even the literature base taken in its entirety is partial: The research lens is often directed by funding toward politically expedient topics, issues, and accountability structures. The focus here has been studies with groups of participants, and programs with articulated goals or outcomes, rather than the everyday moment-to-moment interactions that form the deceptively simple social spaces for learning over time.

REVIEW METHOD: CONSTRUCTING A MULTIPHASE APPROACH

As a means of ensuring that the process for identifying materials was comprehensive, a method for conducting the review was generated, incorporating four phases: searching, reviewing, sorting, and confirming. Initially, this review of research in education was framed by the topic "adolescent learning in informal and nonschool contexts," yielding several key search words: "adolescent," "youth," "learning," "informal learning," "nonschool," "after-school programs," and "community organizations." Recognizing that no single search engine or database provides access to the complete research corpus, I selected several search engines and databases to provide access across education and psychology. As a result of differences in purposes and selection processes, and as well as representational differences in fields, associations, publishers, and publication types, different search engines access a different range of materials, and different databases archive different materials. In addition, under the Education Sciences Reform Act of 2002, access to the Education Resources Information Center (ERIC) database and the range of publications represented has been limited.

The *searching* phase included three steps. First, a broad search was conducted across two academic search engines, Academic Search Premier and Google Scholar, and three databases, ERIC, PsycARTICLES, and PsycINFO. Academic Search Premier provided access to full texts for selected journals, and Google Scholar included references to a wide range of abstracts, articles, books, and theses. For this review, ERIC provided access to both journal and nonjournal education literature, including conference proceedings, research reports, and U.S. Department of Education and contractor reports. PsycARTICLES provided articles from journals published by the American Psychological Association (APA), the Canadian Psychological Association, and the APA Educational Publishing Foundation. PsycINFO provided abstracts from the psychological literature. These different searches yielded 253 to more than 10,000 potential references.

Additional criteria were used to reduce the searches to a manageable size, such as limiting the time frame to 1990–2005 (the previously indicated period of expansion) and limiting the search to refereed journal articles, research-based books, formal reviews of research, conference presentations of research, and research and evaluation reports of federally and privately funded programs. As an approach to checking the extent to which the different search engines and databases provided convergent results as well as unique results, a cross-checking or contrastive analysis approach was developed to ensure that established researchers in the field were represented. Materials that listed research presentations, along with names of contributors identified from reference lists, were also contrasted. This second level of the search led to the identification of 175 potential references.

Second, four literature reviews were identified as "anchor" texts to provide a second approach for entering the literature and identifying additional sources to review. They represented more than two decades of research on learning in informal settings and recursively guided the searches (Fashola, 1998; Honig & McDonald, 2005;

McLaughlin, 2000; Scott-Little, Hamann, & Jurs, 2002). Third, educational organizations that conduct programs and program evaluations were identified on the Web, and their most recent reports on the topic of learning in informal contexts were reviewed. Organizational reports and evaluation research included, for example, publications produced for the Robert Bowne Foundation, the Harvard Family Research Project, the National Research Council, the Afterschool Alliance, and the National Institute on Out-of-School Time. Although these publications have historically been perceived to hold less credibility than peer-reviewed research studies, evaluation studies have become a key area of scholarship for ongoing funding and as a reflection of the social and political foundation underpinning the field. Such reports have an impact on educational practice and program design and they make an important, albeit frequently overlooked, contribution to programmatic research and evaluation. The final two steps of the search phase yielded 21 additional potential references, including the four anchor texts.

The second phase, *reviewing* the 196 documents gathered to represent the current state of the field (research articles, research-based books, review articles, conference presentations, and research and evaluation reports), raised a number of issues. Immediately, it was apparent that publications differed according to the theoretical frameworks and methodologies used and with regard to the organization and purpose of the programs. Information was gathered from each publication, when possible, including theoretical framework, methodology, definition of learning, age group of participants, program type, location, and outcomes. To create a record of publications, I used this information, along with a general summary, to construct an annotated bibliography. Unfortunately, much of this information was not articulated, and, in particular, theoretical frameworks, methodologies, and terms such as learning were not defined or described, making these key dimensions of research invisible. Transparency in terms of theoretical, methodological, and conceptual orientations would have allowed additional sense making across research studies and traditions. During this phase, documents were excluded (47 in total) as outside the scope of the present review for three reasons: if the age group of the participants did not include young people between the ages of 12 and 18 years, if the context of the research was not a structured program, or if the theoretical framework and methodology were not at least stated.

Sorting the documents, the third phase, was undertaken as a method for organizing the remaining 149 articles. This process produced four general categories: (a) reviews of research literature or programs, (b) single program descriptions that included evaluation reports, (c) issues in measurement and research, and (d) research-based advice for educators, program designers, and policymakers. The second category included four subcategories, organized by type of structured program: the arts, music, and dance; literacy, science, and technology; museums and science centers; and youth development programs. Although Honig and McDonald (2005) suggested that reviews of research such as this one be organized according to the types of participation in which young people engage, there were so few articles that included enough detail to construct categories on the basis of participation that this structure was not possible for the current review. There were few publications that provided the kind of detail necessary to make evaluations of learning. Therefore, this review reflects the common approach of categorizing according to program type.

The fourth phase, *confirming* the documents, was a final check for saturation of the general categories and of the data set selected for this review. It included re-searching across types of publications: research articles and reviews published in peer-reviewed journals, a variety of research-based books, conference presentations, and government and nongovernment research and evaluation reports. It also involved a process of chaining articles, from and across reference lists, to examine intertextual links in general and the way ideas were taken up and used more specifically (Fairclough, 1992). Ultimately, however, the documents gathered included topics too broad to manage, and two additional criteria for exclusion were used to ensure that this review was accessible and adhered to common practices in terms of page length. The fourth subcategory, "youth development programs" (e.g., studies of social and emotional "development" rather than "learning"), was excluded as outside the scope of this review. In addition, the fourth category, "research-based advice for educators, program designers, and policymakers," was reduced to a total of 14 articles on the basis of relevance to the topics addressed here. The final number of documents reviewed was 133.

A HISTORICAL PERSPECTIVE: GROUNDING TERMS, CATEGORIES, AND FRAMES

Taken together, the hours spent outside of school are the largest block of time in young people's lives (Council on Adolescent Development, 1992), and, as noted earlier, these hours have become quite interesting to adults concerned about the welfare and safety of youth, as well as potential educational opportunities. Rather than being a new interest, however, the subject of engagement in after-school, out-of-school, and community-based programs is a result of a resurgence of interest that has intensified and decreased in relation to cultural-historical events and issues faced by the other institutions with a vested interest in young people, namely families and schools.

Around the same time that formal schooling was established, local after-school programs were founded to provide an alternative to the perceived structure and rigidity of schools while also attempting to make up for the perceived deficiencies of families (Halpern, 2002). After-school programs have had a history of shifting purposes in relation to families and schools, although, as noted by Halpern (2002), since the 1950s they have commonly advocated that young people be recognized and respected; that they be given a safe space to play, explore interests, develop talents, and express themselves; and that part of growing up well is participating in activities with peers and adults that allow rehearsals and performances of newly learned abilities, roles, and literacies (see also Halpern, Barker, & Mollard, 2000; Spielberger & Halpern, 2002).

Over the past several decades, multiple categories have surfaced to define and qualify the general terms *education* and *learning* as well as a related corollary, *teaching* (e.g., Eraut, 2000). The interest in categorizing different types of education, learning, and teaching was catalyzed by conversations regarding education worldwide, given comparisons between institutional arrangements for education in different cultures and countries. In addition, attention to education over the life span in terms of "lifelong learning" and facilitating adult learning was driven by a pragmatic need to focus on reskilling and reeducating adults for positions in the workforce (e.g., Aspin, Chapman, Hatton, & Sawano, 2001; Knowles, 1980; Livingstone, 1999).

Although the topic of adult education is outside the scope of this chapter, developments in the field of adult education mirrored developments in the conceptualization of education for young people. The conventional trajectory from formal education to nonformal education and, finally, informal education, which identified schooling as the institutional basis for formal education, led to the construction of a similar trajectory in relation to learning (Eraut, 2000). Three early studies, represented in Table 1, were instrumental in conceptualizing these categories, each from a different theoretical frame. The authors sought to clarify the distinctions among *education, learning,* and *teaching* in school or formal contexts and nonschool or informal contexts. As exemplars, they illustrate what has become an often taken-for-granted foundation for this developing area of research and program development, although they do not reflect a single theoretical, methodological, or conceptual orientation.

In an early study of the cognitive aspects of informal education, Greenfield and Lave (1982) highlighted eight idealized characteristics of formal and informal education positioned as two poles in a typology with opposite characteristics and based on earlier cognitive and anthropological research conducted in Samoa, Papua New Guinea, and Liberia. These characteristics provide a series of distinctions between types of education, leading to characterizations of schooling as separate from everyday life and bounded by explicitly structured pedagogical relationships and curricula and characterizations of nonschool or informal education as embedded in daily life and bounded by implicitly structured pedagogical relationships and curricula. As noted by Greenfield and Lave (1982), the formal/informal dichotomy has proven useful in the conceptualization of education beyond the boundaries of "Western-style" schools. However, on the basis of their own research in both Mexico and Liberia, they argued that these categories easily become stereotyped, in particular hiding the variety of instructional techniques used within each category of education.

In a second article, a review of research by cognitive anthropologists, sociologists, and psychologists, Resnick (1987) compared learning both inside and outside of school. From this review, she identified four dimensions of difference emphasizing, for example, that activities outside of school (a) engage young people in social groups and function collaboratively, (b) rely on tools to shape and facilitate cognitive activity and engagement, (c) are embedded within contexts and incorporate the use of artifacts and practices that surface within a particular activity, and (d) develop specific competencies. Working across theoretical perspectives, Resnick noted that "school is a special place and time for people—discontinuous in some important ways with daily

TABLE 1   Comparing Across Formal, Nonformal, and Informal Categories

Formal	Nonformal	Informal

Greenfield and Lave (1982):
eight idealized characteristics of formal and informal *education* (p. 183)

Formal	Informal
• Set apart from the context of everyday life	• Embedded in activities of daily life
• Teacher imparts knowledge	• Learner is responsible for obtaining knowledge and skill
• Impersonal, teachers should not be relatives	• Personal relatives are appropriate teachers
• Explicit pedagogy and curriculum	• Implicit pedagogy and curriculum
• Change/discontinuity are valued	• Maintenance of continuity and tradition
• Learning by verbal exchange	• Learning by observation/ imitation
• Teaching by verbal presentation	• Teaching by demonstration
• Less strong social motivation	• Motivated by social contribution of novices to adult life

Resnick (1987):
four dimensions of comparison for formal and informal *learning*

Formal	Informal
• Individual cognition	• Shared cognition
• "Pure mentation"	• Tool manipulation
• Symbolic manipulation	• Contextualized reasoning
• Generalized skills and knowledge	• Specific competencies

Maarschalk (1988):
comparison of formal, nonformal, and informal science *teaching*[a]

Formal	Nonformal	Informal
• Takes place in a planned way in schools, colleges, and universities	• Proceeds in a planned but adaptable way in institutions and organizations, such as in-service training, field trips, museum visits, and educational television and radio	• Occurs in situations in life that come about spontaneously, for example, within the family circle and neighborhood

Formal, nonformal, and informal science teaching are interdependent, as noted in this example: Discussion in school . . . of an idea from a television program . . . that occurred spontaneously.

[a]The Human Sciences Research Council's (1981) categories of education, cited in Maarschalk (1988, p. 137).

life and work" (p. 13), and she challenged readers to consider reorganizing learning in schools by redirecting "the focus of schooling to encompass more of the features of successful out-of-school functioning" (p. 19). While Resnick's review was based on a substantial research base, educational researchers have taken up these "idealized" categories, in many instances, with little attention paid to anything other than *location:* in school or not in school. In addition, narrowing the research lens from *education* in general to *learning* more specifically shifts the object of study from a socially and historically constructed institution to a process of learners. A semantic change from education to learning becomes an epistemic claim. At issue here are the limits of language available to discuss different categories of learning and, indeed, whether thinking in such categories of learning advances our scholarship.

In contrast to both Greenfield and Lave (1982) and Resnick (1987), work by Maarschalk (1988) on scientific literacy identified "interdependent but clearly distinguishable forms" of formal, nonformal, and informal science teaching (p. 137). On the basis of research with the Rand Afrikaans University Scientific Literacy Research Project focusing on students in Grades 10 and 11, Maarschalk argued that many researchers use the terms nonformal and informal interchangeably and categorized museum visits, which are classified in this review as informal contexts, as nonformal science teaching. The explicitly chosen term, *informal science teaching,* was advanced by Maarschalk to denote that *teaching,* as opposed to *learning,* needs to be examined and explicated in science teaching research. According to Maarschalk, it is teaching that is extended long after the physical absence of the teacher, for example, a professor or another student who explains a science concept to a peer.

These three publications foreground education, learning, or teaching, and the categories "formal," "nonformal," and "informal," in heterogeneous ways. What they converge upon is, in fact, the way they have become stereotyped: as naively contrasting the location of education, learning, or teaching, which is just one feature of a context. This contrast makes visible the way these categories have been taken up by educational researchers more than the intentions of the authors, as well as the ease of slipping among terms such as education, learning, and teaching and applying qualifiers from one to the other. Although Table 1 highlights similarities across conceptions, and general themes can be traced down the formal and informal columns in particular, there are differences that ought not to be overlooked. The categories are useful for research only in certain circumstances and only as long as we do not begin to think and act like they are real.

Some authors explicitly challenge the usefulness of the formal/informal dichotomy in relation to *learning* and argue for using labels such as "incidental" and "implicit" to better describe types of learning (Eraut, 2000). A second type of challenge, consistent with the discussion articulated here, questions the usefulness of the formal/informal dichotomy altogether on the grounds that "there is no consensus about what informal learning might be" (Sefton-Green, 2003, p. 40). Nor, I would add, is there a shared epistemological basis, an explicit role for teachers and students, clarification on the defining features of teacher and student relationships, or a sense of how something called informal learning might be grounded in social and discursive practices, among other things.

Attention to social practices is central to a set of related interdisciplinary frameworks that incorporate perspectives from cultural anthropology, sociology, psychology, and linguistics to explore social practices embedded in everyday life. Education or schooling is just one of a number of social institutions studied alongside the rather ordinary wealth of learning that occurs by virtue of social participation in communities of practice (e.g., Lave, 1988; Lave & Wenger, 1991), as well as funds of knowledge developed in homes, classrooms, and communities (e.g., Gonzalez, Moll, & Amanti, 2005). This research has led to an interest in learning realized through participation in everyday social practices. Commonly referred to as a sociocultural approach or cultural-historical theory, research in this area forms the foundation for the remaining sections of this chapter and the frame needed for understanding the focus on structured contexts for young people between 12 and 18 years of age.

Although not all research on learning in informal contexts involves the use of sociocultural or cultural-historical frameworks, much of it does. Access to the perspectives of L. S. Vygotsky, and his students Leont'ev and Luria, offered a new way of viewing complex human phenomena that required interdisciplinary work and brought together scholars from multiple fields and countries. The availability of translated texts, beginning in the early 1960s, coupled with a desire and a commitment to address social and historical practices as core aspects of individual learning and development, ensured that sociocultural theories[1]—or those theories that foreground human action as socially, culturally, and historically situated—were taken up with interest by researchers, educators, and program developers. Indeed, the current emphasis on learning outside of schools has been influenced by cultural and cross-cultural studies of learning in apprenticeships, as well as studies of learning grounded in extensions of sociocultural and cultural-historical theory across activities and settings (e.g., Chaiklin & Lave, 1996; Engeström, 1987; Lave & Wenger, 1991; Moll & Greenberg, 1990; Rogoff, 1990, 2003; Scribner & Cole, 1973).

Several principles of a sociocultural approach are important here. Most notably, mental functioning in individuals originates in social life, such as the everyday activities and interactions of families, schools, workplaces, and economic institutions, and human action is mediated by cultural tools and signs; that is, from speech and language to our use of machines such as computers, human action is mediated by what we use to make meaning (Wertsch, 1991). From this perspective, at the core of understanding learning is an examination of social practices (generally, what people are doing) and discursive practices (generally, what people are saying) (see Vásquez's chapter in this volume for further explication of this perspective).

Rather than identify new descriptors for education, learning or teaching, I would argue that learning always occurs in context and that contexts define what counts as learning. Indeed, what can be differentiated in a general sense is a context, the features of a context, and how these features are constituted by social and discursive practices. What is needed is an approach to identifying and describing a context, or a participation framework[2] for mapping the context of learning: a frame for identifying patterns of relationships and interactions constituted in social and discursive practices. This is not to say that a context exists a priori, as a given, or as a container for action. Contexts are constituted by participants' actions, physical and verbal, as well as where and when they are acting (see Erickson & Shultz, 1981). Articulating a general participation framework may be one way to study how contexts for learning in general are constituted and sustained by participants across material space and time. I develop this idea over the course of the sections to follow.

THEORETICAL AND METHODOLOGICAL ISSUES: CAPTURING CHANGE OVER TIME

Along with research grounded in sociocultural approaches, the recent literature on learning outside of classroom walls has been augmented by work from other theoretical traditions, for example, research that draws upon traditional cognitive perspectives relying on largely quantifiable data, as well as evaluation studies. Over the past 5 years, given the necessity of responding to policy and funding initiatives with particular kinds of data, research incorporating a range of perspectives and methods has grown. The value of diverse research perspectives is both a function of and a response to the complexity of research questions regarding learning in nonschool contexts. This does not mean that research conducted within schools is easy or straightforward, but it serves to recognize the sheer variation across informal contexts that are "other than" school, from learning in the home to after-school contexts to learning in museums and learning through participation in theater groups and youth organizations. In this section, I review research that highlights theoretical and methodological issues in the field by discussing the methodological limitations of the research that I identified throughout the analyses across studies. On the basis of this, I present some guidelines for conducting research.

The research on learning in structured informal contexts examined here attends to after-school programs and what has come to be called out-of-school time, including participation in community-based youth organizations. Although they have general widespread support, after-school programs are challenged by inconsistent reports regarding their success, as well as a shortage of "transparent," systematic, and comprehensive data regarding terms, research design, implementation, and outcomes. For example, some researchers have found positive learning and social development outcomes related to participation in after-school programs and youth organizations (e.g., Heath, Soep, & Roach, 1998; Honig & McDonald, 2005; Little & Harris, 2003; McLaughlin, 2000; Scott-Little et al., 2002). Furthermore, an evaluation conducted by the After-School Corporation (TASC) indicated that students who participated in TASC consistently and for the longest duration showed the largest gains in mathematics as assessed by standardized achievement tests (Reisner, Russell, Welsh, Birmingham, & White, 2002).

Other researchers have made contradictory claims. For example, Mathematica Policy Research and Decision Information Resources (2003), employed by the U.S.

Department of Education to evaluate 21st Century Community Learning Center programs, found no difference in performance for elementary and middle school students in relation to reading, math, and other subject-area outcomes, as well as social development outcomes, in a comparison of participants and nonparticipants. The organization reinforced this position with its latest report published in October 2004.

The inconsistency in findings across reports may be explained in various ways. Weiss and Little (2003) argued that some studies do not correct for selection bias from participants, that is, the possibility that students with certain characteristics self-select some activities or programs over others. Furthermore, Eccles (2005) noted that this form of selection bias occurs at the level of both program entry and continued participation. In addition, selection bias occurs in sampling, such as in the methods used to establish treatment and comparison groups. This second form of selection bias was the basis for Vandell's (2003) critique of the Mathematica Policy Research and Decision Information Resources (2003) evaluation. At baseline, there were large differences in standardized test scores between the treatment and comparison groups. The mean standardized reading score for participants in the treatment group was at approximately the 40th percentile, and the mean reading score for participants in the comparison group was at the 50th percentile ($p < .00$); for mathematics, the corresponding scores at baseline were at approximately the 34th percentile for the treatment group and the 44th percentile for the comparison group ($p < .00$).

These baseline scores, which favored the comparison group, were not controlled for in the analyses, nor was an analysis conducted to select or match a more appropriate comparison group to the treatment group. Under these conditions, the conclusion that the treatment group did not show gains relative to the comparison group of nonparticipants is not surprising. Following Scott-Little et al. (2002), at minimum quasi-experimental designs require a careful matching process or statistical controls to maximize comparability, a strategy not used in this study or the follow-up study.

While comparability within research studies is an issue, comparability across studies is also needed. Frequently, studies focus on aspects of program design, organization, implementation, or outcomes rather than comprehensively reporting on all areas. Incomplete information is a barrier when attempting to compare across what appear to be similar programs, reducing the likelihood that accurate interpretations can be made (Scott-Little et al., 2002; Weiss & Little, 2003). In addition, differences in data type and collection, as well as favored forms of analyses, tend to hang together under theoretical and methodological umbrellas that make them difficult to compare, particularly when researchers' assumptions and commitments are not made explicit.

Attempting to position these perspectives side by side to address a general research question is a worthwhile pursuit; however, given the incompleteness just mentioned and the lack of explicit theoretical grounding, the overall research picture can become complex, confusing, and even inaccurate. Honig and McDonald (2005) foregrounded the general lack of conceptual framing in their literature review of after-school programs, in particular with regard to "how programs are implemented and organized to support learning outcomes" (p. 3). They made a significant observation: Most studies focus on general program categories, obscuring "the *types of participation* within these categories—what staff and youth actually do day to day—that may help explain variations in results" (p. 4). Being able to compare programs at the level of what participants actually do is an important goal to work toward; it requires the clarification of theoretical and methodological frameworks, the gathering of particular kinds of data, attention to complete data sets (however defined), and a willingness to gather comparable data across research teams.

Finally, when funding organizations and agencies specify criteria for ongoing funding with particular operationalized definitions, data that reflect these criteria tend to find their way into the literature, by necessity, with increasing frequency. At issue is the extent to which funding organization definitions match, parallel, or compete with definitions that arise from research. What comes to mind immediately here are the requirements made by funding organizations that are driven by funding cycles rather than what we know of the time it takes to measure changes in learning and development. For example, the length of time used to gather data, as well as the types of data gathered, may be insufficient to accurately document the learning that occurs in after-school and community-based programs (Fashola, 1998; Granger & Kane, 2004).

As if responding to these concerns, Scott-Little et al. (2002) articulated eight issues that must be addressed to build our knowledge base about effective after-school programs and demonstrate program outcomes. Working with 23 evaluations, they argued for the need for (a) additional evaluations and dissemination of evaluations; (b) evaluations that address the program evaluation standards (Joint Committee on Standards for Educational Evaluation, 1994); (c) evaluations that apply proven evaluation designs; (d) better measures for a variety of student outcomes; (e) attention to attrition from both the program and the research study itself; (f) attention to program quality and composition, including goals, services, staffing patterns, resources, schedules, and group sizes; (g) adequate evaluation reports that provide sufficient detail on basic information, including study design, sample size, descriptive statistics, types of tests and test values, degrees of freedom, and levels of significance; and (h) longitudinal data to represent the long-term impact of participation, cumulative effects, and the significant benefits and for whom. As well as providing principles for the conduct of research, results of this meta-evaluation supported the conclusions of Fashola's (1998) review of after-school and extended-day programs and highlighted their positive effects.

Overall, a number of challenges for research have been identified, including the following:

• The need for theoretically grounded and articulated research that guides the selection and analysis of particular methods, or a stated logic of inquiry for research in informal contexts, a call paralleled more generally in the *Draft Standards for Reporting on Research Methods* (American Educational Research Association, 2006);

- The need for theoretically grounded, articulated, and contextualized definitions for key terms, such as learning and development, as well as their measures or associated variables, such as attendance, participation, and engagement;
- The use of theoretically grounded and articulated models to guide research, to describe contexts, and to explain the learning processes that occur with the richness required to enable interpretations and comparisons by the reader;
- The recognition by funding organizations that learning outcomes may take time to "appear" on measures and may take time to assess, making them difficult or costly to determine;
- The willingness of researchers to undertake longitudinal research that captures change over time, in spite of multiple institutional constraints; and
- The development of collaborations and partnerships to respond to the complexity of research in this field, including the relationships among types of intercontextual learning, or the ways in which learning in one context may support learning in another.

Each of these challenges presents researchers in this area with interesting dilemmas. Although the emphasis in recent years has been to increase the political perception of rigor in studies that capture learning in informal contexts, for example, by increasing the number of studies involving the use of quasi-experimental and experimental designs and by ensuring that even the smallest programs have the tools and information resources necessary to conduct "low-cost, high-yield evaluations" (e.g., Little, DuPree, & Deich, 2002), some researchers have argued for caution. As noted by Walberg, Zins, and Weissberg (2004), randomized experiments may have their own biases such as "Hawthorne" or "hothouse" effects: an improvement in behavior or in quality of work when research participants are being observed or studied. Instead, they proposed that "findings that show consistent benefits notwithstanding variations in research methodology will be most convincing" (p. 212). On the basis of the issues raised in this section, I argue that multiple theoretical perspectives addressing a particular issue in educational research, with articulated logic(s) of inquiry, are needed. These perspectives may make "triangulation" possible on a whole new scale, facilitating the use of different theories, methodologies, data sources, and data-gathering processes to converge on a particular research question or set of questions.

PROMISING PROGRAMS AND AREAS OF RESEARCH

This section highlights structured programs "at promise" and the research studies that support programs for young people and the programs themselves. Three categories were constructed according to program type in an effort to group programs and community-based youth organizations in a manner that reflected, in general, similar participation frameworks. Spanning three general groups of programs— programs in the performing arts; literacy, science, and/or technology programs;

and learning in museums and science centers—this work creates a foundation for the sections that follow and makes visible the current conceptual rationales for the programs selected and for the research associated with these programs.

Learning in Communities of Practice: The Performing Arts

Activities based in the performing arts, including art, music, and dance productions, attract young people to community-based organizations such as theater groups and dance companies. Ethnographic research over the past two decades conducted by Heath and McLaughlin, two prominent researchers working with youth-based organizations (e.g., Heath et al., 1998; McLaughlin, 2000, 2001; McLaughlin, Irby, & Langman, 1994), has made a significant contribution to the research literature by collectively demonstrating the impact of more than 120 youth and community-based programs in approximately 30 regions of the United States that engage young people through the performing arts, as well as research conducted in England, over 5 years, with arts in youth and community development programs.

The current review draws upon this body of work, incorporating, in particular, three documents that compile several years of research: 5 years of field work in youth organizations in inner cities (Ball & Heath, 1993); field work with youth organizations identified as effective by young people from 1988–1993, coupled with a study of students' experiences in secondary school settings (Heath & McLaughlin, 1994); and 15 years of research in U.S.-based performing arts programs, coupled with perspectives from a study in England conducted over 5 years (Heath, 2001). Taken together, this research describes the multiple and varied ways in which community-based organizations support learning and the development of skills valuable in both academic and work settings, including "oral and written language skills, experimentation with mathematical and scientific concepts, regular attendance with sustained commitment, and collaborative planning within a diverse group" (Heath & McLaughlin, 1994, p. 279).

An overview of research studies conducted by Heath (2001) across the United States and England on the role of the performing arts in youth and community development illustrated the power of what she called the "spirit of critique" (p. 12). Programs studied engaged young people in exploring the role of art as social commentary and as a cultural tool that challenged them to open dialogues and to ask questions about topics that were frequently perceived to be above questioning, as well as to engage in sustained explorations of the worlds they inhabited and their roles within these worlds. These studies showed that youth working in programs where the medium of engagement was the visual arts, including sculpture, pottery, photography, painting with both oils and watercolors, and jewelry and fashion design, were exposed to, took up, and mastered the ability to critically perceive, challenge, and ask questions of dominant social practices. Their artwork and exhibitions reflected ways of "making precious the everyday" (p. 12), valuing their own movement across cultural worlds and the impermanence that marked their lives as different from the privileged and stable lives represented in school, advertising, and edutainment texts (Heath, 2001).

Participating youth were able to both critique the limited number of identity positions that were made available to them by the wider adult culture and assert and insert alternative identities, alternative ways of representing, constructing, and authoring themselves through images and collections of images. They were also able to see the effects of partial images, views of young people, for example, that were distorted by advertisers, by adults, and by the news media. As youth engaged in acts of creation and representation and developed expertise in assessing, evaluating, and critiquing the work of others, they began perceiving the world, and their relation to it, in terms of both the ways things were and the way things could be.

Heath (2001) reported similar findings for youth participating in dance rehearsals, recitals, and components of dance within theater, musical, and vocal performances gathered from research conducted across the United States and England. Largely initiated by youth themselves, dance found its way into community-based programs of all kinds, frequently offering flexible roles for young men and women and alternatives to traditional masculinities and femininities. Youth performed together, in multiple small groups, in ways that challenged the notion of a single best participant. Their performances celebrated the different strengths of dancers as well as the visual experience produced by the collective, the harmony created by bodies in motion. According to Heath (2001), the "power of dance" for these participants appeared grounded in "the interpersonal bonding and equitable spread of challenge to exhibit discipline and skill, as well as the mutual engagement in portraying by nonverbal means ideas that cannot be expressed verbally" (p. 14).

In a study with urban youth organizations, Ball and Heath (1993) offered both a cautionary tale about the effects of coordinating too closely with school structures and insights into the central role played by language in informal contexts. They described three distinct programs: a program conducted at the Liberty Theatre for young people from 4 to 18 years old; the Juniors, a program conducted in the Brotherhood Hall with young people from 5 to 18 years old; and a program developed by the director of the Almaz Dance Studio, conducted in an inner-city middle school with students between the ages of 7 and 14 years. Each of these performing arts groups was established to benefit young people and emphasized dance as the central medium for engaging youth.

At the Liberty Theatre, youth and adults produced a videotape as their performance that was filmed, scripted, written, acted, and danced by the young people. The Juniors group foregrounded by this research included performers who danced, sang, and played a musical instrument in more than 40 performances a year, as well as a number of shows at festivals and during meetings with other ensembles. Based on the notion that dance has a positive impact on students, both academically and personally, the program offered in partnership between the Almaz Dance Studio and a local middle school grew to more than 300 students from the mid- to late 1980s and culminated each year with school events or an end-of-the-year production at the dance studio.

While there were commonalities across each of these three programs, including the motivation of program directors to support and engage young people and the use of dance and dance performances as the medium of engagement, Ball and Heath (1993) noted a vital difference: Over time, middle school administrators and teachers began to see participation in Almaz as an incentive program to motivate students in school and to encourage academic achievement. Operating within the constraints of the school day, with dance types, music, and moves under the scrutiny of administrators and parents and with the constant pressure of a 40-minute period, participation in Almaz became, over time, less an experience of embodied musical and physical expression and more an extrinsic reward; only students "who maintained a C average could participate" (p. 85).

Originally, participation in Almaz, with real dancers and choreographers and an emphasis on shared decision making and creativity, was a learning context of value in itself and for the young people who engaged in its programming. Co-opted by the school, it became an uncomfortable compromise: Rather than being legitimated by school administrators and staff, it became accountable to them; rather than inviting all students to participate as originally intended and creating spaces for students to succeed, it became a place for a certain group of students who were already adequately surviving the school environment. Regarding the colonization of informal contexts by the application of formal participation frameworks, or what Nocon and Cole (2006) have called "school's invasion of 'after-school,'" Heath (2001) cautioned against the "urge to merge" learning in informal contexts with learning in schools. Teachers, she argued, already know of the benefits of learning and participating in youth organizations. In fact, many teachers already incorporate activities from other contexts when possible in their own classrooms. Teachers do not need another "add-on" to accomplish alongside their already packed mandate for teaching, testing, and accountability.

In addition, the review of community-based programs generally, and programs in the performing arts in particular, established the central role played by language, especially dialogue, negotiation, and explanation, in learning and the development of metacognitive awareness (e.g., Ball & Heath, 1993; Heath, 2000, 2001). The social and discursive practices that originated in activities in informal contexts were not the setting for learning but the medium through which learning occurred, the way that learning happened. Adults and youth used a "language of practice" that rang "with a sense of family" to support shared decision making along with shared responsibilities in sustained tasks and joint work (Ball & Heath, 1993, p. 81). In the design and creation of sets, the planning and drawing of murals, and the myriad day-to-day and moment-to-moment communicative acts that wove together relationships, words such as "credibility," "connection," and "communication" surfaced most to explain "what counts" in effectiveness with young people (pp. 87–88). After conducting an extensive language analysis of a computerized data bank of transcriptions of talk by program leaders and youth, Ball and Heath found that the importance of both excellence and involvement was evident to the youth.

Fostering Literacy, Science, and/or Technology Exploration

Research representing eight programs is presented in this section, foregrounding informal contexts that fostered literacy, science, and/or technology exploration. These studies reflect diverse purposes and rationales, as well as diverse areas of academic work (i.e., literacy, science, and technology). While all of the programs reviewed mentioned that participation may have had a positive impact on academic achievement, most had more complex goals, for example, developing self-expression and literacy practices by becoming an author during story time (Blackburn, 2002/2003, 2005), constructing apprenticeship and mentoring experiences for university students and school-aged students to support learning of and interest in science (Bieber, Marchese, & Engelberg, 2005; Bruce & Bruce, 2000; Nocon & Cole, 2006; Vásquez, 2003), and engaging and developing scientific and technological literacies with computers and specialized software as well as computer games and educational programs (Nocon & Cole, 2006; Rahm, 2001, 2002; Vásquez, 2003). Programs referenced here and others that fostered exploration in literacy, science, and/or technology are addressed in turn.

Literacy, or the reading and writing of texts such as print-based texts and texts in the form of computer books and programs, is central to academic work and life more generally. Following Moje, Dillon, and O'Brien (2000), "(a) literacy is a cognitive, social, and cultural *practice* as well as *process;* (b) acts of literacy are imbued with power and ideology; and (c) the relationship among contexts, texts, and learners is complex and multidimensional" (p. 177). Engaging with the world through literacy practices formed an implicit foundation for each of the programs discussed here, although it was not necessarily viewed as such by all program developers. Three programs and related research are presented that demonstrate a range of structured non-school programs: The Quantum Opportunity Program (QOP) and TASC were selected because they were explicitly designed to foster a broad range of skills related to academic achievement through the use of a multiservice approach, and The Attic was selected to illustrate the flexibility necessary for some programs, as well as the negotiation of structure.

QOP, a multiservice, year-round demonstration project funded by the Ford Foundation in five communities, focused on young people starting in ninth grade and continuing through high school (Hahn, 1999). Instruction included homework help and tutoring, literacy and life skills, and field trips to museums and opportunities to engage in community service projects. Students earned small stipends in approved services and upon completion of blocks of activities. Most important, QOP was designed to encourage long-term relationships and involvement based on an "anti-attrition philosophy": "Young people were seen as individuals with specific needs and great potential, not as program slots to be filled and replaced" (p. 23). Neither exclusion/expulsion from the program nor the threat of these outcomes was used by the program directors.

Research conducted by Hahn (1999), between 1989 and 1993, included all five sites. At each site, an experimental group and a control group with 25 students in each were created via random assignment, reflecting the number of students allowed to participate by Ford. Students were not allowed to self-select into the program and, instead, were randomly selected from lists of existing eighth-grade students, all of whom were on some form of welfare (Aid to Families with Dependent Children, food stamps, local general assistance, or free school lunch). This way, student willingness to join, given the structure of the program, was measured as well.

After 1 year, according to Hahn (1999), there was not enough evidence to claim a positive influence on the experimental group. However, after 2 years, program differences were apparent between the experimental and control groups, and they accelerated after the first 2 years of high school. The most profound program effects were discovered after the completion of the project. A survey conducted in the fall after scheduled high school graduation showed that 63% of QOP members graduated from high school, as compared with 42% of the control group; 34% of QOP members received an honor or award, as compared with 12% of the control group; and 28% of QOP members had been a volunteer tutor, mentor, or counselor, relative to 8% of the control group. Hahn (1999) argued that, perhaps most important in this "political and cultural climate," "when a quantum opportunity was offered, young people from public assistance backgrounds—African American males, females, whites, Asians, others—took it! They joined the [program] and stayed with it for long periods" (p. 260).

The second program, TASC, served approximately 34,165 youth in 116 projects in New York City during the third-year evaluation in 2000–2001. In addition to exemplifying significant gains for youth in the area of mathematics, as highlighted earlier, TASC showed improvements in overall literacy given a broad array of enrichment activities, including dance, music, and art, along with activities designed to develop literacy skills and mastery such as story-telling, writing, and reading (Moje & Eccles, 2005; Reisner at al., 2002). TASC offered one-on-one teaching using "hands-on" literacy instruction and a variety of other approaches to engage young people and sustain interest, effectively reinforcing the content and material taught in school and the skills necessary for schoolwork. Exhibitions of youth work allowed for authentic assessments of some activities, as well as more conventional forms of assessment.

The evaluation design included multiple forms of data collection, including surveys of TASC site coordinators and staff involved with 96 projects, principals of host schools, and participants in Grades 4–12 from 44 projects; interview, observation, and focus group data from 15 TASC in-depth study sites; a focus group with directors and senior staff of grant organizations; and student enrollment and attendance data from 96 projects. Surveys were collected from 114 coordinators, 1,812 staff members, 80 principals, and 2,103 students. Overall, young people rated the program highly: 85% of high school participants perceived a strong sense of community and 83% were more trusting of staff, and 60% of middle-school participants noted opportunities to contribute to the design or operation of the program itself. Most principals reported that the project enabled students to participate in activities not available during the school day (90%); that it enhanced the overall effectiveness of school (93%), students' motivation to learn (82%), and student attendance (81%); and that the benefits of the project outweighed the costs (93%).

A third program, The Attic, a center for lesbian, gay, bisexual, transgendered, and questioning youth, was based on a youth empowerment model and was youth directed and governed (Blackburn, 2002/2003, 2005). Over 3 years of ethnographic research in which Blackburn (2002/2003) positioned herself as a volunteer, employee, and researcher, she created, together with young people, a literacy group called Story Time, a place where explorations were made into "relationships among literacy performances and identity work . . . that disrupted the hegemonic heteronormative," the assumption and privileging of heteronormativity (p. 315). Young people between 12 and 23 years of age shared journal entries, poems, and short stories, and Blackburn shared her own stories and poems, along with the transcripts of previous meetings, as dialogue material. As this group developed, it became a safe space—a space where participants negotiated the meeting time, the material shared, and the way that support and critique were offered and received.

Alongside discussions of poetic devices, including imagery, metaphor, and alliteration, Story Time became a space for topics such as revenge, loss, and love, with representations that the young people could recognize, respond to, and identify with. Through these literacy practices, the young people became writers and authors, representing themselves, authoring their identities, and reimagining their nonschooled and schooled worlds in validating ways. These acts of creation allowed them to question and critique texts, to see how texts provided a selective version of the world, and to see how representations bestowed privilege (Moje, Young, Readence, & Moore, 2000).

Three programs that fostered exploration in science are discussed next: Project SEARCH (Science Education and Research for Children), the Laser Academy, and City Farmers. Project SEARCH and the Laser Academy shared several similar goals. Project SEARCH was an outreach program designed to facilitate relationships between a research university and its science resources and community centers (Bruce & Bruce, 2000). University students engaged youth between 9 and 13 years of age in activities such as conducting hands-on science experiments, demonstrating microscopes, learning about the planets, playing computer games, and creating Web pages. Collaborating was one of three principles that grounded the program: collaboration between scientists and educators, schools and universities, students and teachers, and among participants in activities. Two other principles guided the program's operation: that young people learn best when engaged in activities that allow them to "ask questions, explore phenomena, construct their own theories, and express their developing understandings in language that is meaningful to them" (p. 243) and that a critical aspect of engagement is the development of positive attitudes toward science learning.

An evaluation conducted from 1994 to 1996 focused on the overall impact of the program and the responses of university students, teachers, and children (Bruce, Bruce, Conrad, & Huang, 1994, 1997). As a result of the wide range of settings in which participants worked, multiple sources of data were used, including field notes of 100 hours of science learning activities; interviews with 48 children regarding their experiences and attitudes toward science and scientists; problem-solving protocols to assess learning and understanding; children's writing, drawing, and other artifacts; interviews with 10 university students; surveys of 24 university students; university course ratings from 30 students; observations of nine project meetings; analysis of e-mail communication; university student projects; and interviews with seven teachers. Bruce and Bruce (2000) found that university students learned a great deal about science and teaching and working with others, and many returned to the project over two or more semesters. For children, the success of Project SEARCH and its participants was a function not of the level of science activities but of the images of science and scientists that were challenged and the simultaneous identity work this process fostered for youth.

Operating for more than 5 years, the Laser Academy also reflected a partnership between higher education and schools, in this case high schools (Bieber et al., 2005). Young people who participated in this program were chosen from those who applied with transcripts, a letter of recommendation from a teacher or administrator, and permission slips from parents; however, preference was "not given to the students with the highest grades" (p. 137). Students were selected on the basis of their interest in science and their interest in working in a technology-related field. In addition, in an effort to address several factors related to the low level of science literacy in the United States—including concerns about teaching quality, classroom climate, quality and extent of counseling regarding career opportunities, and lack of perceived relevance to possible futures (Committee on Science and Mathematics Teacher Preparation, 2001; Seymour & Hewitt, 1994)—as well as the historically skewed demographic profile of employees in technology-related fields, preference was given to women (see also Boudria, 2002).

Working in groups of two to four, students completed lab activities designed to develop a conceptual understanding or a particular skill set identified by the photonics industry as important. Two instructors facilitated the labs—from fiber optics to traditional optics and lasers—through questioning, prompting, and encouraging students to collaborate. Participants learned to make fiber optic connections, including testing, splicing, and coupling cables. They learned about light and its properties, as well as concepts such as refraction, image formation, and polarization. Finally, they learned to align lasers, measure spectral width, and work with a high-powered neodymium-doped yttrium aluminum garnet laser used for holography and as a pump source for other lasers. Through participation, students developed a deeper conceptual understanding of photonics and a number of skills that prepared them for technology programs in community colleges and universities. Students reported that they began to see the equipment and machinery in their lives differently, and high school instructors noted that these students performed better in school as a result of this program.

A summer program called City Farmers was studied by Rahm (2001, 2002, 2004a) using an ethnographic research approach. Rahm identified in depth the operation, participation, and rotation of activities scheduled within this 8-week program.

Twenty-three young people from the ages of 11 to 14 years were in charge of growing, harvesting, and marketing herbs, flowers, and vegetables. The main goal of the program was to establish activities that would enable youth to learn plant science, though this goal was supported by two others: to provide a program that was engaging and modeled positive use of time and to provide activities that allowed for the authentic practice of employment skills. Meetings took place in a community garden 3 days a week for 3.5 hours a day, and the program was scheduled in four rotating activity settings of 2 weeks each: nurturing, harvesting, marketing, and special projects. Four adult team leaders, two master gardeners, and the program director facilitated the activities, including preparing the soil, transplanting seedlings, weeding and watering, harvesting, processing, and marketing, as well as managing the community garden itself by planting trees and creating sandstone walkways.

Working alongside the program, Rahm's research foregrounded the meanings, social structures, and organization of the program from an emic (or insider's) perspective, documenting the social and discursive practices used to convey and make meaning of the science concepts that surfaced through participation. A particularly important contribution of this research was the careful documentation of the sense-making work of the participants, from working definitions for science and doing science to capturing ways of talking about science and using analogies for understanding new concepts. The language and discursive practices constituted in this community of practice were not merely used as a resource to communicate information; they were used more as a tool for the social construction of meaning in science (see Wells, 1992).

The final two programs in this section fostered an exploration of technology, both as an end and as a means to developing literacies: the Fifth Dimension and the Digital Underground Story-Telling for Youth (DUSTY) Project. The Fifth Dimension was developed by Michael Cole and his associates from the Laboratory of Comparative Human Cognition at the University of California, San Diego, and grew to reflect the work of many others. With sites across the United States, in North Carolina, Florida, and Delaware, as well as in various countries such as Brazil, Denmark, and Spain, the Fifth Dimension was an organic after-school program model that relied on community organizations partnering with the university and undergraduate students working in concert with organization leadership to create an activity setting that incorporated computers, computer games, and educational software as a means of engaging young people in a world of inquiry. Working with task cards and activities that were constructed with them in mind, or co-constructing new games and activities with adults, young people were engaged in a collaborative framework that positioned them as adventurers, playing new roles and mastering new identities as learners and contributors to both their computer worlds and their lived worlds.

Along with the apprenticeship structure that grounded interactions between adults and youth—with both adults (program staff, graduate and undergraduate students) and youth taking the lead mentoring under different conditions—a key element of the Fifth Dimension was fantasy woven throughout different aspects of the program.

Youth asked questions of a magical wizard or wizardess, created fantasy environments through gaming and play, and worked their way through a self-directed role-playing game with computer and board games as activities along the way. The object for each player was "to build his or her character into a champion of sorts who accomplishes great feats" (Vásquez, 2003, p. 38).

The fantasy environment was spatially represented as 20 rooms with two or three games assigned to each room, and youth worked toward the goal of completing all "adventures" or games, which could be played at different levels of difficulty. The wizard or wizardess provided sufficient "material and intellectual resources to support the [child's] active involvement in directing his or her progress through the task-laden labyrinth" (p. 38). As a result of a reluctance to use quantitative measures to sort and rank children according to a particular standard of academic success or failure, multiple levels of participation were expected and valued, different and diverse adventures and adventurers were celebrated, and, most important, there was "no failure in the Fifth Dimension" (Nocon & Cole, 2006, p. 106). Along with records of each child's progress through this fantasy world, general program research and evaluation has typically been measured via longitudinal qualitative data to identify change over time (e.g., Nicolopoulou & Cole, 1993), although quantitative studies, showing program outcomes, exist and are increasing (e.g., Blanton, Moorman, Hayes, & Warner, 1997; Mayer, Schustack, & Blanton, 1999).

The DUSTY Project was developed by Glynda Hull and her associates and operated out of a community technology center as a hybrid space coupling traditional school-valued versions of reading and writing with multimedia compositions that included music, video, photographs, and images from popular culture (e.g., Hull & Greeno, 2006; Hull & Zacher, 2002). Youth and adult participants worked together to tell both personal and local stories through multimedia presentations that were shared at a theater and on the Internet. In creative acts of authoring and coauthoring themselves and their worlds, learners were positioned as "capable, intelligent, and creative users of communication technologies" (Hull & Greeno, 2006, p. 91). For some of the participants, this experience was the first time they had perceived themselves, and had been perceived by others, as having expertise, as being experts in the narrating, writing, and presenting of their stories. One of the main goals of the DUSTY Project was to construct bridges between after-school and school learning, developing ways to bring experiences, identities, and learning fostered outside of school into school environments. Rich collaborations that developed among young people, program staff, university students, and local community members enabled participants to broaden their technological skills as they engaged in multimedia literacy practices; such work is foundational to success in schools and workplaces today.

Learning in Museums and Science Centers

Researchers working in the field of learning in museums have argued that much of the work has been descriptive and atheoretical (see Anderson, Lucas, & Ginns, 2003). However, recent work has begun to address this problem by developing theoretical conceptualizations based on empirical research. The work of several different researchers is included here, along with brief descriptions of three current models for learning in museums and science centers. Additional research is reviewed on key elements of learning in these contexts: instructional methods and dialogue.

As a general introduction to this area, researchers have widely reported the impact of learning in art galleries, science and history museums, aquariums, and science centers, a field catalyzed by mandates from the American Association of Museums (1984, 1992). Although educational goals and missions may differ—along with the physical architecture, general "curriculum" topics, and programs—aspects of these sorts of informal contexts for learning are similar, including displays and exhibits that incorporate a variety of textual aids, such as labels, diagrams, background information, and, more recently, interactive components that require action on the part of viewers and visitors (Falk & Dierking, 2000; Rennie & Johnston, 2004). While these contexts may be used by teachers to enhance school learning, much of the time spent in art galleries and aquariums is voluntary: Families, extended families, and friendship groups participate in viewing and interacting with the resources gathered (Falk & Dierking, 2000).

On the basis of a decade of research, Falk and Dierking (2000) developed the contextual learning model, which attempted to combine aspects of Piagetian constructivism with Vygotskian concepts to capture experience across three overlapping contexts—the personal, the sociocultural, and the physical—and across time. Their research showed that the outcomes of visiting and interacting in these contexts were the result of many factors: visitors' personal and collective histories and prior experiences, their interests and motivations, the social and intersubjective situations that arise through participation, the physical space itself, and random factors that cannot easily be explained (Falk & Dierking, 2000). They also emphasized the importance of considering the impact of visits over time.

As an alternative model, Anderson et al. (2003) grounded empirical data in what Mintzes, Wandersee, and Novak (1997) called a "human constructivist perspective" to develop and empirically test a model for learning in science centers. Following Mintzes et al. (1997), this work argued for conceptions of individuals as "products of diverse personal experiences, observations of objects and events, culture, language, and teachers' explanations" (p. 180). From this perspective, individuals' conceptions may or may not be consistent with academic concepts being observed or studied, and indeed instructional practices may themselves be a source of misunderstanding, a parallel that learning in museums has with learning in classrooms. On the basis of this research, these authors found that museum staff and teachers were well situated to query, listen to, and probe students' understandings and that, with a coordinated effort, they might be able to extend learning experiences past the museum gallery.

Building on Falk and Dierking's (2000) model, as well as research by Resnick, Levine, and Teasley (1991) on socially shared cognition, Rennie and Johnston (2004) articulated a model for research and argued that three characteristics of learning serve as research foci—learning is personal, learning is contextualized, and learning takes time. They also raised questions about methods related to each of the foci. Rennie and Johnston (2004) demonstrated the need for data to reflect the personal, "social," and physical contexts, for example, methods such as interviews, survey instruments, and analyses of recorded conversations documented by wireless microphones and corroborated by observation could be used to collect data on the personal nature of learning. They advocated for mixed-method research documenting information about visitors, what they do, with whom they interact, and the physical space of this action while at the same time attempting not to disrupt or influence the experience. And, finally, they argued for longitudinal studies to better understand the impact of visits while recognizing the compound problem of the impact of research itself.

In research on instructional methods in museums conducted by Cox-Petersen, Marsh, Kisiel, and Melber (2003), when features of formal learning contexts were imported for use in a natural history museum, students reported high satisfaction with the tour but low levels of science learning based on the "complexity of their articulation of facts, concepts, and inclusion of multiple concepts" (p. 208). For example, tours directed by a docent were lecture oriented, with little if any connection made to prior knowledge, and were discursively structured following an instructional sequence: docent-delivered content, docent-initiated question, and visitor response with no follow-up, elaboration, or probing. In this situation, students enjoyed the experience but did not learn the material. Dialogue among docents, students, and teachers was constrained by the didactic style used to present the natural history content, a style that runs counter to the national science education standards (National Research Council, 1996).

Cox-Peterson et al. (2003) proposed an "alternative docent-led tour format," an alternative participation framework that addressed research on learning in informal contexts as well as science education reform efforts related to both content and pedagogy (National Research Council, 1996). They began by asking general questions related to concepts, eliciting personal experiences and observations from students, and inviting students to explore the hall. Then the docent's role shifted to facilitator, encouraging students to discuss what they saw, identify differences and similarities across species, and share a few key words such as "habitat" and "adaptation." The tour continued with an investigative task involving open-ended questions, a discussion about findings, and an additional challenge. Although the parallels between the national science education standards and learning in science centers are motivating, these authors warned against attempting to match informal science programs to formal science education goals; the contexts are complementary but different. In addition, the Informal Learning Opportunities Assay, an instrument developed and field tested by Gerber, Marek, and Cavallo (2001) to assess learning that takes place outside classrooms, correlated informal learning throughout everyday social practices with improved scientific reasoning ability (Gerber, Cavallo, & Marek, 2001); again, these are complementary but different contexts for learning.

Museum exhibits, in particular interactive ones, engage visitors in a dialogue, one that is conducted by participants and mediated by the exhibit. An example of this

engagement is Hui's (2003) research on the way in which intersubjectivity was negotiated and managed in a father-son dyad working with an interactive two-dimensional
map, a representation of a three-dimension globe. She noted that while most early
research was concerned with whether or not intersubjectivity was achieved and frequently assumed a unidirectional process of coming to know by the child or less
experienced peer (Rogoff, 1990; Wertsch, 1985), in some cases (e.g., when an adult
does not have a clear understanding of the task at hand) intersubjectivity is a dynamic
process of moment-to-moment and multidirectional (or, in this case, bi-directional)
negotiation.

Research by Ash (2003) with family groups in a museum showed that dialogues
reflected individual and group thematic agendas, the exhibit or museum agenda, and
the specific conversational practices that facilitate or hinder dialogue. Her research
addressed the interaction of content and negotiating strategies, which were documented though representational dialogue segments: segments of talk that included
the "presence of thematic content and differential knowledge of these themes by family members," "use of inquiry skill and differential knowledge of these skills by family members," and "sustained dialogue in which members of the family attempt[ed]
to make sense of themes using inquiry skills" (p. 144). Ash's (2003) research made
visible the complex process of negotiation within the group of visitors and between
the visitors and the museum.

Exploring the engagement and participation of young people with exhibits, Rahm
(2004b) gathered data across multiple modes of meaning making (Wells, 2000),
including artifacts, talk, gestures, and positioning, in collaboration with peers and
with an adult museum guide. Her work highlighted three important points. First, as
exemplified by a participant named Mark, participation may not always be manifested
in dialogue or talk. Mark uttered only one question, and only when his "speaking
agent" (Hatano & Inagaki, 1991), a peer, was not present; however, his active engagement was apparent in his observation and gesturing. Rahm (2004b) documented
how Mark's participation occurred across multiple modes of meaning making and
argued for the importance of various forms of data, including videotape, that enabled
the analysis of meaning making by making visible Mark's presence, gestures, and position in addition to his audiotaped talk. Second, this research emphasized the importance of engaging visitors for longer periods of time; participants became engaged, in
particular, when the museum guide posed a question, which stopped the participants
and became the kernel of a dialogue. Third, following other researchers, Rahm argued
for a notion of learning that is distributed across space and time (e.g., Lave, 1988;
Lave & Wenger, 1991).

Another area of research focused on reflexive museum exhibits, or those that
engaged visitors in a dialogue regarding both the topic of the exhibit and the way the
exhibit was constructed, thus drawing attention to an exhibit's "representational
practice in such a way that visitors can recognize that the material is not just there;
that it is staged, and how" (Styles, 2002, p. 174). This sort of critical dialogue, which
raised the possibility that other perspectives may have led to a different exhibit, was

studied in relation to certain types of exhibits, such as the Australian War Memorial and exhibits that represented the experiences of Aboriginal groups. Styles (2002) argued that when exhibits identified their representations as partial, perhaps because facts were incomplete or aspects of a story were missing, this enabled "visitors to see the questions and tensions arising from the materials, rather than the answers alone" (p. 189). Critical understandings of exhibits emerged in the 1990s, and museums have an opportunity to transform their educational practice to meet this historical shift from didacticism to critical dialogue.

SOCIAL AND DISCURSIVE PRACTICES: LEARNING IN INFORMAL CONTEXTS

This review of research was conducted to understand and conceptualize what counts as learning in informal contexts. In this section, I use the participation framework briefly developed earlier as a general frame to map across the contexts described. This frame is responsive to the challenges of conducting research in the field of learning in informal contexts in at least two ways. First, it is theoretically grounded with an explicit logic of inquiry that articulates the theoretical grounding for the research and definitions of key terms such as learning and development, as well as the method of review. Second, it offers a framework for studying contextual features and the relationships between them. I discuss each in turn and then move to a discussion of the features themselves.

The work in this section is a meta-analysis of the diverse range of research reviewed here. Therefore, I begin with a clarification of the logic of inquiry, the theoretical and conceptual orientation for the work conducted to bring these studies together; the method of this review was discussed in the second section. When grounded in sociocultural theory, social and discursive practices are at the core of understanding learning: What people do and say in their joint work together is the medium of learning. Learning is the individual mastery of joint mental action mediated by cultural artifacts. It is increased participation in social and discursive practices, more complex forms of participation and identity positions, and independent action. Learning forms the leading edge of development, wherein "performance before competence" (Cazden, 1981) allows young people to play a role, or practice taking action, before having developed the necessary capabilities. Learning is the path between the two boundaries of the zone of proximal development: the actual level of development assessed by independent mastery and the potential level of development assessed by joint interaction (Vygotsky, 1978). What holds the most interest from this research perspective is also what holds the most developmental promise: those ways of thinking, performing, and speaking that constitute social and discursive practices and are on the verge of mastery and transformation.

Contexts for learning are typically characterized by a number of features. The five features identified in this review—*location, relationships, content, pedagogy,* and *assessment*—are offered as one possible set of features, rather than an inclusive set. This set is useful for this review because it maintains a link between schooled and nonschooled contexts while avoiding the formal/informal dichotomy. For other discussions, maintaining this link might be less important. To attend to the features that constitute the context of learning, we need data or evidence of these features as well as data that represent the relationships between these features. The social and discursive practices that constitute these features, and the relationships between these features, form a *participation framework* for mapping contexts.

A participation framework for mapping contexts of learning allows for heterogeneity across constellations of features. Certain features may dominate contexts at a particular moment in time, and at other times or within different activities the importance of certain features and the relationships between features may change. For example, it is possible to create an informal context for learning under certain conditions in school settings, perhaps during a particular unit, lesson, or activity when the features of the context come together in a way that allows for flexible participation (e.g., Hirst & Vadeboncoeur, 2006; Vadeboncoeur, 2005). In addition, nonschool contexts may explicitly include specific activities that are based on features of schooling in the hopes of better preparing participants to engage in schoolwork. As with the research conducted by Cox-Peterson et al. (2003) on didactic and alternative docent-led museum tours, this may be more or less successful. Learning contexts are permeable, changing, and open, and the features that constitute them vary by social and discursive practices across time and space.

Using the participation framework defined here, each contextual feature provides the basis for a set of questions to be asked, including questions regarding the *relations between* features and the social and discursive practices that constitute them.

- What is the location? How is it organized?
- How do relationships develop? How are they socially and discursively constituted? What roles and responsibilities are obtained?
- What is the content? Is it disciplinary or nondisciplinary? How is disciplinary knowledge discursively structured? Who has access, and who does not?
- How is the pedagogy organized? What types of speech genres characterize it? What do "teachers" do, and what do "students" do?
- How is assessment conducted? What values are given to oral and written tests and performances? What are assessments taken to mean?

As a flexible configuration that identifies the characteristics of contextual features constituted by patterns of social and discursive practices, this participation framework is valuable not only for explicating the similarities and differences across contexts for learning but also for highlighting the ways in which learning in one context may offer something to learning in another.

Given the review of research here, the articulated sociocultural orientation, and the participation framework described, general descriptions of the contextual features can be synthesized to begin to address the questions "What counts as an informal context?" and "What counts as learning in informal contexts?"

Location

The after-school programs and community organizations included in this review were largely based in community settings such as local community centers and theaters. Many operated using a "home base" and, at the same time, created activities that drew young people from this base and out into the community; for example, designing a mural for a cement wall under the overpass meant returning to the wall repeatedly to outline and paint the mural. Other programs involved a youth-run center, such as The Attic; a community garden, such as City Farmers; or a community technology center, such as DUSTY (Blackburn, 2005; Hull & Greeno, 2006; Rahm, 2004a).

In addition, however, a few programs operated on school grounds, using recreational facilities, libraries, or classrooms. Others used university facilities to provide access to specialized laboratory equipment, such as the Laser Academy (Bieber et al., 2005). The locations of learning reviewed in this chapter were diverse, cutting across community locations as varied as dance halls and community gardens and schools. Interestingly, it appears that the material space of the program mattered less than one might think, given the historical emphasis on location as the defining characteristic of formal and informal contexts for learning.

Relationships

The program leaders from the programs and organizations reviewed explicitly articulated the importance of respecting and valuing young people and acted in ways that communicated this commitment to youth. Some programs existed purposefully as sites to provide safety for and nurture youth, such as the Liberty Theatre and the Quantum Opportunity Program (Ball & Heath, 1993; Hahn, 1999). In these programs, social interactions in caring relationships between adults and young people were not settings for learning but the way learning happened (Packer, 1993). Relationships were a medium of learning that enabled program participants to grow in ways that they themselves might not have anticipated, often meeting and surpassing the goals set for and with them.

This finding is consistent with research emphasizing the importance of caring relationships between youth and adults as the critical ingredient for successful programs (Diversi & Mecham, 2005; Rhodes, 2004) and as the core of young people's mediated agency (Wertsch, Tulviste, & Hagstrom, 1993). Effective programs are led by adults who see potential, rather than problems, in youth; for example, they see young people as positive contributors, they are consistent and flexible, they are committed to and passionate about their work, and they are able to create a safe and positive environment with and for youth (Yohalem, 2003). Through these relationships, program leaders and staff mediate the agency of youth and negotiate enabling conditions for and with youth, allowing them to take up positions that are new or, perhaps, beyond their actual level of development.

Content

The community organizations and youth programs reviewed engaged young people in sustained long-term and comprehensive projects. Working collaboratively, youth and adults planned, designed, engaged in, or performed projects that required a range of capabilities, including physical dexterity and prowess, scientific knowledge, and inquiry-based experiential exploration. This learning, which was more obviously content related, occurred alongside the capacity to work in independent collaborative groups with multiple intangible skills. Indeed, whether or not particular content was identified, there was much to learn in each of these programs.

Young people were engaged in activities from computer games to authors' workshops, but they were also learning the various ways to participate within a particular context, the roles available to participants, the expectations associated with these roles, and the discursive practices that co-occurred. Learning was an integral part of the social and discursive practices that constituted the lived worlds of these programs, and this relationship was recursive. Programs that provided academic and social support were vital sites for youth engagement and learning. Learning occurred when young people co-created authentic projects with built-in academic and social components.

Pedagogy

In general, in the programs and organizations reviewed, the pedagogy offered young people multiple roles and encouraged them to take up, practice, and perform them. The one exception was the didactic pedagogy reported by Cox-Peterson et al. (2003). Generally, youth learned about and through the various roles that were afforded to them, constructing, for example, what it meant to be a writer, a dancer, a biologist, and a friend and the responsibilities these roles entailed. Some young people began by following what others did, and through imitation, play, and performance they constructed something that was unique. This experience was mediated by more experienced peers and caring adults through role modeling, verbal description and explanation, and day-to-day problem solving and decision making. Identity work was part of participation and performance.

Young people were offered different ways of engaging and different levels of engagement. Youth had different strengths and contributions to make, and successful after-school and community-based programs engaged them through multiple and varied "fields of participation." Roles were encouraged and guided through talk, dialogue, negotiation, and discussion. As the medium of everyday social and discursive practices, language enabled young people and adults to share and clarify ideas, create and maintain relationships, and challenge and change structures. Youth learned discursive practices that were considered appropriate in particular contexts, how to inquire, and how to listen. And sometimes, as in the earlier case of Mark, young people engaged, even silently, in the process of learning through attention and observation (Rahm, 2004b).

These community-based programs and after-school programs tended to have different rhythms. For example, in the Fifth Dimension, projects were designed, a process for working through a fantasy labyrinth was identified, and young people made decisions about what to do and how far they would go along the pathways made available, whether jointly or not (Vásquez, 2003). In TASC, young people engaged in highly structured activities that were explicitly linked to school performance. These programs were well suited to travel the road with youth and to make the necessary stops for reflection: The pedagogy encouraged verbal and written reflection on action, both doing and talking about doing.

Assessment

In the programs and organizations reviewed, young people worked toward authentic assessments of their contributions, including dance and choral performances, collaborative computer gaming and program design, marketing and selling herbs, interviews regarding conceptual understandings of science concepts from interactive museum exhibits, and more conventional forms linked to school performance. Each of these forms of assessment was authentic given its relevance to the tasks that engaged youth, as well as in terms of the access provided for youth to relevant and public feedback. When dance performances were scheduled, and when art shows and science fairs loomed, assessments of the contributions of young people followed authentically, in situ, as an outcome of the tasks within which they were engaged, rather than as an add-on. These authentic assessments required risk taking on the part of the participants in making their work public and provided unequaled feedback precisely because of this element.

What becomes clear from this brief exercise is that contexts shared patterns of difference and similarity in terms of location, relationships, content, pedagogy, and assessment. Learning occurred in these diverse contexts through the social and discursive practices that young people were afforded given their engagement and participation. Learning was not confined to one location, schools; to one set of relationships, teacher-student; to one area of content articulated in a curriculum or to one type of conventional didactic pedagogy; or to one form of assessment, standardized. Learning was a contextualized, coincident process with participation in practices. Whether learning took place in after-school programs, community organizations, or schools—even in families—recognition of social and discursive practices as a medium for learning was vital.

Given the diversity of contexts for learning and the sheer difficulty of comparing contexts, one way to move forward may be to conduct research that foregrounds a specific participation framework that links contextual features together. Consistent with this move, Rahm (2004b) suggested a shift of research questions in the field of learning in museums, something that can be extended more generally. Paraphrasing her, the question is no longer *whether* learning happens in particular contexts but *how* different contexts, over time, contribute to learning.[3] To respond to this question, we need to document what it is that young people do in these contexts, how they engage and participate, and how the connections between their joint work with each other and adults are developed and maintained.

ADDITIONAL RESEARCH QUESTIONS: DEVELOPING AND ARTICULATING NEXT STEPS

Schools cannot offer the extensive time for practice and participation and build-up of moral commitment and group discourse needed for students to develop all that employers, policymakers, and philosophers say will mark the future. (Heath, 2000, p. 34)

Fortunately, schools will not have to do the work noted in this quotation alone. Arts-based and performing arts programs, science and technology clubs, museums and science centers, library groups and book clubs, parks, and community organizations of all kinds are part of a "vast educational infrastructure that helps to support the ongoing and continuous learning of American youth and their families," providing "more educational opportunities to more people, more of the time, than schooling or workplace learning combined" (Dierking & Falk, 2003, p. 78). This range of contexts for learning is fortunate for young people as well:

[Children] need space—social as much as physical space—to develop their own thoughts, to daydream and reflect; to dabble and dawdle; to pretend, try on, and rehearse different roles and identities; to learn friendship and to learn how to handle interpersonal conflict; to rest and be quiet; and not least to have fun and take risks of their own design and choosing. (Halpern, 2002, p. 206)

Given the diversity of contexts for learning and the sheer difficulty of comparing contexts, conducting research that uses a theoretically, conceptually, and methodologically grounded participation framework that maps features of contexts may be a method of better understanding what it is that young people and adults do to constitute these contexts: how location contributes to the development of relationships, how content forms the basis for joint pedagogical work, and how assessment provides feedback that is relevant. In the following, I note five sets of questions for future research.

First, in terms of a *sociocultural orientation,* in what ways might using a participation framework enable research? How might using a participation framework constrain research? What factors might constrain a participation framework's usefulness? What sorts of methodologies should guide research, and which data and social and discursive practices should be gathered to represent the features of the context? Ultimately, we may be able to identify participation frameworks that are linked to certain outcomes for particular participants—the contextualized and dynamic processes of social relationships between youth and adults and youth and their peers—and move beyond description to explain why what "works" does. But the questions noted earlier with regard to research and methods would need attention first.

Second, in terms of *theoretical and methodological orientations,* how might the participation framework defined here to map contexts in terms of location, relationships, content, pedagogy, and assessment be useful in research conducted outside of socio-cultural or cultural-historical approaches? If, for example, research is grounded in a different theoretical orientation, would gathering data to reflect these features improve our ability to make comparisons across diverse theoretical orientations? What factors might constrain usefulness? In addition, what types of data are important as evidence for features of contexts from within research traditions? And how might diverse research studies be comprehensively communicated to cautiously bring together perspectives from across traditions? These questions call for detailed and comprehensive data sets to describe how young people and adults engage in participation frameworks and an articulated logic of inquiry to make clear the perspectives and commitments of researchers.

Third, in terms of *conceptual orientations,* how do we define concepts such as "outcomes," "what works," and "participation"? Before we ask "How much participation in after-school programs is required to show a benefit?" we need to ask "How are the terms participation and benefit defined?" If we are to move forward, conversations of this sort must be grounded in particular theoretical and methodological orientations. Perhaps cautious links between them will develop, perhaps not. Currently, competing definitions exist for "attendance" and "participation," for example on the basis of intensity, duration, and breadth, as well as multiple models for describing the relationship between attendance and outcomes (Chaput, Little, & Weiss, 2004). In addition, Bartko (2005) discussed links between participation and outcomes and moving from participation to engagement.

In their review of the concept of school engagement, Fredricks, Blumenfeld, and Paris (2004) noted a need to address the narrow range of methods used to study it and called for thick descriptions of classroom contexts, as well qualitative data reflecting how students behave, feel, and think—a literature base that may offer something to engagement in other contexts. Thinking across contexts, a related question could be asked regarding how definitions of "transfer" might evolve on the basis of research on learning that occurs across contexts, or intercontextually. Currently, there is disagreement on the extent to which young people can transfer learning between school and nonschool contexts, even though there are continued calls to position after-school programs in the service of academic outcomes and achievement. Early research contrasting learning in and out of school contexts suggested that little school knowledge was transferred to and used outside of school (Lave, 1988; Resnick, 1987). In more recent research looking specifically at literacy practices, O'Brien, Stewart, and Moje (1995) also noted the difficulty of integrating these out of school practices into secondary school settings given the structure of schools, as well as beliefs about the discreteness of content areas. Developments in this area of research may have widespread effects on the roles that schools and community organizations play as contexts for learning.

Fourth, from a *programmatic perspective,* how can after-school and community-based youth programs maintain and sustain the distinctiveness that engages young people? "Staying informal" has been identified as a threat that some programs face. Some experts argue that too much structure in after-school programs may stifle creativity or hinder the social and emotional work that young people pursue through participation in activities with others (Ball & Heath, 1993; Heath, 2001; Heckman & Sanger, 2001; McLaughlin et al., 1994). Others argue specifically that programs should be dissimilar to the school environments that students left behind and that students and youth value the differences between school and nonschool contexts for learning (Whalen & Wynn, 1995). However, still others call for a clear alignment between learning in nonschool contexts and learning in schools (Miller, 2001) and argue that the boundary between school and after school could and should be reduced or eliminated, given the argument that "more school is better."

In and of themselves, these differences, and the different participation frameworks that are negotiated and constitute different contexts, may be one of the keys to learning in each context: We grow given different experiences, different roles, different ways of interacting, and different ways of speaking. Whalen and Wynn (1995) argued that different contexts can be considered as complements in an educational network rather than placed in a hierarchy with school positioned on top. This would require, perhaps, that we carve out and appreciate the multiple institutions—families, school, and communities—and the organizations within which children and young people engage and participate rather than assuming that schools, alone, must be responsible for them. Museum outreach programs, including mobile programs, traveling exhibits, kits, and curricula, may be one way that participation across contexts can be extended to young people (Russell, 2002). Outreach programs that link or bridge museums and schools provide "museum-like" experiences for young people who are unable or find it difficult to visit.

Although typically outside the scope of reviews of research, several questions can be addressed by educational researchers from a *policy perspective.* For example, in what ways can programs be funded so that funding initiatives that change from year to year and administration to administration do not drive the self-determined goals and purposes of programs? In what ways can programs be evaluated to ensure that funding cycles do not drive the methodologies used for evaluation? These questions also touch on the time it takes to design, build, and sustain programs that become contexts for learning, as well as the time it takes to engage, participate, and learn. Halpern, Spielberger, and Robb (2001) found that strengthening programs required a "patient, long-term, multifaceted, adequately funded and coordinated approach" (p. 27). Hahn's (1999) research with the Quantum Opportunities Program showed that significant differences were not identified between participants in experimental and control groups until 2 years into the program, and after this point differences accelerated. This set of questions is inherently linked to the work that educational researchers do: gathering data that generates theories of learning, as a process or a product, through the specific lens used to measure it.

I began this review with the following question: What counts as learning in informal contexts? In troubling the categories often applied to education, learning, and teaching—formal, nonformal, and informal—and comparing and contrasting the features of different structured nonschool contexts, I find this question no longer useful. Instead, I offer a different question: How does a particular context contribute to learning? Learning occurs through participation in after-school programs, community organizations, and theater groups. Learning occurs as well during family dinners and chores, negotiations within friendship groups, online chats, and all of the activities that make up living day to day. Mapping contexts using detailed participation frameworks of and across features is a method for examining how contexts contribute to learning, a method for comparing contexts, and a method for evaluating learning. For the time being, a focus on how different contexts contribute to learning may be the best way to appreciate what it is that families, schools, and after-school and community-based programs offer to young people.

ACKNOWLEDGMENTS

This chapter benefited from the scholarly advice and kind support of Judith Green, Allan Luke, Mollie Blackburn, and Elizabeth Moje.

NOTES

[1] Sociocultural approaches, described by Wertsch (1991) as foregrounding "how mental action is situated in cultural, historical and institutional settings" (p. 15), are based on ideas and practices emerging from the work of Vygotsky (e.g., 1978, 1987) and Bakhtin (e.g., 1981, 1986). Scholars worldwide have translated, interpreted, and extended this work, including Cole (1996), Wertsch (1985), Kozulin (1990, 1998), John-Steiner (2000), Daniels (2001), Hedegaard (2001), and Wells (1999).

[2] See also Hirst and Vadeboncoeur (2006). I acknowledge the authors whose work supported use of this concept, including Philips (1972), who coined the term "participant structures"; Erickson (1977) and Erickson and Shultz (1981), who elaborated "participation structures"; and Hanks (1991), who employed the term "participation frameworks" and embedded learning more fully in a theory of social practice, namely Lave and Wenger's (1991) legitimate peripheral participation.

[3] "The question is no longer whether learning happens in science museums but how science museums, among many other institutions and resources, over time, come to contribute to youth's science literacy development" (Rahm, 2004b, p. 242).

REFERENCES

Afterschool Alliance. (2006). *Bush budget proposal will leave millions of children without the afterschool programs they need: Statement of Jodi Grant.* Retrieved March 31, 2006, from http://www.afterschoolalliance.org/press_archives/Budget_FY07.pdf
American Association of Museums. (1984). *Museums for a new century.* Washington, DC: Author.
American Association of Museums. (1992). *Excellence and equity: Education and the public dimensions of museums.* Washington, DC: Author.
American Educational Research Association. (2006). *Draft standards for reporting on research methods.* Retrieved April 23, 2006, from http://www.aera.net
Anderson, D., Lucas, K. B., & Ginns, I. S. (2003). Theoretical perspectives on learning in an informal setting. *Journal of Research in Science Teaching, 40,* 177–199.
Ash, D. (2003). Dialogic inquiry in life science conversations of family groups in a museum. *Journal of Research in Science Teaching, 40,* 138–162.
Aspin, D. N., Chapman, J., Hatton, M., & Sawano, Y. (Eds.). (2001). *International handbook of lifelong learning.* Boston: Kluwer.

Bakhtin, M. M. (1981). *The dialogic imagination: Four essays* (C. Emerson & M. Holquist, Trans., M. Holquist, Ed.). Austin: University of Texas Press.

Bakhtin, M. M. (1986). *Speech genres and other late essays.* (V. W. McGee, Trans., C. Emerson & M. Holquist, Eds.). Austin: University of Texas Press.

Ball, A., & Heath, S. B. (1993). Dances of identity: Finding an ethnic self in the arts. In S. B. Heath & M. W. McLaughlin (Eds.), *Identity and inner-city youth: Beyond ethnicity and gender* (pp. 69–93). New York: Teachers College Press.

Bartko, W. T. (2005). The ABCs of engagement in out-of-school-time programs. *New Directions for Youth Development, 105,* 109–120.

Bieber, A. E., Marchese, P., & Engelberg, D. (2005). The Laser Academy: An after-school program to promote interest in tech careers. *Journal of Science Education and Technology, 14,* 135–142.

Blackburn, M. V. (2002/2003). Disrupting the (hetero)normative: Exploring literacy performances and identity work with queer youth. *Journal of Adolescent and Adult Literacy, 46,* 312–324.

Blackburn, M. V. (2005). Co-constructing space for literacy and identity work with LGBTQ youth. *Afterschool Matters, 4,* 17–23.

Blanton, W. E., Moorman, G. B., Hayes, B. A., & Warner, M. L. (1997). Effects of participation in the Fifth Dimension on far transfer. *Journal of Educational Computing Research, 16,* 371–396.

Boudria, T. (2002). Implementing a project-based technology program for high school women. *Community College Journal of Research and Practice, 26,* 709–722.

Bruce, B. C., Bruce, S., Conrad, R., & Huang, H. (1994). *Evaluation of Project SEARCH (Science Education and Research for Children): 1993–94.* Urbana: University of Illinois College of Education.

Bruce, B. C., Bruce, S., Conrad, R., & Huang, H. (1997). University science students as curriculum planners, teachers, and role models in elementary school classrooms. *Journal of Research on Science Teaching, 34,* 69–88.

Bruce, S. P., & Bruce, B. C. (2000). Constructing images of science, people, technologies, and practices. *Computers in Human Behavior, 16,* 241–256.

Cazden, C. (1981). Performance before competence: Assistance to child discourse in the zone of proximal development. *Quarterly Newsletter of the Laboratory of Comparative Human Cognition, 3,* 5–8.

Chaiklin, S., & Lave, J. (1996). *Understanding practice: Perspectives on activity and context.* New York: Cambridge University Press.

Chaput, S. S., Little, P. M. D., & Weiss, H. (2004). Understanding and measuring attendance in out-of-school time programs. *Issues and Opportunities in Out-of-School Time Evaluation, 7,* 1–6.

Cole, M. (1996). *Cultural psychology: A once and future discipline.* Cambridge, MA: Belknap Press of Harvard University Press.

Committee on Science and Mathematics Teacher Preparation, National Research Council. (2001). *Educating teachers of science, mathematics, and technology: New practices for the new millennium.* Washington, DC: National Academy Press.

Council on Adolescent Development. (1992). *A matter of time: Risk and opportunity in the non-school hours.* New York: Carnegie Corporation.

Cox-Petersen, A. M., Marsh, D. D., Kisiel, J., & Melber, L. M. (2003). Investigation of guided school tours, student learning, and science reform: Recommendations at a museum of natural history. *Journal of Research in Science Teaching, 40,* 200–218.

Daniels, H. (2001). *Vygotsky and pedagogy.* London: RoutledgeFalmer.

de Kanter, A., Williams, R., Cohen, G., & Stonehill, R. (2000). *21st Century Learning Centers: Providing quality after-school learning opportunities for America's families.* Washington, DC: U.S. Department of Education.

Dierking, L. D., & Falk, J. H. (2003). Optimizing out-of-school time: The role of free-choice learning. *New Directions for Youth Development, 97,* 75–88.

Diversi, M., & Mecham, C. (2005). Latino(a) students and Caucasian mentors in a rural after-school program. *Journal of Community Psychology, 33,* 31–40.

Eccles, J. S. (2005). The present and future of research on activity settings as developmental contexts. In J. L. Mahoney, R. W. Larson, & J. S. Eccles (Eds.), *Organized activities as contexts of development: Extracurricular activities, after-school and community programs* (pp. 353–371). Mahwah, NJ: Erlbaum.

Engeström, Y. (1987). *Learning by expanding: An activity-theoretical approach to developmental research.* Helsinki: Orienta-Konsultit.

Eraut, M. (2000). Non-formal learning, implicit learning and tacit knowledge. In F. Coffield (Ed.), *The necessity of informal learning* (pp. 12–31). Bristol, England: Policy Press.

Erickson, F. (1977). Some approaches to inquiry in school-community ethnography. *Anthropology and Education Quarterly, 8,* 58–69.

Erickson, F., & Shultz, J. (1981). When is a context? Some issues and methods in the analysis of social competence. In J. L. Green & C. Wallat (Eds.), *Ethnography and language in educational settings* (pp. 147–160). Norwood, NJ: Ablex.

Fairclough, N. (1992). Intertextuality in critical discourse analysis. *Linguistics and Education, 4,* 269–293.

Falk, J. H., & Dierking, L. D. (2000). *Learning from museums: Visitor experiences and the making of meaning.* Walnut Creek, CA: AltaMira Press.

Fashola, O. S. (1998). *Review of extended day and after-school programs and their effectiveness.* Baltimore: Center for Research on the Education of Students Placed at Risk.

Fredricks, J. A., Blumenfeld, P. C., & Paris, A. H. (2004). School engagement: Potential of the concept, state of the evidence. *Review of Educational Research, 74,* 59–109.

Gerber, B. L., Cavallo, A. M. L., & Marek, E. A. (2001). Relationships among informal learning environments, teaching procedures and scientific reasoning ability. *International Journal of Science Education, 23,* 535–549.

Gerber, B. L., Marek, E. A., & Cavallo, A. M. L. (2001). Development of an informal learning opportunities assay. *International Journal of Science Education, 23,* 569–583.

Gonzalez, N., Moll, L. C., & Amanti, C. (2005). *Funds of knowledge: Theorizing practices in households and classrooms.* Mahwah, NJ: Erlbaum.

Granger, R. C., & Kane, T. (2004). Improving the quality of after-school programs. *Education Week, 23,* 52, 76.

Greenfield, P., & Lave, J. (1982). Cognitive aspects of informal education. In D. A. Wagner & H. W. Stevenson (Eds.), *Cultural perspectives on child development* (pp. 181–207). San Francisco: Freeman.

Hahn, A. (1999). Extending the time of learning. In D. J. Besharov (Ed.), *America's disconnected youth: Toward a preventive strategy* (pp. 233–265). Washington, DC: Child Welfare League of America.

Halpern, R. (2002). A different kind of child development institution: The history of after-school programs for low-income children. *Teachers College Record, 104,* 178–211.

Halpern, R., Barker, G., & Mollard, W. (2000). Youth programs as alternative spaces to be: A study of neighborhood youth programs in Chicago's West Town. *Youth and Society, 31,* 469–506.

Halpern, R., Spielberger, J., & Robb, S. (2001). *Evaluation of the MOST (Making the Most of Out-of-School Time) Initiative: Final report.* Chicago: Chapin Hall Center for Children, University of Chicago.

Hanks, W. F. (1991). Foreword. In J. Lave & E. Wenger, *Situated learning: Legitimate peripheral participation* (pp. 13–24). Cambridge, England: Cambridge University Press.

Hatano, G., & Inagaki, K. (1991). Sharing cognition through collective comprehension activities. In L. B. Resnick, J. M. Levine, & S. D. Teasley (Eds.), *Perspectives on socially shared cognition* (pp. 331–348). Washington, DC: American Psychological Association.

Heath, S. B. (2000). Making learning work. *Afterschool Matters, 1,* 33–45.

Heath, S. B. (2001). Three's not a crowd: Plans, roles, and focus in the arts. *Educational Researcher, 30*(7), 10–17.

Heath, S. B., & McLaughlin, M. W. (1994). The best of both worlds: Connecting schools and community youth organizations for all-day, all-year learning. *Educational Administration Quarterly, 30,* 278–300.

Heath, S. B., Soep, E., & Roach, A. (1998). Living the arts through language-learning: A report on community-based organizations. *Americans for the Arts, 2*(7), 1–20.

Heckman, P. E., & Sanger, C. (2001). LA's BEST—Beyond school as usual. *Educational Leadership, 58*(7), 46–49.

Hedegaard, M. (2001). *Learning in classrooms: A cultural-historical approach.* Aarhus, Denmark: Aarhus University Press.

Hirst, E., & Vadeboncoeur, J. A. (2006). Patrolling the borders of otherness: Dis/placed identity positions for teachers and students in schooled spaces. *Mind, Culture, and Activity: An International Journal, 13,* 203–225.

Honig, M. I., & McDonald, M. A. (2005). *From promise to participation: Afterschool programs through the lens of socio-cultural learning theory.* New York: Robert Bowne Foundation.

Hui, D. (2003, April). *Managing intersubjectivity in the context of an informal learning environment.* Paper presented at the annual meeting of the American Educational Research Association, Chicago, IL.

Hull, G. A., & Greeno, J. G. (2006). Identity and agency in nonschool and school worlds. In Z. Bekerman, N. C. Burbules, & D. Silberman-Keller (Eds.), *Learning in places: The informal education reader* (pp. 77–97). New York: Peter Lang.

Hull, G. A., & Zacher, J. (2002, April). *New literacies, new selves, and second chances: Exploring possibilities for self-representation through writing and multi-media in a community technology center.* Paper presented at the annual meeting of the American Educational Research Association, New Orleans, LA.

John-Steiner, V. (2000). *Creative collaboration.* Oxford, England: Oxford University Press.

Joint Committee on Standards for Educational Evaluation. (1994). *The program evaluation standards* (2nd ed.). Thousand Oaks, CA: Sage.

Knowles, M. S. (1980). *The modern practice of adult education: From pedagogy to andragogy* (rev. ed.). Chicago: Follett.

Kozulin, A. (1990). *Vygotsky's psychology: A biography of ideas.* Cambridge, MA: Harvard University Press.

Kozulin, A. (1998). *Psychological tools: A sociocultural approach to education.* Cambridge, MA: Harvard University Press.

Lave, J. (1988). *Cognition in practice: Mind, mathematics, and culture in everyday life.* Cambridge, England: Cambridge University Press.

Lave, J., & Wenger, E. (1991). *Situated learning: Legitimate peripheral participation.* Cambridge, England: Cambridge University Press.

Little, P., DuPree, S., & Deich, S. (2002). *Documenting progress and demonstrating results: Evaluating local out-of-school time programs.* Cambridge, MA: President and Fellows of Harvard College.

Little, P. M. D., & Harris, E. (2003). A review of out-of-school time program quasi-experimental and experimental evaluation results. *Out-of-School Evaluation Snapshot, 1,* 1–12.

Livingstone, D. W. (1999). Exploring the icebergs of adult learning: Findings of the first Canadian survey of informal learning practices. *Canadian Journal for the Study of Adult Education, 13*(2), 49–72.

Maarschalk, J. (1988). Scientific literacy and informal science teaching. *Journal of Research in Science Teaching, 25,* 135–146.

Mathematica Policy Research and Decision Information Resources. (2003). *When schools stay open late: The national evaluation of the 21st Century Community Learning Centers program.* Washington, DC: Author.

Mathematica Policy Research and Decision Information Resources. (2004). *When schools stay open late: The national evaluation of the 21st Century Community Learning Centers program, new findings.* Washington, DC: Author.

Mayer, R. E., Schustack, M. W., & Blanton, W. E. (1999). What do children learn from using computers in an informal, collaborative setting? *Educational Technology, 39*(2), 27–31.

McLaughlin, M. W. (2000). *Community counts: How youth organizations matter for youth development.* Washington, DC: Publication Education Network.

McLaughlin, M. W. (2001). Community counts. *Educational Leadership, 58*(7), 14–18.

McLaughlin, M., Irby, M., & Langman, J. (1994). *Urban sanctuaries: Neighborhood organizations in the lives and futures of inner-city youth.* San Francisco: Jossey-Bass.

Miller, B. M. (2001). The promise of after-school programs. *Educational Leadership, 58*(7), 6–12.

Miller, B. M. (2003). *Critical hours: After-school programs and educational success.* Wellesley, MA: National Institute on Out-of-School Time.

Mintzes, J. J., Wandersee, J. H., & Novak, J. D. (1997). Meaningful learning in science: The human constructivist perspective. In G. D. Phye (Ed.), *Handbook of academic learning: Construction of knowledge* (pp. 405–447). San Diego, CA: Academic Press.

Moje, E. B., Dillon, D. R., & O'Brien, D. (2000). Reexamining roles of learner, text, and context in secondary literacy. *Journal of Educational Research, 93,* 165–180.

Moje, E. B. & Eccles, J. S. (2005). *Out-of-school programs for adolescent literacy development: A review of the literature.* New York: Adolescent Literacy Council, Carnegie Corporation.

Moje, E. B., Young, J. P., Readence, J. E., & Moore, D. W. (2000). Reinventing adolescent literacy for new times: Perennial and millennial issues. *Journal of Adolescent and Adult Literacy, 43,* 400–410.

Moll, L. C., & Greenberg, J. B. (1990). Creating zones of possibilities: Combining social contexts for instruction In L. C. Moll (Ed.), *Vygotsky and education: Instructional implications and applications of sociohistorical psychology* (pp. 319–348). Cambridge, England: Cambridge University Press.

National Research Council. (1996). *National science education standards.* Washington, DC: National Academy Press.

Nicolopoulou, A., & Cole, M. (1993). Generation and transmission of shared knowledge in the culture of collaborative learning: The Fifth Dimension, its play-world, and its institutional contexts. In E. A. Forman, N. Minick, & C. A. Stone (Eds.), *Contexts for learning: Sociocultural dynamics in children's development* (pp. 283–314). New York: Oxford University Press.

Nocon, H., & Cole, M. (2006). School's invasion of "after-school": Colonization, rationalization, or expansion of access? In Z. Bekerman, N. C. Burbules, & D. Silberman-Keller (Eds.), *Learning in places: The informal education reader* (pp. 99–121). New York: Peter Lang.

O'Brien, D. G., Stewart, R. A., & Moje, E. B. (1995). Why content literacy is difficult to infuse into the secondary school: Complexities of curriculum, pedagogy, and school culture. *Reading Research Quarterly, 30,* 442–463.

Packer, M. J. (1993). Commentary: Away from internalization. In E. A. Forman, N. Minick, & C. A. Stone (Eds.), *Contexts for learning: Sociocultural dynamics in children's development* (pp. 254–265). New York: Oxford University Press.

Perry, M., Teague, J., & Frey, S. (2002). *Expansion of after-school programs aims at improving student achievement.* Palo Alto, CA: EdSource.

Philips, S. U. (1972). Participant structures and communicative competence: Warm Springs children in community and classroom. In C. Cazden, V. John, & D. Hymes (Eds.), *Functions of language in the classroom* (pp. 370–394). New York: Teachers College Press.

Rahm, J. (2001). Science literacy in the making in an inner-city youth programme: They take time to show us how a plant grows. In M. Hedegaard (Ed.), *Learning in classrooms: A cultural-historical approach* (pp. 145–165). Aarhus, Denmark: Aarhus University.

Rahm, J. (2002). Emergent learning opportunities in an inner-city youth gardening program. *Journal of Research in Science Teaching, 39,* 164–184.

Rahm, J. (2004a). Community-gardens and science laboratories as texts for science literacy development. In A. Peacock & A. Cleghorn (Eds.), *Missing the meaning: The development and use of print and non-print text materials in diverse school settings* (pp. 47–60). New York: Palgrave-Macmillan.

Rahm, J. (2004b). Multiple modes of meaning-making in a science center. *Science Education, 88,* 223–247.

Reisner, E. R., Russell, C. A., Welsh, M. E., Birmingham, J., & White, R. N. (2002). *Supporting quality and scale in after-school services to urban youth: Evaluation of program implementation and student engagement in TASC After-School Program's third year.* Washington, DC: Policy Studies Associates.

Rennie, L. J., & Johnston, D. J. (2004). The nature of learning and its implications for research on learning from museums. *Science Education, 88*(Suppl. 1), S4–S16.

Resnick, L. B. (1987). The 1987 presidential address: Learning in school and out. *Educational Researcher, 16*(9), 13–20, 54.

Resnick, L. B., Levine, J. M., & Teasley, S. D. (1991). *Perspectives on socially shared cognition.* Washington, DC: American Psychological Association.

Rhodes, J. E. (2004). The critical ingredient: Caring youth-staff relationships in after-school settings. *New Directions for Youth Development, 101,* 145–161.

Rogoff, B. (1990). *Apprenticeship in thinking: Cognitive development in social context.* New York: Oxford University Press.

Rogoff, B. (2003). *The cultural nature of human development.* New York: Oxford University Press.

Russell, R. L. (2002). Museum outreach. *Informal Learning, 52,* 12–17.

Scott-Little, C., Hamann, M. S., & Jurs, S. G. (2002). Evaluations of after-school programs: A meta-evaluation of methodologies and narrative synthesis of findings. *American Journal of Evaluation, 23,* 387–419.

Scribner, S., & Cole, M. (1973). Cognitive consequence of formal and informal education. *Science, 182,* 553–559.

Sefton-Green, J. (2003). Informal learning: Substance or style? *Teaching Education, 14*(1), 37–51.

Seymour, E., & Hewitt, N. (1994). *Talking about leaving: Factors contributing to high attrition rates among science, mathematics, and engineering undergraduate majors.* Boulder: Bureau of Sociological Research, University of Colorado.

Spielberger, J., & Halpern, R. (2002). *The role of after-school programs in children's literacy development.* Chicago: Chapin Hall Center for Children, University of Chicago.

Styles, C. (2002). Dialogic learning in museum space. *Australian Journal of Adult Learning, 42,* 169–191.

Vadeboncoeur, J. A. (2005). The difference that time and space make: An analysis of institutional and narrative landscapes. In J. A. Vadeboncoeur & L. P. Stevens (Eds.), *Re/constructing "the adolescent": Sign, symbol and body* (pp. 123–152). New York: Peter Lang.

Vandell, D. L. (2003). Playing by the rules: The 21st CCLC program evaluation violates established research standards. *Issues and Opportunities in Out-of-School Time Evaluation Briefs, 5,* 5–8.

Vásquez, O. A. (2003). *La Clase Magica: Imagining optimal possibilities in a bilingual community of learners.* Mahwah, NJ: Erlbaum.

Vygotsky, L. S. (1978). *Mind in society: The development of higher psychological processes* (M. Cole, V. John-Steiner, S. Scribner, & E. Souberman, Eds.). Cambridge, MA: Harvard University Press.

Vygotsky, L. S. (1987). Thinking and speech. In *The collected works of L. S. Vygotsky: Vol. 1. Problems of general psychology* (N. Minick, Trans., R. W. Rieber & A. S. Carton, Eds., pp. 39–285). New York: Plenum.

Walberg, H. J., Zins, J. E., & Weissberg, R. P. (2004). Recommendations and conclusions: Implications for practice, training, research, and policy. In J. E. Zins, R. P. Weissberg, M. C. Wang, & H. J. Walberg (Eds.), *Building academic success on social and emotional learning: What does the research say?* (pp. 209–218). New York: Teachers College, Columbia University.

Weiss, H., & Little, P. (2003). Why, when, and how to use evaluation: Experts speak out. *Issues and Opportunities in Out-of-School Time Evaluation Briefs, 5,* 1–12.

Wells, G. (1992). The centrality of talk in education. In K. Norman (Ed.), *Thinking voices: The work of the National Oracy Project* (pp. 283–310). London: Hodder & Stoughton.

Wells, G. (1999). *Dialogic inquiry: Towards a sociocultural practice and theory of education.* Cambridge, England: Cambridge University Press.

Wells, G. (2000). Modes of meaning in a science activity. *Linguistics and Education, 10,* 307–334.

Wertsch, J. V. (1985). *Vygotsky and the social formation of mind.* Cambridge, MA: Harvard University Press.

Wertsch, J. V. (1991). *Voices of the mind: A sociocultural approach to mediated action.* Cambridge, MA: Harvard University Press.

Wertsch, J. V., Tulviste, P., & Hagstrom, F. (1993). A sociocultural approach to agency. In A. Forman, N. Minick, & C. Addison (Eds.), *Contexts for learning* (pp. 336–356). New York: Oxford University Press.

Whalen, S. P., & Wynn, J. R. (1995). Enhancing primary services for youth through an infrastructure of social services. *Journal of Adolescent Research, 10,* 88–110.

Yohalem, N. (2003). Adults who make a difference: Identifying the skills and characteristics of successful youth workers. In F. A. Villarruel, D. F. Perkins, L. M. Borden, & J. G. Keith (Eds.), *Community youth development: Programs, policies, and practices* (pp. 358–372). Thousand Oaks, CA: Sage.

Chapter 8

Youth, Technology, and Media Cultures

JULIAN SEFTON-GREEN
University of South Australia

In Miranda July's film *You, Me and Everyone We Know* (2005), a young child, Robby, is initiated into and then takes over from his big brother a "chat" with an anonymous respondent who (we later find out) turns out to be an older woman. In unsupervised experiences online, and through cutting and pasting text, the young child effectively teaches himself to "write" and manages to "seduce" the chat respondent. This satire of contemporary anxiety about children's online vulnerability plays into current press saturation and television's focus on online pornography and pedophilia.

In July's film, the boy's play with the projected identity afforded him in the "chat room," the image of him learning to write and communicate, offers a very different image of the modern child. His agency, symbolized in his control of the computer and its communicative possibilities and in his sexual desire (however "appropriate"), can be contrasted with the child transfixed by the TV in the 1982 film *Poltergeist*. There the image of the blank flickering white screen beckons a toddler away from the warmth of her family into its evil heart. This is an image of the media intruding into the family and taking over a child's mind.

The screen has changed from 1982 to 2005. In 2005 it is now more "interactive," more dominant of the visual field (Manovich, 2002), and it is a principal means of communication beyond the living room walls. Although these two film excerpts are clearly fictional representations of child and screen, I want to take them as the organizing themes for this review in an attempt to explore research about young people and the media over the past approximately 20 years. This is not a story of enlightenment as if we have moved from the notion of an evil magic to one of sophisticated play. The scholarship and research in this field does not follow such a simple trajectory. Indeed, we encounter anxiety about the negative *effects* of the media current in contemporary debate—for example, around the role of the media in childhood obesity. However, the current levels of attention to learning to write, to "master" the technology, to appropriate a play with identity, and to act in the sexualized adult world are all important in current debates around how young people use the media. They also frame how we now theorize and study children's interactions with the media as pedagogic relationships with significant educational potential.

279

Contextualizing these debates is central to my argument, and in general this means that my approach is slightly different from some of the other contributors to this volume. I am not offering a comprehensive study of recent research in this field but more an overview of thematic arguments designed to question how education research in this area intersects with changes in policy and public debate. As I explain subsequently, my analysis is broadly constructed out of cultural studies paradigms, and I am thus interested in focusing attention on attempting to understand why certain kinds of analysis and research have been popular over the past 20 years and how such interest affects broad attitudes toward learning, education, schools, and culture beyond the narrower interest of professional education researchers. I argue that an interest in forms of media culture helps us understand wider notions of learning beyond education or school systems and shows how these models of learning may from time to time conflict, support, or be in tension with each other as the media now actively "compete" with schooling as a key learning domain. I believe that this approach is useful in helping us understand not only changing fashions in educational theory but what kinds of arguments may help us create social and political change.

My account is organized into four sections. First, I discuss some of the broad research paradigms and key concepts underpinning research on young people, technology, and media cultures. The second and third sections focus more specifically on two key areas of what is an expanding field: video games and media production. My discussion of computer game marks out continuity and difference from earlier studies of young people and the media (TV and film). I then turn to the current interest in young people as producers, authors, and makers of media. This work exemplifies a shift from work on youth as passive consumers to media-producing agents. Both of these areas, I argue, are central to debates about how to remake elements of schooling, curriculum, and pedagogy.

Much of the key literature about youth, media, and technology is not traditional educational research but work undertaken in the emerging fields of media and cultural studies. This work is sociological and ethnographic in orientation, featuring quantitative studies that document media use by young people and qualitative studies that describe media interactions and model their social, cultural, and political consequences. This review is clearly selective in scope as it engages with two broad areas of inquiry and takes a historical view in exploring literature over the past 20 years. In addition, more detailed accounts of media use and interaction are undertaken by educationalists, particularly those who approach the challenge of describing and defining learning from sociocultural perspectives. These efforts entail ethnographic studies of cultural uses of media in social contexts and their implications for learning.

HISTORICAL CONTEXTS

As with the introduction of mass literacy in the 19th century (Barker, 1989; Luke, 1989), the introduction of each new medium (radio, film, television, and finally the Internet) during the 20th century has been accompanied by anxiety about its imagined effect on less educated, "vulnerable" social groupings. This story has been well told (Kress, 2003; A. Luke, 2003; Marvin, 1988; Winston, 1998) and in popular political discourse the media have been held responsible for the destruction of political culture (Postman, 1985; Sanders, 1995), the vulgarity of popular culture, and a host of other particular and general social evils. Taking as its paradigm the role of Nazi propaganda (symbolized in George Orwell's screen in *1984*), most early theorists of the media tended to stress the power of the text (and its message) and the ignorance and passivity of the viewer or reader. The negative thesis of media effects crosses both traditional psychological studies and early critical cultural analyses informed by the Frankfurt school's critique of the "culture industry" (Adorno, 1991).

This tradition is still extraordinarily powerful in popular debate about the role of the media in young people's lives and is a recognized school of research (e.g., Kirsch, 2006). Typically, research in this tradition is underpinned by kinds of medical authority (Goswami, 2005), and reports (however humorous, such as the story of the Russian parent taking the makers of the Fox TV show *The Simpsons* to the Court of Human Rights for undermining family values [Ananova, 2006]) continue to proliferate across the world.[1] In recent years, concern with violence as an effect of exposure to the media has seen a definite swing toward an interest in the role of media in influencing consumption—as media research has responded to public concern about obesity across developed nations (for a summary of this debate, see S. Livingstone, 2006).

In the 1980s, empirical studies of the actual meanings audiences make of the media slowly began to unsettle and question this consensus. These studies were grounded in changing theoretical paradigms about the relationships among reader, text, and meaning affiliated with the Birmingham School for Cultural Studies (Hall, 1980). Early studies of audiences broke down the monolithic power of the media and began the process of explicating how individual or smaller social groupings began to make meanings from the interaction of text and context (Morley, 1980, 1986). Following key feminist studies of marginalized audiences (Ang, 1985; Hobson, 1982), there was a shift toward viewing audiences as active participants in and constructors of media messages and codes.

The newfound rationale for the power of the audience, underpinned by the theories of the emerging discipline of cultural studies (Grossberg, Nelson, & Treichler, 1992), began to locate power solely in the agency of the audience and almost to deny the effect of the media themselves (Fiske, 1987, 1989). As has been noted (Buckingham, 2000, 2003a; Buckingham et al., 2005), studies of media and their audiences have tended to seesaw between an effects and an empowerment paradigm. Put simply, the former (which tended to rely on psychological and experimental research models [e.g., Gerbner, 1997]) emphasized the power of the media. The latter (which tended to be more sociological and to use qualitative research methods [e.g., Hodge & Tripp, 1986]) emphasized the power of the individual reader or audience grouping (Gauntlett, 1995).

The dialectical nature of this debate—between emphases on media code and decoding, between audience effects and empowerment, between production and reception, between text and receptive context—has not thus far reached a new synthesis. It is clear that such a position is important for exploration of the educational potential of new media; a line needs to be drawn under the effects tradition of earlier generations, if only to qualify the conservative rhetoric and technophobia that can readily inform educational debate and reform. Here the increasing quality and range of empirical study is important because it introduces a very different level of analysis and debate. Yet, both research positions are heavily invested in opposing theoretical models of the meaning and impact of media.

Even during periods of research that celebrated the power of the audience, children and young people tended to be exempt from wider claims about the democratic powers of active resistance. Because we tend to regard young people as vulnerable subjects, research has tended to concentrate on showing how young people can be susceptible to media culture (e.g., Kline's, 1993, study of children and the marketing of toys within the wider media and commercial culture). There are serious questions about the way they are positioned in the marketplace and in consumer culture more generally, as well as traditional research questions about how immersion in media culture might shape their psychological and educational development (Kline, 1993; Meyrowitz, 1985; for more critical analysis, see Seiter, 1993, or Kinder, 1999).

The new sociology of childhood (James & James, 2004; Qvortrup, 2005) has concentrated on the positioning of children and young people as having agency or power in contradistinction to classic descriptions of these social groups as passive objects of adult supervision. In the context of debates about the effects and use of the media and new technologies, this approach has recapitulated the discovery of the audience suggested earlier. This means that children and young people are defined as active agents in the meaning-making process. However, a salient point of difference between research on child and adult audiences is attention to how the young media consumer or user is positioned as a learner. In this way, the power relationship between text and audience is constructed in pedagogic terms. At a theoretical level, this approach begins to conceptualize power in pedagogic terms, which has a number of implications for what we can discern about children's out-of-school learning (from the media).[2]

It is also possible to see in this tension the familiar terrain of debate around traditional and progressive views of education and learning (for an overview of this educational debate, see Egan, 1997, chap. 1). The notion of simple direct media effects restates a transmission view of pedagogy, while more complex ideas about meaning making by active audiences echo ideas about work done by learners in the construction of their learning. More recent studies of media pedagogy (e.g., Goldfarb, 2002) have explicated this analogy further.

Assumptions about power underpin such a comparison. Buckingham and Sefton-Green (2004) attempted to show how the theories of learning implicit in pedagogic relationships offer a more subtle and nuanced understanding in regard to theorizing about the relationship between media and user. Their study of the Pokemon phenomenon tried to move beyond a simple effects paradigm locating power as immanent properties of either the text (or, in this case, the variety of cross-media and marketing products) or the user/reader (the watcher of the TV series or player of the

Nintendo game) to show how the relationship between individuals and social phenomena can be analyzed in the same way as pedagogy (i.e., as an interactive, iterative process rather than a simple, crude "effect"). This forms part of a more general notion of how it is now impossible to separate assumptions about learning and education from the wider media culture. In light of this volume's overarching focus— "What counts as learning?"—here I concentrate on showing how media and popular culture research explicitly or implicitly are premised on theories and models of learning as a necessary and intrinsic part of engagement with forms of media culture.

These issues have been complicated further by the effects of digitalization and "media convergence."[3] My opening images of child and screen contrast 1982 and 2005, and the key issue here is how the Internet and other allied production technologies have affected the transmissive "power" of the screen. Obviously, one issue is the variation and the range and quantity of screens now available to young people in the developing world. Mobile phones are a key area of research, as is the way in which "new" technologies supplement or complement older technologies—especially given the extreme claims in advertising, popular literature, and, indeed, media reporting about the impact of such changes (Negroponte, 1996; Snyder, 1997a; Tapscott, 1998). Some of the claims for technological change are peculiar to the technologies themselves (e.g., debates about the use of community in social networking, Web 2.0 technologies), while others tend to restate earlier arguments about effects. For example, anxiety about children's exposure to sexually explicit material online conforms to patterns of explanation and research followed by scholars concerned about the impact of adult material on broadcast TV (e.g., Meyrowitz, 1985).

But new media do not simply repeat old arguments. Equally, it is not true that new media in and of themselves create new conditions for the consumption and circulation of meanings. In an early study of television, Raymond Williams (1974) pointed out that there was (at that time) no reason why TV had to develop simply as a mass broadcast medium; this was a consequence of competing economic and political factors. Because the democratic potential of mass communications is now much more accessible to many more people, it appears to have unlocked a conundrum central to democratic aims of mass education across the developing world: that many can now communicate with many. At the same time as new media expand access, they do so selectively (Hellawell, 2001; Warschauer, 2003). Mass culture is commercially produced and privately owned, and this too has to be factored into our assessment of how media culture and technology are or are not changing the communicative landscape for young people today (Rifkin, 2000; Schiller, 1996).

PLAYING GAMES WITH PARADIGMS

A history of the study of computer games provides an excellent example of both the utopian aspirations for new media and the dystopian apocalyptic sermonizing that characterizes extremes of the literature. Because the field of study can be isolated to the past 20 years or so, it is also useful to see the underpinning disciplines, methods, and assumptions. In so doing, we can study how continuity or rupture with earlier studies of (comparable) media does or does not translate into the developing field. Furthermore, the fact that modern computer games are a new technical medium (see Wardrip-Fruin & Harrigan, 2004; Wolf, 2003; Wolf & Perron, 2003) allows us to explore how changing technologies also influence research on the meaning of an emergent form. In my conclusion to this section, I argue that the findings of research into computer games, the orientation of such research, and the methods of research are all indicative of the ways in which studies of media and technology carry with them the burden of "overrepresentation" (i.e., overdetermination of meaning in relation to debates about education).

The emergence of computer (or video) games in the mass market appeared to offer a "baseline" for research on the effects of a new media form and indeed a new social-media practice (cf. Charlton's, 2001, work on the impact of TV in St. Helena). By the early years of this century, the games industry had outgrown Hollywood in terms of turnover (see http://www.theesa.com and http://www.elspa.co.uk) and had expanded rapidly into international markets. This only enhanced the view that the study of computer games represents a classic "before and after" opportunity to explore the impact of a new media technology in terms of both the changing nature of youth and childhood and the effects of globalization. Here I explore literature investigating new or different computer games in relation to preceding forms and practices.

Early games were not, of course, rich in visual or narrative complexity, and their abstractness may have influenced the orientation toward the cognitive rather than the sensual. Greenfield's (1984) early study offered a psychological evaluation of the broadly "beneficial" benefits of playing computer games, conceptualizing the interrelationships among text, player, and context as an abstract engagement between mind and symbolic interaction. This situated the effect of computer games in a profoundly educational light, setting the scene for a pedagogic relationship between text and child/youth and decontextualizing the relationship from social milieu and setting. Although later forms of mediation theory (e.g., Wertch, 1998) drawn from more sociocultural and sociological traditions come into play in analyzing the learning afforded by playing games, present advocates for the educational benefits of computer games tend to draw from assumptions set by this paradigm.

In contrast, Provenzo's (1991) critique of Nintendo worked in the negative effects tradition. This study focused on the Nintendo phenomenon from an economic and institutional perspective. Here anxiety about the role of large corporate institutions (inflected by concern about Japan's economic dominance; see Iwabuchi, 2004) meshed with burgeoning concern about children's contradictory position as consumers in the marketplace (e.g., Kline, 1993). By the end of the 1990s, the metaphor of the computer addict (Walkerdine, 1999; Walkerdine, Thomas, & Studdert, n.d.) had emerged as the defining relationship between computer games and their players (or so the players' agency was constructed). Again, as with Greenfield's study, the actual games or texts under discussion were relatively "immature." Nonetheless, Provenzo focused on broader notions of effect, picking up on not only consumption behaviors but other "antisocial" features of game playing. This effectively involved a tradition popularized by Postman (1985) that took a highly proscriptive view toward the place of popular culture in education. The pedagogy of popular culture from this perspective was characterized in terms of its vulgar appeal to pleasure and an adult seduction of the young (see Buckingham, 2003a, 2003b, for critiques of this position and its platonic antecedents).

This approach to the effect of computer games reached a height in the wake of the tragic events at Columbine High School and the resulting discussion and analysis of the causes of the perpetrators' actions. This is not the place to revise the intricacies of that debate (see especially the contribution of Henry Jenkins at http://web.mit.edu/comm-forum/papers/jenkins_ct.html). However, in general, as Jenkins argued, the events at Columbine were explained by the media as a direct consequence—as an effect—of playing violent computer games, especially, it was alleged, the game *Doom*. Coverage of this event bore all of the hallmarks of a classic "moral panic" (Barker & Petley, 1997), and, as Jenkins showed, the attribution of blame to the media, and computer games in particular, bore scant relation to the facts. This was not an isolated example of poor press coverage but a classic displacement whereby problematic coverage was made to take the blame for complex social events. The Barker and Petley collection (1997) contains studies of a number of examples of this process in relation to older media such as TV and film, primarily in the United Kingdom. My point here is that research in the media field, and especially computer games, inherits spurious claims about alleged violent, sensational, and traumatic effects. It is not premised on a basis of objective inquiry; rather, as I argue subsequently, it can give rise to a form of academic inquiry that is significantly interested in rebuttal and justification and cannot adopt the pretense of a disinterested investigation of current phenomena. It also places media research squarely in the political arena.

Study of the textual nature and structure of games and the experiences of game playing argues that computer games have relied on preceding forms and traditions (much like the relationship of films to novels [Bordwell, 1987]). A wide range of critical theory has been employed to describe narrative, ludology, genre, and so on (see Carr, Buckingham, Burn, & Schott, 2006; Wardrip-Fruin & Harrigan, 2004; Wolf, 2001; Wolf & Perron, 2003). All of these studies and collections are highly theoretical in orientation. They effectively take the form of textual study, although (as noted subsequently) this is more complex than in relation to predigital texts because the player's experience is an integral part of the way the text constructs itself. The approach to games across these traditions is primarily literary. There are studies of specific games or of visual themes or tropes; for example, Wolf (2001) explored abstraction and Filiciak (2003), among others, examined changing models of postmodern identity as constructed though the use of game avatars. A key debate is the distinction between the structure of games as narrative forms and as "games" (e.g., Frasca, 2003). This argument focuses on exploring whether games can best be analyzed formally as rule-based systems or as other kinds of narrative text. However, there are few qualitative or quantitative interpretive studies of game playing (either observational or experimental), and even ethnographies are virtually nonexistent here. Research has concentrated on structural formal issues, containing little sociology and none of the uses and gratifications work that characterized the development of the feminist and audience studies described in the previous section. Games here are constructed as complex and at times avant-garde textual forms; they are not examined in terms of youth culture, and even studies of economics and media institutions are rare.

More popular studies of games concentrate on technical developments and computer technologies (Herz, 1997; Poole, 2000). In this tradition, developments in graphic display or computer processing power as well as institutional studies of early game companies (like Atari) are used to explain the game phenomenon, with an emphasis being placed on describing the rapid rise of computer games in terms of revenues generated.

Together, this work concentrates on content and technical form, paying little attention to how players *learn* to play games or the impact of such learning and play on the lives of young people. Similar to studies of film and television, the research focus has neglected young people as members of the audience and, in particular, their experience of game playing. Only in the past 10 or so years have empirical studies of children and young people playing games begun to emerge (e.g., Beavis, 1997, 2001; Facer, Sutherland, Furlong, & Furlong, 2003; Nixon, Beavis, & Atkinson, 2003; Sefton-Green, 2004a), and theorization about both the pedagogy and the effect of game playing is still developing.

Researching computer games does pose methodological challenges. For example, as noted by Fiske (1989), the notion of a text is a problematic construct (as the object of study) in that it is "completed" through the process of being played—thus changing the fixed object of study common to all readers' experiences—and the actual process of game playing is difficult to research (as acknowledged in Aarseth's, 2001, call to the field of study). Part of the problem is that game playing is difficult to observe (it frequently takes place in the home), difficult to capture (a game can take weeks to play as it unfolds), and difficult to interpret, in that the interaction between player and screen is private and needs to be made active for research purposes. Although there is considerable industry-supported research on sales volumes and time spent playing games (showing, for example, that 31% of game players are less than 18 years of age and that 62% are male [http://www.theesa.com/archives/]), these kinds of statistics do not tell us much about meaning or pleasure—the problem identified in the new audience studies described earlier. While we know that the gaming industry now exceeds Hollywood (in terms of turnover), what does this mean for young people? Some academic research focuses on young people's use of time, and we do have some accounts describing how young people report their game playing outside school (http://www.children-go-online.net/). A recent European comparative study, for example, suggested that young people 6–16 years old spent on average 32 minutes a day playing games, as compared with 136 minutes watching TV (Kirriemuir & McFarlane, 2003, p. 10).

Because these kinds of studies provide little insight into the specific pleasures afforded by particular games and we can only infer effects and consequences (what else might these young people be doing if they did not use their time in this way?), there is a tendency to use interview and case studies to shed light on questions of purpose and significance (Beavis, 1997; Nixon et al., 2003). These studies are necessarily small scale and qualitative. Findings tend to be less descriptive and more suggestive in terms of models of what actually happens during game playing and how the text-user interaction might work in practice. Sefton-Green's (2004a) ethnographic account of a young child learning to play Pokemon described the learning process and contextualized that learning within the child's life. Beavis (1997) and Nixon et al. (2003) explored the meaning and pleasure small groups of male players derived from game playing. All three of these studies examined the significance of mastery and control and focused on the nature of the "reading" process, leading to a need to theorize how a multimodal text might work in practice. Facer et al.'s (2003) research was part of a larger quantitative 2-year study that looked at game playing in the context of other kinds of home computer and information and communication technology use. Again there was an attempt to account for pleasure and meaning (in terms of the cultural studies paradigm described earlier).

The main exception to this is in the area of gender, where anxiety about violence in computer games and the evident gendered split in game-playing uptake provoked huge debate. The statistics cited here about the gendered nature of game playing break down to confound popular expectations that game playing is an exclusively male preserve. Bryce and Rutter (2002) argued that discussions about the nature of gendered game playing tend to focus on game content rather than looking at the factors that might determine specific gender-related pleasures and motivations, and they concluded that game playing is more evenly spread across genders than is commonly supposed.

The collection edited by Cassell and Jenkins (1998) not only effectively summarized the range of discussion in this area but explored the development of an alternative production infrastructure (games made for girls) in what can almost be seen as an academic intervention in the field of popular culture. Jenkins's essays in that collection and in other work (Fuller & Jenkins, 1995) proposed an explanation for the popularity of games through a historical review of adventure play spaces, arguing that the virtual adventures provided by games, with their capacity to offer "safe" yet imaginatively challenging landscapes, "compensate" for the more enclosed childhoods experienced by young people in more built-up environments. I return to his attention to the pleasures of investigative exploration and the implicitly experiential modes of learning through such exploration later. Much of the rest of the collection explored the relationship between the supply and demand of pleasure as provided by the market. For example, detailed case studies of the "pink" games movement, such as Mattel's *Barbie* games and Brenda Laurel's *Purple Moon* (Cassell & Jenkins, 1998, chaps. 5–10), were included. Exploration and development of other kinds of games (some presumed to appeal more to girls) represent attempts to provide alternative spaces for young people. Academic debate here circles the uneasy configuration of cause and effect in ways that echo other radical interventions around social change. Are the games gendered, or is market demand the determining factor? What is it about games that is appealing? Will alternative games stimulate changes in demand?

At the same time, changes in the "media mix," as Ito termed the contemporary media environment, further problematize the nature of a computer game text. Ito's nuanced studies of Japanese-originated global children's culture, especially *Yugioh* (Ito, in press), have developed Kinder's (1993) notion of "transmedia intertextuality." Her study of the reception and development of TV, games, toys, and trading cards aimed at the child market developed Kinder's study of the interrelationships among toys, TV, and films. This model is, as shown by Ito, complicated by the arrival of computer games. Not only does this analytical approach direct attention toward the entire regime of consumption present in children's experiences of media culture, it further "complexifies" our understanding of text in this new media environment as story and character are "delivered" across a range of media. In contrast to the studies mentioned earlier, these authors employed more of an institutional analysis, examining how media industries work in practice and describing the history and development of the TV series and the marketing of action figurines, associated computer games, and other play toys. Both Kinder and Ito are also particularly interested in exploring the globalization of culture, given that the series they assessed were of Japanese origin. This trend reached its height in studies of the Pokemon phenomenon and directed research interest toward the institutional matrix of marketing and media-industry crossovers and tie-ins—an approach that is clearly global in scope and orientation (see Tobin, 2004). Here study has moved away from simply exploring the text-reader relationship toward a broader sociological inquiry into audience reception and economic impact.

Although work around *Yugioh* is more rooted in studies of children than in youth media, Ito's work is especially important in that it also draws attention to the changing nature of the media themselves and helps us explore the meaning of sociotechnical form as well as content. Ito and colleagues frame their work from a cultural-anthropological tradition. The focus is not so much on quantitative research on use or qualitative studies on text-user relationships as on providing "thick description" of technosocial uses and meanings. Coupled with attention to cross-cultural or intercultural uses, this tradition offers a great deal to media studies. Further developing the study of games and game playing, a recent focus of this approach has been to explore how the mobile phone, as a "point of delivery," is changing how media or techno-culture constitutes itself in social contexts (Ito, Okabe, & Matsuda, 2005). For example, Okabe (2004) sought to look at the implications of the new generation of camera phones. Although the sample was small ($n = 7$), he collected data directly from informants in the form of camera pictures and then followed up with interviews. This work was intensive, but, like the qualitative studies of computer games and unlike much of the mass media studies described in the previous section, it offered ways of understanding cultural meanings. In this instance, findings related to the growing importance of visual data in the creation of personal narratives of everyday life.

This attention to the social function of new technology use has driven much of the recent research on mobile technologies, in which the changing meaning of community is an important study theme (e.g., Harkin, 2003; Rheingold, 1993). Cultural-anthropological research methods combine with traditional sociological research methods in attempts to capture these changes For example, Geser (2004) advocated the use of quantitative methods to capture varieties, ranges, and intensities of usage, concentrating on isolating shifts of time and space from traditional communication patterns. Harkin (2003) showed how mobile phones reinforce local immediate social networks in his small-scale study of mobile phone users. However, despite the fact that computer games are part of the same shift in configurations of text, use, medium, and technology, it is notable that, on the whole, they are not subjected to the same sociocultural empirical approaches, remaining more rooted in literary and text-based studies.

This shows up particularly clearly in recent discussions of computer games and learning or education. I suggest that, especially in the literature most explicitly addressing games and learning, the neglect of this social context or "envelope" (Giacquinta, Bauer, & Levin, 1993) in favor of an interest in text and effects arises out of ways in which game study has developed as a way of redressing anxiety about negative effects. I also suggest that there is a paradigm conflict between the work described earlier that emerged out of a media or cultural studies tradition and work that explores games and learning from the perspective of educational technology. As mentioned, early study of computer games was bound up with consideration of their pedagogic effects (both positive and negative). However, opportunities for educational interventions (frequently commercially motivated) noted in the work on gender and game play continue to exert an influence in conceptualizing the field. Study here is not so much interested in the social effects of games as a cultural form or necessarily the politico-sociological discussion of the games and entertainment industries but, rather, in making a case for the learning benefits (variously conceptualized) derived from playing games. Two of the most developed theories and interventions in this area are the project initiated at the Massachusetts Institute of Technology (http://www.educationarcade.org) and the recent work of James Paul Gee (especially his 2003 book *What Video Games Have to Teach Us About Learning and Literacy*) and fellow scholars as part of the Games and Professional Practice Simulations project discussed subsequently (http://www.academiccolab.org/initiatives/gapps.html). In different ways, the research and writing represented by these initiatives exemplify the learning-related possibilities and challenges of computer games.

Before looking at these approaches in more detail, I want to repeat the argument, made earlier in regard to media such as film and television, that popular culture frequently defined the success of computer games in market terms by contrast with that of mass schooling. Rampton (2006) argued that educational research conducted in the 1970s and 1980s implicitly but consistently articulated an opposition between home and school and between popular and official culture across a variety of domains. In contrast, as I have noted, forms of popular culture can be characterized in terms of market success (although, of course, popularity is not always regarded as an indi-cator of a school's effectiveness). Educational research on games thus inherited an idea that games "work," and a key research interest in early study revolved around the tricky, commonsense concept of "motivation" or "engagement." Put crudely, popu-lar (and commercially motivated) research has tended simply to celebrate playing games as a "better" motivator than learning in school. Yet, there has been little theo-retical investigation of this kind of comparison, and there is no doubt that contrast-ing game playing with other kinds of activity (especially school activities) constitutes a kind of rhetorical move. Walkerdine's (1999) Foucauldian analysis of the "addict" as a normative construct in the literature on gamers could certainly be applied to the less extreme proposition about games being intrinsically motivating, in direct contrast to school being intrinsically unengaging (see Green & Bigum, 1993).

I cannot quite trace the sleight of hand that led the absence of such engagement in school to act as a substitute for the game player (and vice versa), but the 1990s were characterized by a binary opposition between the appeal of popular culture and a rhetoric that loudly castigated failures in school systems across the developed world. Nixon's (1998) discourse analysis of the computer versus school rhetoric in Australia in the late 1990s showed how the home computer had become a privileged site for learning over and above that provided by "basic" schooling. Indeed, reviewing the "ideological work" of that period, we could suggest that games were at the forefront of a technologically determinist critique of the form and function of modern school-ing but were only part of a series of changes in the educational landscape (of which the Internet was obviously the most important) that could be seen as challenging schooling. And of course, like other technological "inventions" of this period, com-puter games were tainted by their associations with violent and problematic effects.

The education/games approach follows two paths: looking at how games played outside of school support different kinds of learning and determining how games as a cultural form can be adapted for work within the curriculum or as pedagogy. I do not discuss this second approach here.[4] However, interest in game playing in the home has given rise to an understanding of how games work as a form of learning technology, even if such research does not follow the methods and approaches of media/cultural studies.

This is the stated aim of James Gee's well-received and important *What Video Games Have to Teach Us About Learning and Literacy* and the work of his colleagues in the Games and Professional Practice Simulations project, especially Shaffer and Squire (see Shaffer, Squire, Halverson, & Gee, 2005; Squire, 2006a, 2006b). Gee is an educational sociolinguist and, as such, sees games (and game playing) as a new arena for theorizing about learning in and through semiotic processes. This kind of approach offers different kinds of insights than those offered by media or cultural studies, but I also suggest that it is symptomatic of debates about learning in society more generally that games now receive such attention from educational theorists and carry such appeal as educational experiences. For example, Gee engages directly with the unfashionable and "unacceptable" face of "violent" and "sexist" video games by arguing that, in and of themselves, they require a kind of "reading." Furthermore, this reading is demanding, structured, and progressive (in the sense of offering development), and it can lead to deep or authentic learning. This offers a different way of engaging with arguments about negative effects. However, Gee's approach is based on his own experiences of game playing, and his book is fundamentally a form of textual exegesis (although, because an account of a game text must include a detailed explanation of how a game is played, the texts studied in the book are not stable entities even as they are being "read" by the author). As an autobiographical study, this approach begs questions about generalizability, not only in terms of scale but in terms of diversity. That is, to what extent would Gee's experiences be common among other kinds of players, and would they mean the same thing?

Building on other kinds of work in learning theory and critical literacy education, Gee is interested in exploring games as a form of literacy. The use of this term is intended both to normalize a proscribed cultural activity (playing games) and to critique normative uses of the concept of literacy as it conventionally applies in education. Gee suggests that learning to play the games themselves constitutes a demanding, rigorous (and exclusive) kind of literacy and should therefore in and of itself demand the serious attention of educationalists. While Gee wants to avoid the position that games offer an attractive way of seducing students disenchanted with schools into new kinds of learning, his research does not avoid the accusation that although he might prove the existence of games as a kind of literacy, it is a literacy that cannot do anything other than support the playing of more games. Gee himself is sensitive about this problem. His chapter on cultural models, for example, and his discussion of the way that all learning is "about something" are persuasive in making the case that video games are not a waste of time. He claims an implicit learning/cognitive benefit but leaves the argument open to the challenge that making the case for theorizing game playing as a learning experience may be no more than rebutting the negative effects agenda. In other words, literacy as entitlement, as the historically singular means of understanding all sorts of things and participating fully in modern society, may be the wrong term to use here, however analogous the processes of understanding might be between literacy learning and game playing. Indeed, this kind of criticism raises the more challenging question (explored in more detail in the following section) as to what the more ubiquitous uses of literacy as a way of explaining media use and interpretation might offer us in general.

Some of these arguments come down to how educationalists believe that their studies can affect policy and the wider culture more generally. Similar to my skepticism about initiatives intended to recuperate computer games into a more sanctioned and "worthwhile" environment, this research is predicated on the notion that the production of learning principles (in Gee's case based on a fusion of contemporary learning theories) will constitute adequate evidence of policy change. In other words, if our starting point for the theorization and conceptualization of computer games is an acceptance of the alleged failure of the educational system (schools in particular) combined with concern about the "success" of different forms of popular culture in communicating with our young, then are we likely to be convinced by this kind of academic work? Not only might it make sense to question these assumptions, but it strikes me as fundamentally problematic to begin analyzing computer games with this weight of expectation bearing down on an analytical perspective.

The other challenge here is that claims about learning needs to be supported by a wider and more imaginative range of research approaches. Empirical (qualitative and quantitative) studies (both observational and experimental) and interpretative research, including single-subject case and larger scale sociological studies, would benefit from longer term comparative work exploring how game players do learn *across* home and school. The important insights gained about the relation of text to audience and the need to contextualize understanding of the media with economic and institutional analyses have played only a small part in approaches to date. Considering commercial games as a form of educational technology is instructive and provocative, but educationalists interested in games would benefit from considering them (and their players) as cultural products as well as abstract interactions.

My purpose has been to explore, first, some of the debates around the reception and use of new (digital) media and, second, how the research agenda has been shaped by its dialogic position within the more public effects discourse. I have suggested that the history of research on computer games is similar to that of research on film images, moving from a negative effects agenda to a model of interactivity. We have seen scholarship explore the effects position (often starting from a defensive position) and now reach heights of enthusiastic advocacy. Research methods are varied and, because of enduring methodological challenges, rarely offer a synthesis of empirical study sensitive to the material conditions of reception in the home and analyses designed to uncover new and changing forms of texts and interactions. In general, I have argued that as a case study the reception of computer games by the research community points toward a consistent interest in the ways in which the role of media culture in everyday life is conceptualized as a form of literacy learning and how commercial and academic interventions focusing on that relationship have attempted to shape learning, opening up media culture as in some ways analogous to the institution of schooling.

CREATIVE MEDIA: FROM READING TO WRITING AND BACK AGAIN

The previous section concluded with a look at the ways in which the playing of computer games has been described as a form of literacy. Indeed, there are now studies of game literacy (see Kirriemuir & McFarlane, 2003) attempting to articulate the salient features of playing games as a form of multimodal reading (see also Burn & Parker, 2003). However, as long noted by media educators, conceptualizations of media consumption as a kind of reading need to account for types of "writing" in the range of media forms now available (for a historical study on this topic, see Sefton-Green, 1996; see Buckingham et al., 2005, for an up-to-date review of media literacy).

One of the distinguishing features of attention to new media, and one of the key effects of the penetration of computers into the home, has been this renewed focus on young people as "writers" or producers. This section reviews research on young people as media producers and writers. Studies in this area have argued that changing technological regimes (those afforded by the Internet in particular) offer young people a new "agency" and new power within the contemporary media environment.

These features are central to any way we might want to think about education in relation to media culture for a variety of reasons. The first is that exploring young people as actors within the techno-media culture circumvents the effects paradigm in that young people are shown as "active" rather than being constructed as merely consumers. Second, as with the work of Holland, Jenkins, and Squire (2003) on making games, such features allow us a qualitatively different insight into how young people might make sense of media culture; in other words, such work serves as a "research heuristic" offering us insight into the meaning-making process. Holland et al. (2003) reviewed four initiatives that developed forms of game-based educational software. They found that reviewing the design process undertaken by the software developers and testers helped trace how games were played and thus what they might mean for players. This study especially focused on the learning process undertaken by players as they grappled with the form and content of new game experiences (see also Making Games project at http://www.childrenyouthandmediacentre.co.uk/projects.asp?Completed=no; Willet & Sefton-Green, 2002). Third, such work points to a crucial and developing area of curriculum study in which we need to ensure that young people can communicate within this new culture (Snyder & Beavis, 2004). Finally, this area is of great interest in that it supports "writing" in nonprint forms, also pointing to the nature of changing textual regimes in general as a defining feature of contemporary literacies (Cope & Kalantzis, 2000).

The evidence for young people making media is contested at an empirical as well as a theoretical level. The 2005 Pew Internet Survey, for example, claimed that more than half of teen Internet users are content creators (Lenhart & Madden, 2005), while U.K.-based surveys of this nature are more skeptical about such claims (Livingstone & Bober, 2005) and suggest that children lack the skills to evaluate online content, let alone create it. Some of the Pew findings describe a more "intermediate" kind of production, namely downloading and remixing existing content. Following Willis (1990), there has been a tendency to describe forms of creative consumption as production. This is part of the remix culture (Miller, 2004), but the Pew survey is indicative of this tendency to blur such distinctions given headline findings (such as those mentioned earlier) that create a picture of agency and activity, confirming the youthful activity of the digital domain.

This distinction between creative consumption and production is, in reality, more complicated than common sense might suggest, because researchers interested in the agency of the remix culture (mainly following Birmingham school studies of encoded meaning in processes such as bricolage; Hebdige, 1979; McRobbie, 1990) have focused on the active nature of consumption. Studies such as that of Ito (2005) or even Gee's analysis of computer games are good examples of analyses conducted on the active side of media consumption. Indeed, as I have suggested, computer games themselves blur this distinction. One of the most interesting foci for research in this area is how forms of media culture are themselves worked and reworked as part of this consumption process.

For example, Rampton's (2006) sociolinguistic study looking at how snatches of music, common phrases, and so forth are reworked, contested, negotiated, and "accommodated" in the day-to-day linguistic interactions of an urban classroom provides excellent insight into the meanings of media culture at a micro level. The classroom studies by Anne Haas Dyson (e.g., 1997) and associated youth-focused scholarship (e.g. Hicks, 2001) also explore the ways in which media culture provides key material for identity work. Dyson explored young children's writing and their surrounding talk through ethnographic immersion in the classroom and playground of an urban school. Her work examined how forms of popular culture are appropriated, written, and rewritten by children in play or composition as well-structured forms of talk and playground interaction. Studies of children and young people's writing (within conventional curriculum areas) have begun to acknowledge how media-determined narratives and texts—including form (e.g., horror genres; Bragg, 2000, 2002) character, and genre—can be absorbed, internalized, and then re-"written" by young people and how these narratives and texts now need to be considered as central to children's changing imaginative and textual universe (Willet, 2006). From this point of view, studies of creative consumption also offer important points of entry for curriculum development and educators in general, as they provide insight into meaning-making processes. Indeed, understanding media culture is a key element of any kind of child- or learner-centered curriculum.

I am more interested in two key features of digital production. The first involves how young people can use the communicative possibilities of the Internet as a way of reaching and interacting with wider audiences than had been possible in the predigital era. Second, there are clearly new kinds of production made possible with digital technologies, of which blogging is fashionable at the moment; work in video, multimedia, and even software development also exemplifies this trend. Although a key element of media literacy is its visual and multimodal nature (Jewitt, 2005; Kress & Van Leeuwen, 2001), as has been noted by numerous commentators, the Internet is still primarily a text-based medium, and any new-media writing continues to take the form of conventional writing (Snyder, 1997b).

Although it is easy to understand why educators might be interested in the growth of media writing, it is worthwhile spending a little time exploring the motives of research in this field. Young people are both a key target group for product marketing and a means to commodify new technologies. They also embody notions of authentic and original experiences, as shown with more independent but popular media such as the documentary film *Born to Brothels*. Here the validation of young people's voices represents a key indicator of value. And, as exemplified by Tapscott (1998), the creative production of young people validates itself by virtue of its path-breaking role in opening up new markets, with iconic youth such as Shaun Fanning (the inventor of Napster) serving almost as case studies. Of course, as has been argued (Fleetwood, 2005), the use of new youth voices and experiences may appear to offer up simply new or "exotic" experiences for consumption, and the increasing exposure of youth may be no more than the marketization of new experiences in an increasingly desperate search for commodification of new material.

In a recent special issue of *Reading Research Quarterly*, both Nixon (2003) and C. Luke (2003) made a plea for new research methodologies to explore young people's changing literacy practices in new media. Such requests are qualified given that part of the problem in exploring young people's media production is working out what might be the significant effects of the explosion in young people's quantity of production, while some of the understandings we have about the meaning of texts can now be tested more thoroughly rather than theorized anew.

One key area of difference between work conducted today and earlier research is how we account for the level of what might be called the "institutional mediation" required by production technologies. By this I refer to the fact that the production process is now "imagined" to be virtually transparent so that authors can manage to "talk" to audiences directly in one-to-one relationships. Previously, forms of media production not only required access to a more highly capitalized production system but also required forms of social organization. Goodman's (2003) account of the New York–based Educational Video Center is a good example of the processes, procedures, and mediation required to support young people in reaching audiences by creating and expressing themselves through various kinds of video production.

Investigations of these kinds of settings and these kinds of productions typically describe community settings (Tyner, 2003) or media education work in school and forms of semiformal educational work (Buckingham & Sefton-Green, 1994). Here analysis is focused on a wide range of social and educational outcomes, exploring how texts are constructed, learning processes, group processes, and reception and circulation. By contrast, production in the contemporary era is significantly more individualized (than simplified traditional preconceptions about personal voice) and predicated on a direct author-audience relationship (although, of course, the audience is imagined as an aggregation of individuals rather than as a mass entity; Alasuutari, 1999; Neuman, 1991).

The key medium for research in this area has been video or film (first in analogue formats but now more widespread in digital forms), although more recent research has investigated Web authorship and the various hybrid textual forms now available through convergence (e.g., Stern, 1999, 2004). Video has been especially important because of its visual nature, not only allowing young people the ability to represent themselves using the forms and conventions of popular culture but offering a seemingly more intuitive and natural (Messaris, 1994) medium than writing and a contrast with more "schooled" literacies. Much research has in fact explored the assumptions behind the "naturalness" of video and the distinct opportunities it offers young people from a culturalist perspective. Here the opportunities for young people who typically are perceived as failing in terms of formal education or being excluded from success by virtue of race, gender, or sexual orientation are also highlighted as if media making can circumvent such social barriers.

Recent work in this tradition has been qualitative and ethnographic (raising a number of political and methodological challenges; Fleetwood, 2005). Soep's (in press) and Chan's (in press) accounts of video-making experiences exemplify this approach. Chan explored how Hong Kong youth use forms of aesthetic coding as a way of exploring identity under repressive circumstances, and Soep built on earlier work exploring the meaning of video as a site for identity work (Soep, 2005). Both studies were qualitative and semi-ethnographic (participant observation), comprising detailed case studies involving author analyses of a created artifact (in these examples, video) along with interviews and observations. Both authors employed some form of discourse analysis to avoid a naive interpretation of interview data and to allow generalization and extrapolation of themes and findings about learning processes. Research in this tradition frequently explores marginalized youth (de Castell & Jenson, in press; Hull & Greeno, 2006; Hull & James, 2006), assessing how engagement with media images and representations from the mainstream can be subverted and "rewritten" in these circumstances.

In recent years, there has been a resurgence of qualitative work in this area, extending an interest in video to other media, graffiti (Forman, 2005), Web pages (O'Hear & Sefton-Green, 2004; Stern, 1999, 2004; Walton, 2004), and now, of course, blogging. Unlike some of the research described in the preceding paragraph, much of this material is produced by young people for young people in a youth sphere; that is, it is not made, produced, or circulated within the constraints of an educational institution. Although we might be interested in such work as educationalists, and although scholars of this work are often located within educational facilities, there is also a sense that such work has been explicated from an ethnographic and cultural-anthropological perspective. The current interest in MySpace and other similar phenomena has now penetrated public debates to the extent that there is a common perception that young people can act naturally and spontaneously as authors in these new and developing spheres. This zeitgeist was captured by Prensky's (2001) popularization of the phrase "digital natives," again articulating the academic gaze as that of a kind of foreign explorer.

However, even the cultural-anthropological tradition is very much concerned with defining and describing participation as a kind of learning. At times, certain writers espouse a notion of auto-didacticism (Katz, 2000), while others imply romantic notions of genius (Tapscott, 1998). Some scholars focus more skeptically on interpreting such work within a developing kind of writing theory (Abbott, 1998, 1999; Atkinson & Nixon, 2005), showing how young people are appropriating and using knowledge from outside the digital domain for use within it. Scholars are also intrigued by the ways in which globalization offers access to new audiences and influences constructions of identity (Maira & Soep, 2005). For some commentators, this kind of production renaissance demonstrates only an ability to begin to participate fully in the consumerist competencies defining youth today; others are concerned with identifying the processes of transfer and generalizability that can be said to result from the expertise gained in these new communication relationships (Sefton-Green, 2004b).

In general, and as a conclusion to this section, it can be said that public debate is much more accepting of the idea that participating in digital culture is in some way an educational experience. It is still unclear how digital technologies support the idea that such production is more widespread and more varied, although this assumption seems widely supported. Research exploring production is sensitive to questions of genre, form, and especially globalized identities and audiences. Its main impact is that of aggregating qualitative, small-scale work. A key area for future research is providing critical understandings of the metaphor (or analogy) of literacy as a way of conceptualizing changes in the new communications order, especially in relation to the function, purpose, and power of literacy as it is used within conventional schooling. I have suggested that production (or writing) is a key attribute of this formulation, but as yet there is very little study exploring what this might mean for teaching or curriculum reform and even less research exploring young people's literacy formation across home and school domains.

MEDIA CULTURE OR EDUCATION? THE POLICY CHALLENGE

Taken together, these case studies give rise to a final set of challenges for education policy. First, we need to ask, generally, what is the place of theories of learning in analyzing young people's use of media culture? Why are they important to our understanding of media culture? What implicit or explicit pedagogic relationships and notions of learning do we use when modeling our understanding of how young people use, respond to, or are affected by media? Second, and more specifically, recent research is clearly interested in the "effect" of the digital difference, that is, the impact of digital technologies on predigital theorizations of media culture. How have recent development in technologies and media convergence changed or affected conflicting or consensual paradigms of media effect or influence? How does the richness of the new media ecology create new opportunities for communication and creativity, and how do the new forms of information poverty shape social exclusion and alienation? Finally, we need to be reflexive and ask what roles research and reporting in this field—especially in response to public concern—play in creating assumptions and norms about media, children, and effects. And, of course, what might be the causal relationships among these sets of questions?

There seem to be two particular inflections to these challenges. The first deals with the explicit relationship between research and developments in education policy (from the more micro level of curriculum development to the macro frames of school reform), and the second deals with the broader relationship of research to public debate. I have argued here, especially in the section focusing on computer games, that a significant amount of research not only is motivated by the desire to repudiate popular opinion (especially in terms of the "effects position") but seeks to intervene in the field by providing alternatives.

It could be argued that studies directed toward education reform (Gee's latest book on computer games and learning [2005] is subtitled "a critique of traditional schooling") and the "computer games in education movement" (Monihan, 2006) demonstrate the tendency to credentialize all aspects of experience and learning as part of a lifelong learning agenda (Edwards, 1994). As critics of that agenda have noted (in parallel with some of the debates about the politics of childhood; Ennew, 1994), young people's out-of-school lives and their informal (nonaccredited) learning are affected by the need to insert learning into all aspects of human life (Coffield, 2000a, 2000b). If all forms of media consumption are now "curricularized" as useful knowledge or deep learning, then how do we define formal or informal modes of learning? And, indeed, are such distinctions important or viable (D. Livingstone, 2006; Sefton-Green, 2003)? There seems to be real difficulty in defining "lines of responsibility" here, of making a meaningful demarcation between life worlds as the desire to accredit (or even to "educationalize") reaches into previously "private" and discrete life experiences. In other words, recuperating the pleasures of play or leisure-time activity raises a political set of questions about public and private boundaries. This blurring of boundaries also makes it difficult to develop education policy or school reform because such policy or reform would seek to intervene in the home and beyond the school.

Part of this problem comes down to a fundamental challenge for schooling itself. My interest in popular media culture is only part of the broader transformation of teaching and learning underpinning reconfiguration of knowledge industries in the era of hypercapitalism (Graham, 2005). Paying attention to the learning structuring young people's uses of mass media as either cognitive or sociocultural processes directs us to the organization of that learning—and, by implication, to how school works. Just as early research on the uses of popular culture implicitly registered high culture as the absent presence, so exploring the learning or educational nature of mass culture dialogically involves schools as the unsaid "other." Schools are always a key index of learning, and given that much of the research on learning of media culture demonstrates the importance of contexts and freedoms for individual or social networks to act in collective virtual domains, so again the perceived constraints of formal schooling are exposed. Research on media culture has located the home (Livingstone's, 2002, "digital bedroom"), the mall, and the friendship network as the most vibrant kinds of "learning spaces." This is one of the most significant findings from studies of computer games and forms of creative production and consumption. And, as has been repeatedly noted, these locations and contexts seem to possess attributes that are almost the reverse of the disciplinary regime of mass schooling.

The discussions of agency and power that dominate all media research (positively and negatively with respect to the effects tradition) subject learners to a different regime than that experienced within mass education systems. Even when that power relationship is expressed in market terms (see Kenway & Bullen, 2001), the market-place purports to address or construct the consumer with greater "respect" than in education.[5] The literature recognizing and validating other kinds of learning thus reads like the work of more utopian, idealistic educators, such as Dewey or Illich, who deliberately worked in nonschooled environments to promote conceptualizations of learning as broader (or deeper) than simple academic achievement. As with that progressivist tradition, research on media learning seems to find limited opportunities to negotiate with the regimes of more formal and narrowly defined schooling. There may be only a limited opportunity for a synthesis between different theories of learning to develop if the institutional regimes of popular media culture and schools are separately and jointly impervious to change. Or, to pose this as a challenge: Can the narratives of learning that appear to underpin how young people work in these apparently distinct domains—in school and not in school, at home and at play—really be developed in ways that offer structural change across learning contexts? Can we escape these "binary" oppositions, or will they remain parallel, mirror theories?

The focus of debate needs to turn away from what counts as learning towards who is doing the counting, when, how often, and so forth. We need to reflect critically on those researchers and critics who are validating new kinds of media learning, and it should be acknowledged that there is a danger that appraising these kinds of learning not only will normalize contemporary childhood (as argued by Buckingham, 2000) but will lead to a new form of progressivism wherein (similar to the arguments pursued by Delpit, 1995, and Walkerdine & Lucy, 1989) new kinds of digital learning—even "digital literacy"—will simply serve to rationalize the changing nature of middle-class childhood and youth. For this reason, it is important to explore what kinds of protocols could link home, school, and peer cultures and to develop research methods and programs that look at large numbers of young people across different social worlds in an attempt to understand fully the effects and limitations of immersion in media cultures.

A final way of framing this challenge is to consider discussions about the nature of the learning presumed to transfer across and between the domains of school and media culture and to reflect on the use of literacy as a way of characterizing transferability. Setting aside the tendency of both "sides" (home and school) to exaggerate their distinctiveness from each other—as if the different types and mechanisms of formal and nonformal learning do not occur in each setting—this problem is a thorny challenge for all educators because it is difficult to assess whether transfer occurs and is extremely difficult to provide evidence that this is the case (Bruner, 1996). This theoretical stand-off is rather obscured by the use of literacy (or literacies) as a way of characterizing the learning presumed to be occurring. Because most uses of literacy imply (and are indeed predicated upon) the concept of transformative use of skills and understanding, there is no suggestion of finite limitations in terms of application of new understandings. On the whole, the use of various types of media literary as a foundational term in this debate has become a new orthodoxy, as in media literacy or digital literacy. Although it is often used in a shorthand way to describe the

nature of the learning relationship between reader and text, it may conceal important assumptions about learning as much as it appears to reveal alternatives.

This is most evident in attempts to reconcile learning processes between and across
experiences. Educational theory is keen on describing and analyzing the role of context, for example with respect to the cultural dimensions of popular media and technology use. A conservative interpretation of this approach would argue that, however
complex or sophisticated our analysis of the pedagogic relationship within media culture, the cultural experience (playing the computer game, being in a chat room)
remains the end of the learning. That transfer may be inferred or desired, but it cannot be deduced from one context to another. A progressivist (or post-progressivist[6])
interpretation (e.g., Gee's, 2005, analysis of computer game playing) suggests that
such learning has a kind of permanent value that is transformative of individual capacities and identities. This review points to research theorizing such change for young
people through their "learning lives," but it has also argued that there is an absence of
studies exploring the kind of longer term change suggested by these claims. It must
also be noted that we do not currently inhabit a political culture interested in developing strategies to help us move beyond this traditional impasse.

I began this chapter by contrasting two seemingly different images of child and
media from before and after the "digital revolution." I have argued that there is much
greater continuity in how we conceptualize this relationship over the period than is
commonly imagined. I have also suggested that we now tend to characterize the relationship in more positive terms as research and popular debate have "replaced" the
simple notion of negative media effects with one of beneficial learning effects. I have
attempted to emphasize how the politics of privatized media consumption make new
demands on the values and practices of formal learning. This creates a series of theoretical (and practical) challenges for schools, just as it has helped us conceptualize
other educational transactions in the home and in peer cultures. My final argument
is that we need more methodologically imaginative and complex studies of diverse
young people *learning across* all kinds of social domains so that we can gain an
enhanced understanding of the meaning of media culture for young people. There is
still an imbalance of speculation and "evidence." The past 10 to 15 years have been
very exciting in theoretical terms as we have attempted to imagine the implications of
media convergence and the penetration of popular media culture, but we now need
more holistic investigations of young people's cultural lives if we are to uncover the
significance of learning across schools and media cultures.

ACKNOWLEDGMENT

I would like to thank Donna Alvermann, Jim Gee, Judith Green, Allan Luke, and Helen Nixon
for their close reading of earlier versions of this chapter.

NOTES

[1] See, for example, the scope and spread of research in this effects tradition found at the
Nordic Clearinghouse (http://www.nordicom.gu.se/clear.php?).

[2] One interesting implication of this attention to the pedagogic relationship between media and audience should be that of conceptualizing learning as equally central to adult readers; however, this "invitation" has not been taken up to any great degree, possibly suggesting an implicitly "developmentalist" assumption in the use of learning here.

[3] These terms describe both the technological processes by which all media (text, sound, image, and moving image) can now be converted into digital formats, thus allowing for the delivery of media across a range of platforms (e.g., computers, digital televisions); and the emergence of new textual forms such as computer games; and the changing socioeconomic regimes of control and ownership that allow global corporations authority across national boundaries; and the ways in which media content is managed across previously discrete media.

[4] See Kirriemuir and McFarlane (2003), http://www.digra.org/, or Mor, Winters, Cerulli, and Björk (2006) for introductions to this field. Shaffer's (2005) critique of authenticity and professionalism in made-for-teaching-games is also helpful.

[5] See http://www.cluetrain.com for an extreme statement of this position.

[6] This term goes beyond the conventional Deweyian sense of social learning in real-world activities to encompass a synthesis of such values with contemporary theories about situated learning, semiosis and the sociocultural, neo-Vygotskian principles of guided instruction.

REFERENCES

Aarseth, E. (2001). *Computer games studies, Year 1.* Retrieved August 26, 2006, from http://www.gamestudies.org/0101/editorial.html

Abbott, C. (1998). Making connections: Young people and the Internet. In J. Sefton-Green (Ed.), *Digital diversions: Youth culture in the age of multimedia* (pp. 84–105). London: UCL Press.

Abbott, C. (1999). Web publishing by young people. In J. Sefton-Green (Ed.), *Young people, creativity and new technologies: The challenge of digital arts* (pp. 111–121). London: Routledge.

Adorno, T. (1991). *The culture industry.* London: Routledge.

Alasuutari, P. (Ed.). (1999). *Rethinking the media audience: The new agenda.* London: Sage.

Ananova. (2006). *Simpsons row heads to European Court of Human Rights.* Retrieved August 26, 2006, from http://www.ananova.com/news/story/sm_1625169.html

Ang, I. (1985). *Watching Dallas: Soap opera and the melodramatic imagination.* London: Methuen.

Atkinson, S., & Nixon, H. (2005). Locating the subject: Teens online @ninemsn. *Discourse: Studies in the Cultural Politics of Education, 26,* 387–409.

Barker, M. (1989). *Comics, ideology, power and the critics.* Manchester, England: Manchester University Press.

Barker, M., & Petley, J. (Eds.). (1997). *Ill effects: The media/violence debate.* London: Routledge.

Beavis, C. (1997). Computer games, culture and the curriculum. In I. Snyder (Ed.), *Page to screen: Taking literacy into the electronic age* (pp. 234–255). Sydney: Allen & Unwin.

Beavis, C. (2001). Digital cultures, digital literacies. In C. Durrant & C. Beavis (Eds.), *P(ict)ures of English: Teachers, learners and technology* (pp. 145–161). Norwood, South Australia: Wakefield Press.

Bordwell, D. (1987). *Narration in the fiction film.* London: Routledge.

Bragg, S. (2000). *Media violence and education: A study of youth audiences and the horror genre.* Unpublished doctoral thesis, University of London.

Bragg, S. (2002). Wrestling in woolly gloves: Not just being "critically" media literate. *Journal of Popular Film and Television, 30,* 42–52.

Bruner, J. (1996). *The culture of education.* Cambridge, MA: Harvard University Press.

Bryce, J., & Rutter, J. (2002). *Killing like a girl: Gendered gaming and girl gamers' visibility.* Retrieved August 26, 2006, from www.digiplay.org.uk/media/cgdc/pdf

Buckingham, D. (2000). *After the death of childhood: Growing up in the age of electronic media.* Cambridge, England: Polity Press.

Buckingham, D. (2003a). *Media education: Literacy, learning and contemporary culture.* Cambridge, England: Polity Press.

Buckingham, D. (2003b). Media education and the end of the critical consumer. *Harvard Educational Review, 73,* 309–327.

Buckingham, D., Banaji, S., Burn, A., Carr, D., Cranmer, S., & Willet, R. (2005). *The media literacy of children and young people.* Retrieved August 26, 2006, from http://www.ofcom.org.uk/advice/media_literacy/medlitpub/medlitpubrss/ml_children.pdf

Buckingham, D., & Sefton-Green, J. (1994). *Cultural studies goes to school: Reading and teaching popular media.* London: Taylor & Francis.

Buckingham, D., & Sefton-Green, J. (2004). Structure, agency and culture in children's media culture. In J. Tobin (Ed.), *Pikachu's global adventure: The rise and fall of Pokemon.* Durham, NC: Duke University Press.

Burn, A., & Parker, D. (2003) *Analysing media texts.* London: Continuum.

Carr, D., Buckingham, D., Burn, A., & Schott, G. (2006). *Computer games: Text, narrative and play.* Cambridge, England: Polity Press.

Cassell, J., & Jenkins, H. (Eds.). (1998). *From 'Barbie' to 'Mortal Combat': Gender and computer games.* Cambridge, MA: MIT Press.

Chan, C. (in press). 'Youth voice? Whose voice?' Young people and youth media practice in Hong Kong. *McGill Journal of Education.*

Charlton, T. (2001). *Broadcast television effects in a remote community.* New York: Erlbaum.

Coffield, F. (Ed.). (2000a). *Differing visions of a learning society: Research findings* (Vols. 1 & 2). Bristol, England: Policy Press.

Coffield, F. (Ed.). (2000b). *The necessity of informal learning.* Bristol, England: Policy Press.

Cope, B., & Kalantzis, M. (2000). (Eds.). *Multiliteracies: Literacy learning and the design of social futures.* London: Routledge.

de Castell, S., & Jenson, J. (in press). No place like home: Sexuality, community and identity among street involved queer and questioning youth. *McGill Journal of Education.*

Delpit, L. (1995). *Other people's children.* New York: New Press.

Dyson, A. H. (1997). *Writing super heroes: Contemporary childhood, popular culture and popular literacy.* New York: Teachers College Press.

Edwards, R. (1994). *Changing places: Flexibility, lifelong learning, and a learning society.* London: Routledge.

Egan, K. (1997). *The educated mind: How cognitive tools shape our understanding.* Chicago: University of Chicago Press.

Ennew, J. (1994). Time for children or time for adults. In J. Qvortrup, M. Bardy, G. Sgritta, & H. Wintersberger (Eds.), *Childhood matters, social theory, practice and politics* (pp. 125–144). Aldershot, England: Avebury.

Facer, K., Sutherland, R., Furlong, J., & Furlong, R. (2003). *ScreenPlay: Children and computing in the home.* London: Routledge.

Filiciak, M. (2003). Hyperidentities: Postmodern identity patterns in massively multiplayer online role-playing games. In M. Wolf & B. Perron (Eds.), *The video game theory reader* (pp. 87–102). London: Routledge.

Fiske, J. (1987). *Television culture.* London: Routledge.

Fiske, J. (1989). *Understanding popular culture.* London: Unwin Hyman.

Fleetwood, N. (2005). Authenticating practices: Producing realness, performing youth. In S. Maira & E. Soep (Eds.), *Youthscapes: The popular, the national, the global* (pp. 155–172). Philadelphia: University of Pennsylvania Press.

Forman, M. (2005). Straight outta Mogadishu: Prescribed identities and performative practices among Somali youth in North American high schools. In S. Maira & E. Soep (Eds.), *Youthscapes: The popular, the national, the global* (pp. 3–22). Philadelphia: University of Pennsylvania Press.

Frasca, G. (2003). Simulation versus narrative: Introduction to ludology. In M. Wolf & B. Perron (Eds.), *The video game theory reader* (pp. 221–236). London: Routledge.

Fuller, M., & Jenkins, H. (1995). Nintendo and new world travel writing: A dialogue. In S. Jones (Ed.), *Cyber society computer-mediated communication and community* (pp. 57–72). London: Sage.

Gauntlett, D. (1995). *Moving experiences: Understanding television's influences and effects.* Luton, England: John Libby.

Gee, J. (2003). *What video games have to teach us about literacy and learning.* New York: Palgrave Macmillan.

Gee, J. (2005). *Situated language and learning: A critique of traditional schooling.* London: Routledge.

Gerbner, G. (1997). Violence in TV drama. *News on Children and Violence on the Screen, 3,* 6–7.

Geser, H. (2004). *Towards a sociological theory of the mobile phone.* Retrieved August 26, 2006, from http://socio.ch/mobile/t_geser1.pdf

Goswami, N. (2005). *Too much television slows children's reading.* Retrieved August 26, 2006, from http://www.telegraph.co.uk/news/main.jhtml?xml=/news/2005/11/27/nread27.xml&sSheet=/news/2005/11/27/ixhome.html

Giacquinta, J., Bauer, J., & Levin, J. (1993). *Beyond technology's promise.* Cambridge, England: Cambridge University Press.

Goldfarb, B. (2002). *Visual pedagogy: Media cultures in and beyond the classroom.* Durham, NC: Duke University Press.

Goodman, S. (2003). *Teaching youth media: A critical guide to literacy, video production, and social change.* New York: Teachers College Press.

Graham, P. (2005). *Hypercapitalism: New media, language, and social perceptions of value.* New York: Peter Lang.

Green, B., & Bigum, C. (1993). Aliens in the classroom. *Australian Journal of Education, 37,* 119–141.

Greenfield, P. M. (1984). *Mind and media: The effects of television, computers and video games.* London: Fontana.

Grossberg, L., Nelson, C., & Treichler, P. (Eds.). (1992). *Cultural studies.* London: Routledge.

Hall, S. (1980). Encoding/decoding. In S. Hall, D. Hobson, & P. Willis (Eds.), *Culture, media language* (pp. 128–138). London: Hutchinson.

Harkin, J. (2003). *Mobilisation: The growing public interest in mobile technology.* London: Demos.

Hebdige, D. (1979). *Subculture: The meaning of style.* London: Methuen.

Hellawell, S. (2001). *Beyond access: ICT and social inclusion.* London: Fabian Society.

Herz, J. (1997). *Joystick nation: How videogames ate quarters, won our hearts, and rewired our minds.* Boston: Little, Brown.

Hicks, D. (2001). *Reading lives: Working class children and literacy learning.* New York: Teachers College Press.

Hobson, D. (1982). *Crossroads: The drama of a soap opera.* London: Methuen.

Hodge, R., & Tripp, B. (1986). *Children and television.* Cambridge, England: Polity Press.

Holland, W., Jenkins, H., & Squire, K. (2003). Theory by design. In M. Wolf & B. Perron (Eds.), *The video game theory reader* (pp. 25–46). London: Routledge.

Hull, G., & Greeno, J. (2006). Identity and agency in nonschool and school worlds. In Z. Bekerman, N. Burbules, & D. Silberman-Keller (Eds.), *Learning in places: The informal education reader* (pp. 77–98). New York: Peter Lang.

Hull, G., & James, M. (2006). *Geographies of hope: A study of urban landscapes and a university-community collaborative.* Manuscript in preparation.

Ito, M. (in press). Technologies of the childhood imagination: Yugioh, media mixes, and everyday cultural production. In J. Karaganis & N. Jeremijenko (Eds.), *Structures of participation in digital culture.* Durham, NC: Duke University Press.

Ito, M., Okabe, D., & Matsuda, M. (2005). *Personal, portable, pedestrian: Mobile phones in Japanese life.* Cambridge, MA: MIT Press.

Iwabuchi, I. (2004). How "Japanese" is Pokemon? In J. Tobin (Ed.), *Pikachu's global adventure: The rise and fall of Pokemon* (pp. 53–79). Durham, NC: Duke University Press.

James, A., & James, A. (2004). *Constructing childhood: Theory, policy and social practice.* Basingstoke, England: Palgrave Macmillan

Jewitt, C. (2005). *Technology, literacy learning.* London: Taylor & Francis.

Katz, J. (2000). *Geeks.* New York: Villard Press.

Kenway, J., & Bullen, E. (2001). *Consuming children: Education-entertainment-advertising.* Buckingham, England: Open University Press.

Kinder, M. (1993). *Playing with power in movies, television and video games.* Berkeley: University of California Press.

Kinder, M. (1999). (Ed.). *Kids' media culture.* Durham, NC: Duke University Press.

Kirriemuir, J., & McFarlane, A. E. (2003). *Literature review in games and learning.* Bristol, England: NestaFuturelab.

Kirsch, S. (2006). *Children, adolescents, and media violence: A critical look at the research.* New York: Sage.

Kline, S. (1993). *Out of the garden: Toys and children's culture in the age of TV marketing.* London: Verso.

Kress, G. (2003). *Literacy in the age of new media.* London: RoutledgeFalmer.

Kress, G., & Van Leeuwen, T. (2001). *Reading images: The grammar of visual design.* London: Routledge.

Lenhart, A., & Madden, M. (2005). *Teen content creators and consumers.* Washington, DC: Pew Internet and American Life Project.

Livingstone, D. (2006). Informal learning: Conceptual distinctions and preliminary findings. In Z. Bekerman, N. Burbules, & D. Silberman-Keller (Eds.), *Learning in places: The informal education reader* (pp. 203–228). New York: Peter Lang.

Livingstone, S. (2002). *Young people and new media.* London: Sage.

Livingstone, S. (2006). Does advertising make children fat? *Public Policy Research, 13,* 54–63.

Livingstone, S., & Bober, M. (2005). *UK children go online: Final report of project findings.* Retrieved August 26, 2006, from http://www.children-go-online.net/

Luke, A. (2003). Literacy and the other: A sociological agenda for literacy research and policy in multicultural societies. *Reading Research Quarterly, 38,* 132–141.

Luke, C. (1989). *Pedagogy, printing and Protestantism: The discourse on childhood.* Albany: State University of New York Press.

Luke, C. (2003). Pedagogy, connectivity, multimodality and interdisciplinarity. *Reading Research Quarterly, 38,* 387–403.

Maira, S., & Soep, E. (Eds.). (2005). *Youthscapes: The popular, the national, the global.* Philadelphia: University of Pennsylvania Press.

Manovich, L. (2002). *The language of new media.* Cambridge, MA: MIT Press.

Marvin, C. (1988). *When old technologies were new: Thinking about electronic communication in the late nineteenth century.* Oxford, England: Oxford University Press.

McRobbie, A. (1990). *Feminism and youth culture.* London: Macmillan.

Messaris, P. (1994). *Visual "literacy": Image, mind and reality.* Boulder, CO: Westview Press.

Meyrowitz, J. (1985). *No sense of place: The impact of electronic media on social behaviour.* Oxford, England: Oxford University Press.

Miller, P. (2004). *Rhythm science.* Cambridge, MA: MIT Press.

Monihan, J. (2006). *Game theory makes its mark.* Retrieved August 26, 2006, from http://education.guardian.co.uk/elearning/story/0,10577,1682478,00.html

Mor, Y., Winters, N., Cerulli, M., & Björk, S (2006). *Literature review on the use of games in mathematical learning: Part I. Design* (Report of the Learning Patterns for the Design and Deployment of Mathematical Games Project). Retrieved October 27, 2006, from http://lp.noe-kaleidoscope.org/outcomes/litrev/

Morley, D. (1980). *The 'Nationwide' audience: Structure and decoding.* London: British Film Institute.

Morley, D. (1986). *Family television: Cultural power and domestic leisure.* London: Comedia.

Negroponte, N. (1996). *Being digital.* Rydalmere, New South Wales, Australia: Hodder & Stoughton.

Neuman, W. (1991). *The future of the mass audience.* Cambridge, England: Cambridge University Press.

Nixon, H. (1998). Fun and games are serious business. In J. Sefton-Green (Ed.), *Digital diversions: Youth culture in the age of multimedia* (pp. 21–42). London: UCL Press.

Nixon, H. (2003). New research literacies for contemporary research into literacy and new media. *Reading Research Quarterly, 38,* 407–413.

Nixon, H., Beavis, C., & Atkinson, S. (2003). *Exploring identities and communities with adolescent game players and Web users.* Retrieved August 26, 2006, from http://www.nordicom.gu.se/clear.php?portal=special&main=themes.php&&cat=12&me=14

O'Hear, S., & Sefton-Green, J. (2004). Style, genre and technology: The strange case of youth culture online. In I. Snyder & C. Beavis (Eds.), *Doing literacy online: Teaching, learning and playing in an electronic world* (pp. 121–144). Creskill, NJ: Hampton Press.

Okabe, D. (2004, October). *Emergent social practices, situations and relations through everyday camera phone use.* Paper presented at the International Conference on Mobile Communication, Seoul, Korea.

Poole, S. (2000). *Trigger happy: The inner life of video games.* London: Fourth Estate.

Postman, N. (1985). *Amusing ourselves to death: Public discourse in the age of show business.* New York: Penguin Books.

Prensky, M. (2001). Digital natives, digital immigrants. *On the Horizon, 9*(5), 1–6.

Provenzo, E. (1991). *Video kids: Making sense of Nintendo.* Cambridge, MA: Harvard University Press.

Qvortrup, J. (Ed.). (2005). *Studies in modern childhood: Society, agency, culture.* Basingstoke, England: Palgrave Macmillan.

Rampton, B. (2006). *Language in late modernity: Integration in an urban school.* Cambridge, England: Cambridge University Press.

Rheingold, H. (1993). *The virtual community: Homesteading on the electronic frontier.* Reading, MA: Addison-Wesley.

Rifkin, J. (2000). *The age of access: The new culture of hypercapitalism, where all of life is a paid-for experience.* New York: Tarcher/Putnam.

Sanders, B. (1995). *A is for ox: The collapse of literacy and the rise of violence in an electronic age.* New York: Vintage.

Schiller, H. (1996). *Information inequality.* London: Routledge.

Sefton-Green, J. (1996). Neither 'reading' nor 'writing': The history of practical work in media education. *Media, Culture and the Curriculum, 2,* 77–96.

Sefton-Green, J. (2003). Informal learning: Substance or style? *Teaching Education, 13,* 37–52.

Sefton-Green, J. (2004a). Initiation rites: Small boy in a poke-world. In J. Tobin (Ed.), *Pikachu's global adventure: The rise and fall of Pokemon* (pp. 141–164). Durham, NC: Duke University Press.

Sefton-Green, J. (2004b). *Literature review in informal learning with technology outside school.* Bristol, England: Futurelab.

Seiter, E. (1993). *Sold separately: Parents and children in consumer culture.* New Brunswick, NJ: Rutgers University Press.

Shaffer, D. (2005). Epistemic games. *Innovate, 1*(6). Retrieved August 26, 2006, from http://www.innovateonline.info/index.php?view=article&id=79

Shaffer, D., Squire, K., Halverson, R., & Gee, J. (2005). *Video games and the future of learning.* Retrieved August 26, 2006, from http://www.wcer.wisc.edu/publications/workingPapers/index.php

Snyder, I. (1997a). Beyond the hype. In I. Snyder (Ed.), *Page to screen* (pp. 125–143). Sydney: Allen & Unwin.

Snyder, I. (Ed.). (1997b). *Page to screen.* Sydney: Allen & Unwin.

Snyder, I., & Beavis, C. (2004). *Doing literacy online: Teaching, learning and playing in an electronic world.* Creskill, NJ: Hampton Press.

Soep, E. (2005). Making hard-core masculinity: Teenage boys playing house. In S. Maira & E. Soep (Eds.), *Youthscapes: The popular, the national, the global* (pp. 173–191). Philadelphia: University of Pennsylvania Press.

Soep, E. (in press). Beyond literacy and voice in youth media production. *McGill Journal of Education.*

Squire, K. (2006a). *Changing the game: What happens when video games enter the classroom?* Retrieved August 26, 2006, from http://www.academiccolab.org/resources/documents/Changing%20The%20Game-final_2.pdf

Squire, K. (2006b). *Games as ideological worlds.* Retrieved August 26, 2006, from http://www.academiccolab.org/resources/documents/edreacher-submitted.pdf

Stern, S. (1999). Adolescent girls' expression on Web home pages: Spirited, somber and self-conscious sites. *Convergence, 5*(4), 22–41.

Stern, S. (2004). Expression of identity online: Prominent features and gender differences in adolescents' WWW home pages. *Journal of Broadcasting and Electronic Media 48*(2). Retrieved August 26, 2006, from http://www.highbeam.com/library/doc0.asp?DOCID=1G1:118953908&num=1&ctr Info=Round9b%3Aprod%3ASR%3Aresult&ao=

Tapscott, D. (1998). *Growing up digital: The rise of the Net generation.* New York: McGraw-Hill.

Tobin, J. (Ed.). (2004). *Pikachu's global adventure: The rise and fall of Pokemon.* Durham, NC: Duke University Press.

Tyner, K. (2003). *A closer look: Media arts 2003.* San Francisco: National Alliance for Media Arts and Culture.

Walkerdine, V. (1999). Violent boys and precocious girls: Regulating childhood at the end of the millennium. *Contemporary Issues in Early Childhood, 1,* 3–23.

Walkerdine, V., & Lucy, H. (1989). *Democracy in the kitchen: Regulating mothers and socialising daughters.* London: Virago.

Walkerdine, V., Thomas, A., & Studdert, D. (n.d.). *Young children and video games: Dangerous pleasures and pleasurable danger.* Retrieved August 26, 2006, from http://web.mit.edu/comm-forum/papers/jenkins_ct.html

Walton, M. (2004). Behind the screen: The language of Web design. In I. Snyder & C. Beavis (Eds.), *Doing literacy online: Teaching, learning and playing in an electronic world* (pp. 91–119). Creskill, NJ: Hampton Press.

Wardrip-Fruin, N., & Harrigan, P. (2004). (Eds.). *First person: New media as story, performance and game.* Cambridge, MA: MIT Press.

Warschauer, M. (2003). *Technology and social inclusion: Rethinking the digital divide.* Cambridge, MA: MIT Press.

Wertch, J (1998). *Mind as action.* New York: Oxford University Press.

Willett, R. (2006). *'Baddies' in the classroom: Media education and narrative writing.* Unpublished manuscript.

Willett, R., & Sefton-Green, J. (2002). Living and learning in chatrooms (or does informal learning have anything to teach us?). *Education et Sociétiés, 2,* 57–77.

Williams, R. (1974). *Television: Technology and cultural form.* Glasgow: Fontana.

Willis, P. (1990). *Common culture: Symbolic work and play in the everyday cultures of the young.* Milton Keynes, England: Open University Press.

Winston, B. (1998). *Media, technology and society: A history from the printing press to the super-highway.* London: Routledge.

Wolf, M. (Ed.). (2001). *The medium of the video game.* Austin: University of Texas Press.

Wolf, M., & Perron, B. (Eds.). (2003). *The video game theory reader.* London: Routledge.